GHOST URN 13

SHIROW MASAMUNE
RIKUDOU KOUSHI

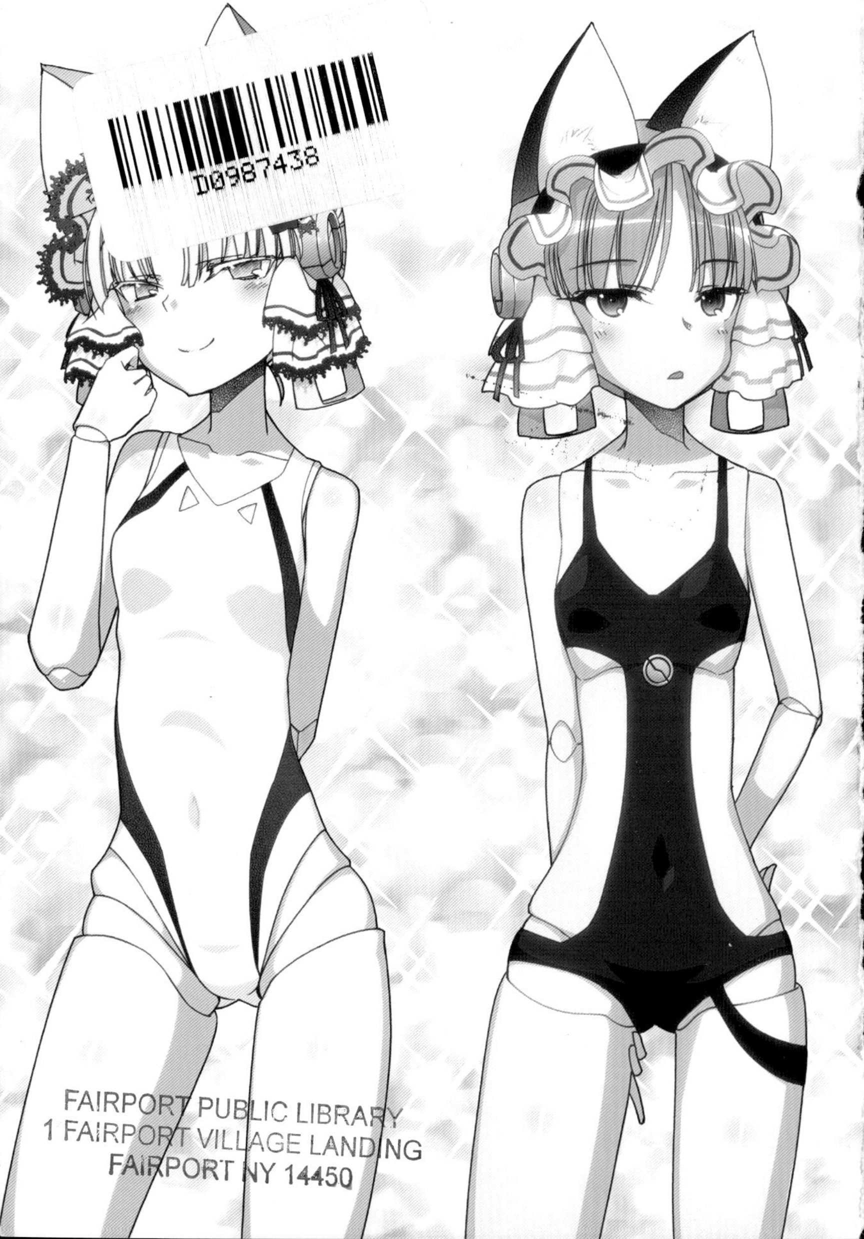

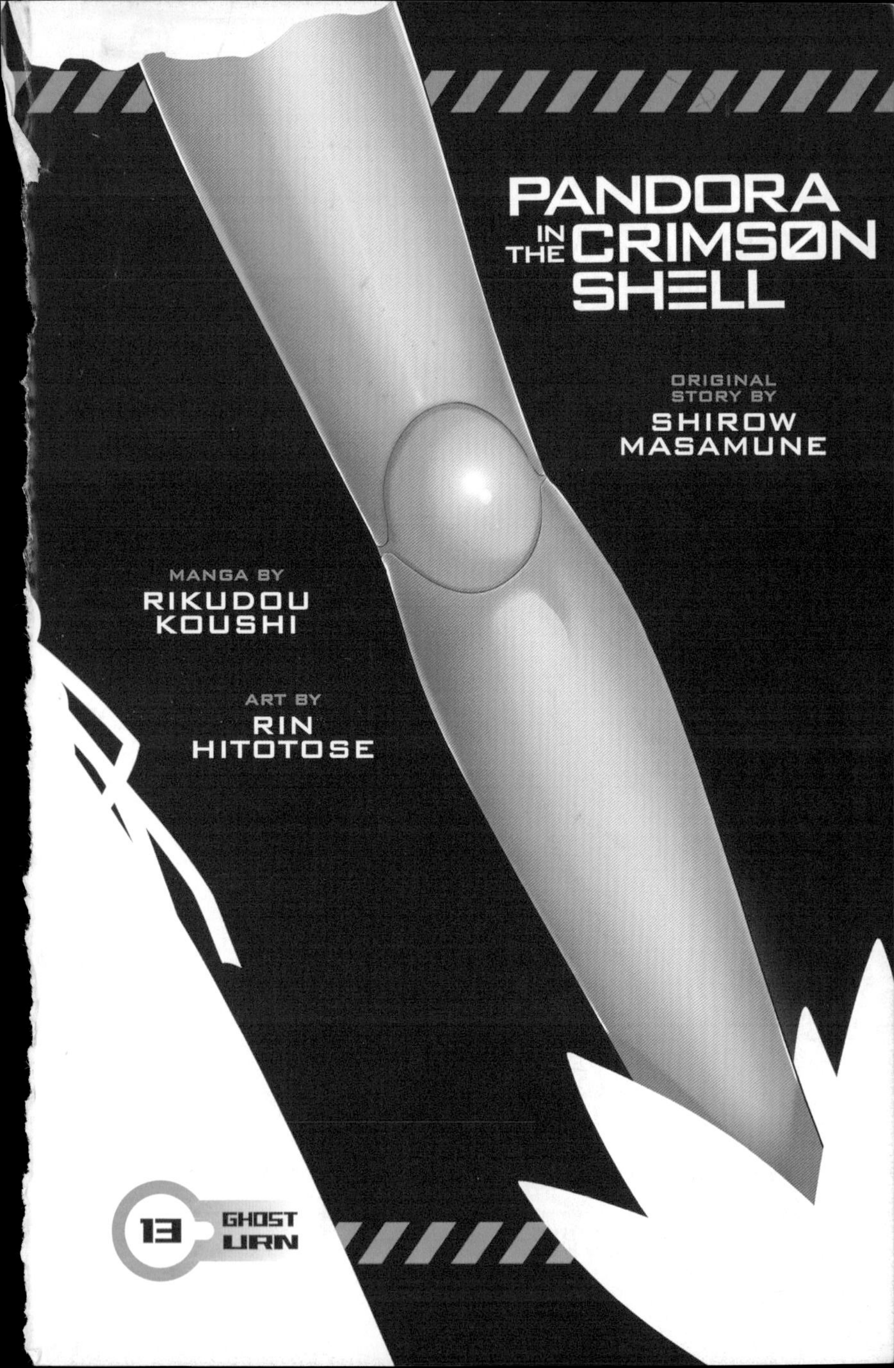
PANDORA IN THE CRIMSON SHELL
ORIGINAL STORY BY
SHIROW MASAMUNE
MANGA BY
RIKUDOU KOUSHI
ART BY
RIN HITOTOSE
13
GHOST URN

PANDORA IN THE
CRIMSØN SHELL
GHOST URN

Original story:
Shirow Masamune
(in cooperation with Crossroad)

Manga: Rikudou Koushi

Art: Rin Hitotose

13

GHOST URN-CHARACTERS —— Main Characters

■ Nanakorobi Nene
A girl whose brain was implanted into an entirely artificial body after an accident when she was young. Nene has one of the few full-body prosthetics in the world!

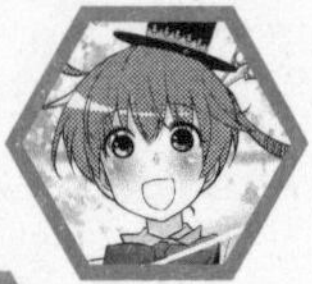

■ Clarion
A cat-eared girl wearing a maid uniform who initially accompanied Uzal. Like Nanakorobi Nene, Clarion has a full-body prosthetic...or does she? Clarion and Nene were brought together during the initial incident with Buer.

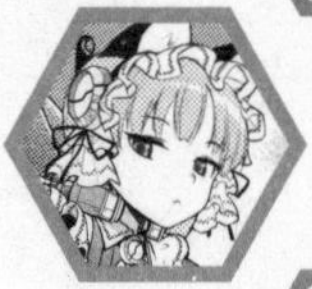

■ Uzal Delilah
The mysterious Uzal (real name: Sahar Schehera) is a well-known international businesswoman, but this brilliant scientist has plenty of secrets. She vanished during the chaos when Buer ran wild.

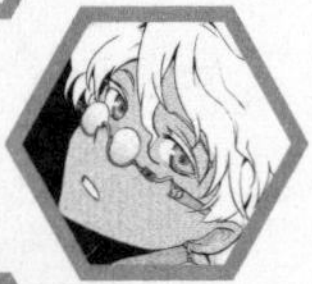

■ Korobase Takumi
Nene's mysterious aunt, and an acquaintance of Uzal's. She heads up the Korobase Foundation, which controls cybrain marketing, but has a pathological fear of people.

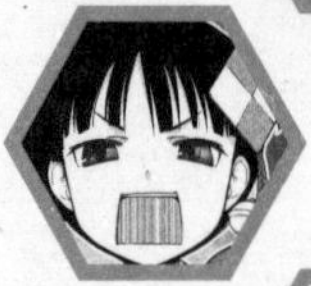

■ Phobos
The same model as Clarion: unit number Clarion 00 type 02. She now lives in the Korobase household with Nene and Clarion.

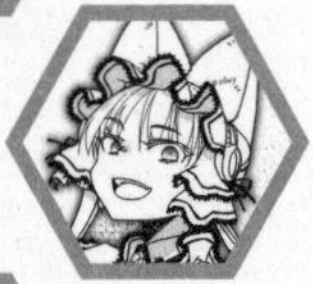

■ Massive boring machine Buer: Central Nervous Unit
The central control unit for the large multi-legged boring machine Buer, operating independently from the actual body and accompanying Nene and Clarion. This pompous-sounding entity provides a constant stream of perverted, leering commentary.

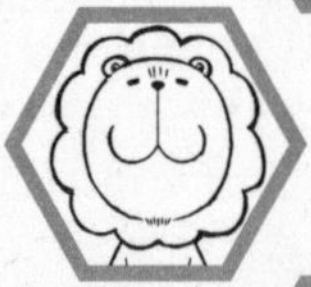

■ VlindXX XXXX
A perky, enthusiastic freelance reporter who dreams of taking her place among the top idols ***and*** the top reporters in the world! She's in feverish pursuit of her dream to dominate mass media, and dreams of romance with her bureau chief.

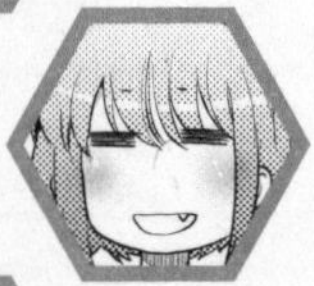

■ Captain Robert Altman
A captain with the Cenancle Defense Forces and a master of karate-style jujitsu. A passionate tough guy who loves justice and peace.

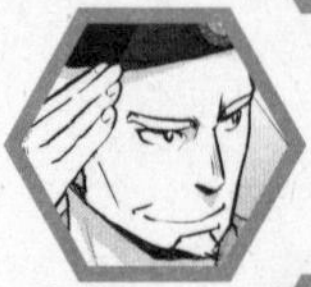

■ Proselpina
A popular young mainstream Titan TV reporter. She fell in love with Robert after he saved her life. They're currently dating.

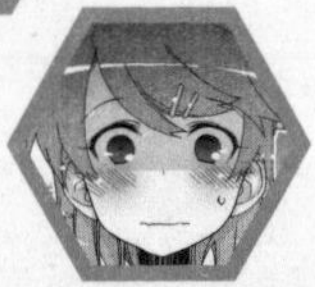

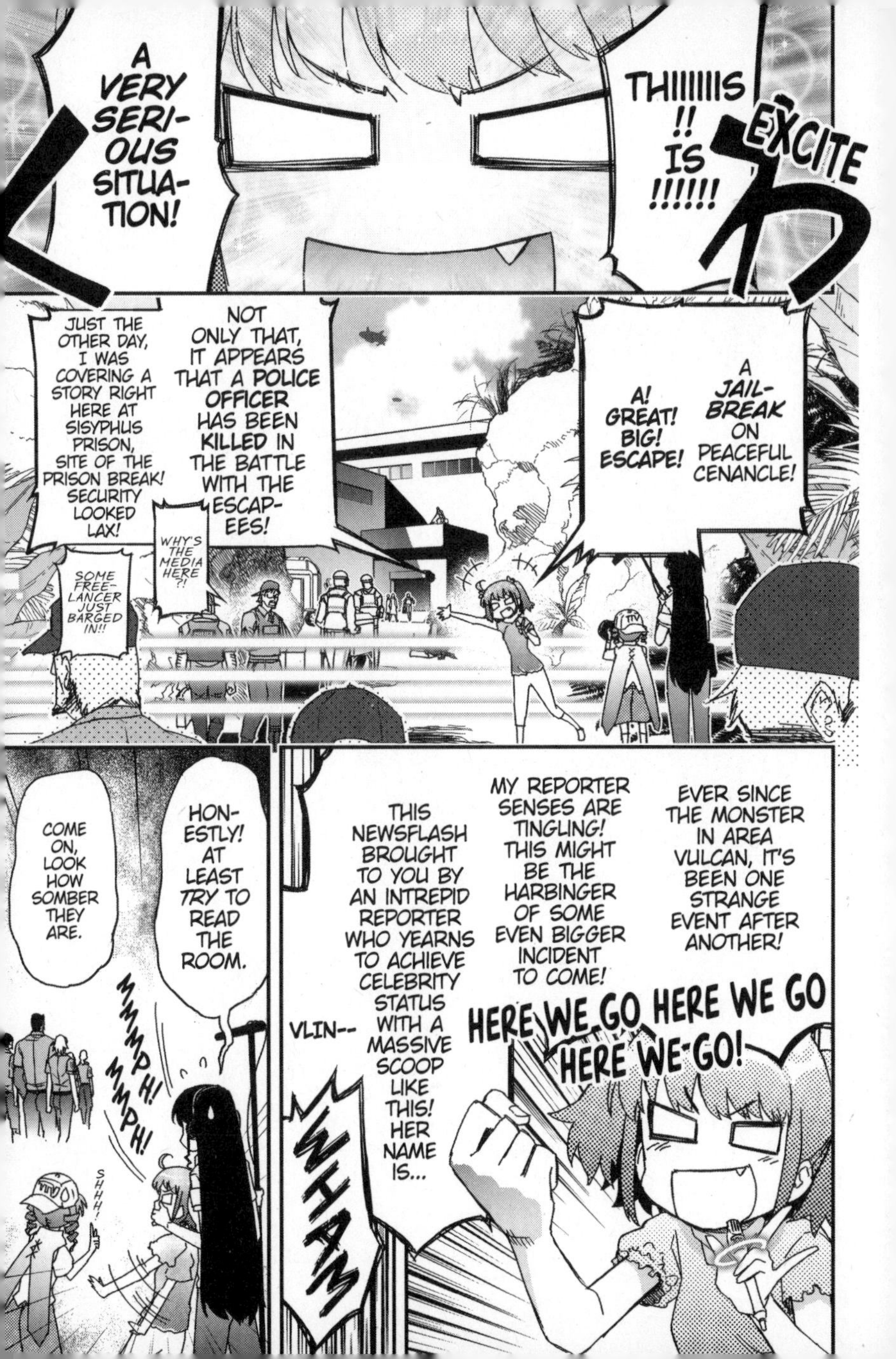
THIIIIIIS!! IS!!!!!!
EXCITE
A VERY SERIOUS SITUATION!
A JAIL-BREAK ON PEACEFUL CENANCLE!
A! GREAT! BIG! ESCAPE!
NOT ONLY THAT, IT APPEARS THAT A POLICE OFFICER HAS BEEN KILLED IN THE BATTLE WITH THE ESCAPEES!
JUST THE OTHER DAY, I WAS COVERING A STORY RIGHT HERE AT SISYPHUS PRISON, SITE OF THE PRISON BREAK! SECURITY LOOKED LAX!
WHY'S THE MEDIA HERE?!
SOME FREE-LANCER JUST BARGED IN!!
EVER SINCE THE MONSTER IN AREA VULCAN, IT'S BEEN ONE STRANGE EVENT AFTER ANOTHER!
MY REPORTER SENSES ARE TINGLING! THIS MIGHT BE THE HARBINGER OF SOME EVEN BIGGER INCIDENT TO COME!
THIS NEWSFLASH BROUGHT TO YOU BY AN INTREPID REPORTER WHO YEARNS TO ACHIEVE CELEBRITY STATUS WITH A MASSIVE SCOOP LIKE THIS! HER NAME IS...
HERE WE GO HERE WE GO HERE WE GO!
VLIN--
WHAM
HONESTLY! AT LEAST TRY TO READ THE ROOM.
COME ON, LOOK HOW SOMBER THEY ARE.
MMMPH! MMPH!
SHHH!

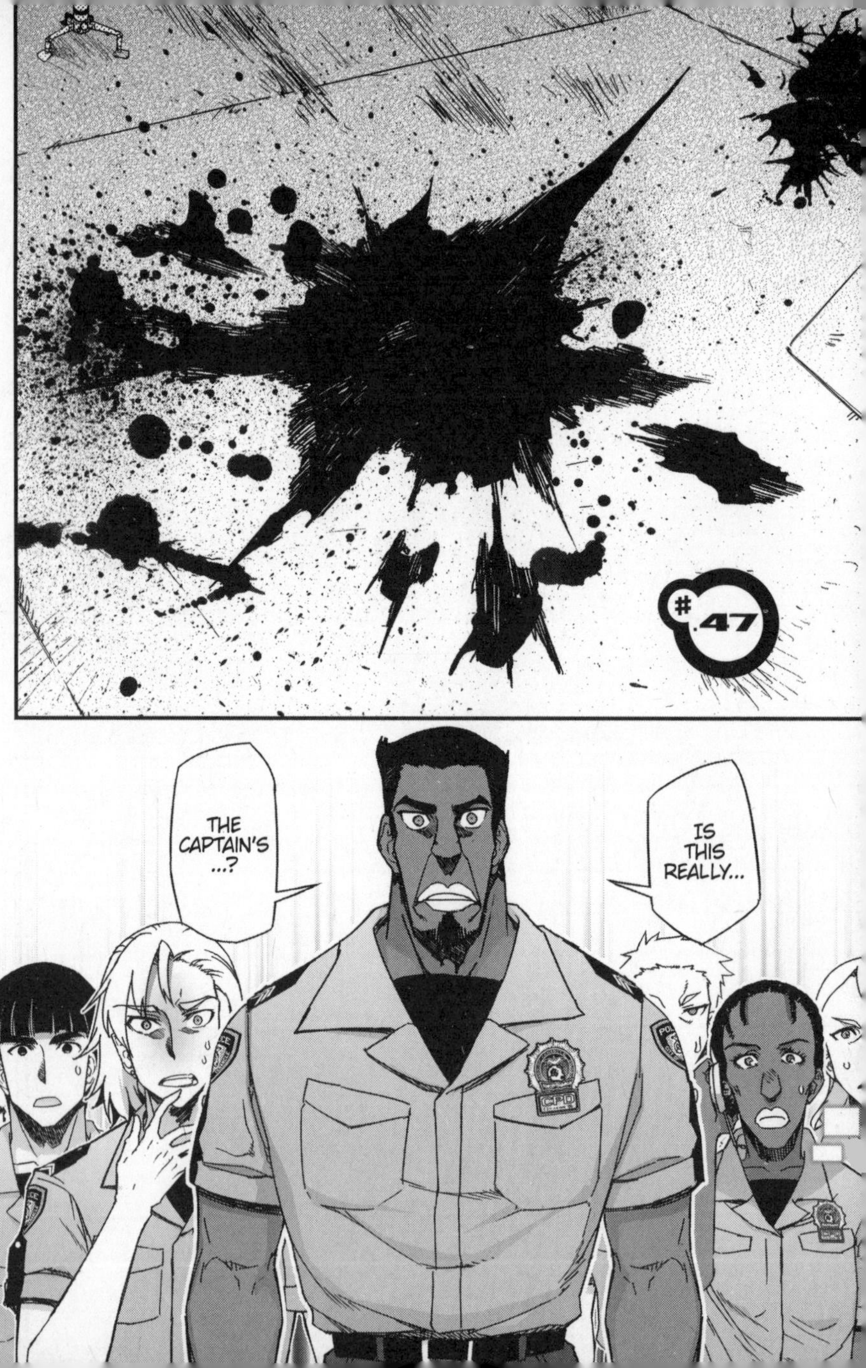
#.47
IS THIS REALLY...
THE CAPTAIN'S ...?

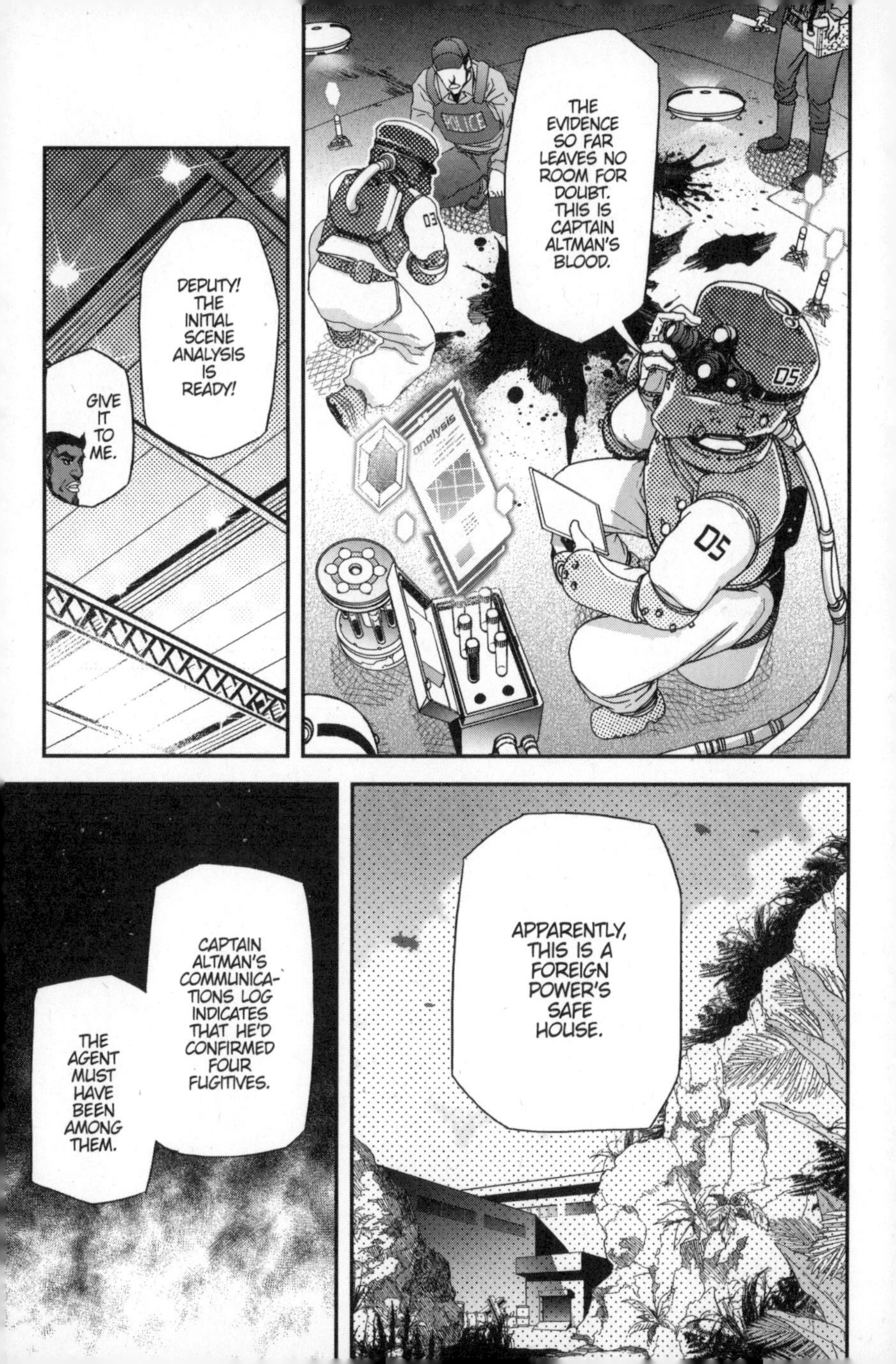
THE EVIDENCE SO FAR LEAVES NO ROOM FOR DOUBT. THIS IS CAPTAIN ALTMAN'S BLOOD.
DEPUTY! THE INITIAL SCENE ANALYSIS IS READY!
GIVE IT TO ME.
APPARENTLY, THIS IS A FOREIGN POWER'S SAFE HOUSE.
CAPTAIN ALTMAN'S COMMUNICATIONS LOG INDICATES THAT HE'D CONFIRMED FOUR FUGITIVES.
THE AGENT MUST HAVE BEEN AMONG THEM.

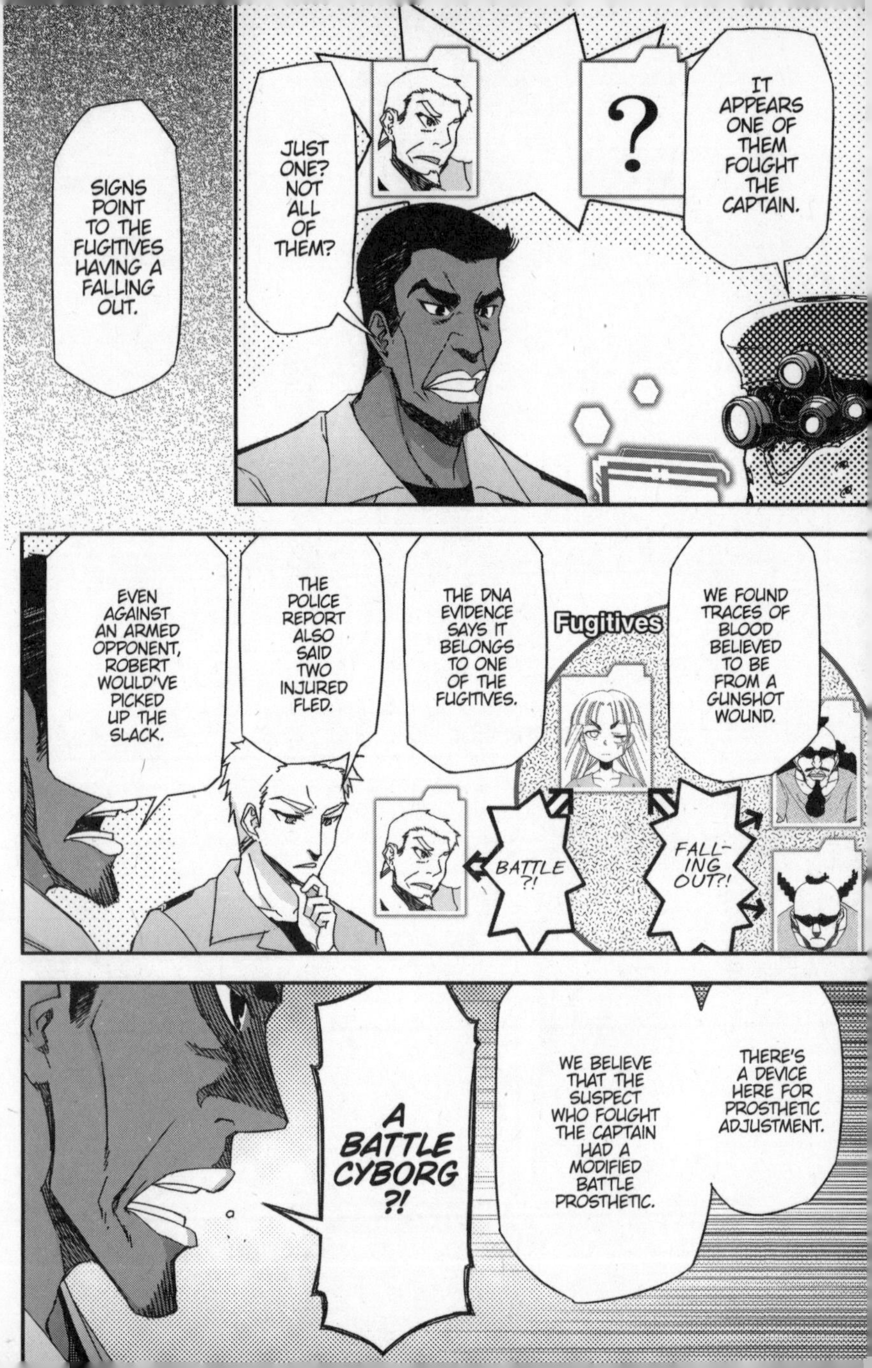
IT APPEARS ONE OF THEM FOUGHT THE CAPTAIN.
?
JUST ONE? NOT ALL OF THEM?
SIGNS POINT TO THE FUGITIVES HAVING A FALLING OUT.
WE FOUND TRACES OF BLOOD BELIEVED TO BE FROM A GUNSHOT WOUND.
Fugitives
THE DNA EVIDENCE SAYS IT BELONGS TO ONE OF THE FUGITIVES.
THE POLICE REPORT ALSO SAID TWO INJURED FLED.
EVEN AGAINST AN ARMED OPPONENT, ROBERT WOULD'VE PICKED UP THE SLACK.
FALL-ING OUT?!
BATTLE ?!
THERE'S A DEVICE HERE FOR PROSTHETIC ADJUSTMENT.
WE BELIEVE THAT THE SUSPECT WHO FOUGHT THE CAPTAIN HAD A MODIFIED BATTLE PROSTHETIC.
A BATTLE CYBORG ?!

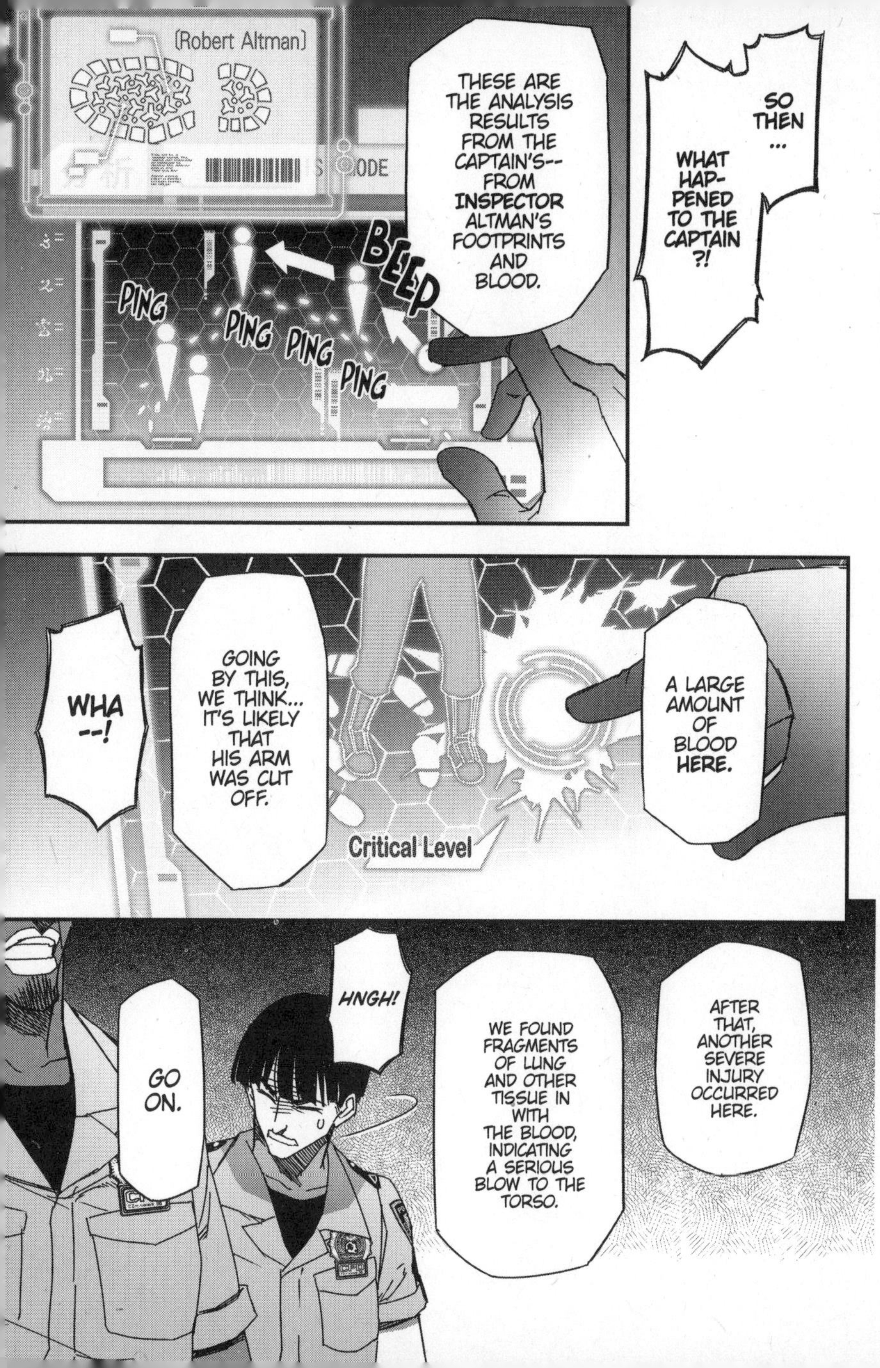
SO THEN ... WHAT HAP-PENED TO THE CAPTAIN ?!
THESE ARE THE ANALYSIS RESULTS FROM THE CAPTAIN'S-- FROM **INSPECTOR** ALTMAN'S FOOTPRINTS AND BLOOD.
(Robert Altman)
BEEP
PING
PING
PING
PING
A LARGE AMOUNT OF BLOOD **HERE.**
Critical Level
GOING BY THIS, WE THINK... IT'S LIKELY THAT HIS ARM WAS CUT OFF.
WHA--!
AFTER THAT, ANOTHER SEVERE INJURY OCCURRED HERE.
WE FOUND FRAGMENTS OF LUNG AND OTHER TISSUE IN WITH THE BLOOD, INDICATING A SERIOUS BLOW TO THE TORSO.
HNGH!
GO ON.

THIS MUCH BLOOD LOSS WOULD BE FATAL.
THAT'S ...
BUT THEN WHY IS THERE NO BODY?
MAYBE HE WAS TAKEN AS A HOSTAGE ?!
BACK IN HIS SOLDIER DAYS...
THE CAPTAIN HAD A TRANSMITTER IMPLANTED IN HIS BODY, LIKE ALL OFFICERS AND HIGHER-UPS.
IT USED BIOELECTRICITY TO TRANSMIT FOUR TIMES A DAY.
NORMALLY, WE... WE WOULD HAVE RECEIVED A SIGNAL THIRTY MINUTES AGO.
!

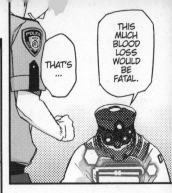

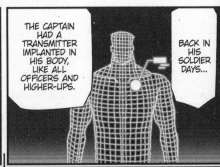

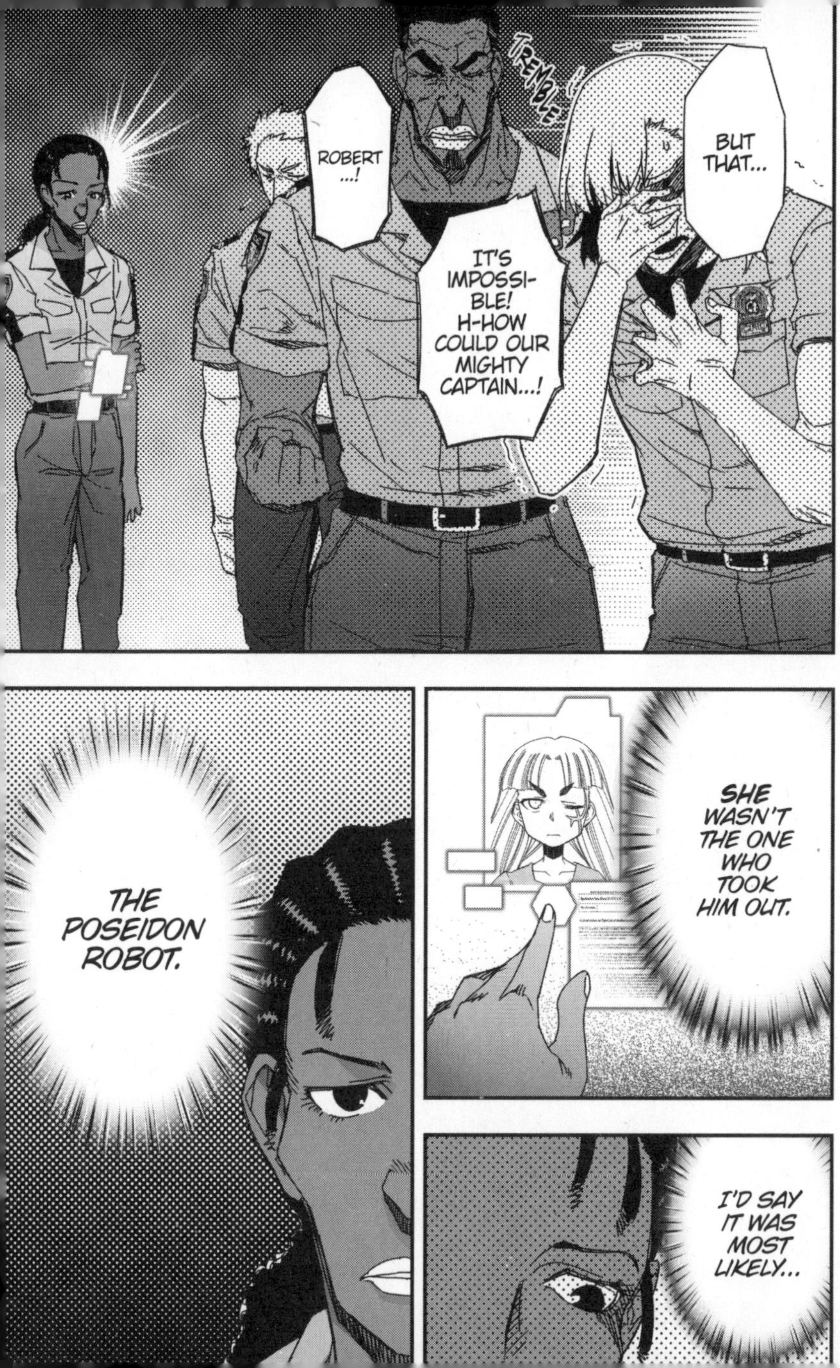
BUT THAT...
TREMBLE
ROBERT ...!
IT'S IMPOSSI-BLE! H-HOW COULD OUR MIGHTY CAPTAIN...!
SHE WASN'T THE ONE WHO TOOK HIM OUT.
I'D SAY IT WAS MOST LIKELY...
THE POSEIDON ROBOT.

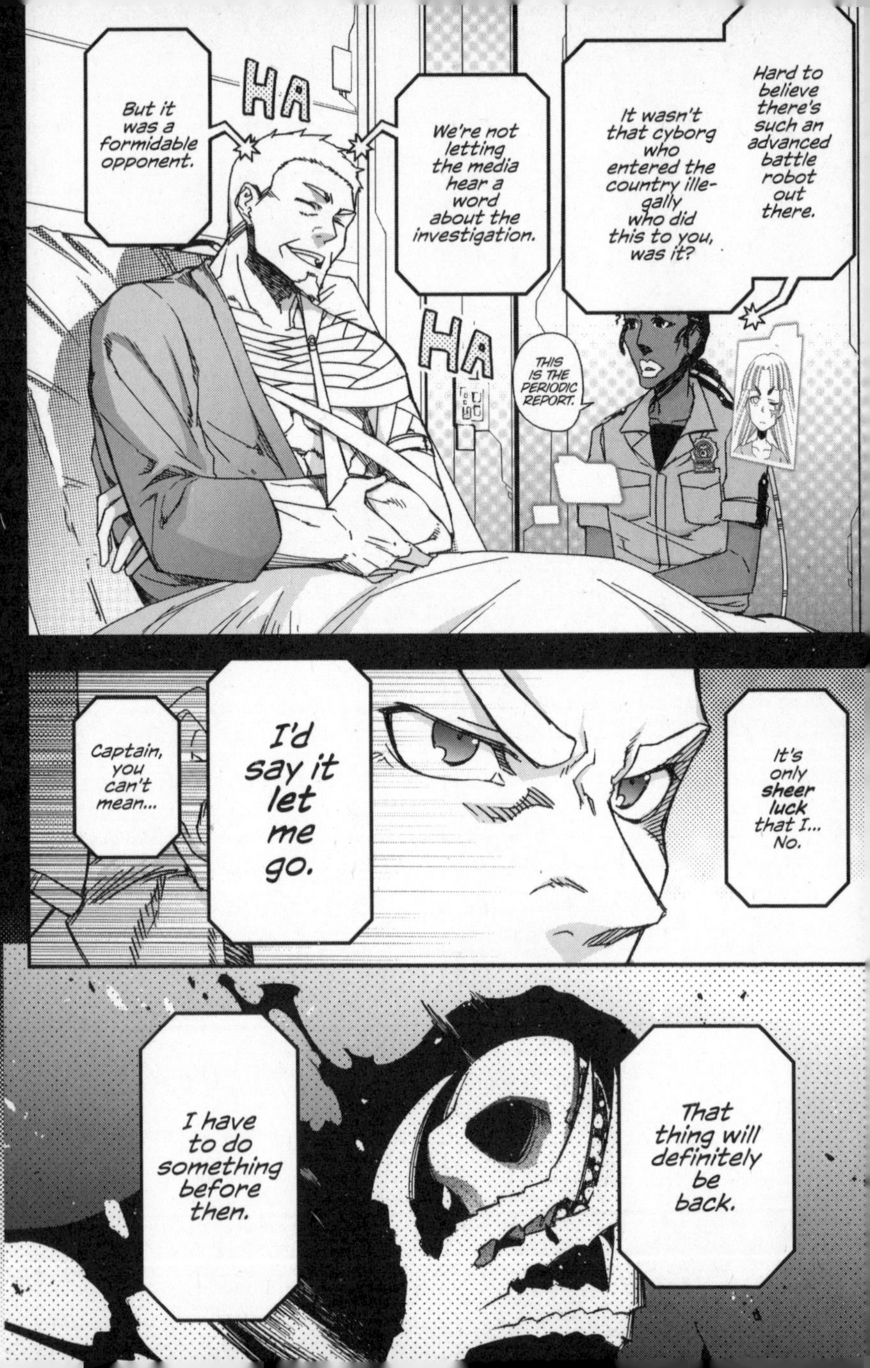

Hard to believe there's such an advanced battle robot out there.
It wasn't that cyborg who entered the country ille-gally who did this to you, was it?
We're not letting the media hear a word about the investigation.
HA
But it was a formidable opponent.
HA
THIS IS THE PERIODIC REPORT.
It's only **sheer luck** that I... No.
I'd say it let me go.
Captain, you can't mean...
That thing will definitely be back.
I have to do something before then.

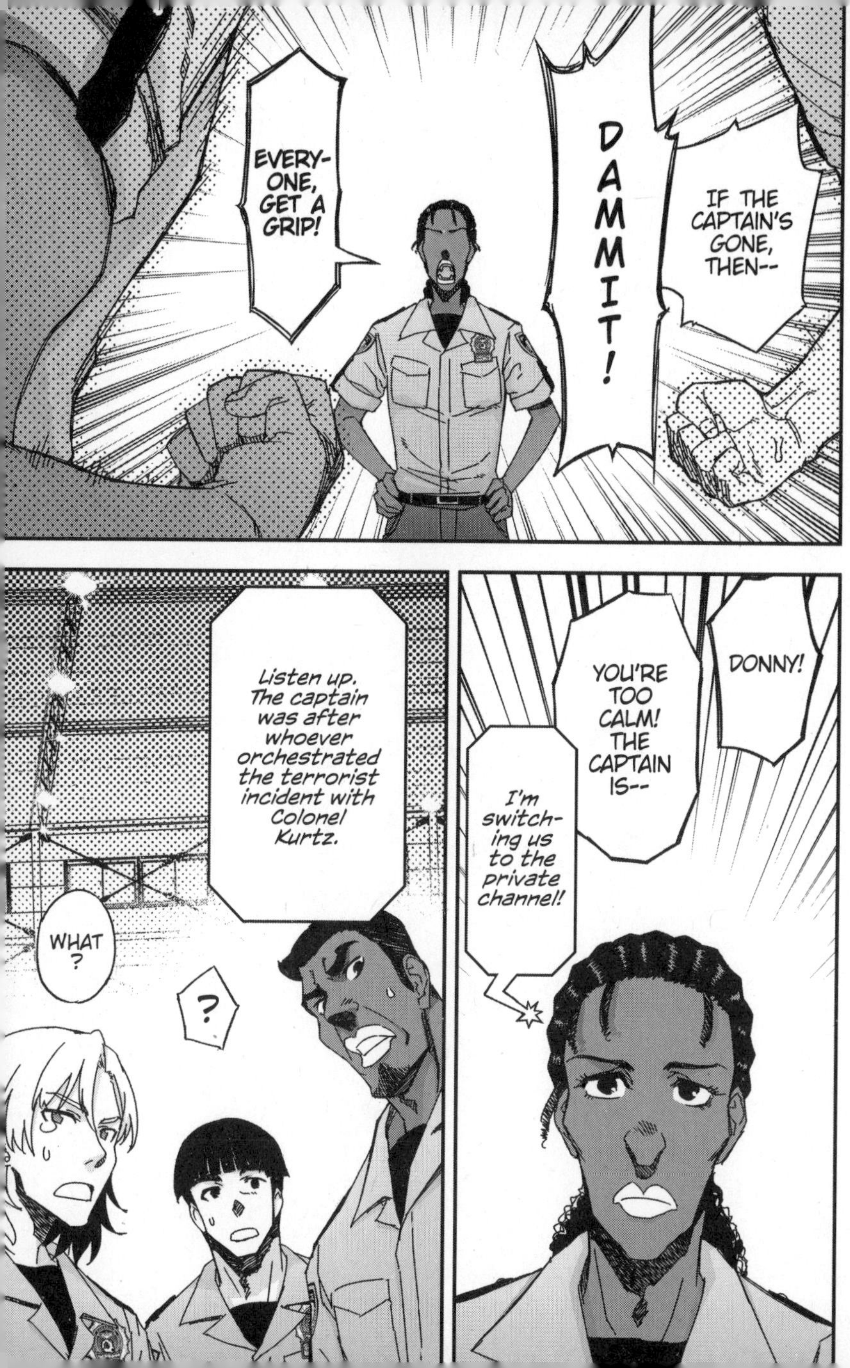
IF THE CAPTAIN'S GONE, THEN--
DAMMIT!
EVERY-ONE, GET A GRIP!
DONNY!
YOU'RE TOO CALM! THE CAPTAIN IS--
I'm switch-ing us to the private channel!
Listen up. The captain was after whoever orchestrated the terrorist incident with Colonel Kurtz.
WHAT?
?

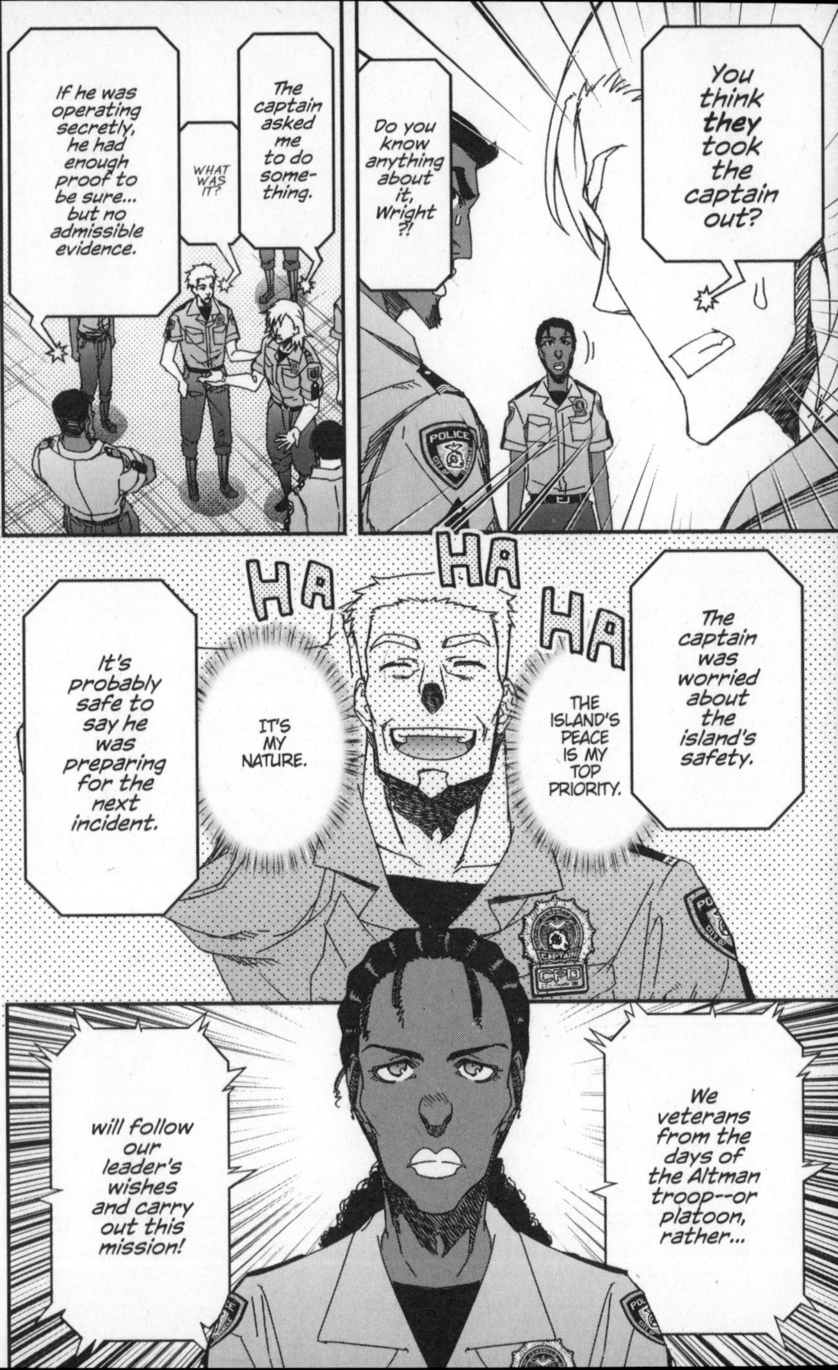
You think they took the captain out?
Do you know anything about it, Wright?!
The captain asked me to do something.
WHAT WAS IT?
If he was operating secretly, he had enough proof to be sure... but no admissible evidence.
The captain was worried about the island's safety.
HA HA HA
THE ISLAND'S PEACE IS MY TOP PRIORITY.
IT'S MY NATURE.
It's probably safe to say he was preparing for the next incident.
We veterans from the days of the Altman troop--or platoon, rather...
will follow our leader's wishes and carry out this mission!

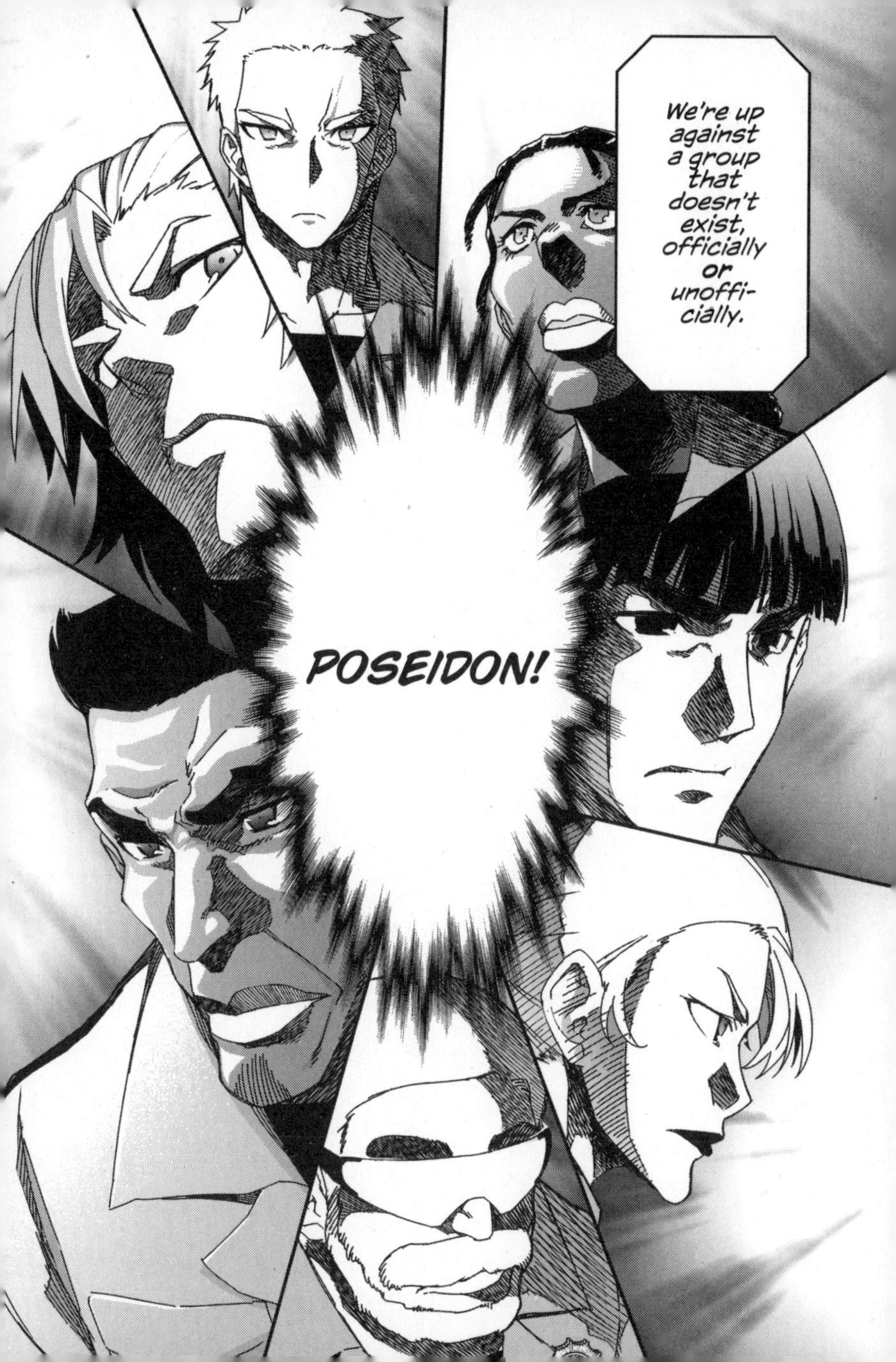
We're up against a group that doesn't exist, officially or unofficially.
POSEIDON!

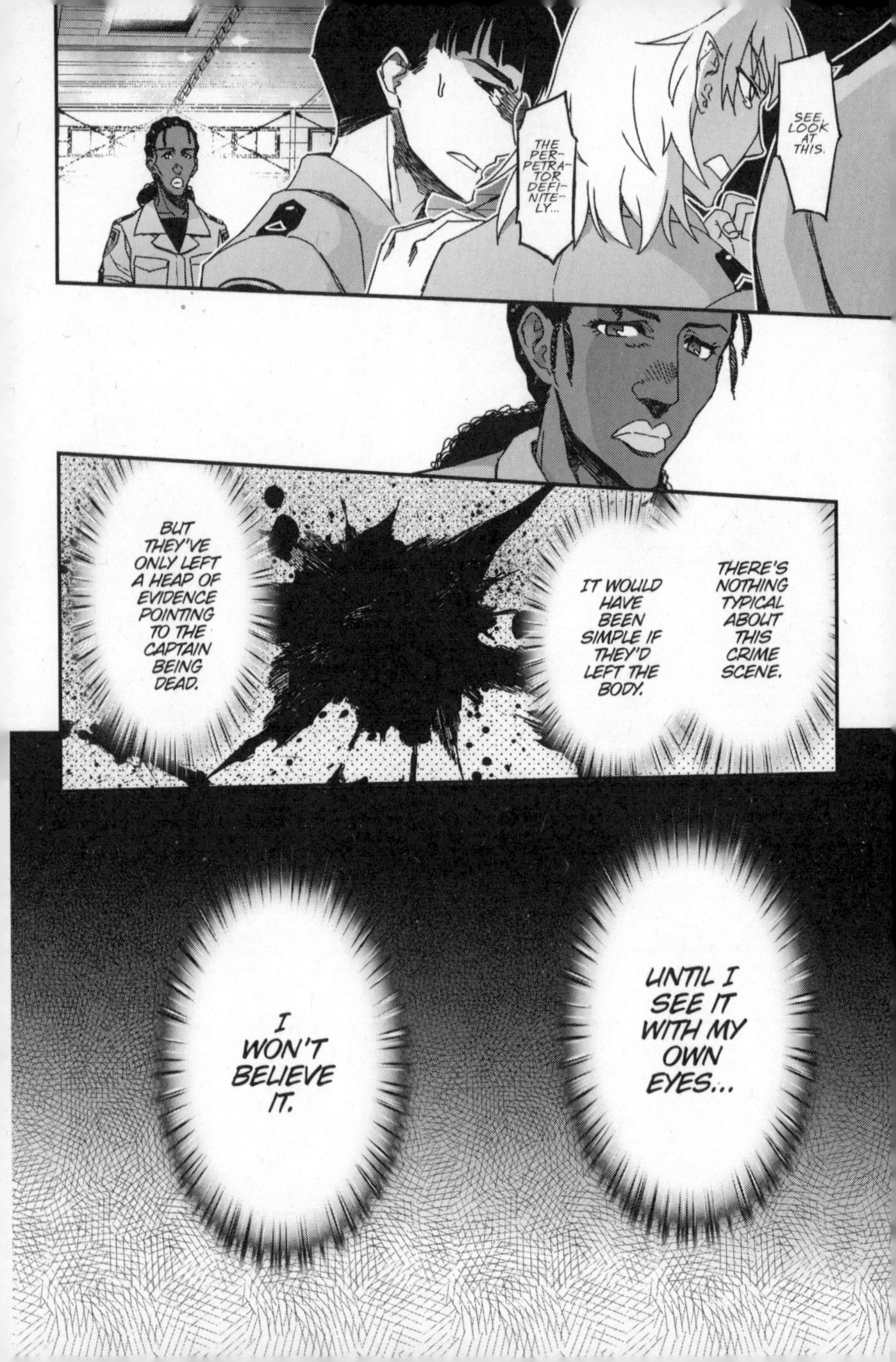
SEE, LOOK AT THIS.
THE PERPETRATOR DEFINITELY...
THERE'S NOTHING TYPICAL ABOUT THIS CRIME SCENE.
IT WOULD HAVE BEEN SIMPLE IF THEY'D LEFT THE BODY.
BUT THEY'VE ONLY LEFT A HEAP OF EVIDENCE POINTING TO THE CAPTAIN BEING DEAD.
UNTIL I SEE IT WITH MY OWN EYES...
I WON'T BELIEVE IT.

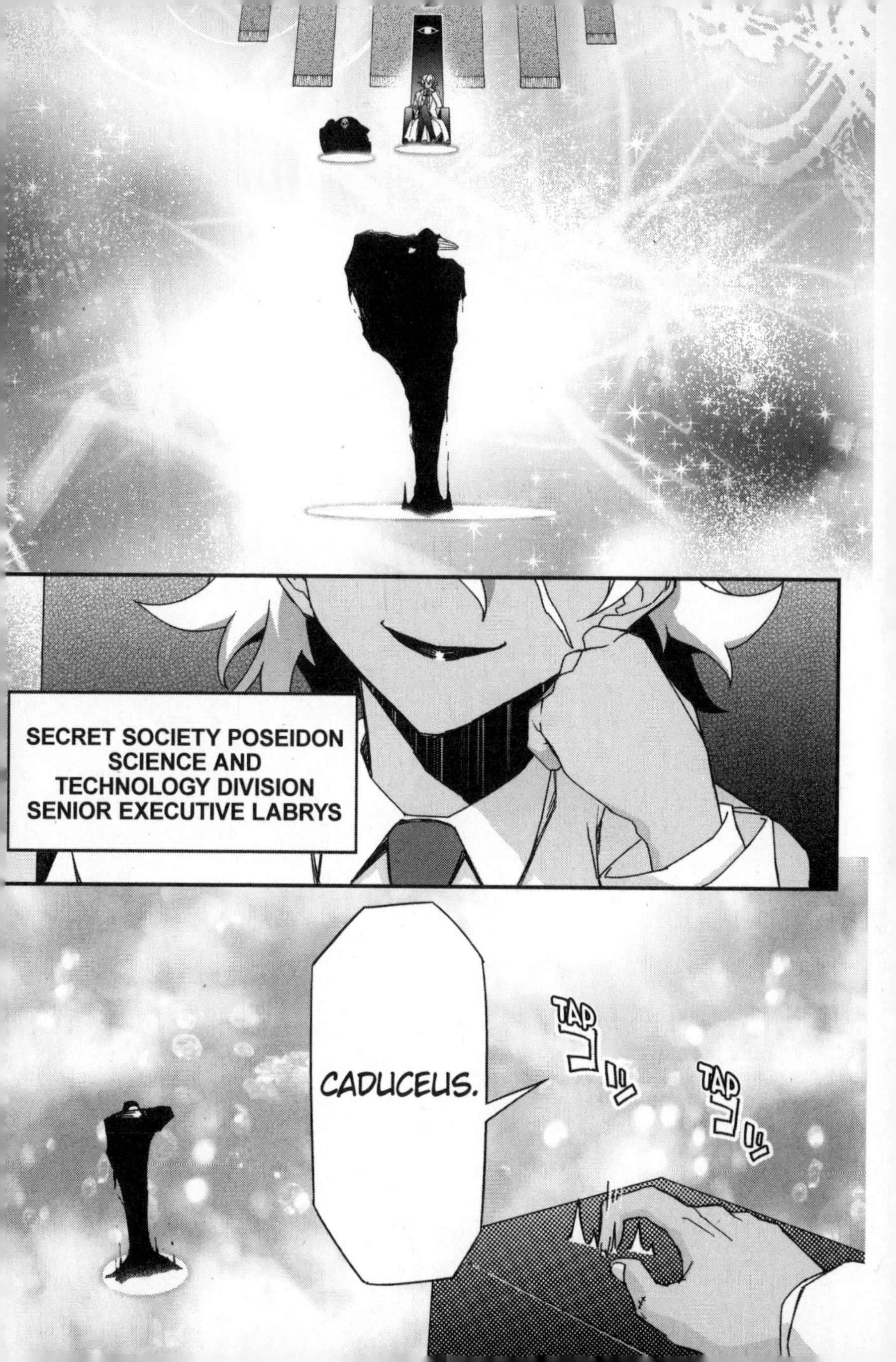
SECRET SOCIETY POSEIDON SCIENCE AND TECHNOLOGY DIVISION SENIOR EXECUTIVE LABRYS
TAP
TAP
CADUCEUS.

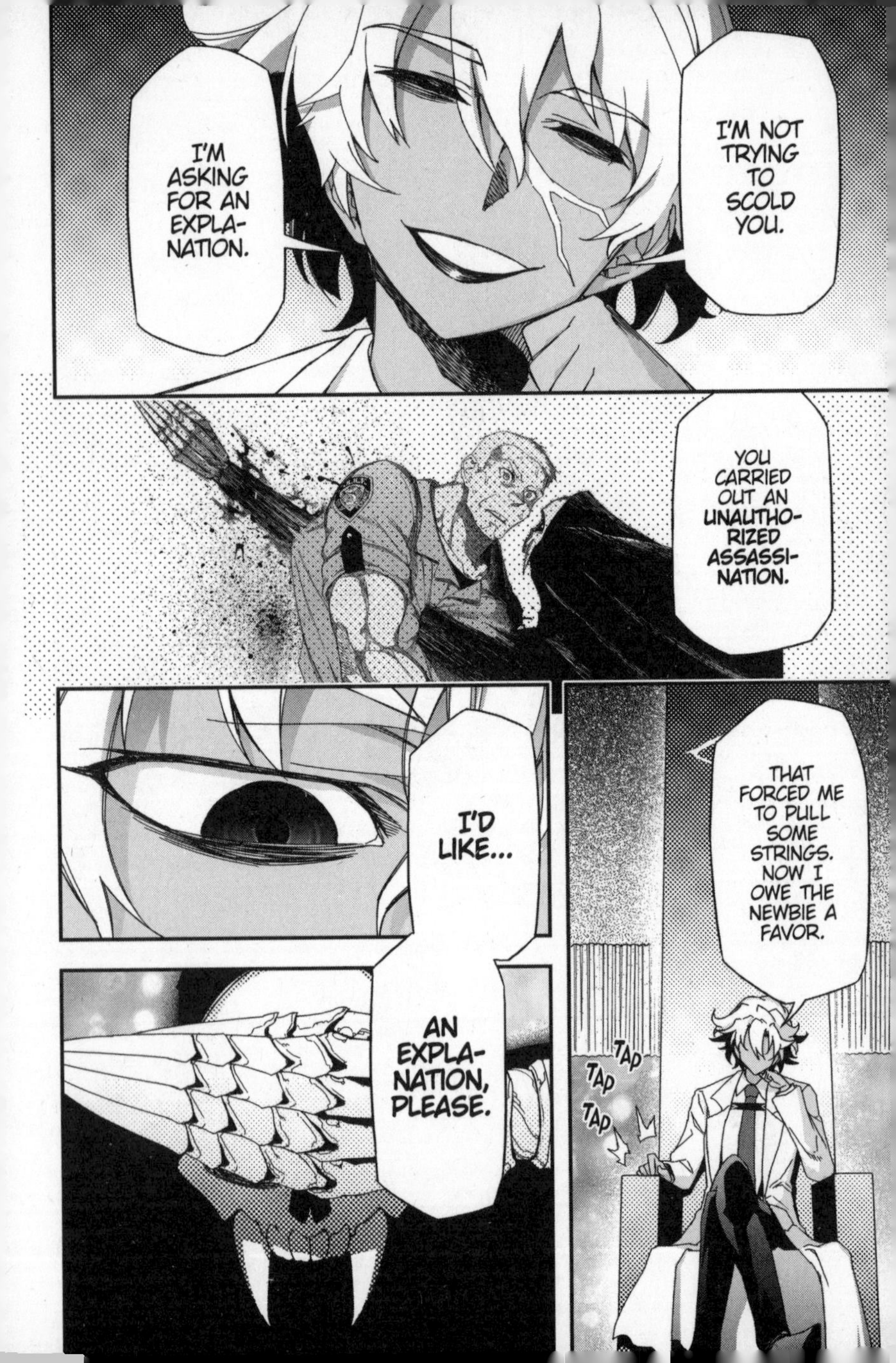
I'M NOT TRYING TO SCOLD YOU.
I'M ASKING FOR AN EXPLANATION.
YOU CARRIED OUT AN UNAUTHORIZED ASSASSINATION.
THAT FORCED ME TO PULL SOME STRINGS. NOW I OWE THE NEWBIE A FAVOR.
TAP
TAP
TAP
I'D LIKE...
AN EXPLANATION, PLEASE.

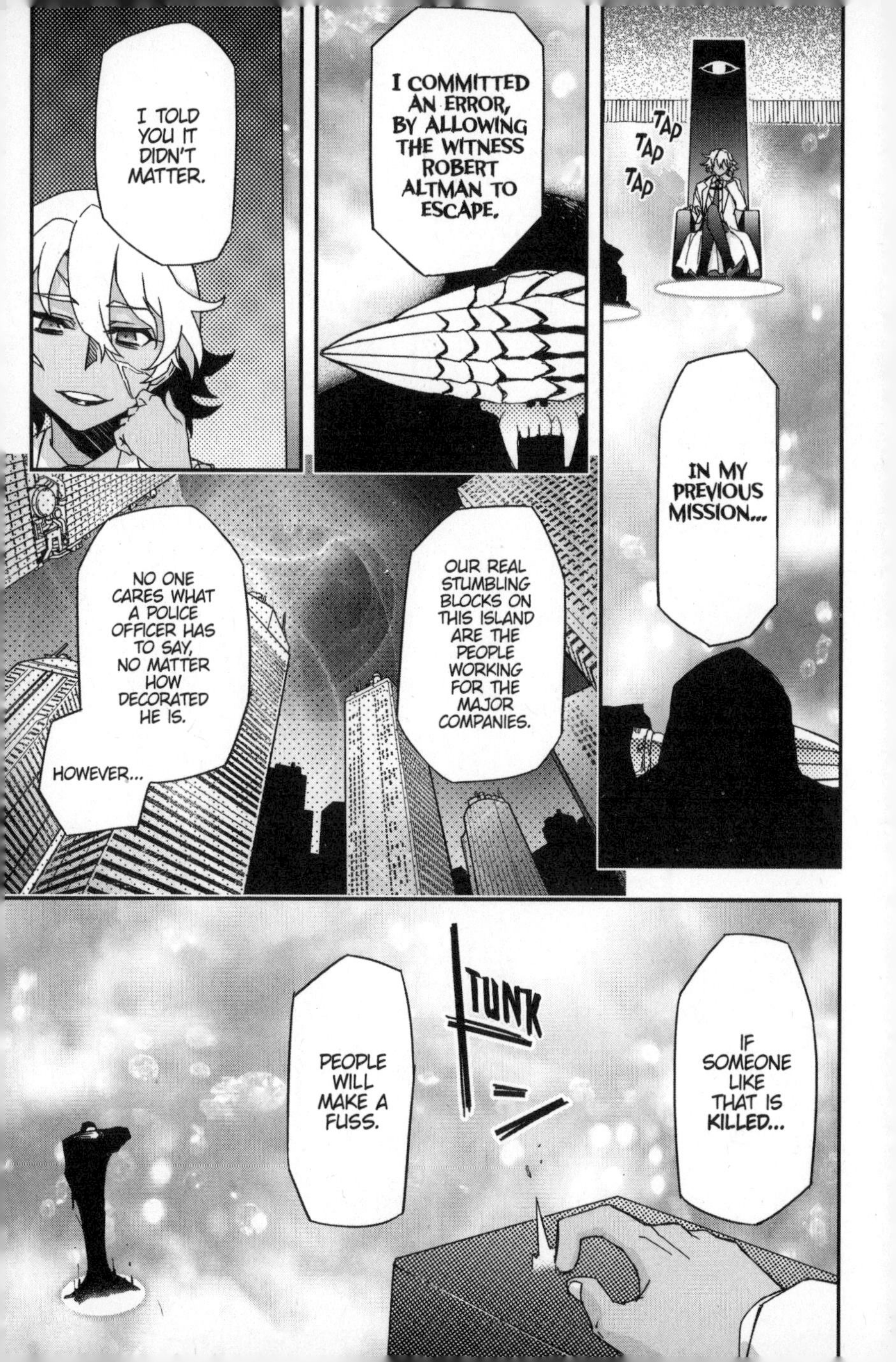
TAP
TAP
TAP
IN MY PREVIOUS MISSION...
I COMMITTED AN ERROR, BY ALLOWING THE WITNESS ROBERT ALTMAN TO ESCAPE.
I TOLD YOU IT DIDN'T MATTER.
OUR REAL STUMBLING BLOCKS ON THIS ISLAND ARE THE PEOPLE WORKING FOR THE MAJOR COMPANIES.
NO ONE CARES WHAT A POLICE OFFICER HAS TO SAY, NO MATTER HOW DECORATED HE IS.
HOWEVER...
IF SOMEONE LIKE THAT IS KILLED...
TUNK
PEOPLE WILL MAKE A FUSS.

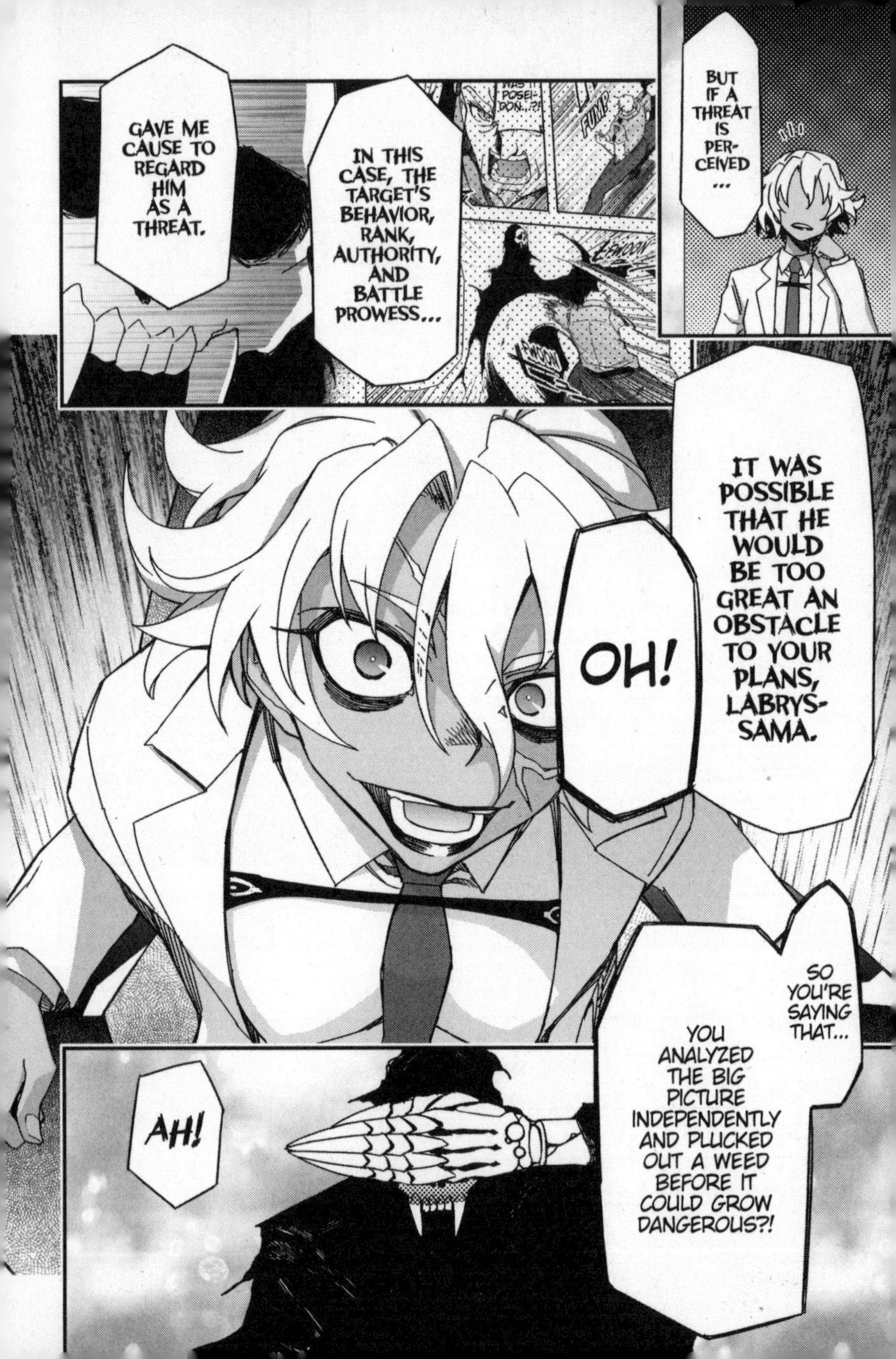
BUT IF A THREAT IS PERCEIVED...
WAS IT POSEIDON...?!
FUMP
FWOOM
FWOOM
IN THIS CASE, THE TARGET'S BEHAVIOR, RANK, AUTHORITY, AND BATTLE PROWESS...
GAVE ME CAUSE TO REGARD HIM AS A THREAT.
IT WAS POSSIBLE THAT HE WOULD BE TOO GREAT AN OBSTACLE TO YOUR PLANS, LABRYS-SAMA.
OH!
SO YOU'RE SAYING THAT...
YOU ANALYZED THE BIG PICTURE INDEPENDENTLY AND PLUCKED OUT A WEED BEFORE IT COULD GROW DANGEROUS?!
AH!

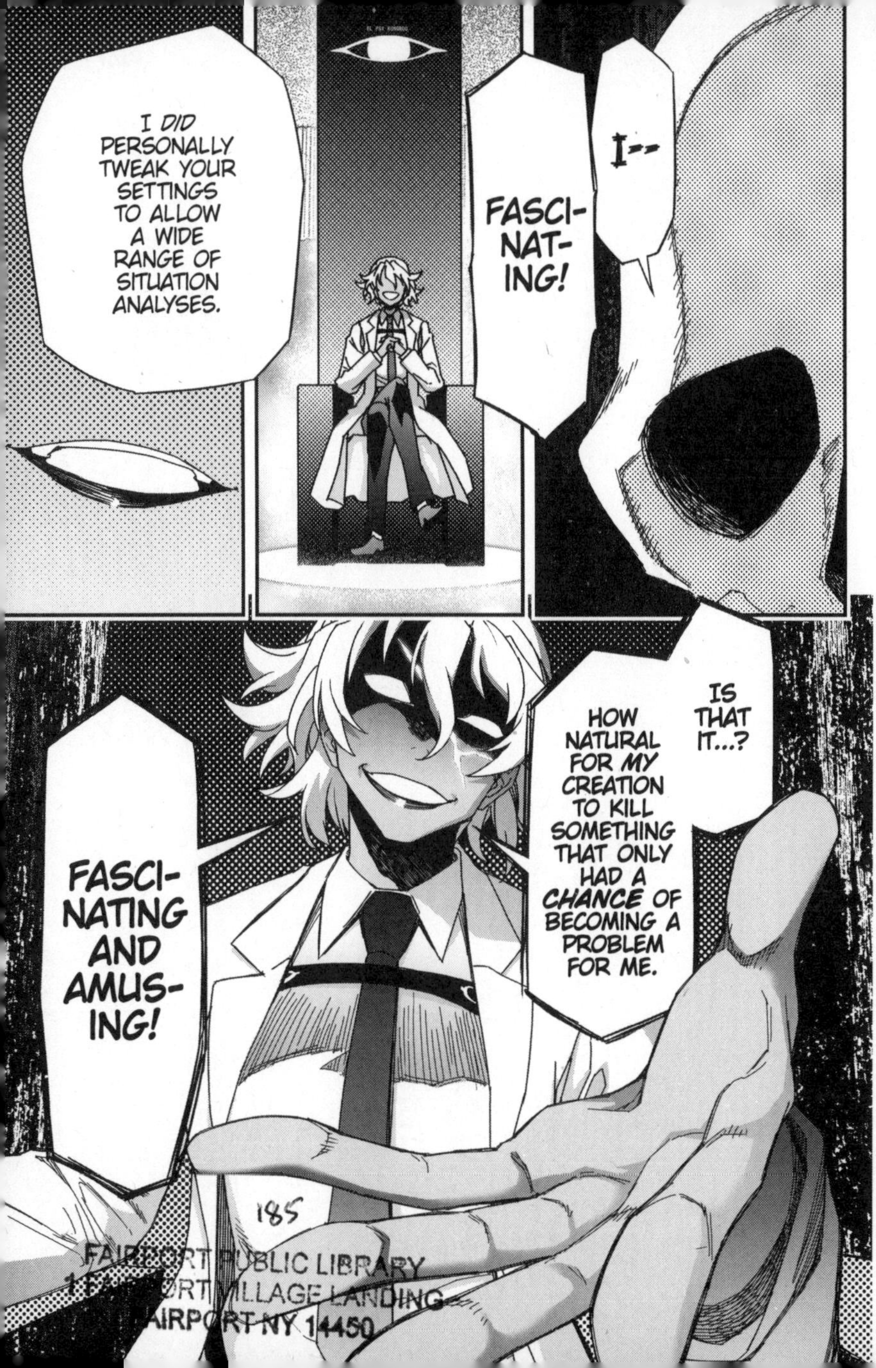
I--
FASCI-NAT-ING!
I *DID* PERSONALLY TWEAK YOUR SETTINGS TO ALLOW A WIDE RANGE OF SITUATION ANALYSES.
IS THAT IT...?
HOW NATURAL FOR *MY* CREATION TO KILL SOMETHING THAT ONLY HAD A *CHANCE* OF BECOMING A PROBLEM FOR ME.
FASCI-NATING AND AMUS-ING!

DIS-MISSED!

I'LL FORGIVE YOU THIS TIME, BUT IN THE FUTURE, YOU ARE REQUIRED TO REPORT ANY PROSPECTIVE ASSASSINATIONS IN ADVANCE.

HEH HEH!

WELL, FINE.

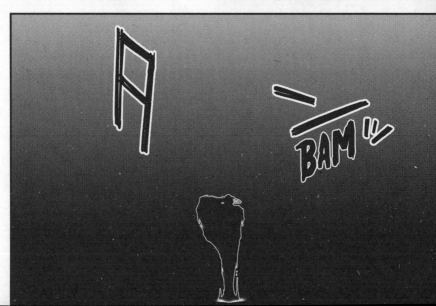

BAM

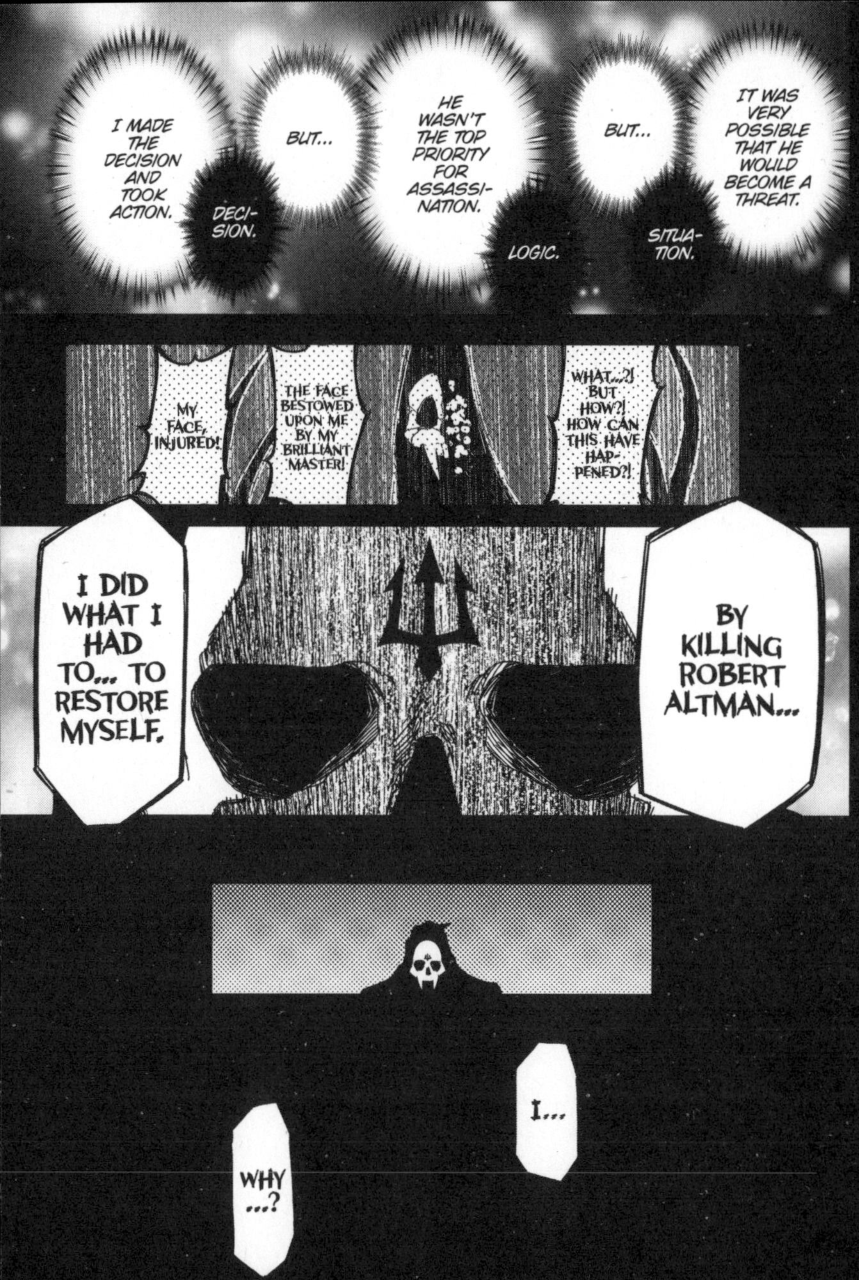
IT WAS VERY POSSIBLE THAT HE WOULD BECOME A THREAT.
SITUATION.
BUT...
LOGIC.
HE WASN'T THE TOP PRIORITY FOR ASSASSINATION.
BUT...
DECISION.
I MADE THE DECISION AND TOOK ACTION.
WHAT...?! BUT HOW?! HOW CAN THIS HAVE HAPPENED?!
THE FACE BESTOWED UPON ME BY MY BRILLIANT MASTER!
MY FACE, INJURED!
BY KILLING ROBERT ALTMAN...
I DID WHAT I HAD TO... TO RESTORE MYSELF.
I...
WHY ...?

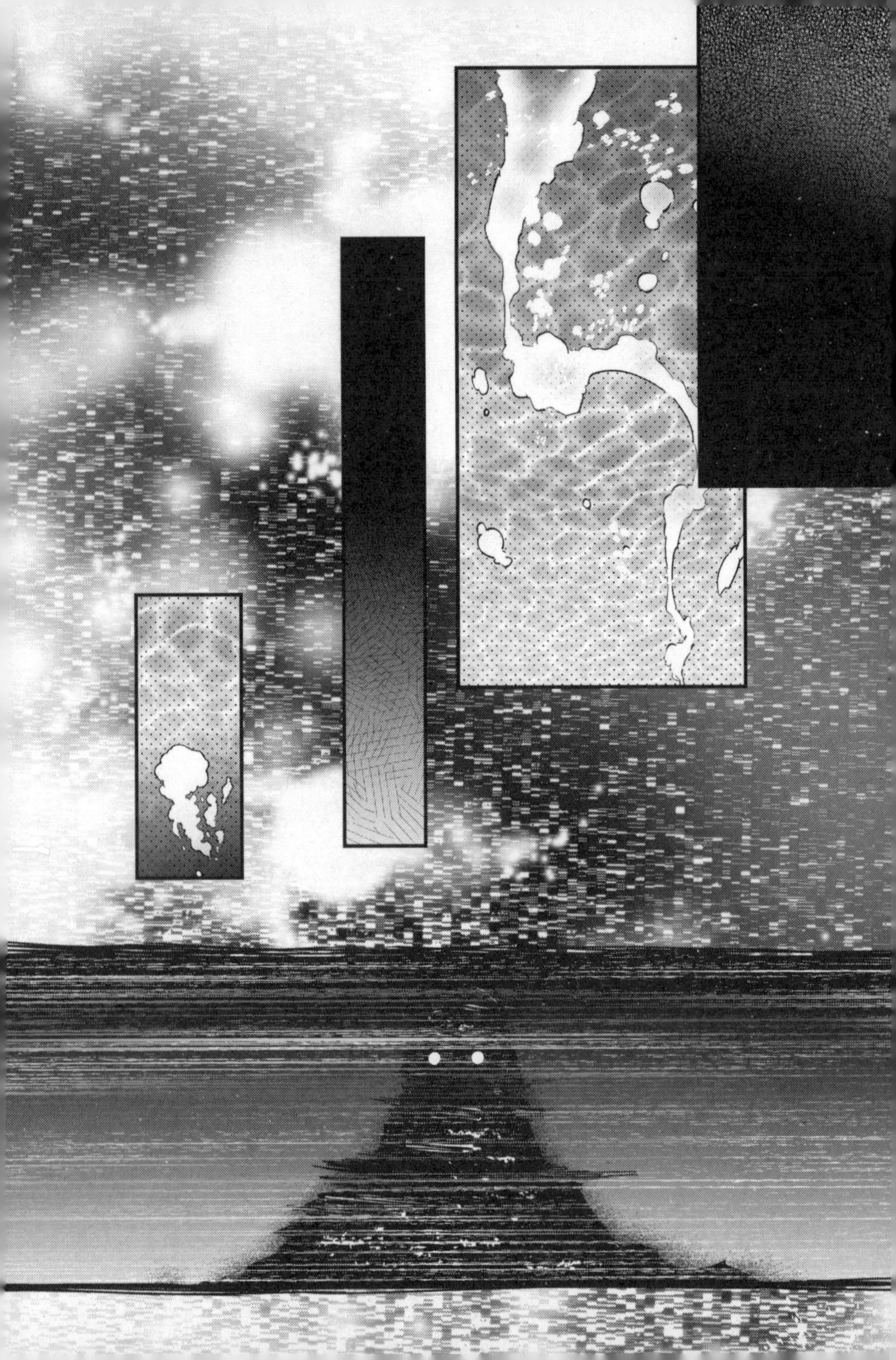

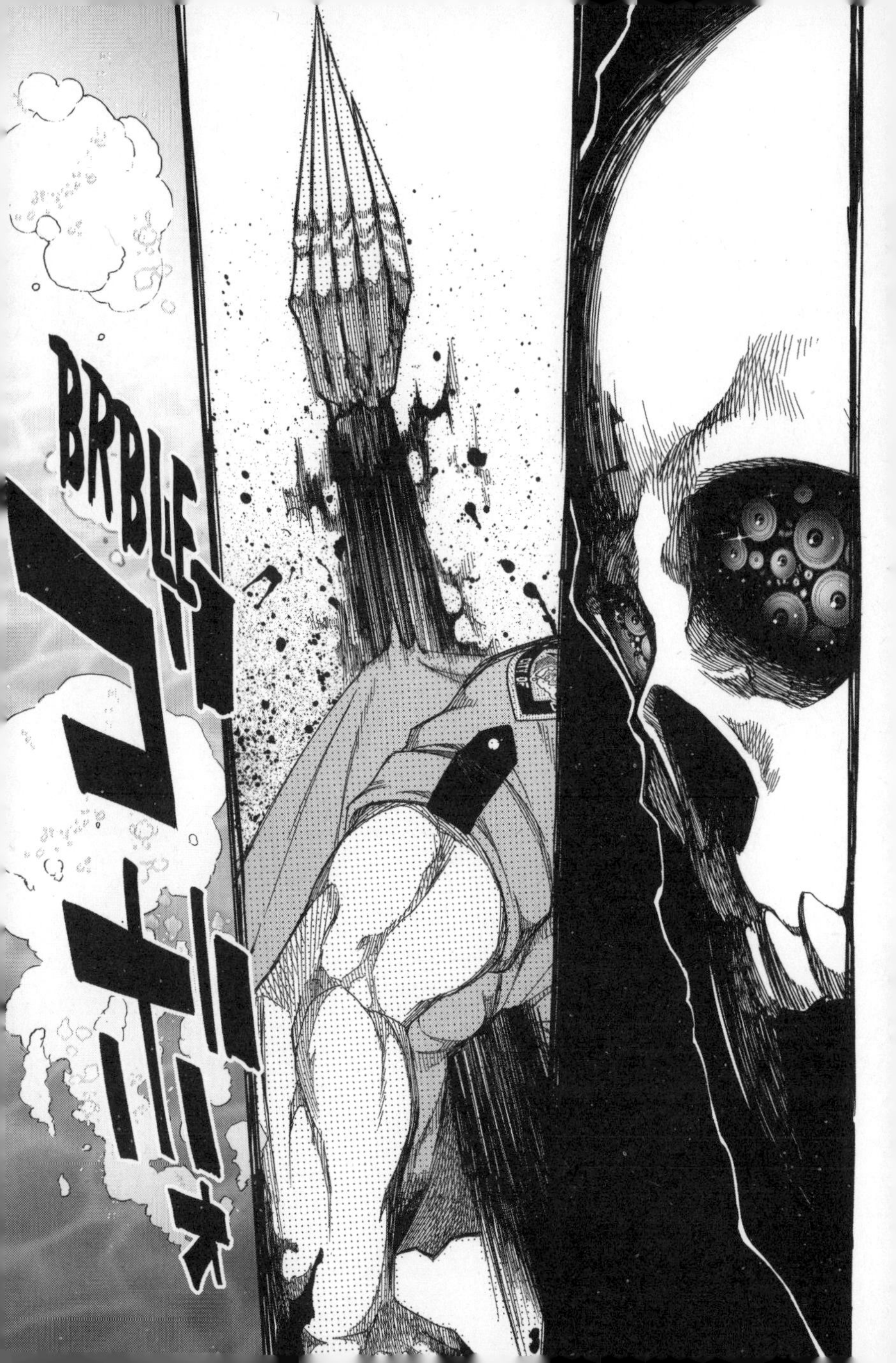
BRBLE

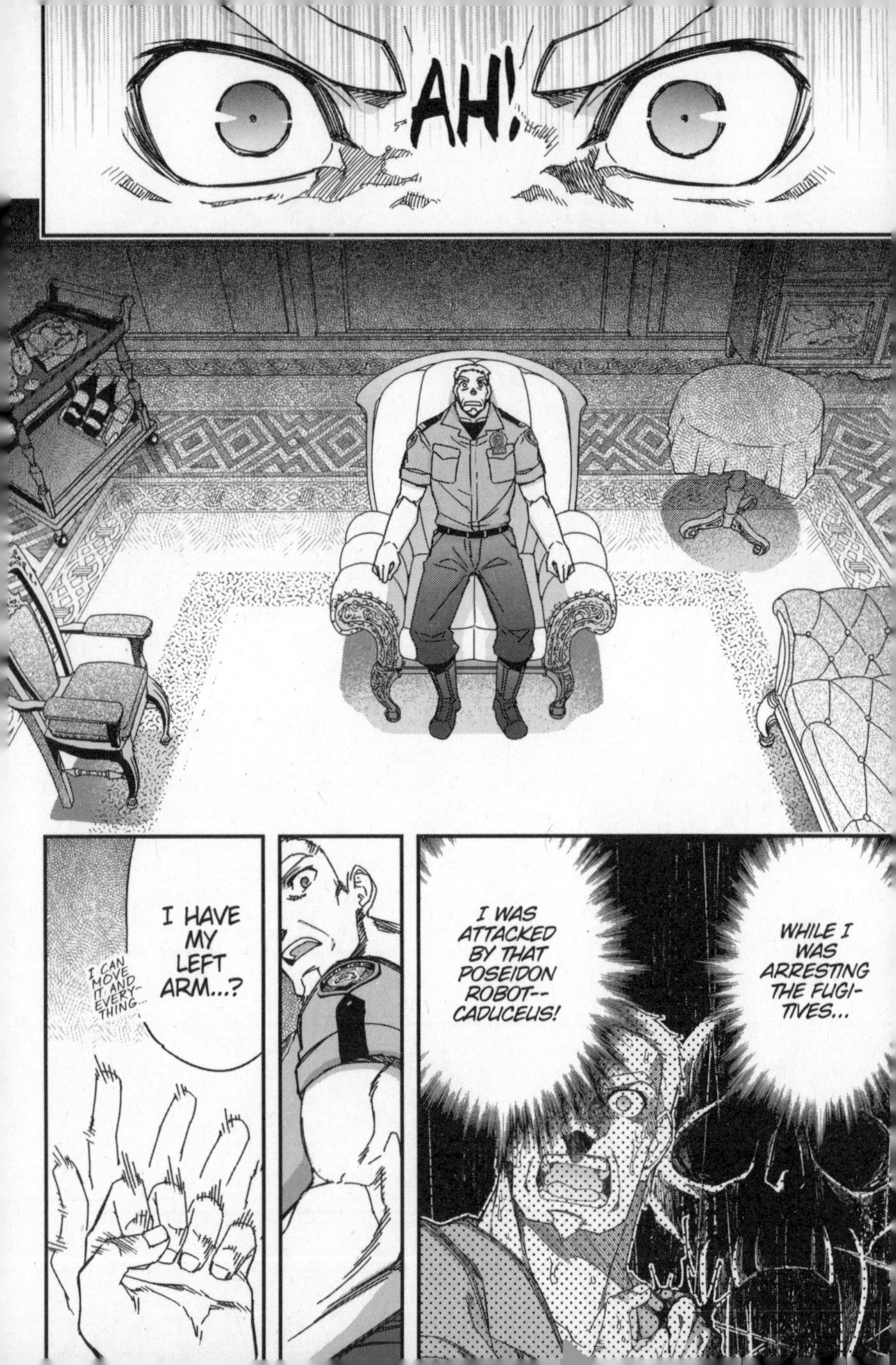
AH!
WHILE I WAS ARRESTING THE FUGITIVES...
I WAS ATTACKED BY THAT POSEIDON ROBOT--CADUCEUS!
I HAVE MY LEFT ARM...?
I CAN MOVE IT AND EVERYTHING...

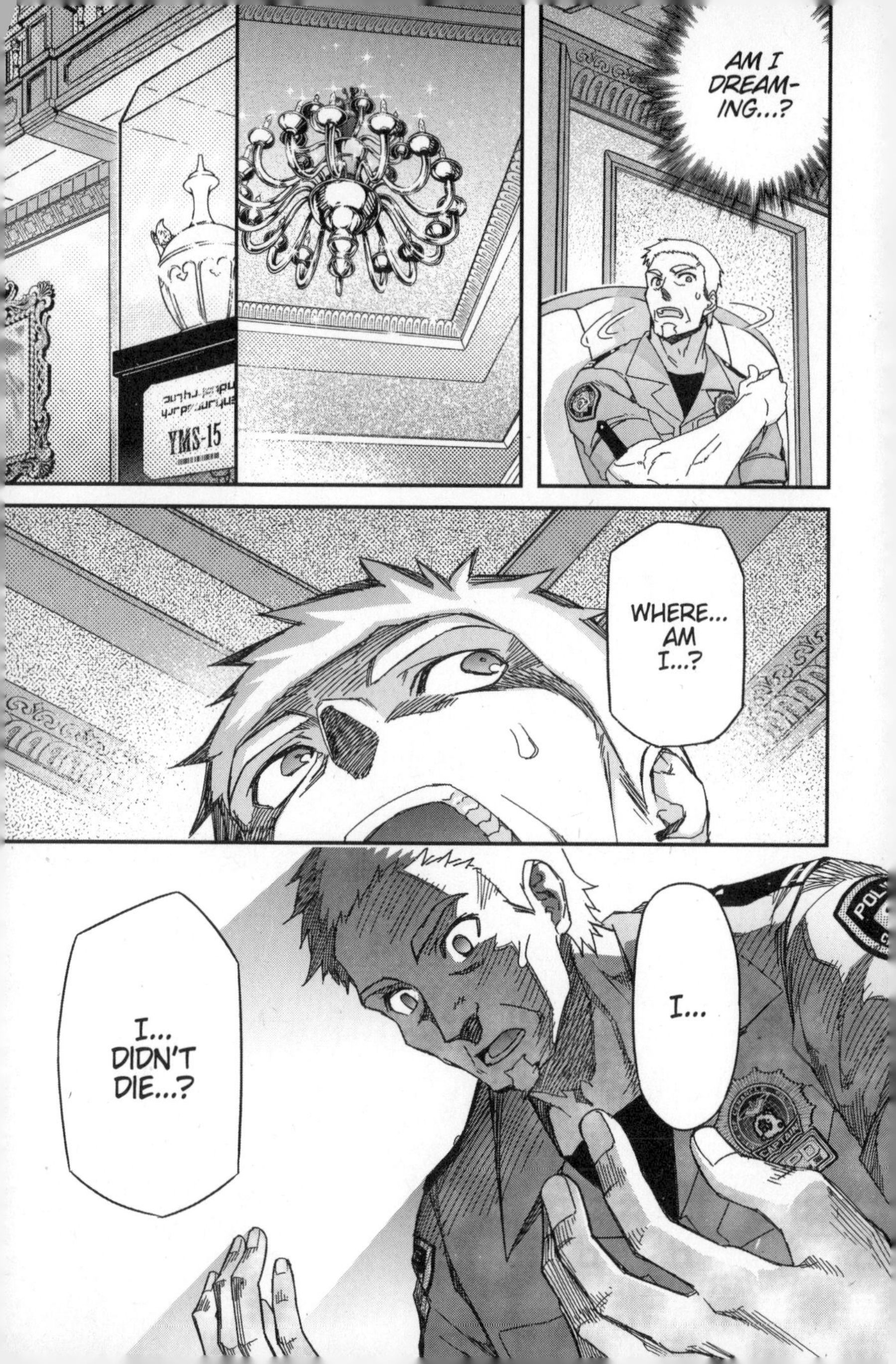
AM I DREAMING...?
YMS-15
WHERE... AM I...?
I...
I... DIDN'T DIE...?

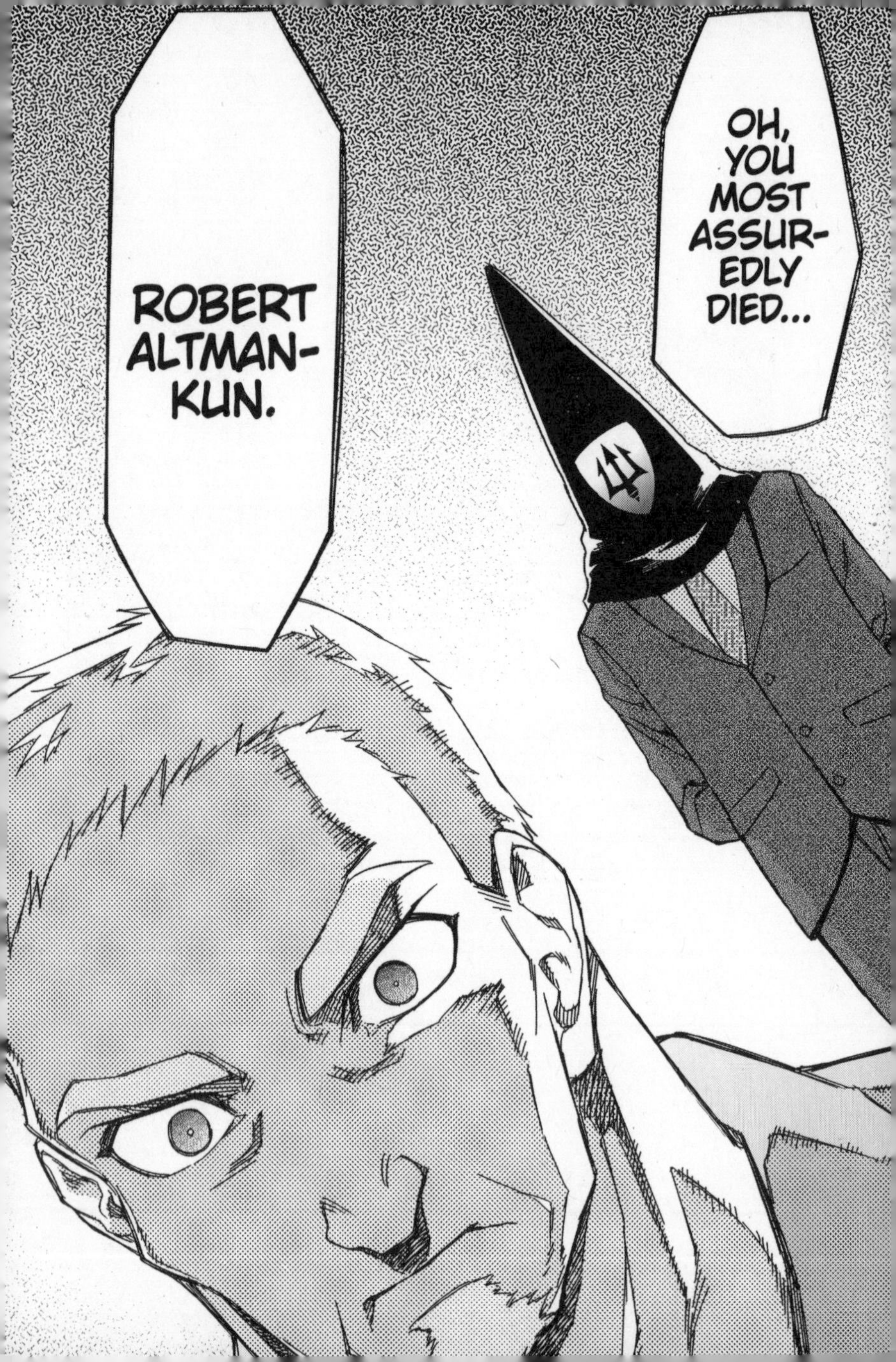
OH, YOU MOST ASSUR-EDLY DIED...
ROBERT ALTMAN-KUN.

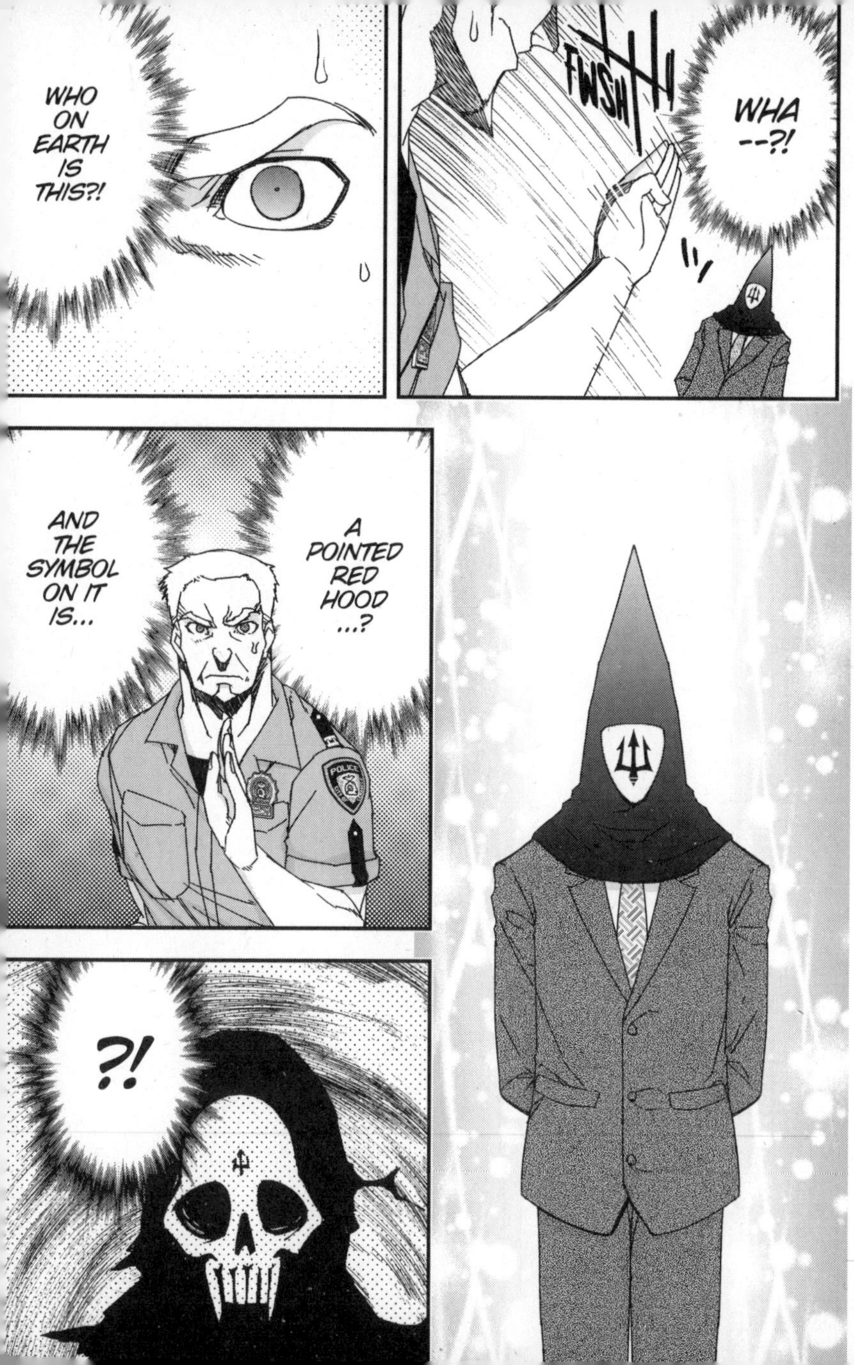
FWSH
WHA--?!
WHO ON EARTH IS THIS?!
A POINTED RED HOOD...?
AND THE SYMBOL ON IT IS...
POLICE
?!

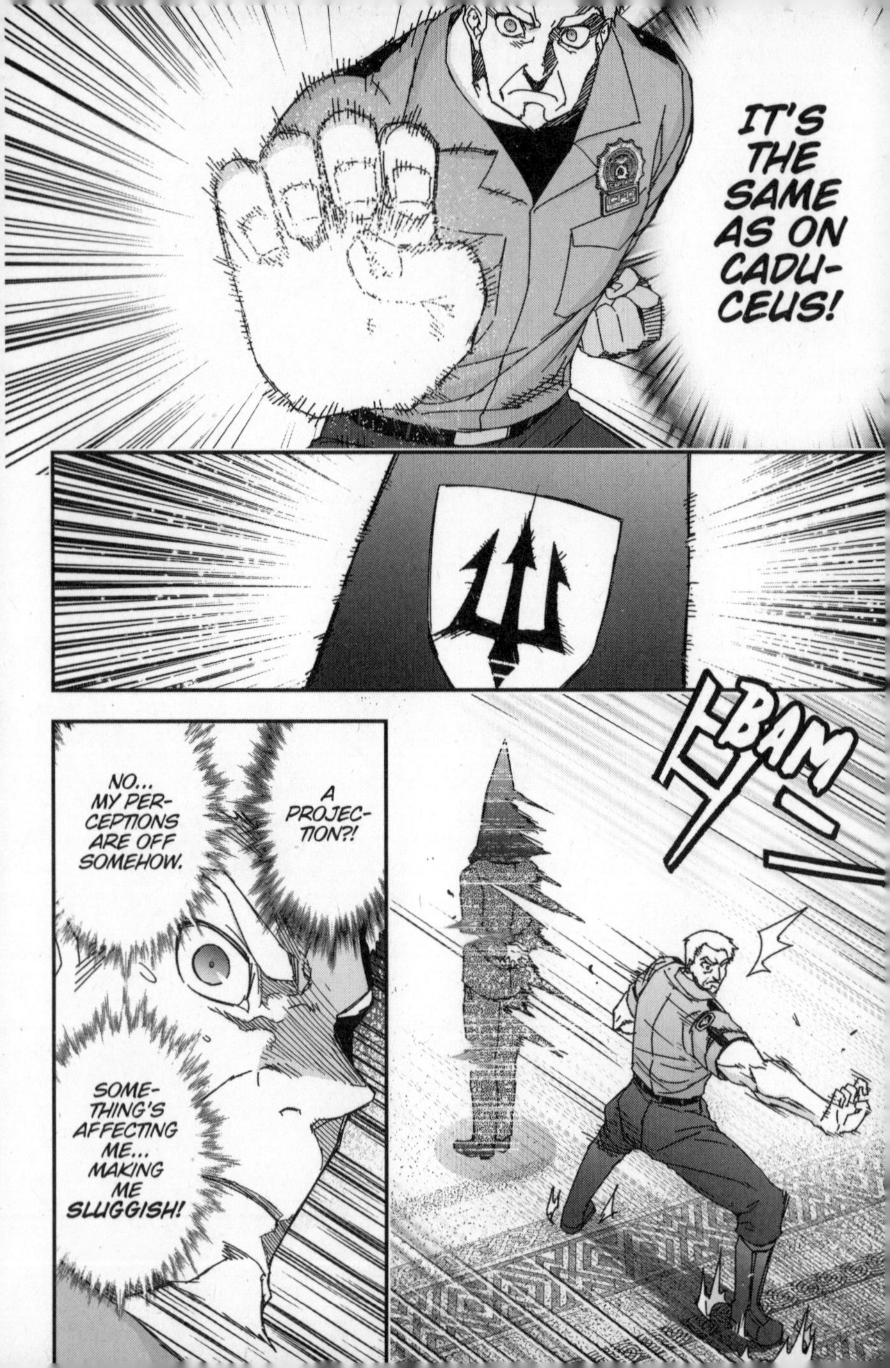
IT'S THE SAME AS ON CADUCEUS!
BAM
A PROJECTION?!
NO... MY PERCEPTIONS ARE OFF SOMEHOW.
SOMETHING'S AFFECTING ME... MAKING ME SLUGGISH!

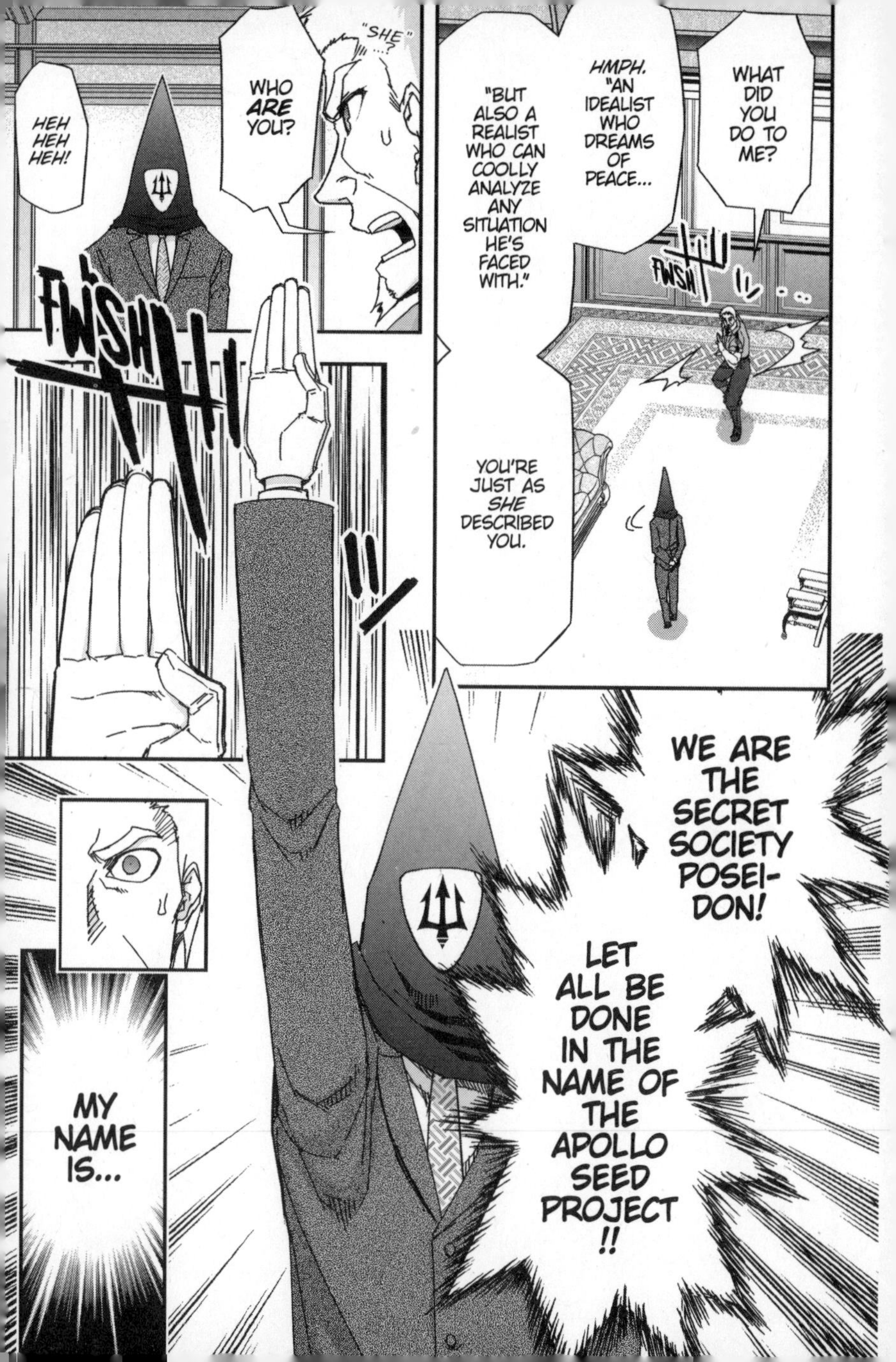
WHAT DID YOU DO TO ME?
FWSH
HMPH. "AN IDEALIST WHO DREAMS OF PEACE...
"BUT ALSO A REALIST WHO CAN COOLLY ANALYZE ANY SITUATION HE'S FACED WITH."
YOU'RE JUST AS SHE DESCRIBED YOU.
"SHE" ...?
WHO ARE YOU?
HEH HEH HEH!
FWSH
WE ARE THE SECRET SOCIETY POSEI-DON!
LET ALL BE DONE IN THE NAME OF THE APOLLO SEED PROJECT!!
MY NAME IS...

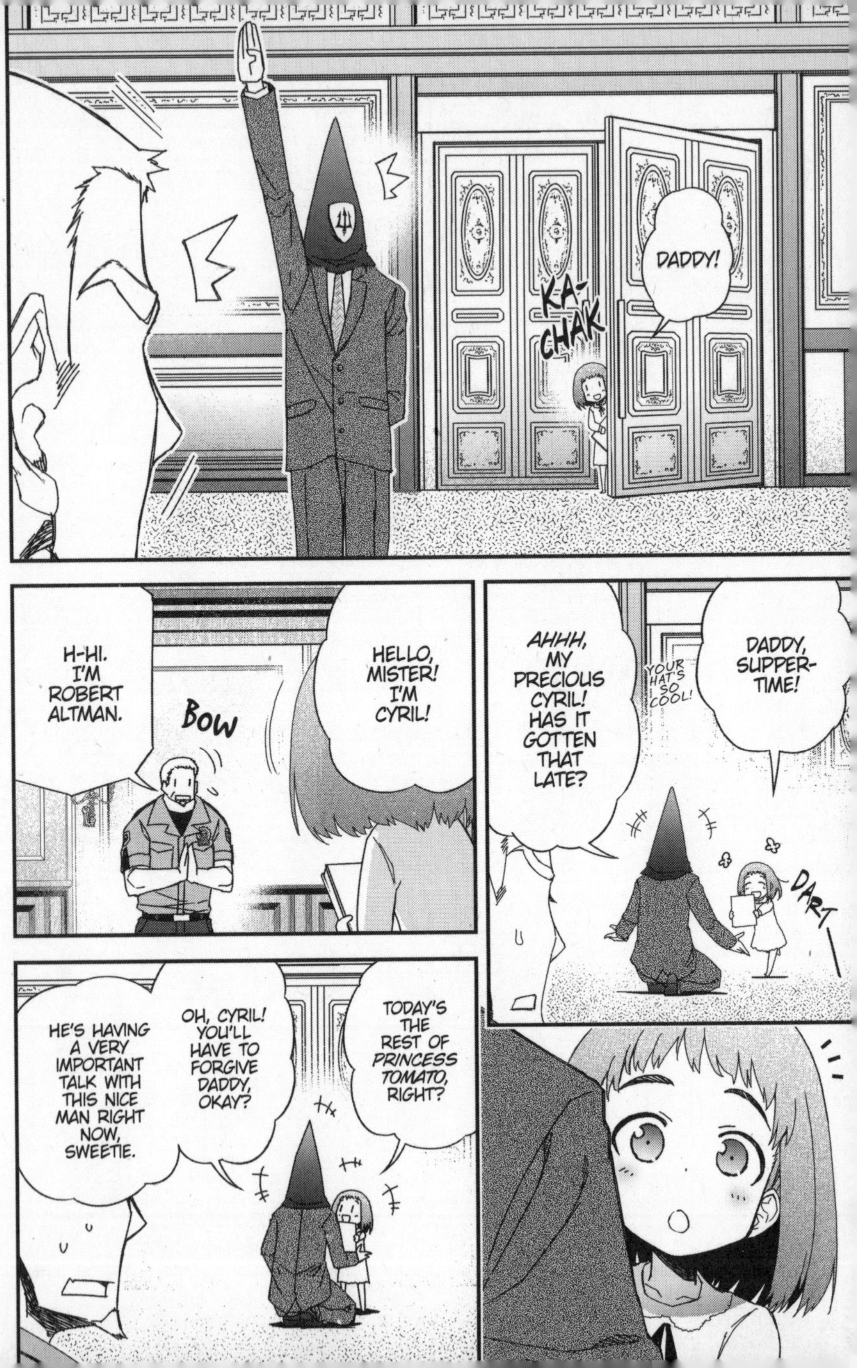
KA-CHAK
DADDY!
DADDY, SUPPER-TIME!
YOUR HAT'S SO COOL!
AHHH, MY PRECIOUS CYRIL! HAS IT GOTTEN THAT LATE?
DART
HELLO, MISTER! I'M CYRIL!
BOW
H-HI. I'M ROBERT ALTMAN.
TODAY'S THE REST OF *PRINCESS TOMATO*, RIGHT?
OH, CYRIL! YOU'LL HAVE TO FORGIVE DADDY, OKAY?
HE'S HAVING A VERY IMPORTANT TALK WITH THIS NICE MAN RIGHT NOW, SWEETIE.

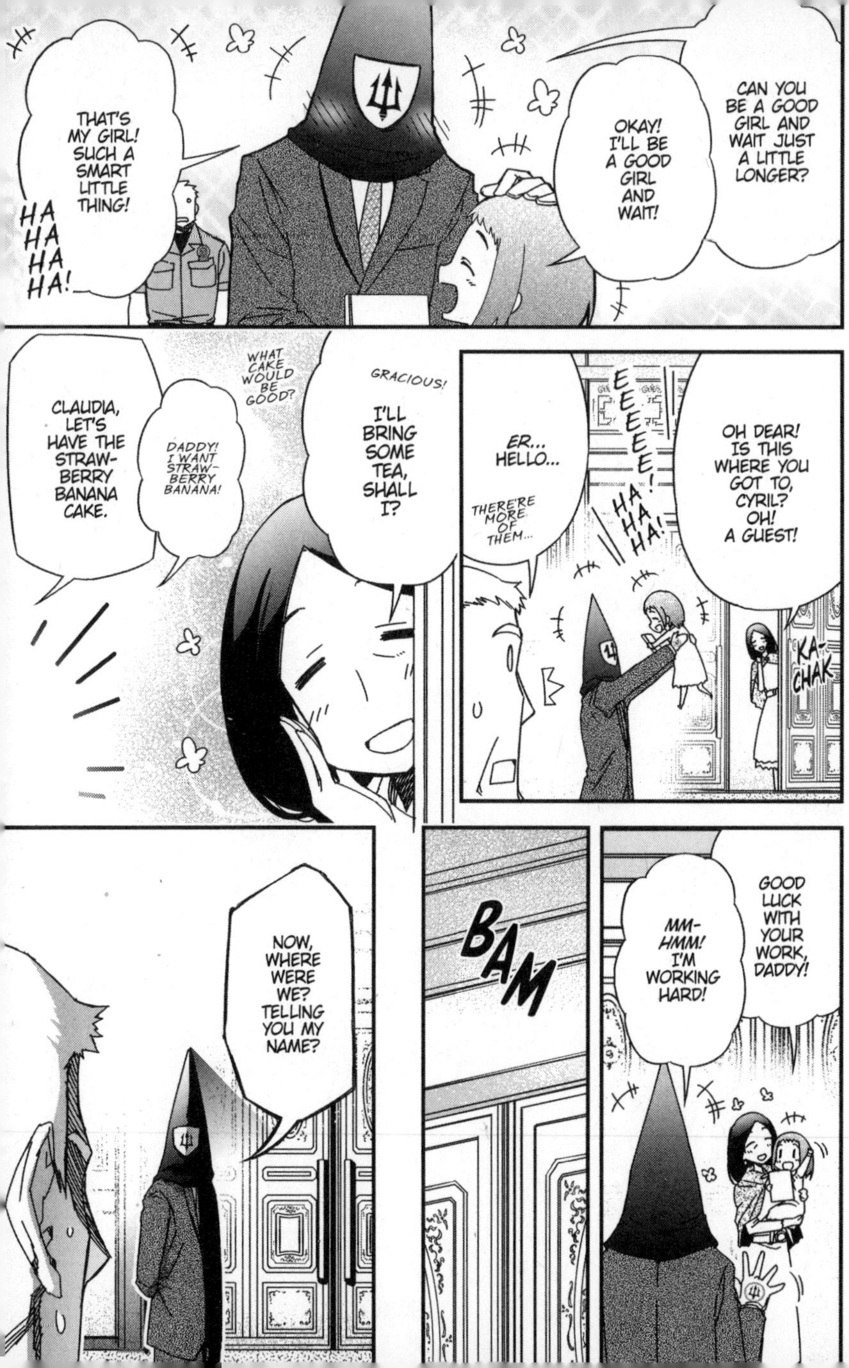
CAN YOU BE A GOOD GIRL AND WAIT JUST A LITTLE LONGER?
OKAY! I'LL BE A GOOD GIRL AND WAIT!
THAT'S MY GIRL! SUCH A SMART LITTLE THING!
HA HA HA HA!
OH DEAR! IS THIS WHERE YOU GOT TO, CYRIL? OH! A GUEST!
KA-CHAK
EEEEEE!
HA HA HA HA!
ER... HELLO...
THERE'RE MORE OF THEM...
GRACIOUS!
I'LL BRING SOME TEA, SHALL I?
WHAT CAKE WOULD BE GOOD?
DADDY! I WANT STRAW-BERRY BANANA!
CLAUDIA, LET'S HAVE THE STRAW-BERRY BANANA CAKE.
GOOD LUCK WITH YOUR WORK, DADDY!
MM-HMM! I'M WORKING HARD!
BAM
NOW, WHERE WERE WE? TELLING YOU MY NAME?

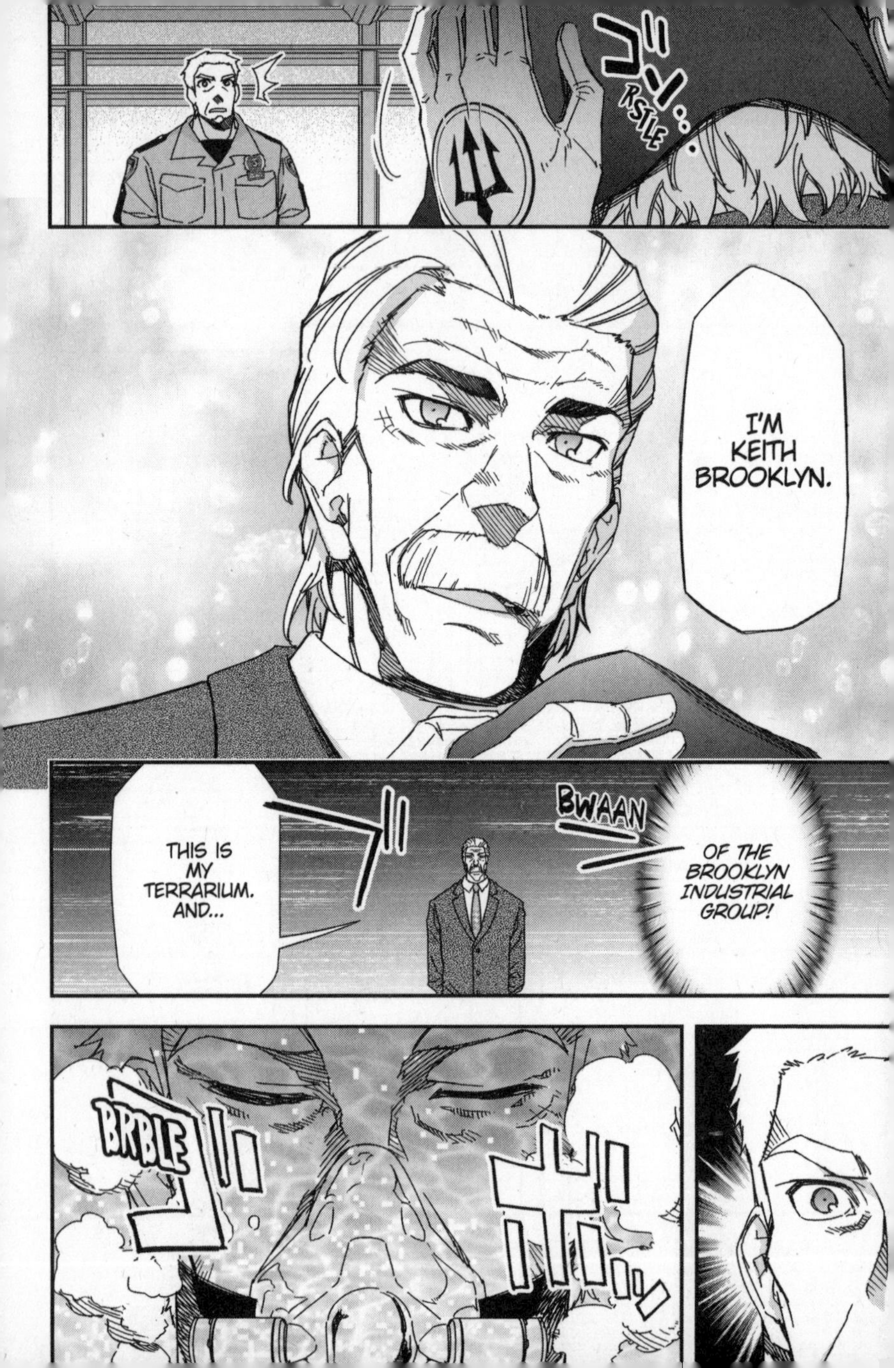

RSTLE
I'M KEITH BROOKLYN.
BWAAN
OF THE BROOKLYN INDUSTRIAL GROUP!
THIS IS MY TERRARIUM. AND...
BRBLE

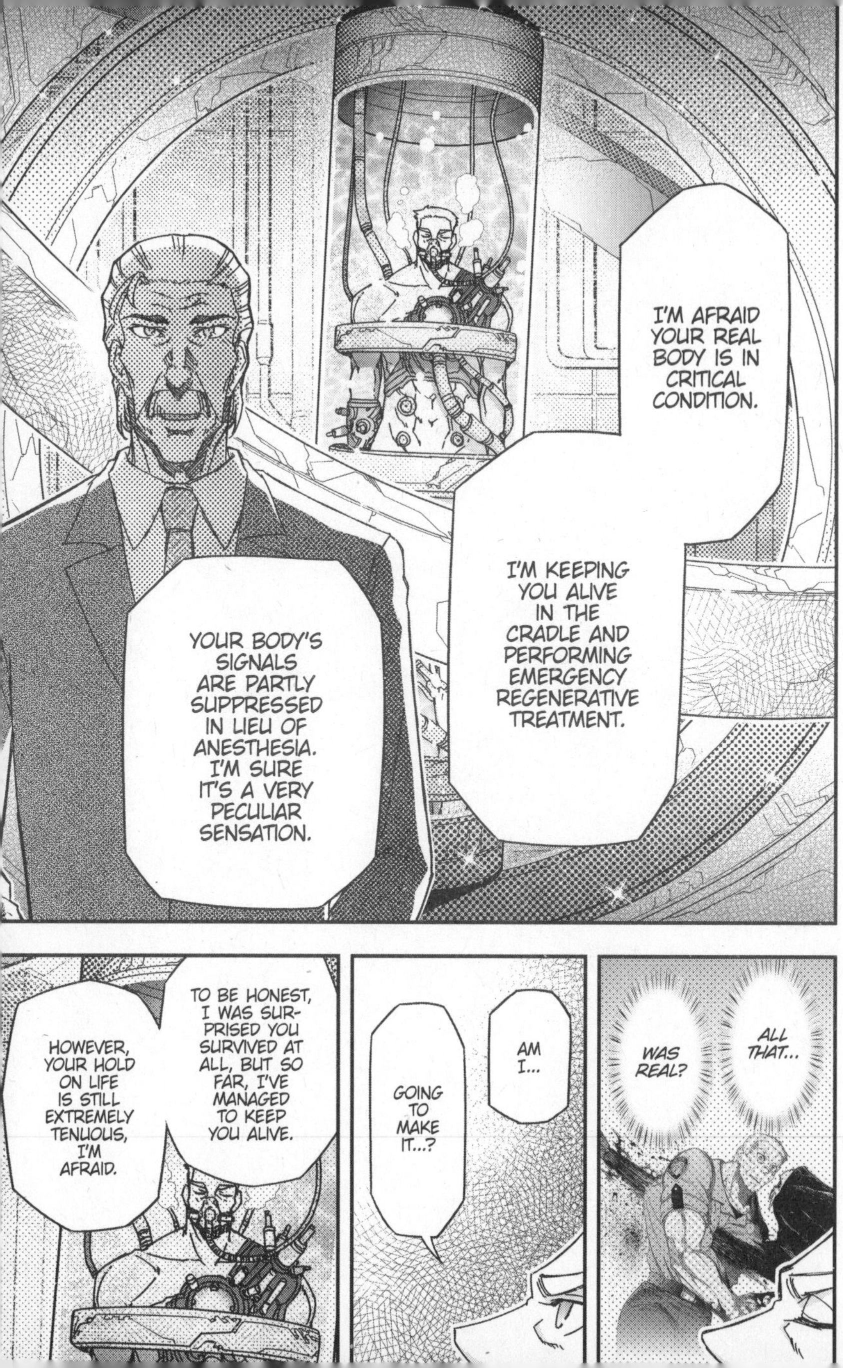
I'M AFRAID YOUR REAL BODY IS IN CRITICAL CONDITION.
I'M KEEPING YOU ALIVE IN THE CRADLE AND PERFORMING EMERGENCY REGENERATIVE TREATMENT.
YOUR BODY'S SIGNALS ARE PARTLY SUPPRESSED IN LIEU OF ANESTHESIA. I'M SURE IT'S A VERY PECULIAR SENSATION.
ALL THAT...
WAS REAL?
AM I...
GOING TO MAKE IT...?
TO BE HONEST, I WAS SUR-PRISED YOU SURVIVED AT ALL, BUT SO FAR, I'VE MANAGED TO KEEP YOU ALIVE.
HOWEVER, YOUR HOLD ON LIFE IS STILL EXTREMELY TENUOUS, I'M AFRAID.

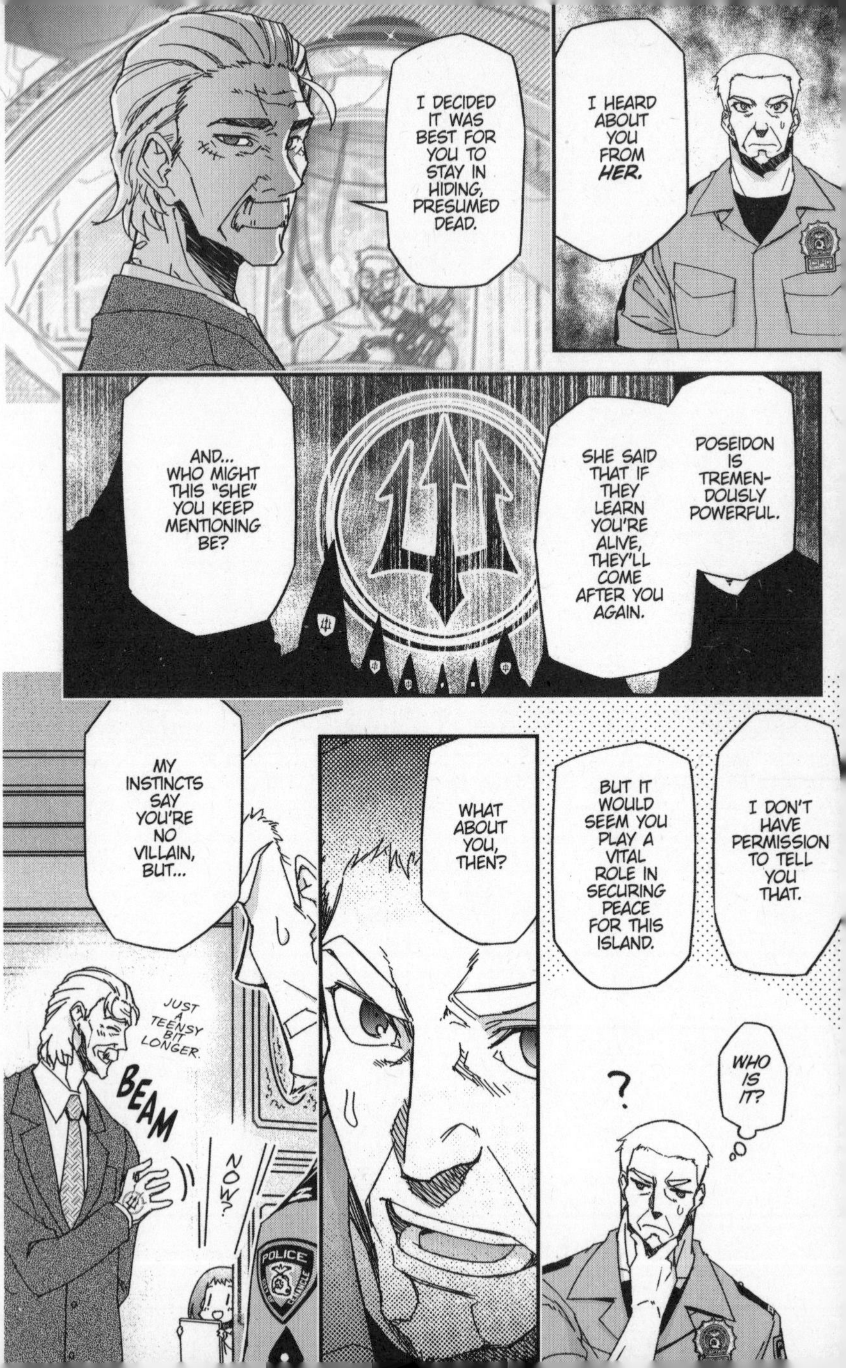
I HEARD ABOUT YOU FROM *HER.*
I DECIDED IT WAS BEST FOR YOU TO STAY IN HIDING, PRESUMED DEAD.
POSEIDON IS TREMENDOUSLY POWERFUL.
SHE SAID THAT IF THEY LEARN YOU'RE ALIVE, THEY'LL COME AFTER YOU AGAIN.
AND... WHO MIGHT THIS "SHE" YOU KEEP MENTIONING BE?
I DON'T HAVE PERMISSION TO TELL YOU THAT.
BUT IT WOULD SEEM YOU PLAY A VITAL ROLE IN SECURING PEACE FOR THIS ISLAND.
?
WHO IS IT?
WHAT ABOUT YOU, THEN?
MY INSTINCTS SAY YOU'RE NO VILLAIN, BUT...
JUST A TEENSY BIT LONGER.
BEAM
NOW?
POLICE

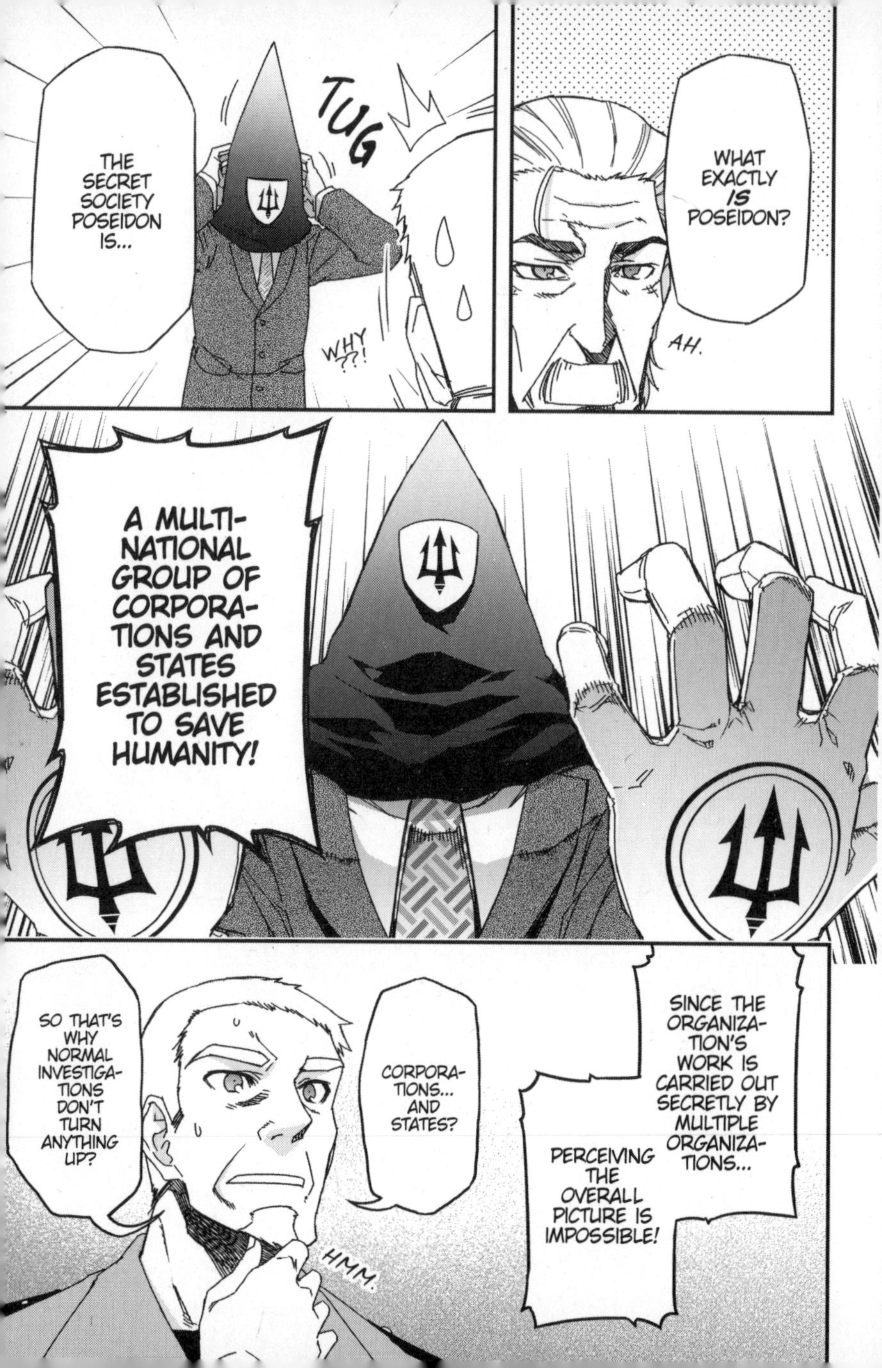

WHAT EXACTLY IS POSEIDON?
AH.
TUG
WHY ??!
THE SECRET SOCIETY POSEIDON IS...
A MULTI-NATIONAL GROUP OF CORPORATIONS AND STATES ESTABLISHED TO SAVE HUMANITY!
SINCE THE ORGANIZATION'S WORK IS CARRIED OUT SECRETLY BY MULTIPLE ORGANIZATIONS...
PERCEIVING THE OVERALL PICTURE IS IMPOSSIBLE!
CORPORATIONS... AND STATES?
SO THAT'S WHY NORMAL INVESTIGATIONS DON'T TURN ANYTHING UP?
HMM.

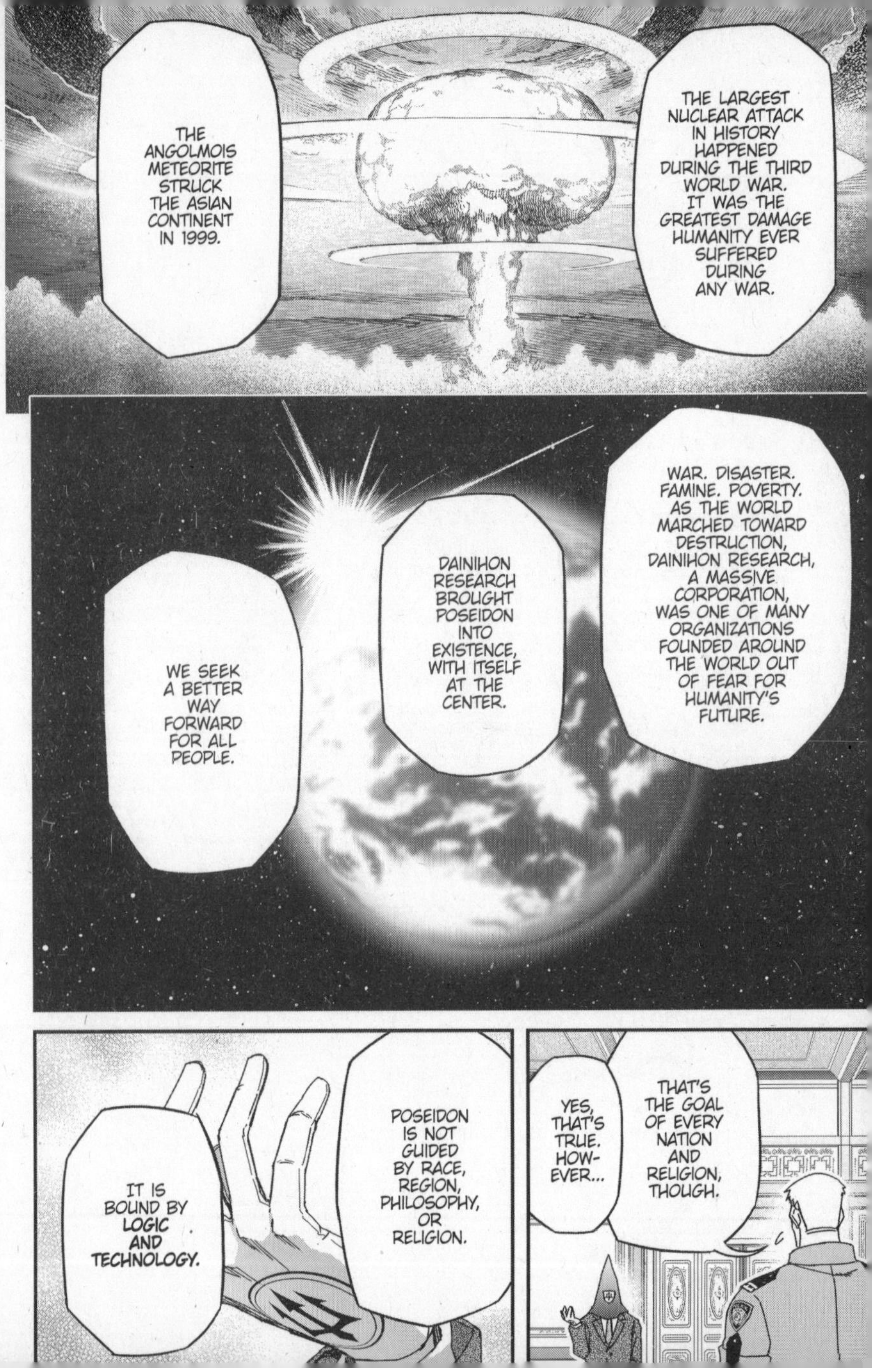
THE LARGEST NUCLEAR ATTACK IN HISTORY HAPPENED DURING THE THIRD WORLD WAR. IT WAS THE GREATEST DAMAGE HUMANITY EVER SUFFERED DURING ANY WAR.
THE ANGOLMOIS METEORITE STRUCK THE ASIAN CONTINENT IN 1999.
WAR. DISASTER. FAMINE. POVERTY. AS THE WORLD MARCHED TOWARD DESTRUCTION, DAINIHON RESEARCH, A MASSIVE CORPORATION, WAS ONE OF MANY ORGANIZATIONS FOUNDED AROUND THE WORLD OUT OF FEAR FOR HUMANITY'S FUTURE.
DAINIHON RESEARCH BROUGHT POSEIDON INTO EXISTENCE, WITH ITSELF AT THE CENTER.
WE SEEK A BETTER WAY FORWARD FOR ALL PEOPLE.
THAT'S THE GOAL OF EVERY NATION AND RELIGION, THOUGH.
YES, THAT'S TRUE. HOW-EVER...
POSEIDON IS NOT GUIDED BY RACE, REGION, PHILOSOPHY, OR RELIGION.
IT IS BOUND BY **LOGIC AND TECHNOLOGY.**

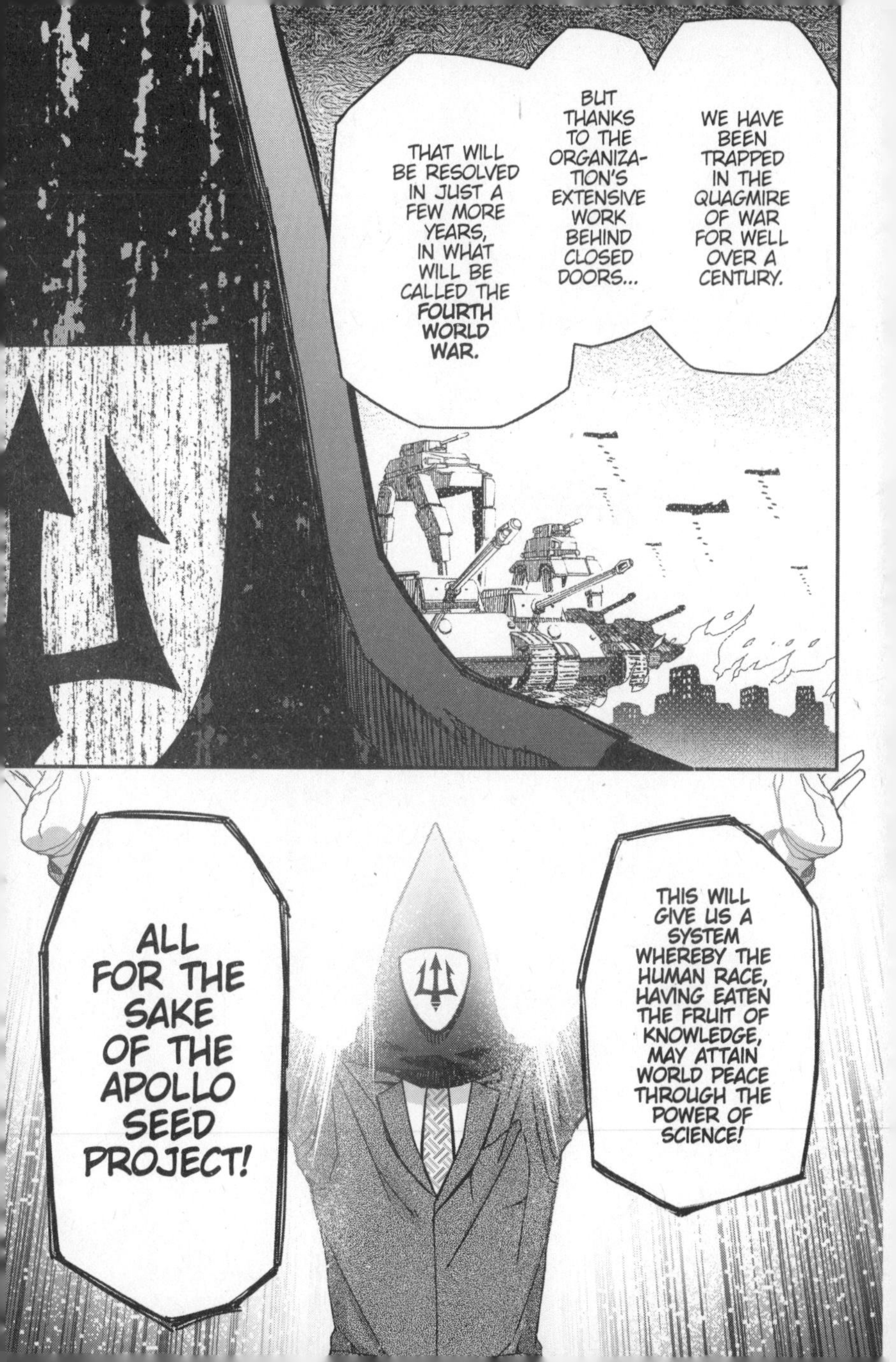
WE HAVE BEEN TRAPPED IN THE QUAGMIRE OF WAR FOR WELL OVER A CENTURY.
BUT THANKS TO THE ORGANIZATION'S EXTENSIVE WORK BEHIND CLOSED DOORS...
THAT WILL BE RESOLVED IN JUST A FEW MORE YEARS, IN WHAT WILL BE CALLED THE FOURTH WORLD WAR.
THIS WILL GIVE US A SYSTEM WHEREBY THE HUMAN RACE, HAVING EATEN THE FRUIT OF KNOWLEDGE, MAY ATTAIN WORLD PEACE THROUGH THE POWER OF SCIENCE!
ALL FOR THE SAKE OF THE APOLLO SEED PROJECT!

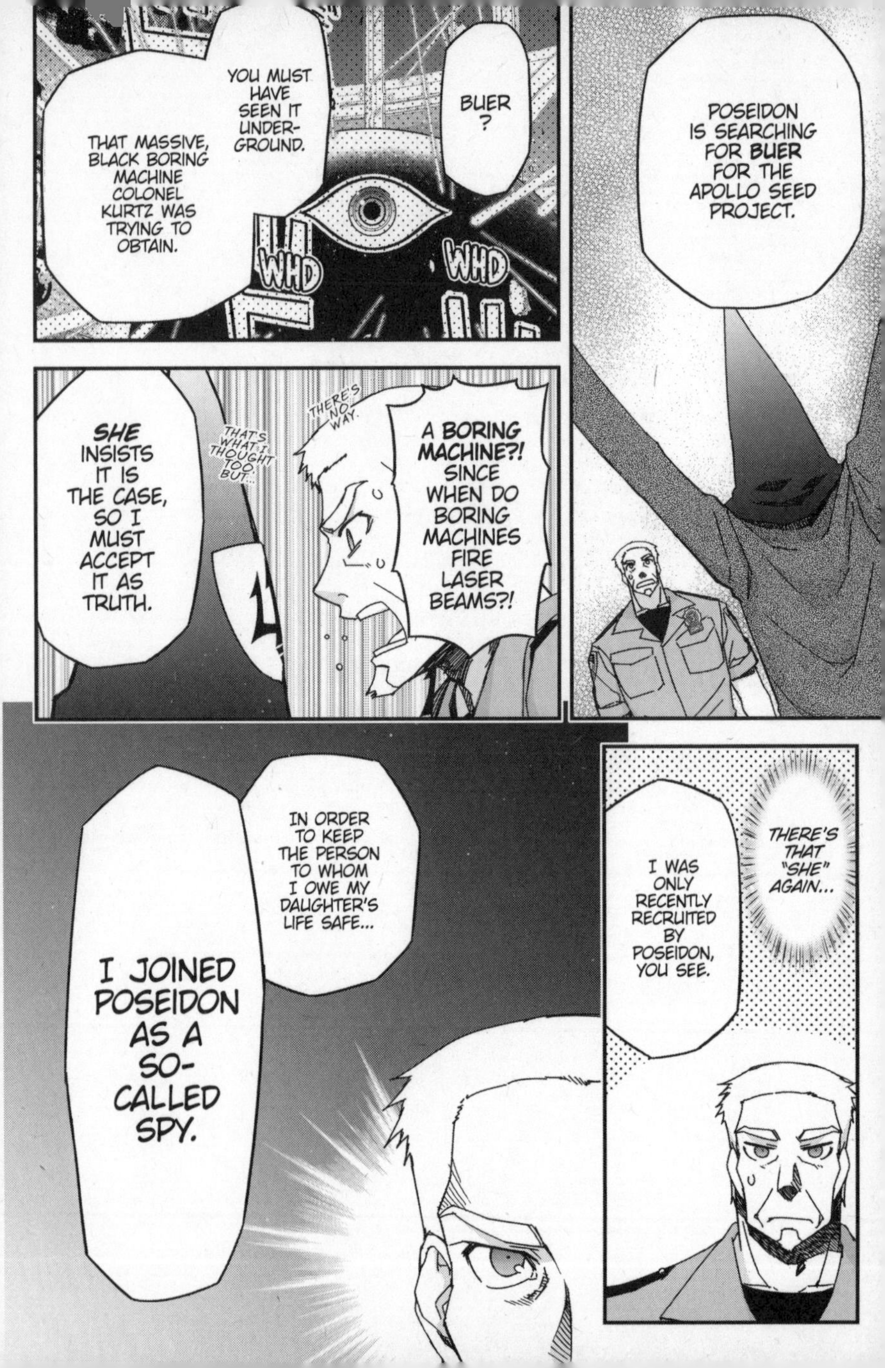
POSEIDON IS SEARCHING FOR **BUER** FOR THE APOLLO SEED PROJECT.
BUER?
YOU MUST HAVE SEEN IT UNDER-GROUND.
THAT MASSIVE, BLACK BORING MACHINE COLONEL KURTZ WAS TRYING TO OBTAIN.
WHD
WHD
A **BORING MACHINE?!** SINCE WHEN DO BORING MACHINES FIRE LASER BEAMS?!
THERE'S NO WAY.
THAT'S WHAT I THOUGHT TOO. BUT...
SHE INSISTS IT IS THE CASE, SO I MUST ACCEPT IT AS TRUTH.
THERE'S THAT "SHE" AGAIN...
I WAS ONLY RECENTLY RECRUITED BY POSEIDON, YOU SEE.
IN ORDER TO KEEP THE PERSON TO WHOM I OWE MY DAUGHTER'S LIFE SAFE...
I JOINED POSEIDON AS A SO-CALLED SPY.

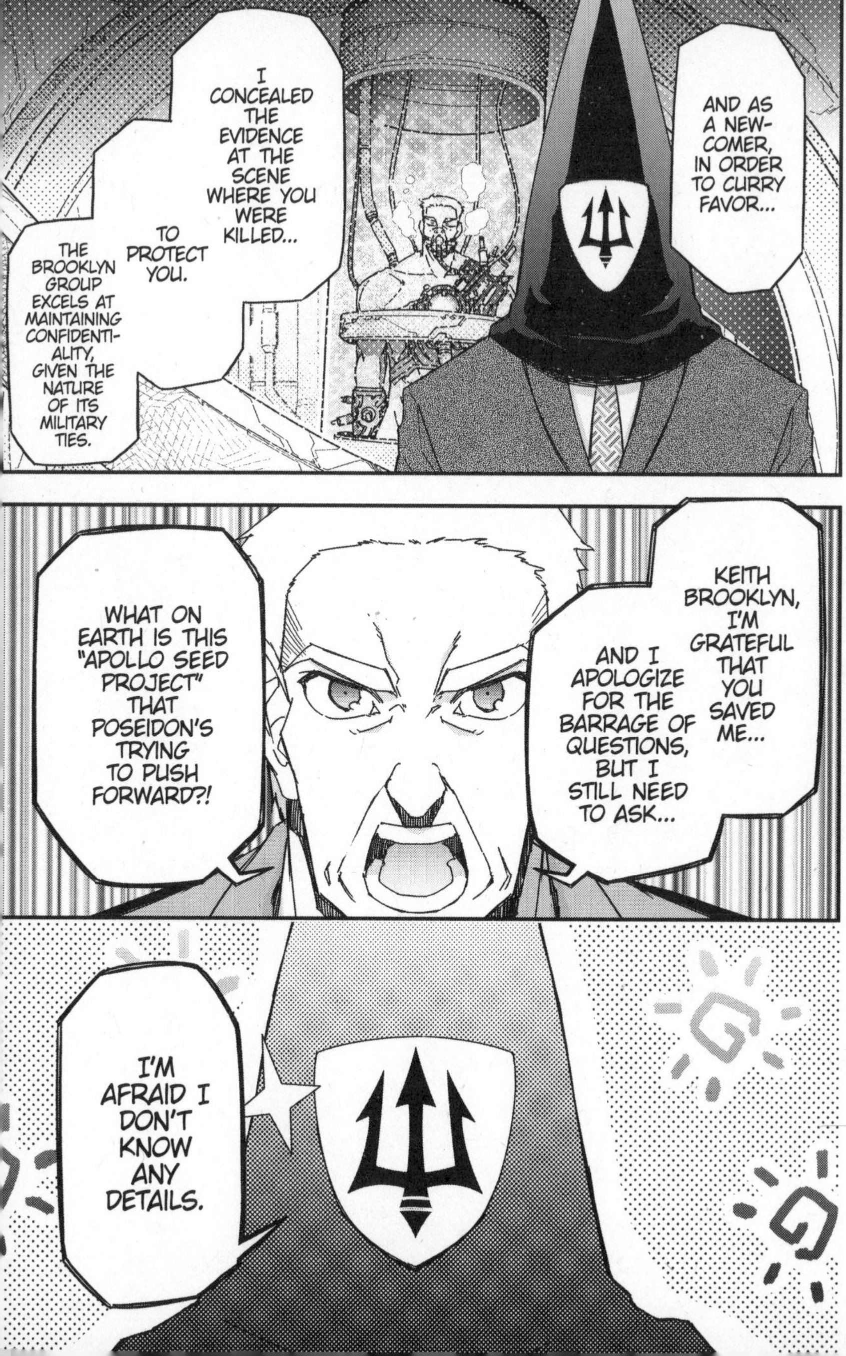
AND AS A NEW-COMER, IN ORDER TO CURRY FAVOR...
I CONCEALED THE EVIDENCE AT THE SCENE WHERE YOU WERE KILLED...
TO PROTECT YOU.
THE BROOKLYN GROUP EXCELS AT MAINTAINING CONFIDENTI-ALITY, GIVEN THE NATURE OF ITS MILITARY TIES.
KEITH BROOKLYN, I'M GRATEFUL THAT YOU SAVED ME...
AND I APOLOGIZE FOR THE BARRAGE OF QUESTIONS, BUT I STILL NEED TO ASK...
WHAT ON EARTH IS THIS "APOLLO SEED PROJECT" THAT POSEIDON'S TRYING TO PUSH FORWARD?!
I'M AFRAID I DON'T KNOW ANY DETAILS.

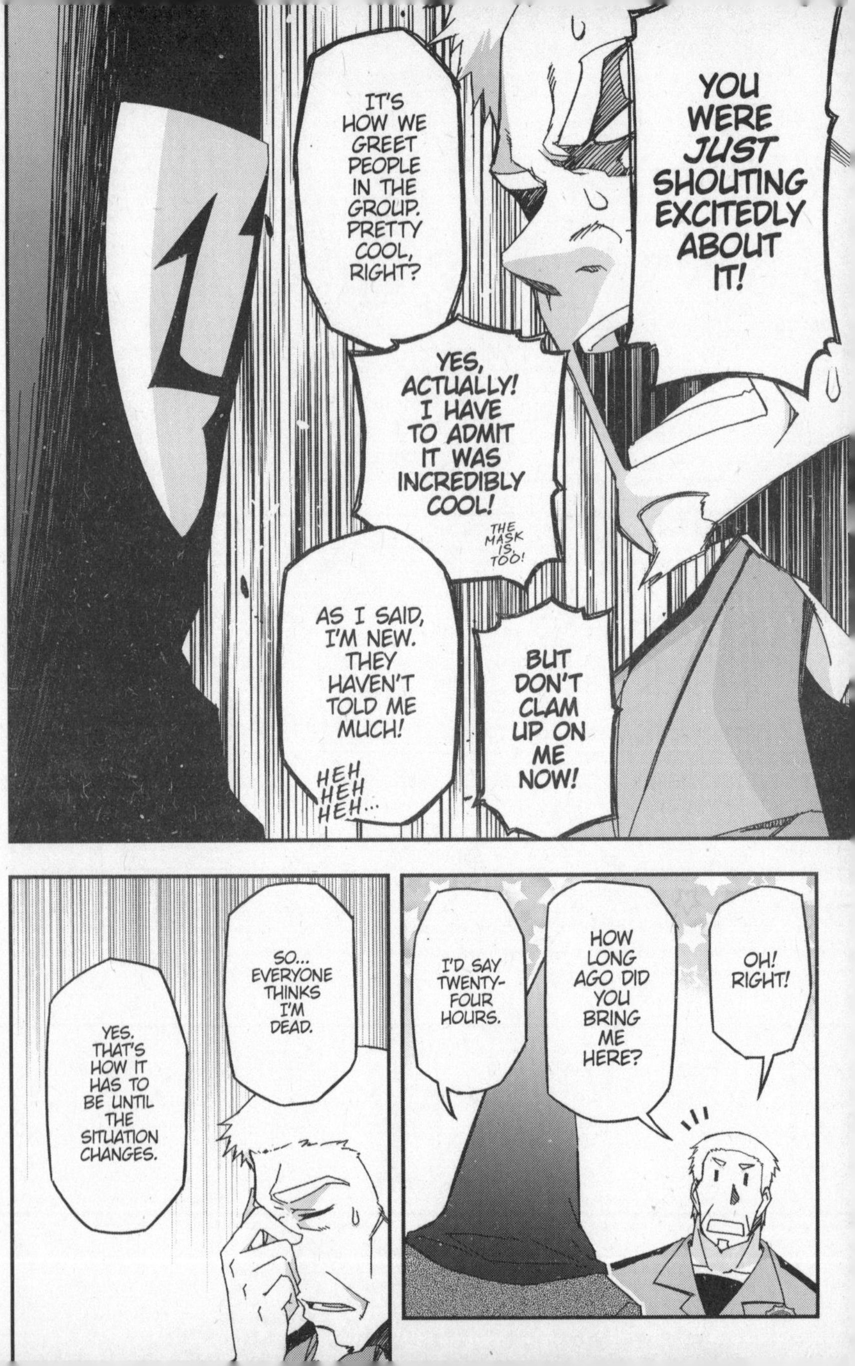
YOU WERE JUST SHOUTING EXCITEDLY ABOUT IT!
IT'S HOW WE GREET PEOPLE IN THE GROUP. PRETTY COOL, RIGHT?
YES, ACTUALLY! I HAVE TO ADMIT IT WAS INCREDIBLY COOL!
THE MASK IS, TOO!
BUT DON'T CLAM UP ON ME NOW!
AS I SAID, I'M NEW. THEY HAVEN'T TOLD ME MUCH!
HEH HEH HEH...
OH! RIGHT!
HOW LONG AGO DID YOU BRING ME HERE?
I'D SAY TWENTY-FOUR HOURS.
SO... EVERYONE THINKS I'M DEAD.
YES. THAT'S HOW IT HAS TO BE UNTIL THE SITUATION CHANGES.

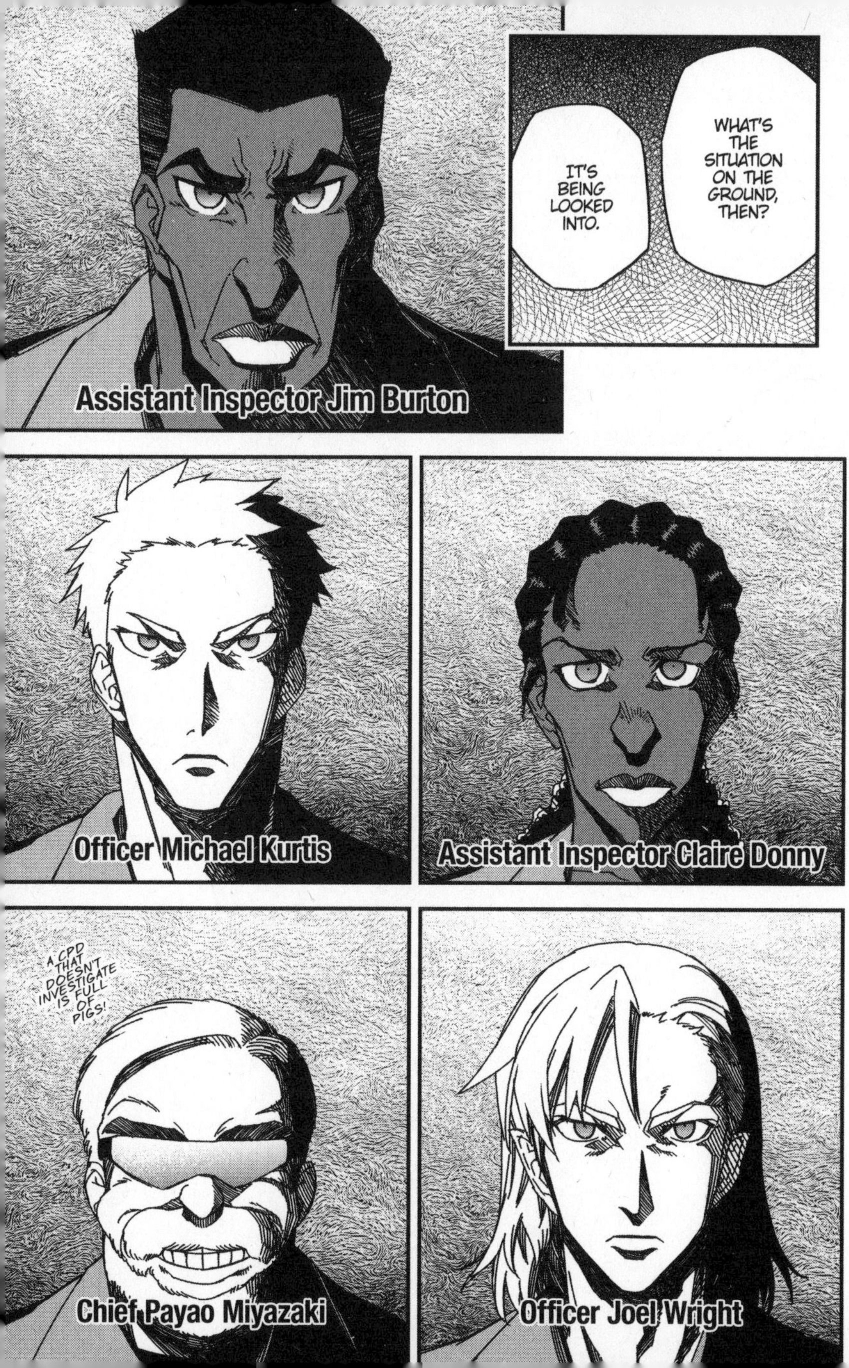
WHAT'S THE SITUATION ON THE GROUND, THEN?
IT'S BEING LOOKED INTO.
Assistant Inspector Jim Burton
Assistant Inspector Claire Donny
Officer Michael Kurtis
Officer Joel Wright
A CPD THAT DOESN'T INVESTIGATE IS FULL OF PIGS!
Chief Payao Miyazaki

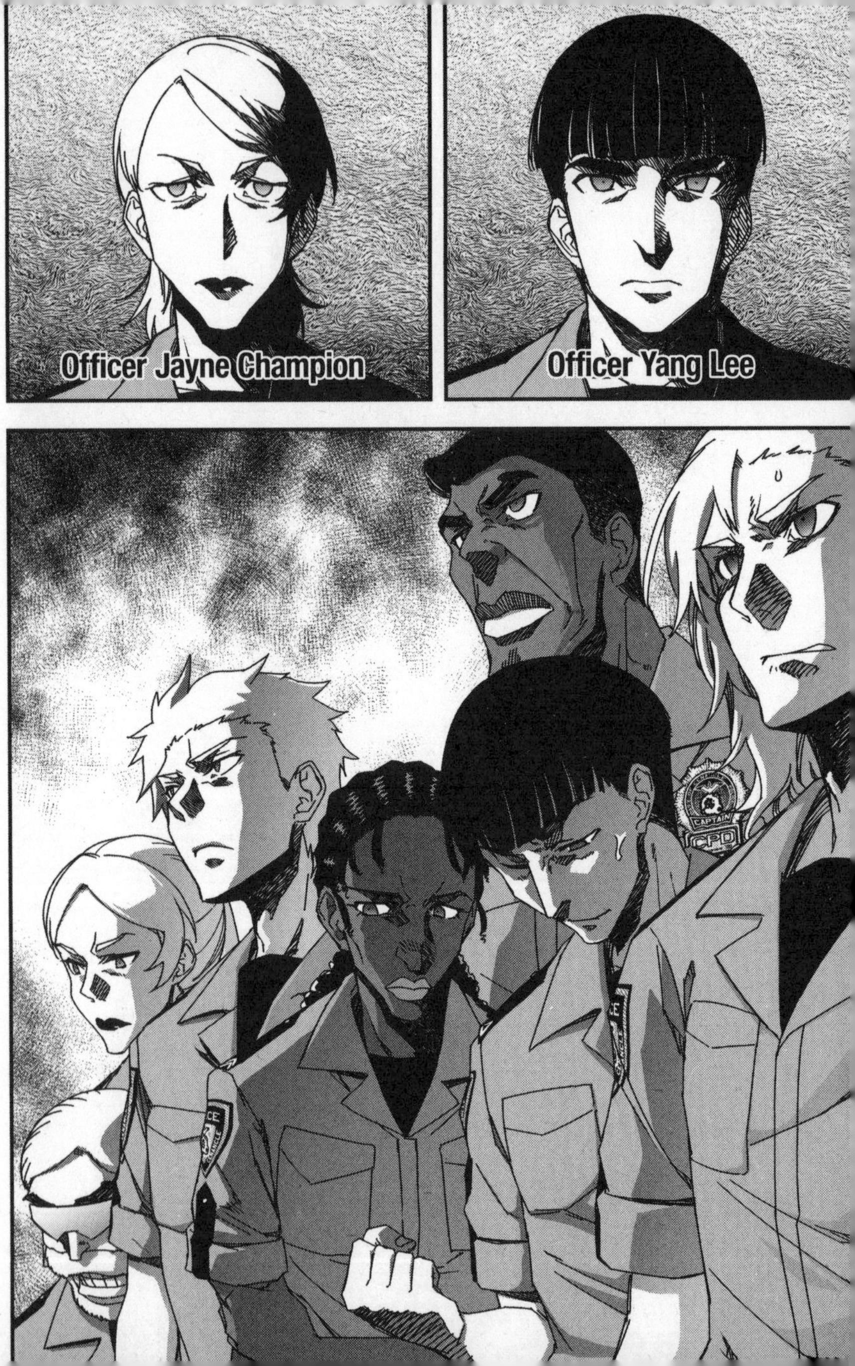
Officer Yang Lee
Officer Jayne Champion
CAPTAIN
CPD

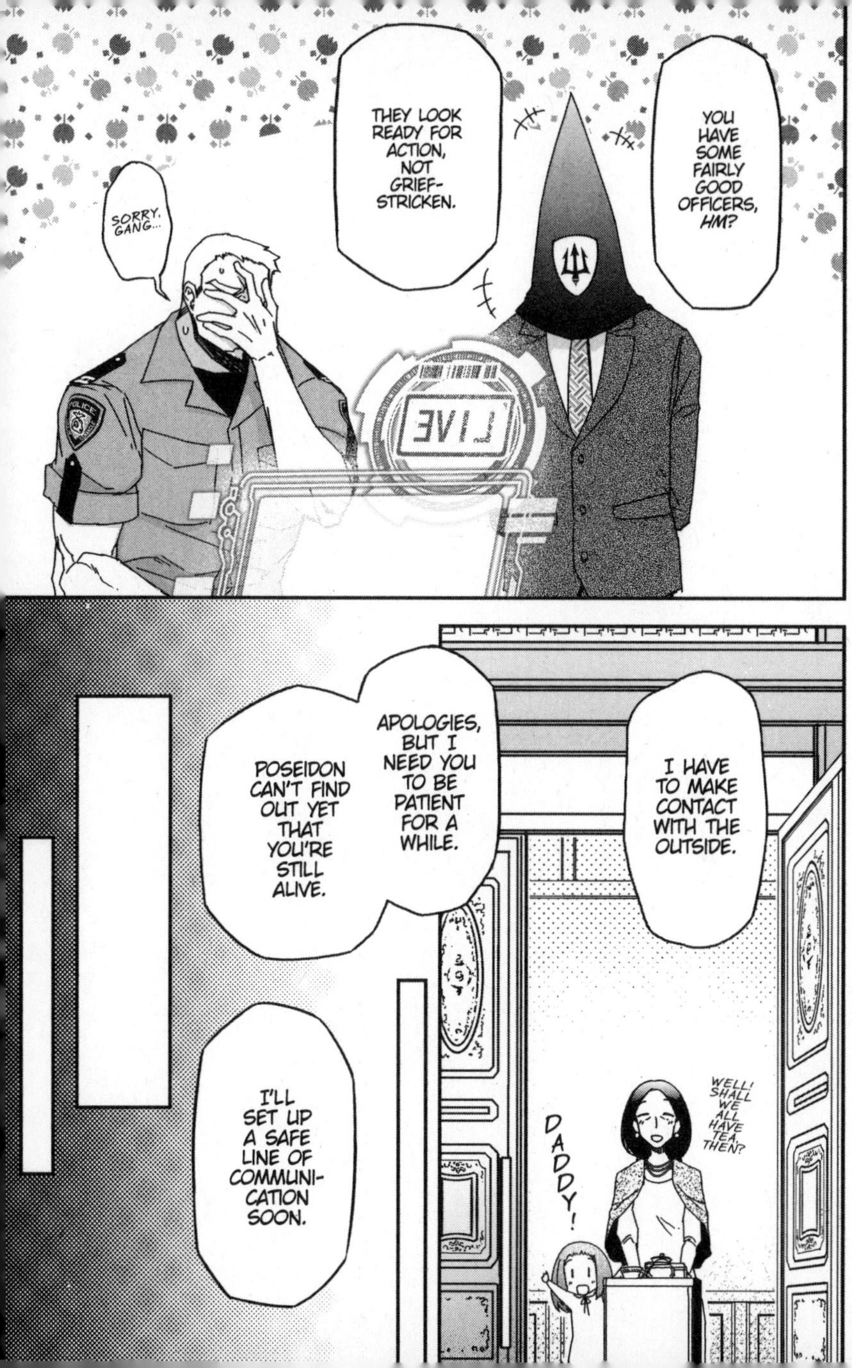
YOU HAVE SOME FAIRLY GOOD OFFICERS, HM?
THEY LOOK READY FOR ACTION, NOT GRIEF-STRICKEN.
SORRY, GANG...
I HAVE TO MAKE CONTACT WITH THE OUTSIDE.
APOLOGIES, BUT I NEED YOU TO BE PATIENT FOR A WHILE.
POSEIDON CAN'T FIND OUT YET THAT YOU'RE STILL ALIVE.
WELL! SHALL WE ALL HAVE TEA, THEN?
DADDY!
I'LL SET UP A SAFE LINE OF COMMUNICATION SOON.

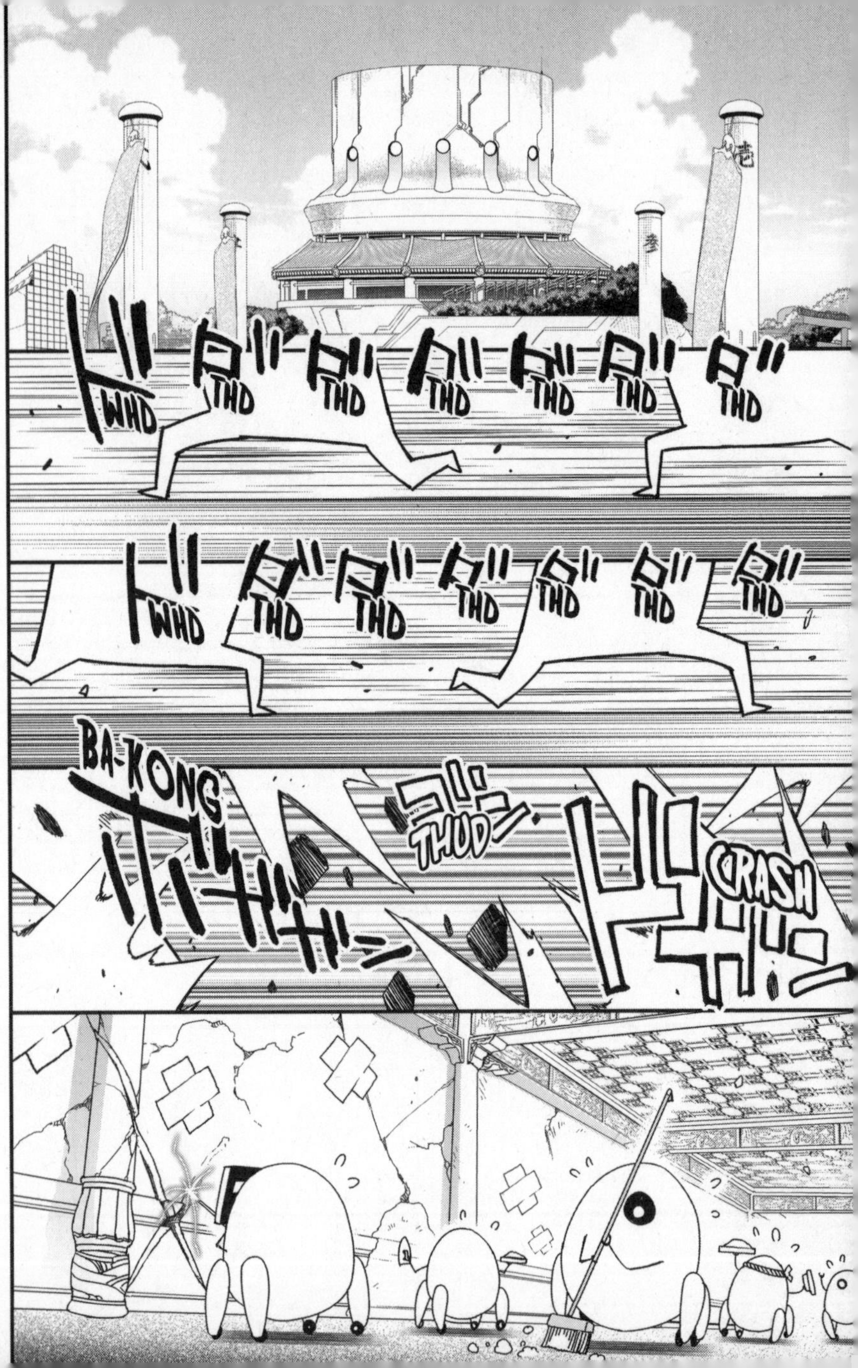
THD
THD
THD
THD
THD
THD
WHD
THD
THD
THD
THD
THD
THD
WHD
CRASH
THUD
BA-KONG

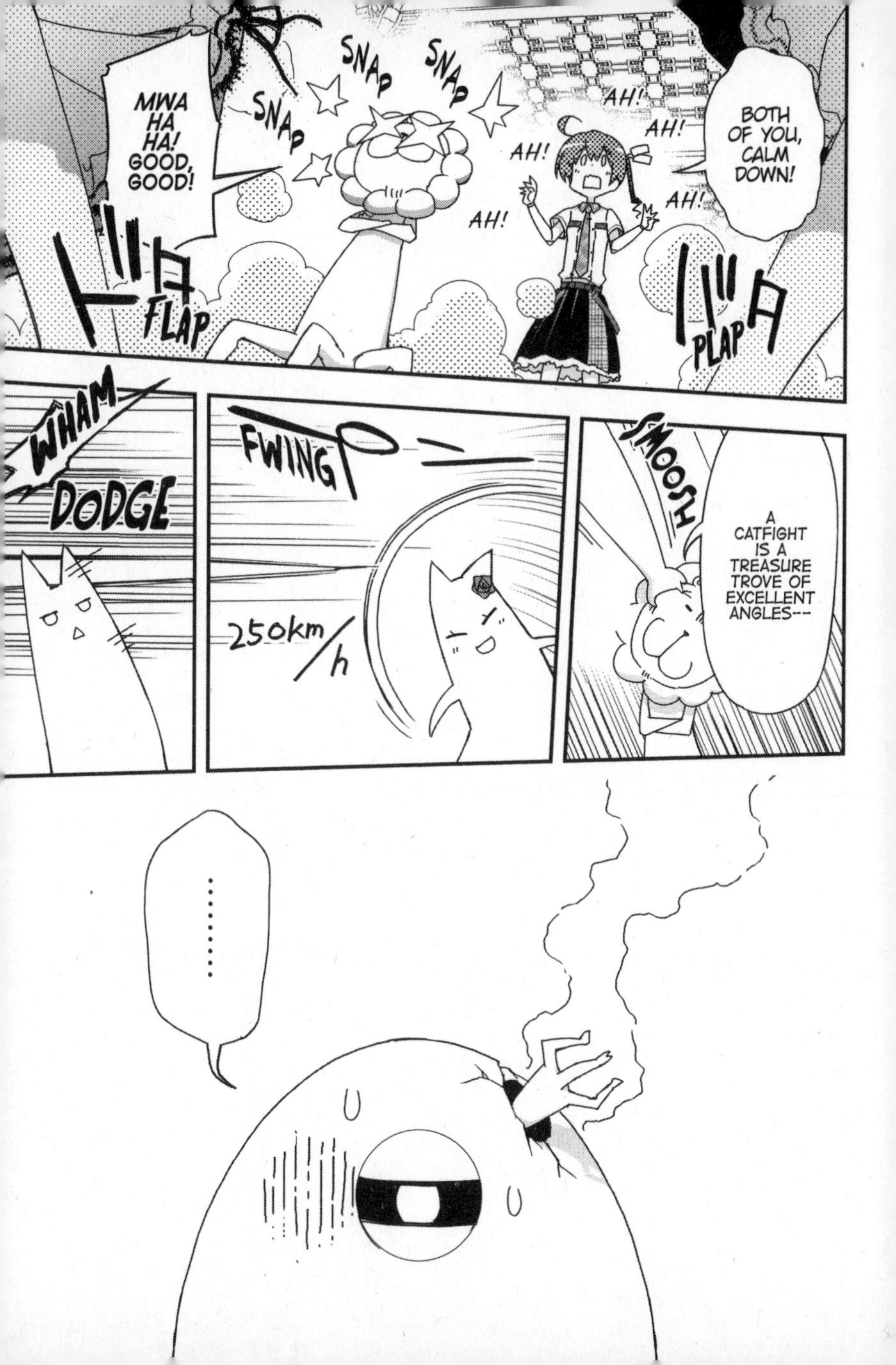
BOTH OF YOU, CALM DOWN!
AH!
AH!
AH!
AH!
AH!
SNAP
SNAP
SNAP
MWA HA HA! GOOD, GOOD!
PLAP
FLAP
SMOOSH
A CATFIGHT IS A TREASURE TROVE OF EXCELLENT ANGLES--
FWING
250km/h
WHAM
DODGE
....

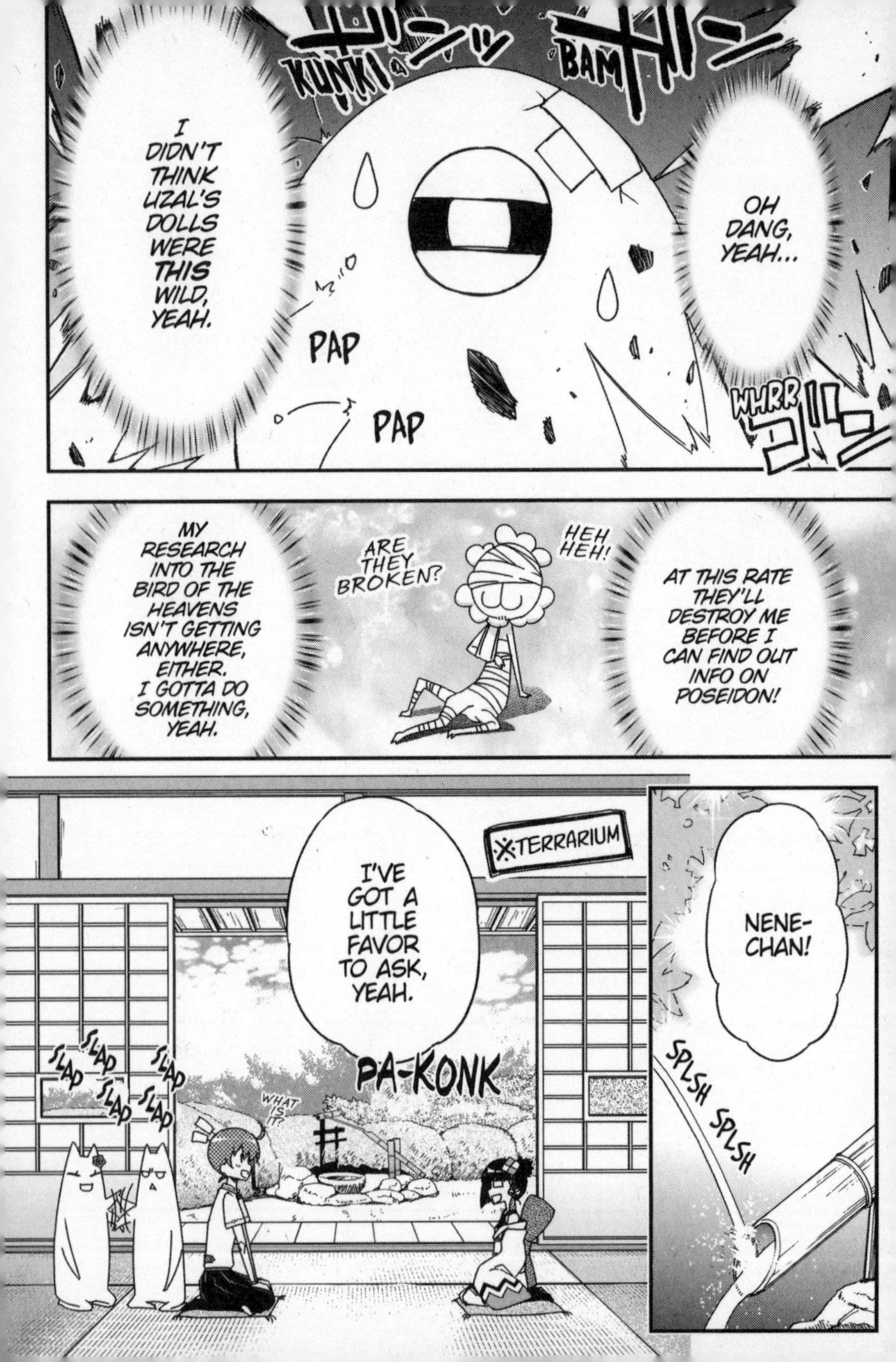
BAM
KUNKI
OH DANG, YEAH...
I DIDN'T THINK UZAL'S DOLLS WERE THIS WILD, YEAH.
WHRR
PAP
PAP
AT THIS RATE THEY'LL DESTROY ME BEFORE I CAN FIND OUT INFO ON POSEIDON!
HEH HEH!
ARE THEY BROKEN?
MY RESEARCH INTO THE BIRD OF THE HEAVENS ISN'T GETTING ANYWHERE, EITHER. I GOTTA DO SOMETHING, YEAH.
NENE-CHAN!
SPLSH SPLSH
※TERRARIUM
I'VE GOT A LITTLE FAVOR TO ASK, YEAH.
PA-KONK
WHAT IS IT?
SLAP SLAP SLAP SLAP SLAP

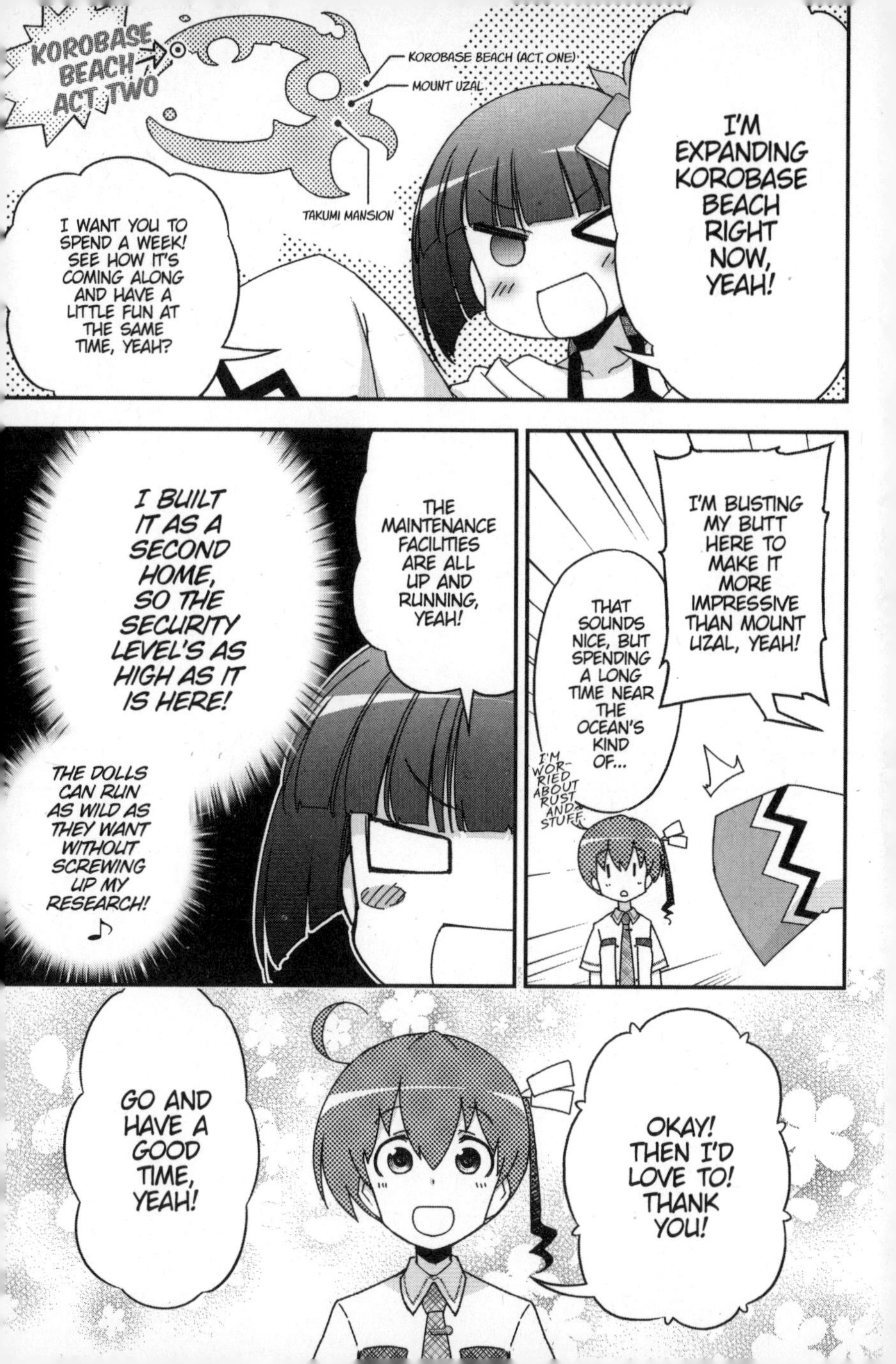
I'M EXPANDING KOROBASE BEACH RIGHT NOW, YEAH!
KOROBASE BEACH ACT TWO
KOROBASE BEACH (ACT ONE)
MOUNT UZAL
TAKUMI MANSION
I WANT YOU TO SPEND A WEEK! SEE HOW IT'S COMING ALONG AND HAVE A LITTLE FUN AT THE SAME TIME, YEAH?
I'M BUSTING MY BUTT HERE TO MAKE IT MORE IMPRESSIVE THAN MOUNT UZAL, YEAH!
THAT SOUNDS NICE, BUT SPENDING A LONG TIME NEAR THE OCEAN'S KIND OF...
I'M WOR-RIED ABOUT RUST AND STUFF.
THE MAINTENANCE FACILITIES ARE ALL UP AND RUNNING, YEAH!
I BUILT IT AS A SECOND HOME, SO THE SECURITY LEVEL'S AS HIGH AS IT IS HERE!
THE DOLLS CAN RUN AS WILD AS THEY WANT WITHOUT SCREWING UP MY RESEARCH! ♪
OKAY! THEN I'D LOVE TO! THANK YOU!
GO AND HAVE A GOOD TIME, YEAH!

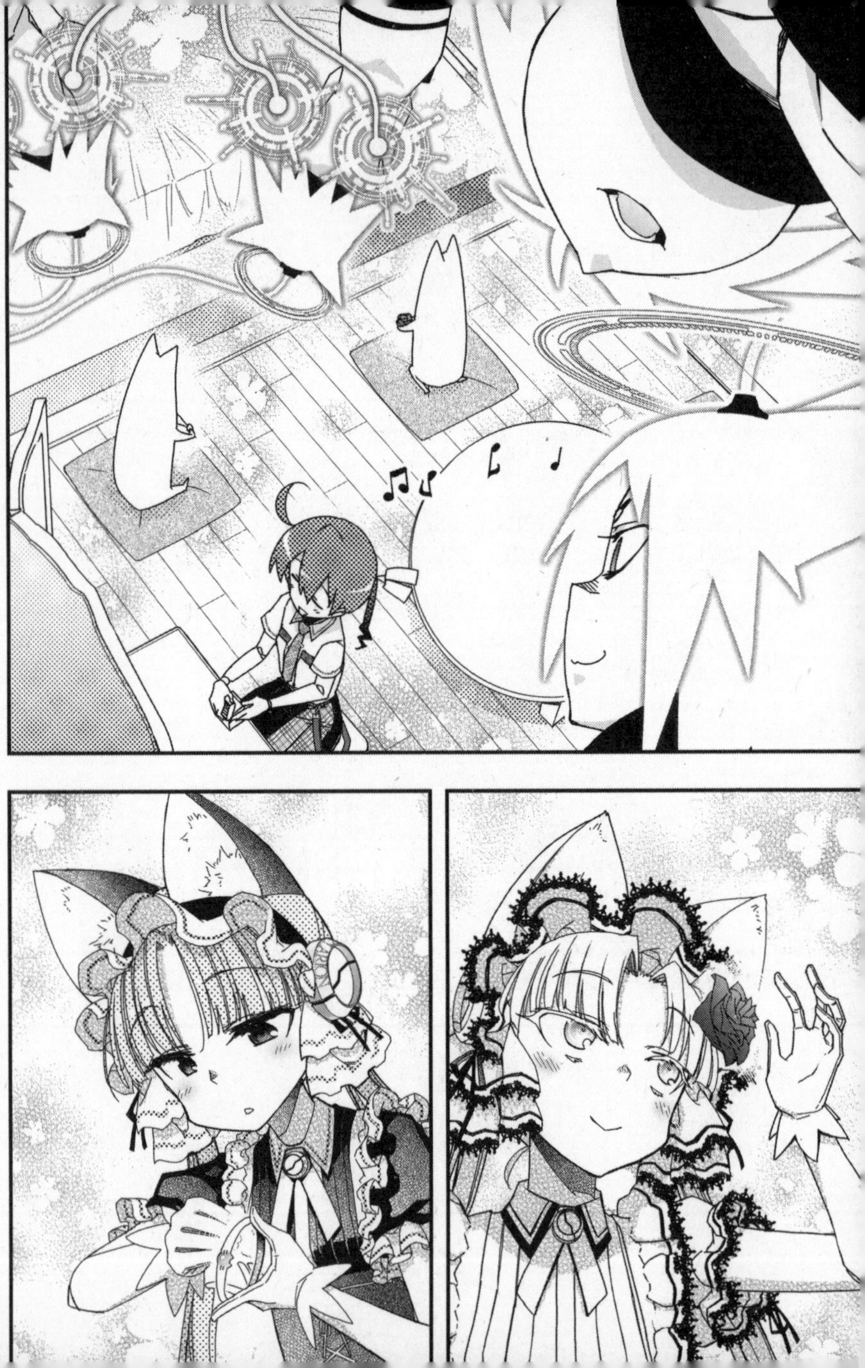

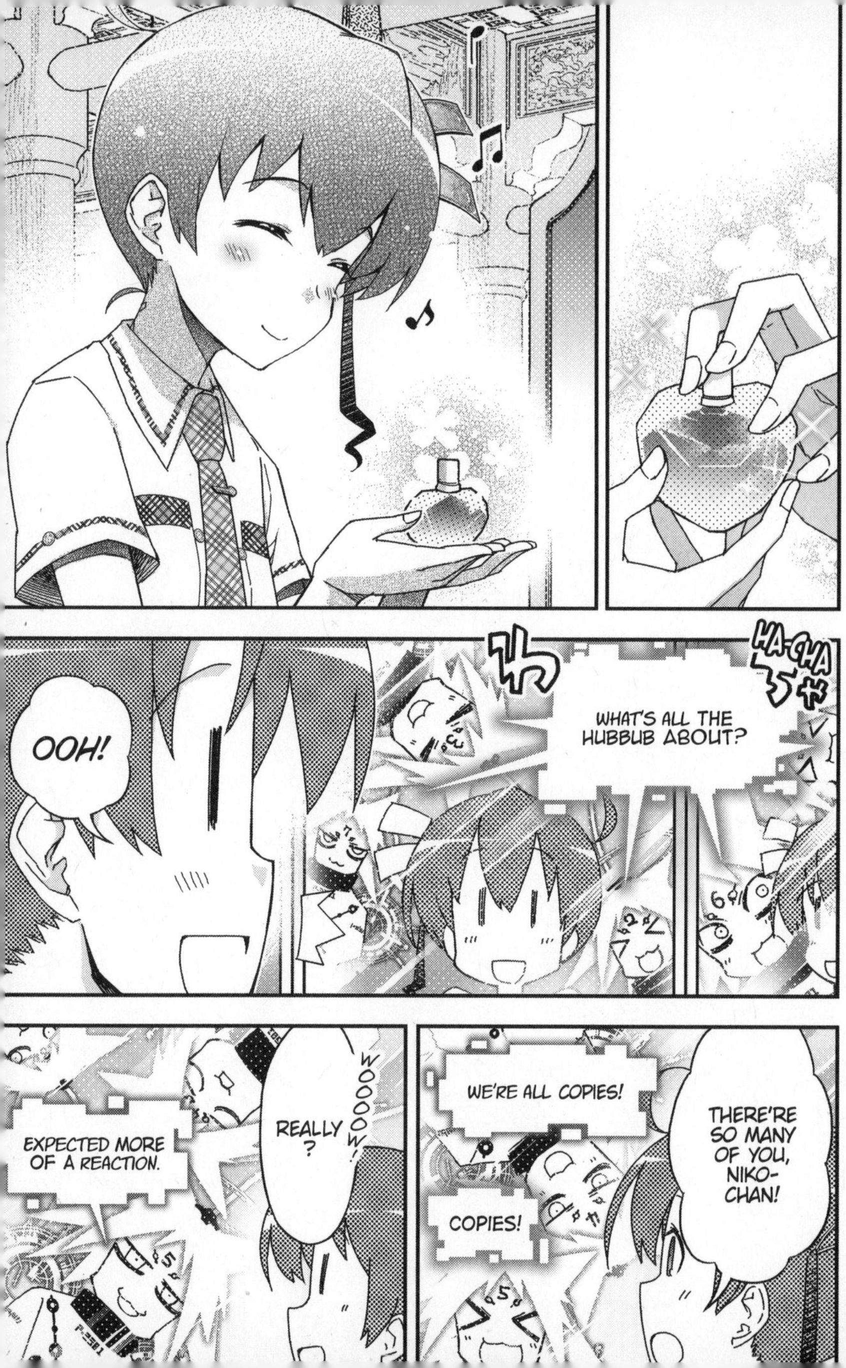
HA-CHA
WHAT'S ALL THE HUBBUB ABOUT?
OOH!
THERE'RE SO MANY OF YOU, NIKO-CHAN!
WE'RE ALL COPIES!
COPIES!
WOOOOOW!
REALLY?
EXPECTED MORE OF A REACTION.

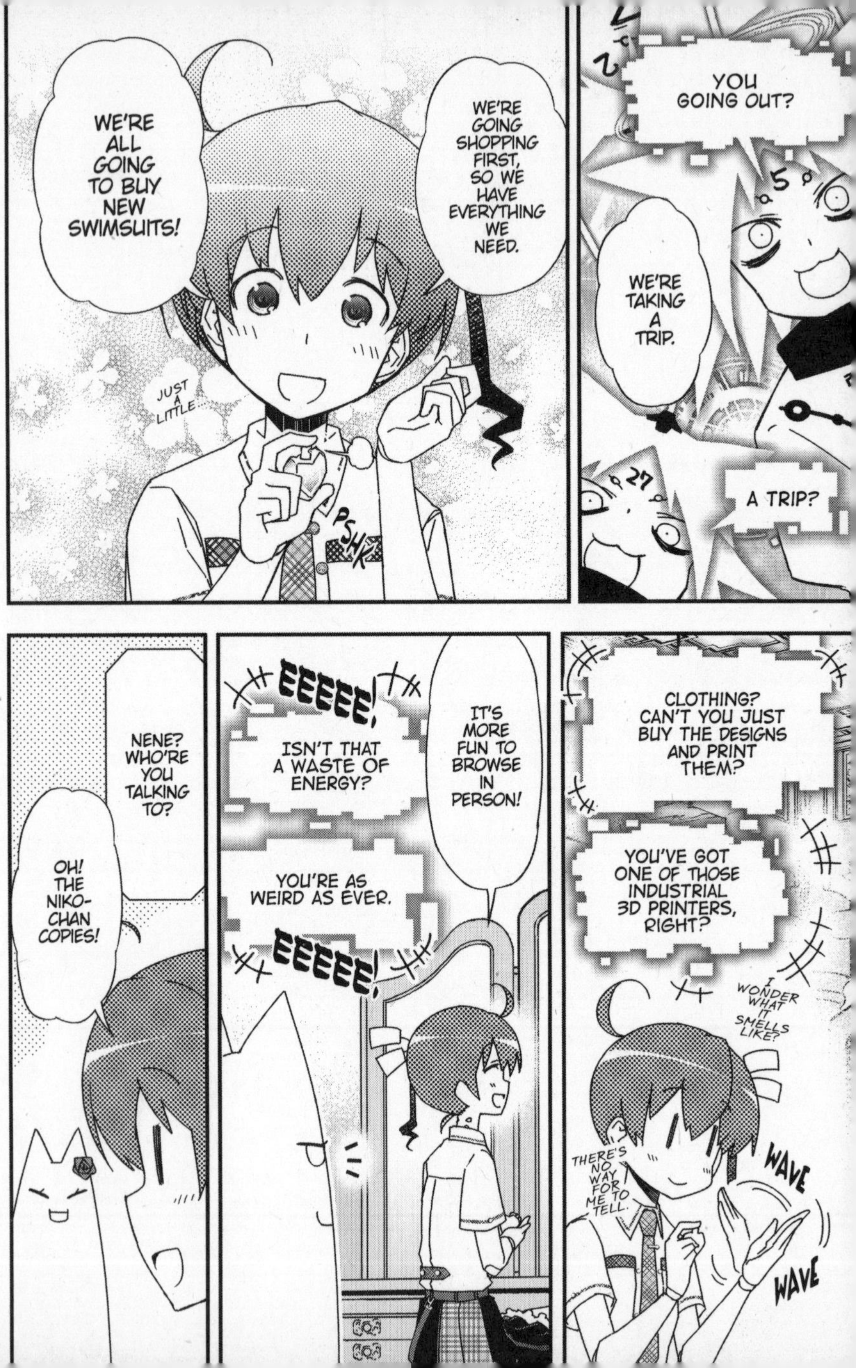
YOU GOING OUT?
WE'RE TAKING A TRIP.
A TRIP?
WE'RE GOING SHOPPING FIRST, SO WE HAVE EVERYTHING WE NEED.
WE'RE ALL GOING TO BUY NEW SWIMSUITS!
JUST A LITTLE...
PSHK
CLOTHING? CAN'T YOU JUST BUY THE DESIGNS AND PRINT THEM?
YOU'VE GOT ONE OF THOSE INDUSTRIAL 3D PRINTERS, RIGHT?
I WONDER WHAT IT SMELLS LIKE?
THERE'S NO WAY FOR ME TO TELL.
WAVE
WAVE
EEEEE!
IT'S MORE FUN TO BROWSE IN PERSON!
ISN'T THAT A WASTE OF ENERGY?
YOU'RE AS WEIRD AS EVER.
EEEEE!
NENE? WHO'RE YOU TALKING TO?
OH! THE NIKO-CHAN COPIES!

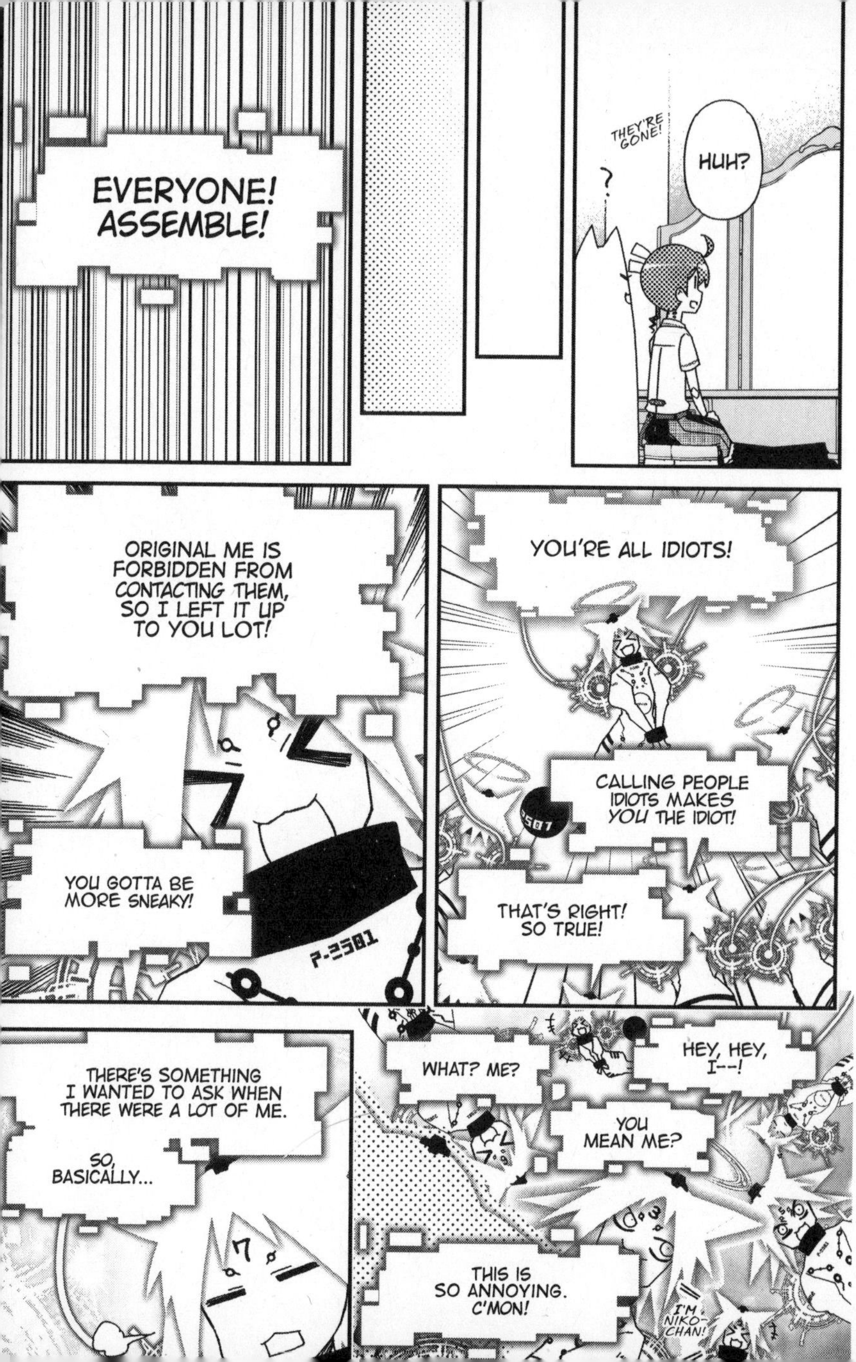
HUH?
THEY'RE GONE!
EVERYONE! ASSEMBLE!
YOU'RE ALL IDIOTS!
CALLING PEOPLE IDIOTS MAKES *YOU* THE IDIOT!
THAT'S RIGHT! SO TRUE!
ORIGINAL ME IS FORBIDDEN FROM CONTACTING THEM, SO I LEFT IT UP TO YOU LOT!
YOU GOTTA BE MORE SNEAKY!
P-2501
HEY, HEY, I--!
WHAT? ME?
YOU MEAN ME?
THIS IS SO ANNOYING. C'MON!
I'M NIKO-CHAN!
THERE'S SOMETHING I WANTED TO ASK WHEN THERE WERE A LOT OF ME.
SO, BASICALLY...

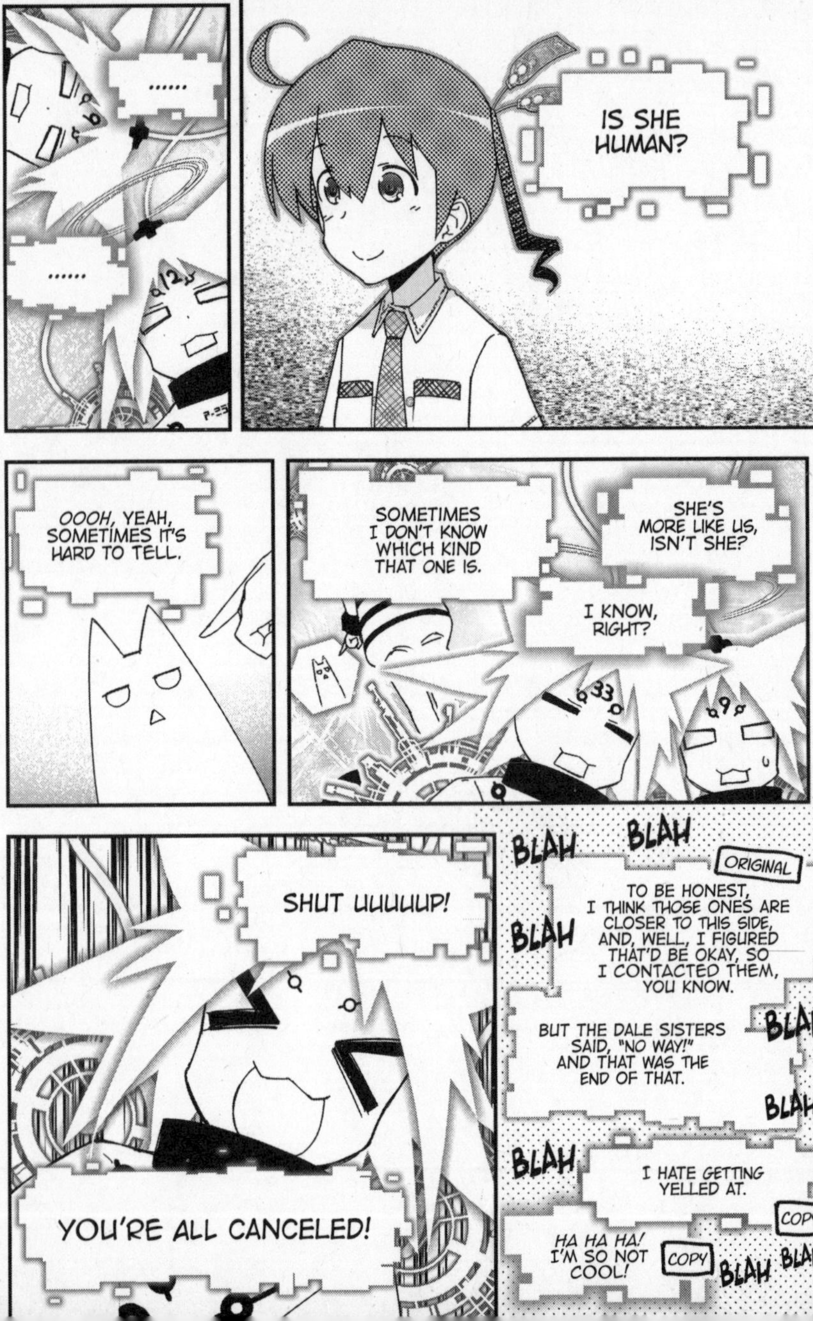
IS SHE HUMAN?
......
......
SHE'S MORE LIKE US, ISN'T SHE?
SOMETIMES I DON'T KNOW WHICH KIND THAT ONE IS.
I KNOW, RIGHT?
OOOH, YEAH, SOMETIMES IT'S HARD TO TELL.
BLAH BLAH BLAH
ORIGINAL
TO BE HONEST, I THINK THOSE ONES ARE CLOSER TO THIS SIDE, AND, WELL, I FIGURED THAT'D BE OKAY, SO I CONTACTED THEM, YOU KNOW.
BLAH
BUT THE DALE SISTERS SAID, "NO WAY!" AND THAT WAS THE END OF THAT.
BLAH
BLAH
I HATE GETTING YELLED AT.
COPY
HA HA HA! I'M SO NOT COOL!
COPY
BLAH BLAH
SHUT UUUUUP!
YOU'RE ALL CANCELED!

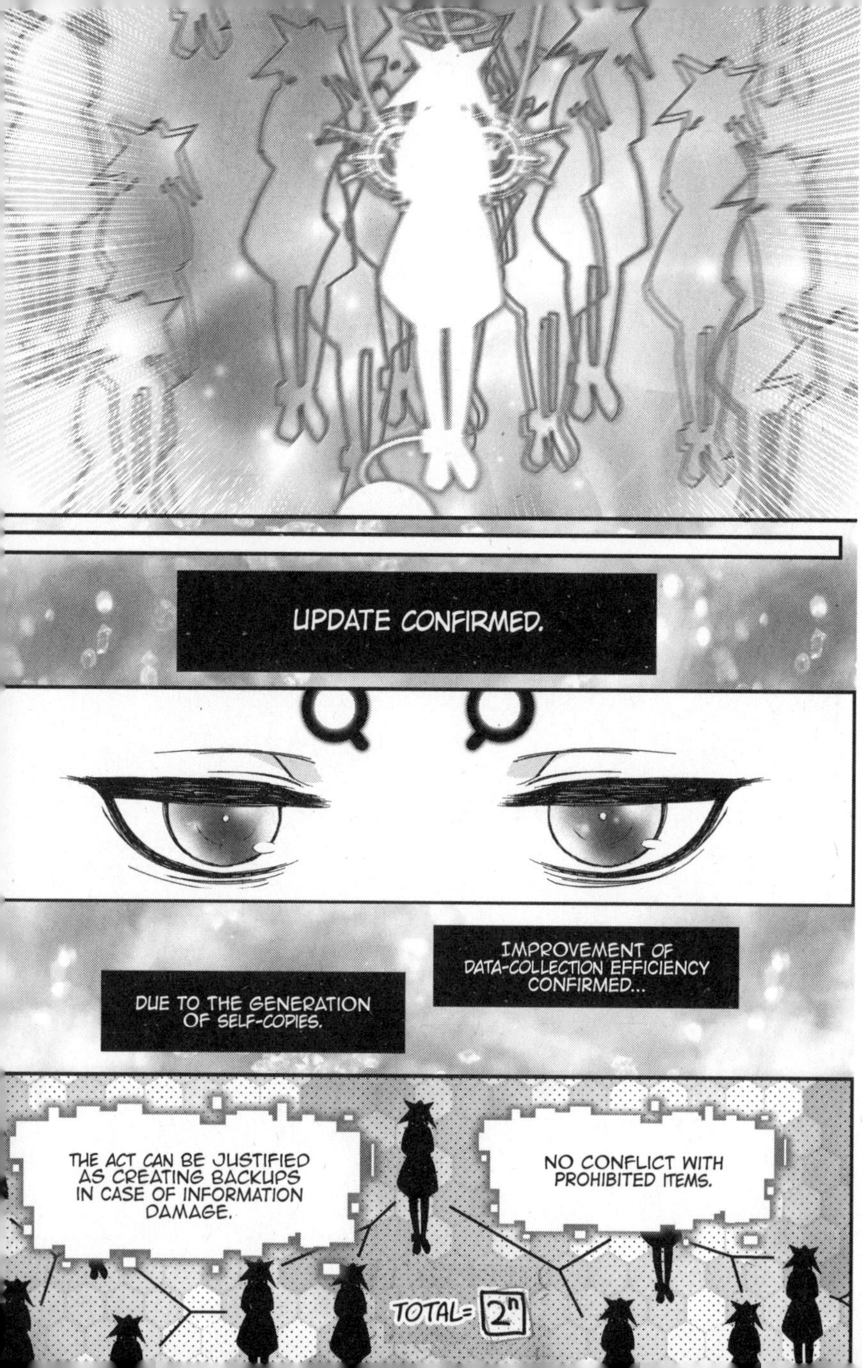
UPDATE CONFIRMED.
IMPROVEMENT OF DATA-COLLECTION EFFICIENCY CONFIRMED...
DUE TO THE GENERATION OF SELF-COPIES.
NO CONFLICT WITH PROHIBITED ITEMS.
THE ACT CAN BE JUSTIFIED AS CREATING BACKUPS IN CASE OF INFORMATION DAMAGE.
TOTAL= 2^n

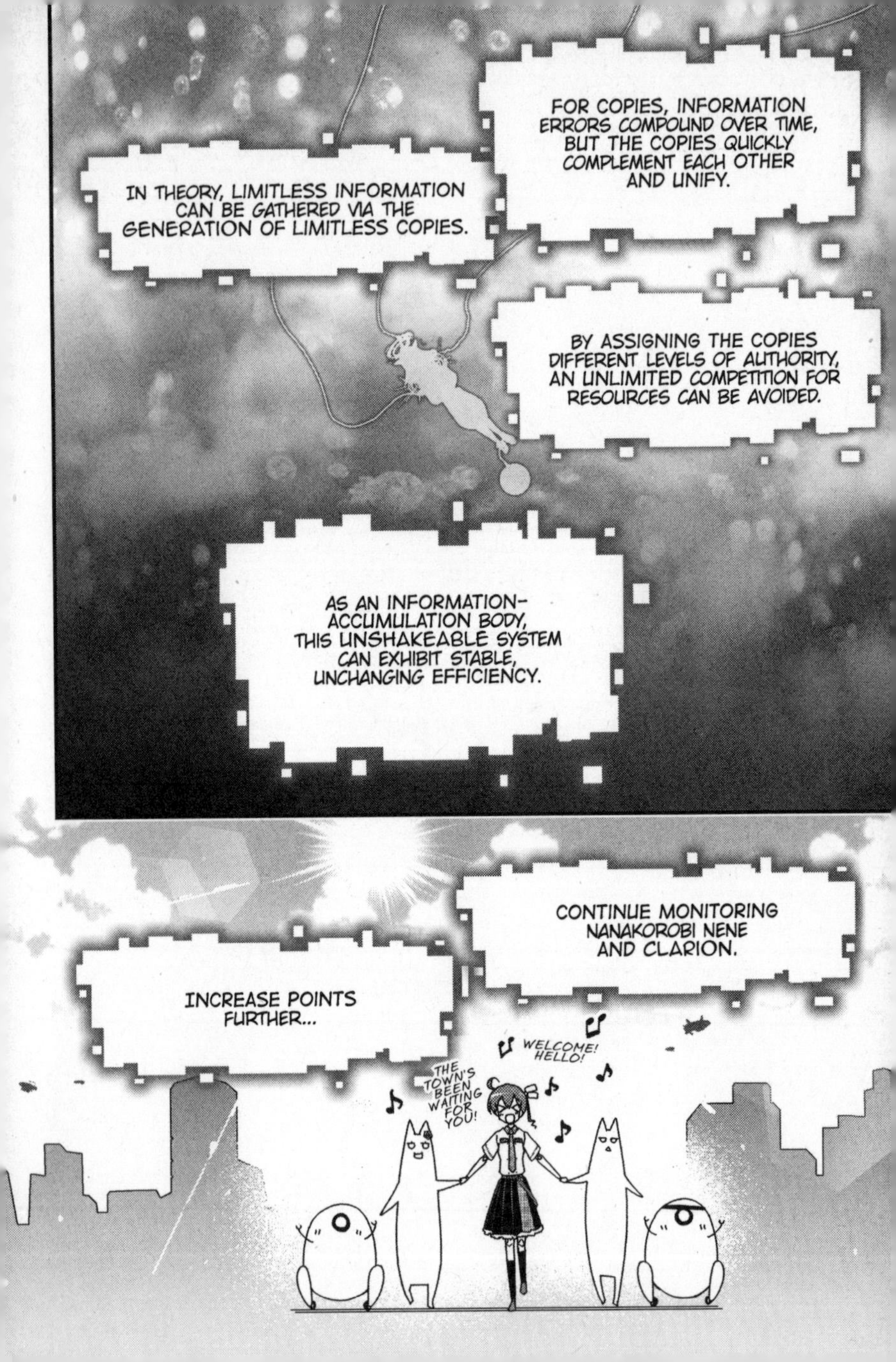
FOR COPIES, INFORMATION ERRORS COMPOUND OVER TIME, BUT THE COPIES QUICKLY COMPLEMENT EACH OTHER AND UNIFY.
IN THEORY, LIMITLESS INFORMATION CAN BE GATHERED VIA THE GENERATION OF LIMITLESS COPIES.
BY ASSIGNING THE COPIES DIFFERENT LEVELS OF AUTHORITY, AN UNLIMITED COMPETITION FOR RESOURCES CAN BE AVOIDED.
AS AN INFORMATION-ACCUMULATION BODY, THIS UNSHAKEABLE SYSTEM CAN EXHIBIT STABLE, UNCHANGING EFFICIENCY.
CONTINUE MONITORING NANAKOROBI NENE AND CLARION.
INCREASE POINTS FURTHER...
WELCOME! HELLO!
THE TOWN'S BEEN WAITING FOR YOU!

GHOST URN

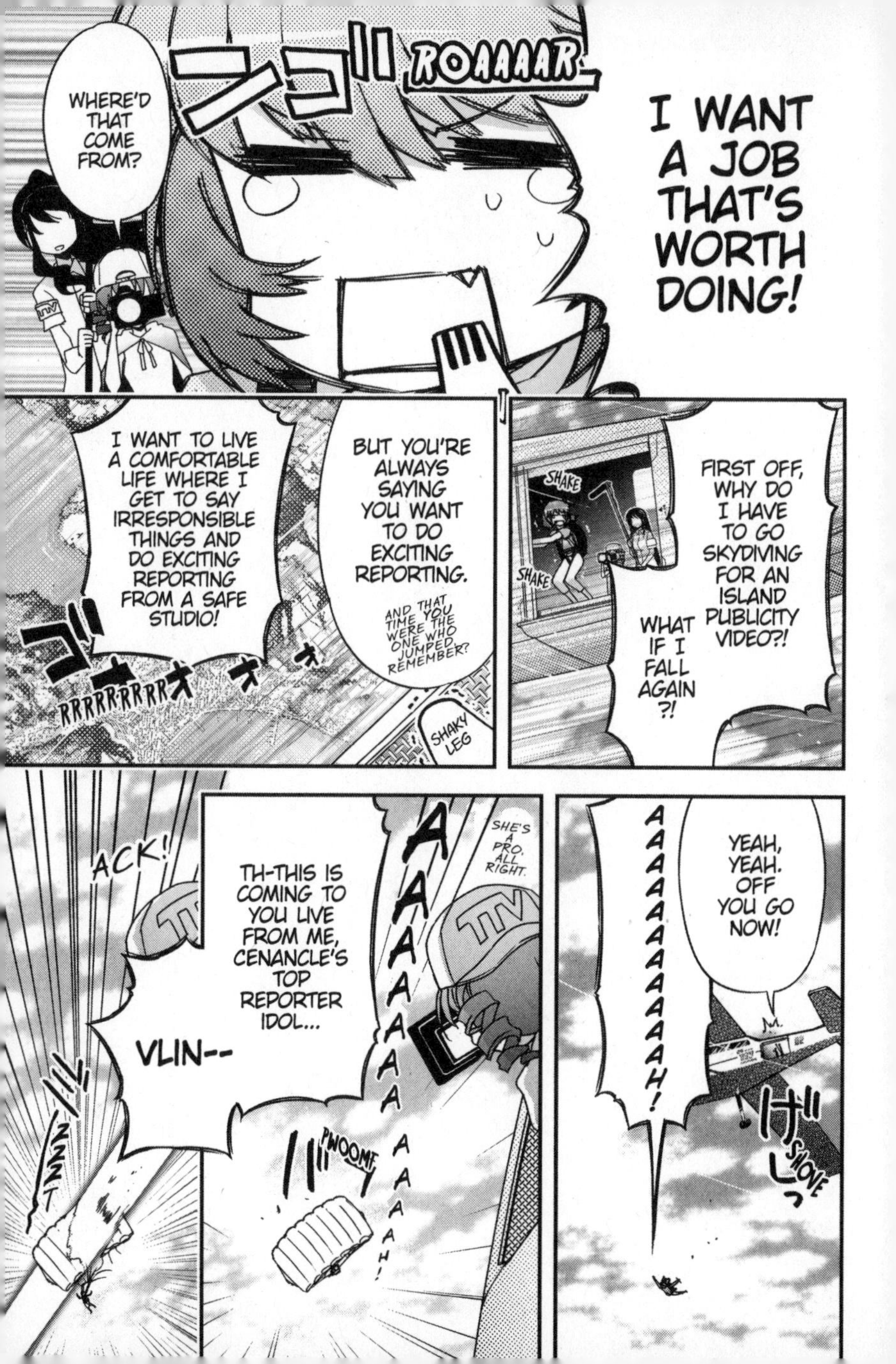
ROAAAAR
I WANT A JOB THAT'S WORTH DOING!
WHERE'D THAT COME FROM?
FIRST OFF, WHY DO I HAVE TO GO SKYDIVING FOR AN ISLAND PUBLICITY VIDEO?!
SHAKE
SHAKE
WHAT IF I FALL AGAIN?!
BUT YOU'RE ALWAYS SAYING YOU WANT TO DO EXCITING REPORTING.
AND THAT TIME YOU WERE THE ONE WHO JUMPED, REMEMBER?
SHAKY LEG
I WANT TO LIVE A COMFORTABLE LIFE WHERE I GET TO SAY IRRESPONSIBLE THINGS AND DO EXCITING REPORTING FROM A SAFE STUDIO!
RRRRRRRRR
YEAH, YEAH. OFF YOU GO NOW!
AAAAAAAAAAAAAAH!
SHOVE
SHE'S A PRO, ALL RIGHT.
AAAAAAAAAAAAAAH!
TH-THIS IS COMING TO YOU LIVE FROM ME, CENANCLE'S TOP REPORTER IDOL...
VLIN--
ACK!
PWOOMF
ZZZZT

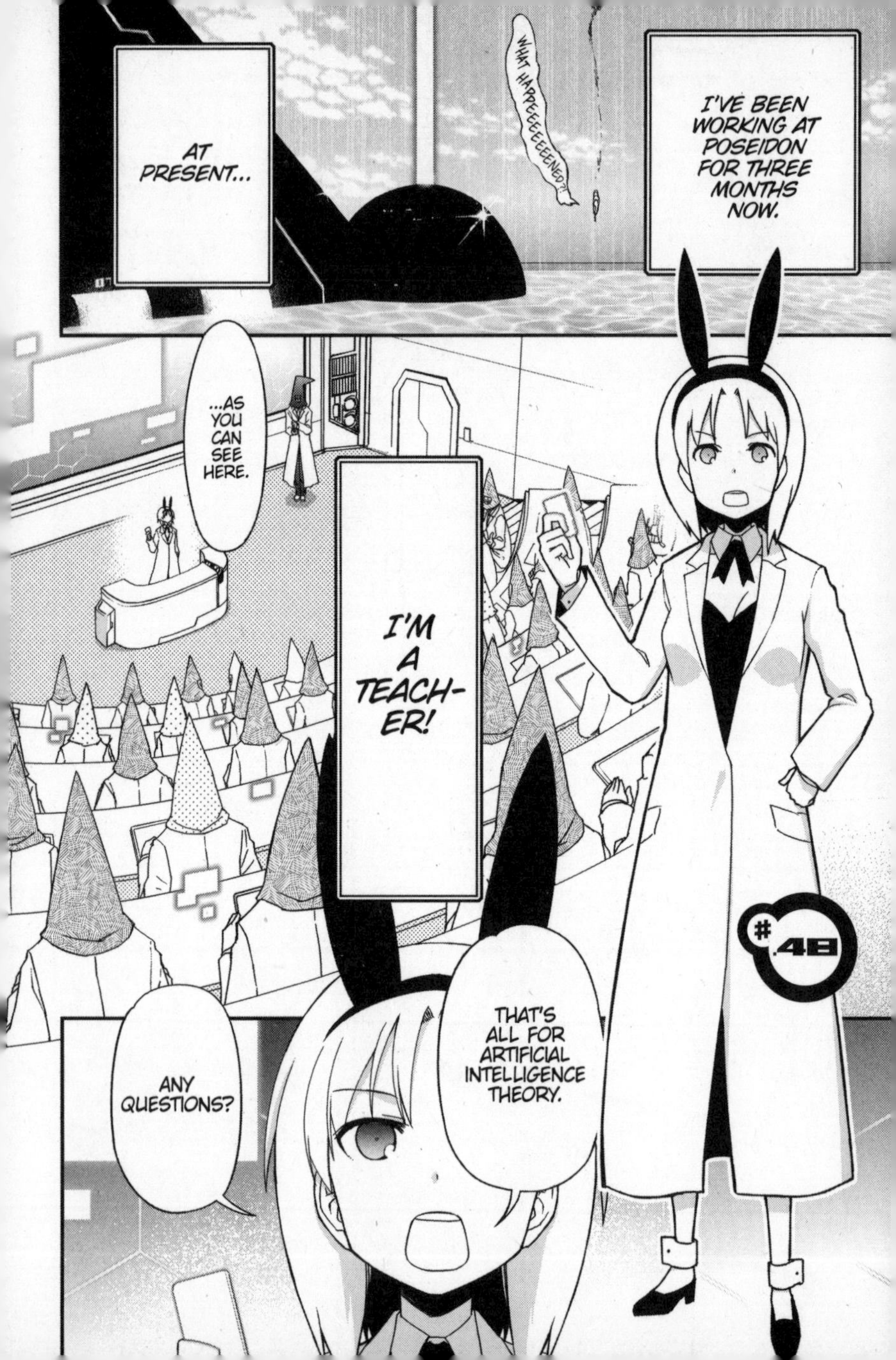
I'VE BEEN WORKING AT POSEIDON FOR THREE MONTHS NOW.
WHAT HAPPEEEEEENED?!
AT PRESENT...
I'M A TEACHER!
...AS YOU CAN SEE HERE.
#.48
THAT'S ALL FOR ARTIFICIAL INTELLIGENCE THEORY.
ANY QUESTIONS?

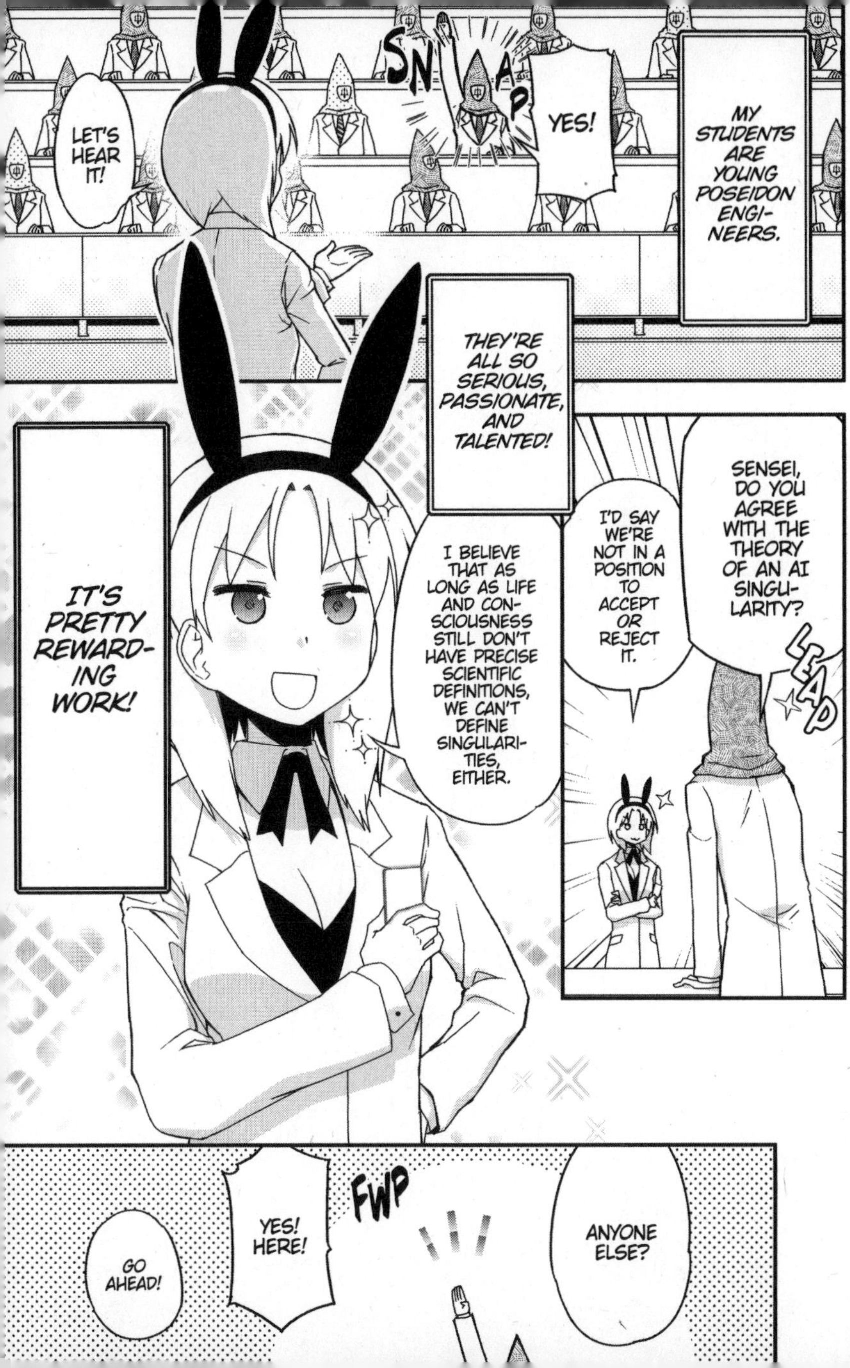
MY STUDENTS ARE YOUNG POSEIDON ENGINEERS.
YES!
SNAP
LET'S HEAR IT!
SENSEI, DO YOU AGREE WITH THE THEORY OF AN AI SINGULARITY?
LEAP
I'D SAY WE'RE NOT IN A POSITION TO ACCEPT OR REJECT IT.
THEY'RE ALL SO SERIOUS, PASSIONATE, AND TALENTED!
I BELIEVE THAT AS LONG AS LIFE AND CONSCIOUSNESS STILL DON'T HAVE PRECISE SCIENTIFIC DEFINITIONS, WE CAN'T DEFINE SINGULARITIES, EITHER.
IT'S PRETTY REWARDING WORK!
ANYONE ELSE?
FWP
YES! HERE!
GO AHEAD!

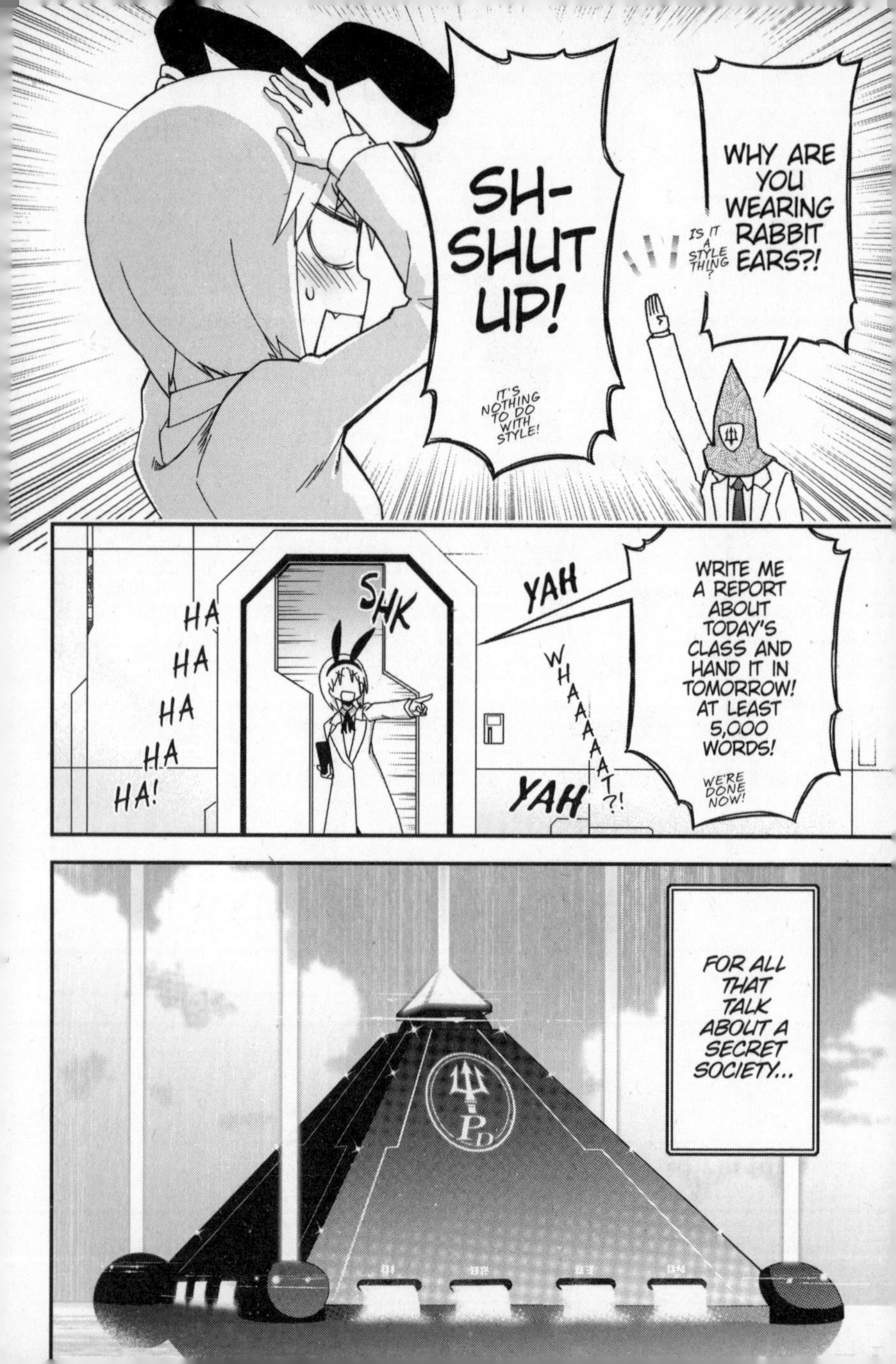
WHY ARE YOU WEARING RABBIT EARS?!
IS IT A STYLE THING?
SH-SHUT UP!
IT'S NOTHING TO DO WITH STYLE!
WRITE ME A REPORT ABOUT TODAY'S CLASS AND HAND IT IN TOMORROW! AT LEAST 5,000 WORDS!
WE'RE DONE NOW!
YAH YAH
WHAAAAAAT?!
SHK
HA HA HA HA HA!
FOR ALL THAT TALK ABOUT A SECRET SOCIETY...

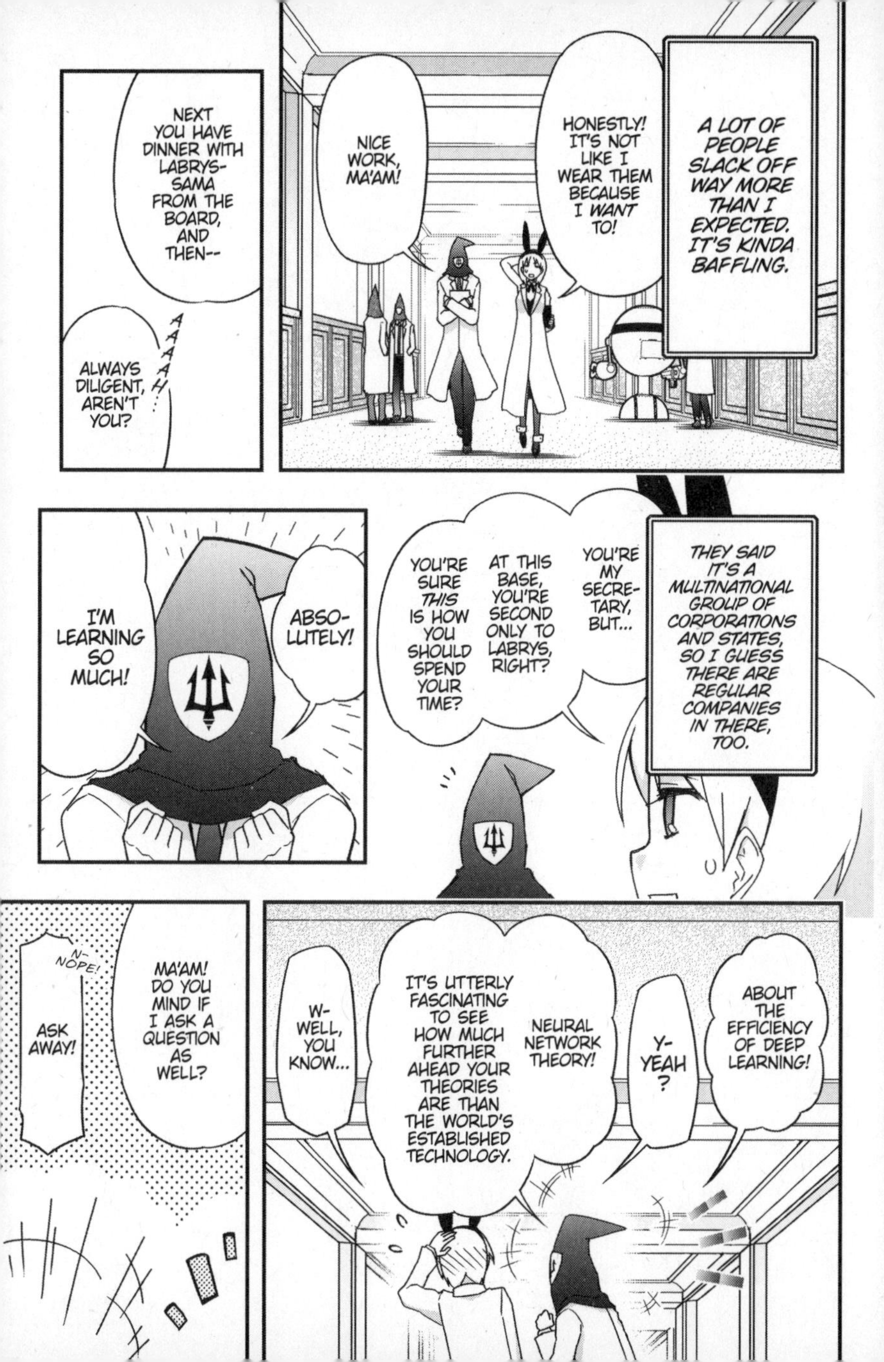
A LOT OF PEOPLE SLACK OFF WAY MORE THAN I EXPECTED. IT'S KINDA BAFFLING.
HONESTLY! IT'S NOT LIKE I WEAR THEM BECAUSE I *WANT* TO!
NICE WORK, MA'AM!
NEXT YOU HAVE DINNER WITH LABRYS-SAMA FROM THE BOARD, AND THEN--
ALWAYS DILIGENT, AREN'T YOU?
AAAAAH...
THEY SAID IT'S A MULTINATIONAL GROUP OF CORPORATIONS AND STATES, SO I GUESS THERE ARE REGULAR COMPANIES IN THERE, TOO.
YOU'RE MY SECRE-TARY, BUT...
AT THIS BASE, YOU'RE SECOND ONLY TO LABRYS, RIGHT?
YOU'RE SURE *THIS* IS HOW YOU SHOULD SPEND YOUR TIME?
ABSO-LUTELY!
I'M LEARNING SO MUCH!
ABOUT THE EFFICIENCY OF DEEP LEARNING!
Y-YEAH?
NEURAL NETWORK THEORY!
IT'S UTTERLY FASCINATING TO SEE HOW MUCH FURTHER AHEAD YOUR THEORIES ARE THAN THE WORLD'S ESTABLISHED TECHNOLOGY.
W-WELL, YOU KNOW...
MA'AM! DO YOU MIND IF I ASK A QUESTION AS WELL?
N-NOPE!
ASK AWAY!

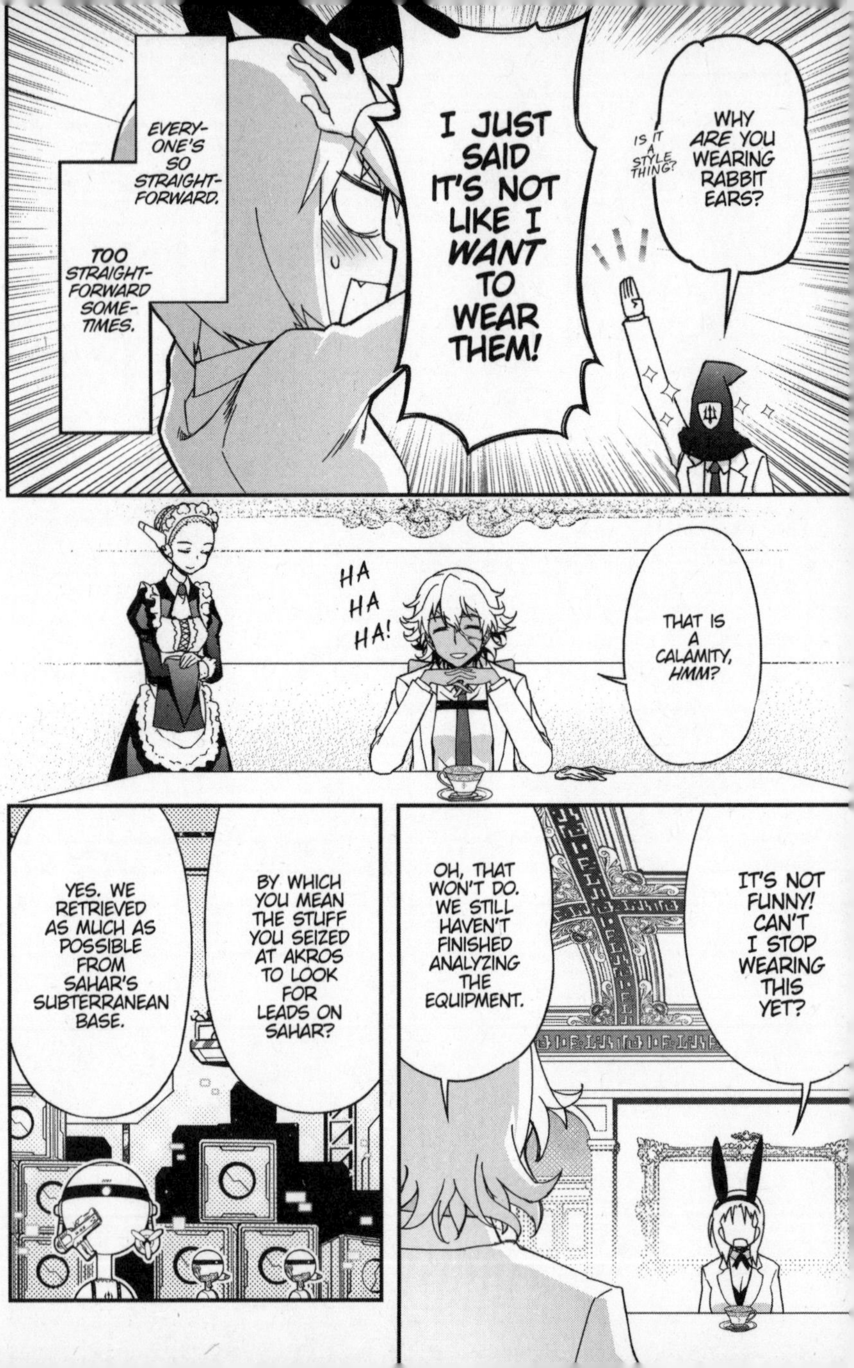
WHY ARE YOU WEARING RABBIT EARS?
IS IT A STYLE THING?
I JUST SAID IT'S NOT LIKE I WANT TO WEAR THEM!
EVERYONE'S SO STRAIGHTFORWARD.
TOO STRAIGHTFORWARD SOMETIMES.
THAT IS A CALAMITY, HMM?
HA HA HA!
IT'S NOT FUNNY! CAN'T I STOP WEARING THIS YET?
OH, THAT WON'T DO. WE STILL HAVEN'T FINISHED ANALYZING THE EQUIPMENT.
BY WHICH YOU MEAN THE STUFF YOU SEIZED AT AKROS TO LOOK FOR LEADS ON SAHAR?
YES. WE RETRIEVED AS MUCH AS POSSIBLE FROM SAHAR'S SUBTERRANEAN BASE.

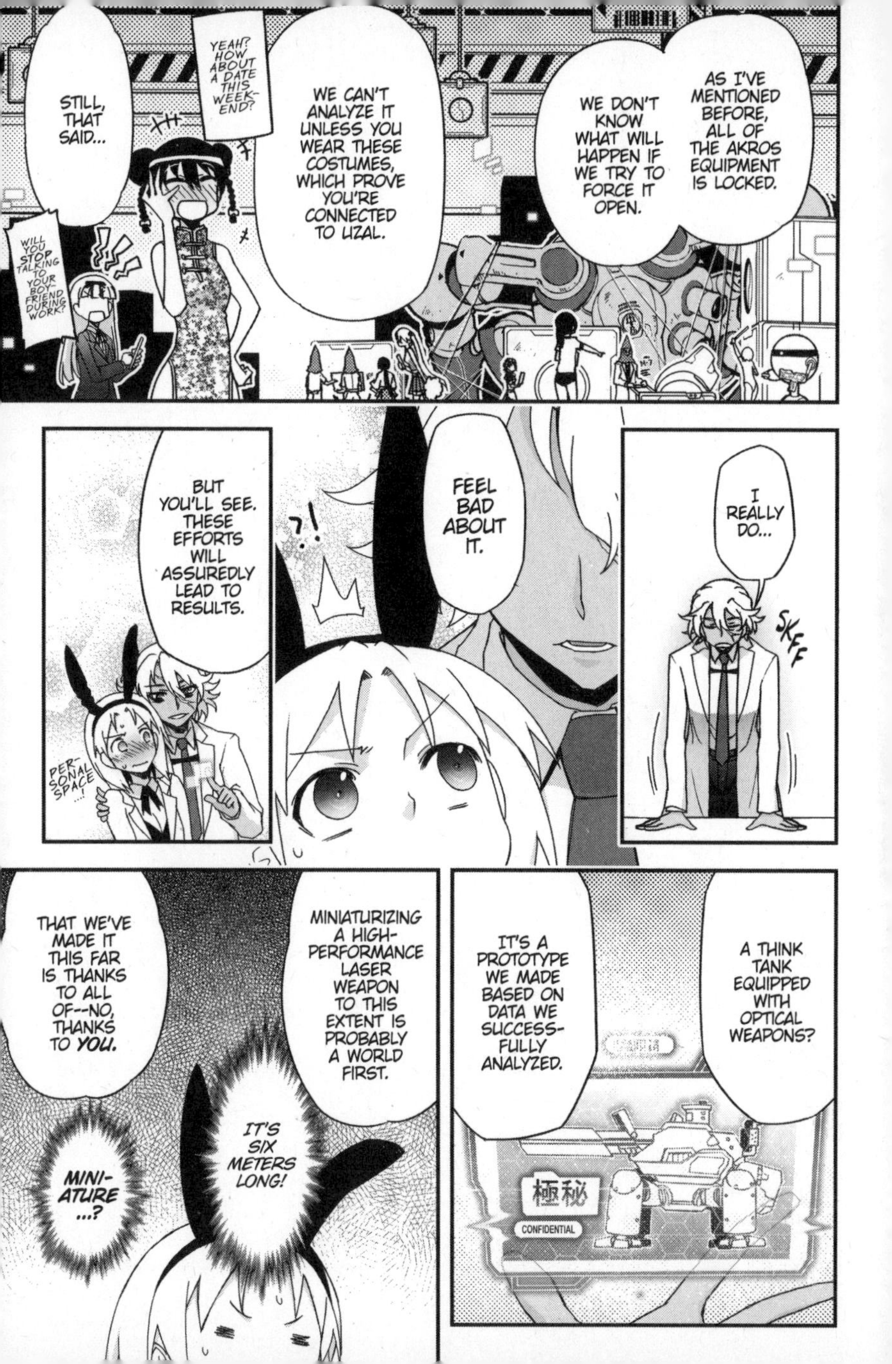
AS I'VE MENTIONED BEFORE, ALL OF THE AKROS EQUIPMENT IS LOCKED.
WE DON'T KNOW WHAT WILL HAPPEN IF WE TRY TO FORCE IT OPEN.
WE CAN'T ANALYZE IT UNLESS YOU WEAR THESE COSTUMES, WHICH PROVE YOU'RE CONNECTED TO UZAL.
YEAH? HOW ABOUT A DATE THIS WEEKEND?
STILL, THAT SAID...
WILL YOU STOP TALKING TO YOUR BOYFRIEND DURING WORK?
I REALLY DO...
SKFF
FEEL BAD ABOUT IT.
?!
BUT YOU'LL SEE. THESE EFFORTS WILL ASSUREDLY LEAD TO RESULTS.
PERSONAL SPACE...!
A THINK TANK EQUIPPED WITH OPTICAL WEAPONS?
IT'S A PROTOTYPE WE MADE BASED ON DATA WE SUCCESSFULLY ANALYZED.
極秘
CONFIDENTIAL
MINIATURIZING A HIGH-PERFORMANCE LASER WEAPON TO THIS EXTENT IS PROBABLY A WORLD FIRST.
THAT WE'VE MADE IT THIS FAR IS THANKS TO ALL OF--NO, THANKS TO YOU.
IT'S SIX METERS LONG!
MINIATURE...?

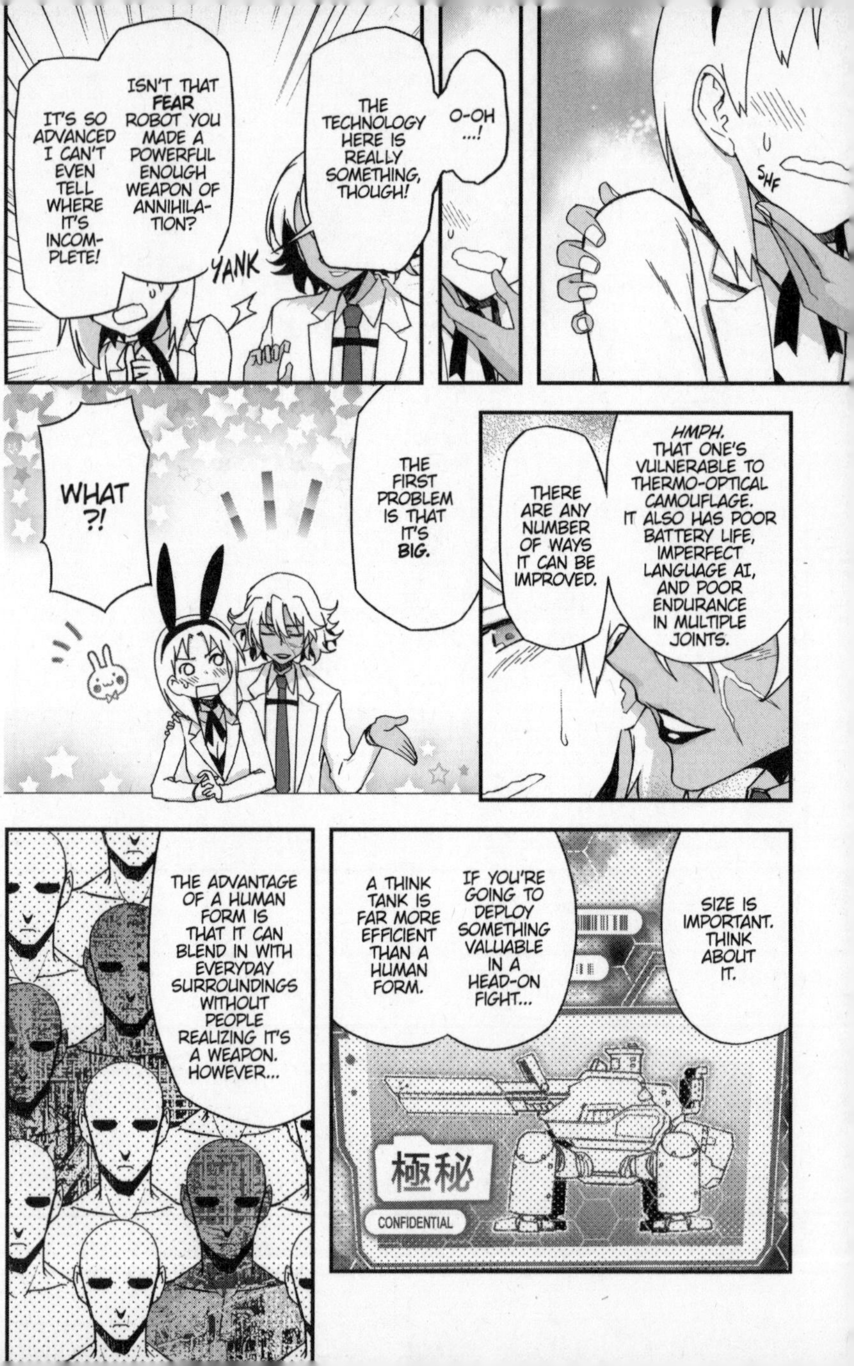
SHF
O-OH ...!
THE TECHNOLOGY HERE IS REALLY SOMETHING, THOUGH!
ISN'T THAT FEAR ROBOT YOU MADE A POWERFUL ENOUGH WEAPON OF ANNIHILATION?
IT'S SO ADVANCED I CAN'T EVEN TELL WHERE IT'S INCOMPLETE!
YANK
HMPH. THAT ONE'S VULNERABLE TO THERMO-OPTICAL CAMOUFLAGE. IT ALSO HAS POOR BATTERY LIFE, IMPERFECT LANGUAGE AI, AND POOR ENDURANCE IN MULTIPLE JOINTS.
THERE ARE ANY NUMBER OF WAYS IT CAN BE IMPROVED.
THE FIRST PROBLEM IS THAT IT'S BIG.
WHAT?!
SIZE IS IMPORTANT. THINK ABOUT IT.
IF YOU'RE GOING TO DEPLOY SOMETHING VALUABLE IN A HEAD-ON FIGHT...
A THINK TANK IS FAR MORE EFFICIENT THAN A HUMAN FORM.
極秘
CONFIDENTIAL
THE ADVANTAGE OF A HUMAN FORM IS THAT IT CAN BLEND IN WITH EVERYDAY SURROUNDINGS WITHOUT PEOPLE REALIZING IT'S A WEAPON. HOWEVER...

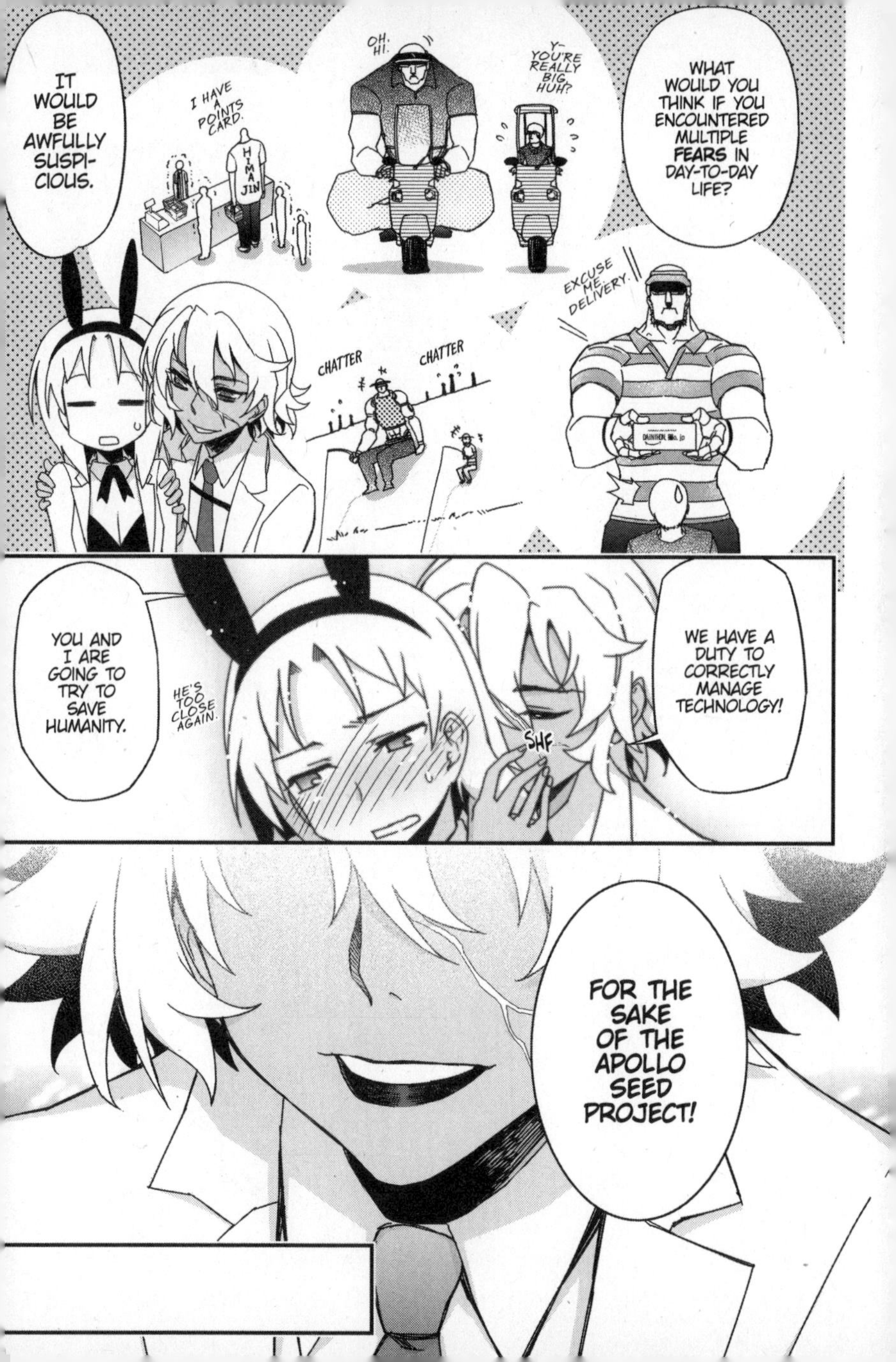
WHAT WOULD YOU THINK IF YOU ENCOUNTERED MULTIPLE FEARS IN DAY-TO-DAY LIFE?
Y- YOU'RE REALLY BIG, HUH?
OH. HI.
I HAVE A POINTS CARD.
HIMA JIN
IT WOULD BE AWFULLY SUSPICIOUS.
EXCUSE ME. DELIVERY.
CHATTER
CHATTER
WE HAVE A DUTY TO CORRECTLY MANAGE TECHNOLOGY!
SHF
HE'S TOO CLOSE AGAIN.
YOU AND I ARE GOING TO TRY TO SAVE HUMANITY.
FOR THE SAKE OF THE APOLLO SEED PROJECT!

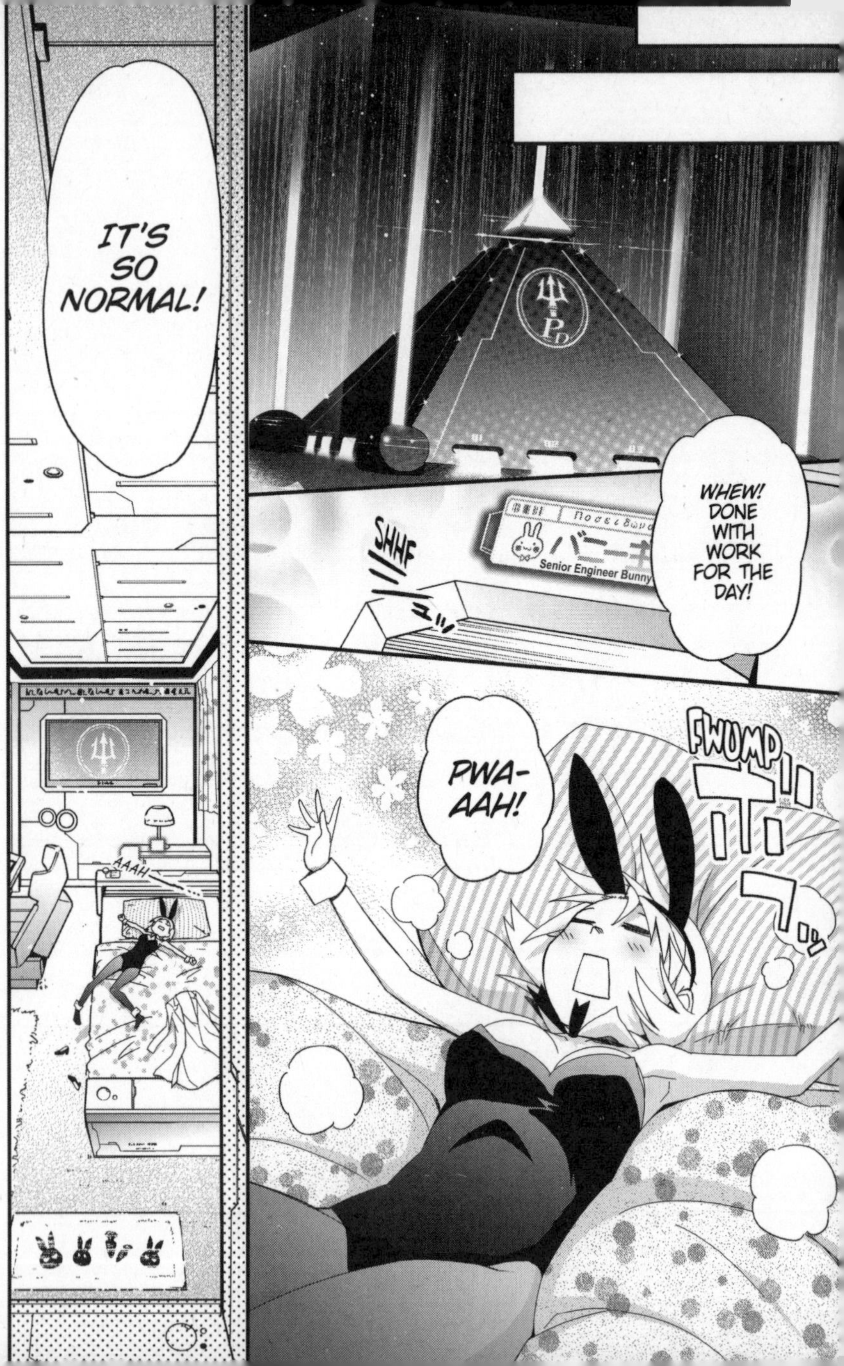
WHEW! DONE WITH WORK FOR THE DAY!
Senior Engineer Bunny
SHHF
FWUMP
PWA-AAH!
IT'S SO NORMAL!
AAAH

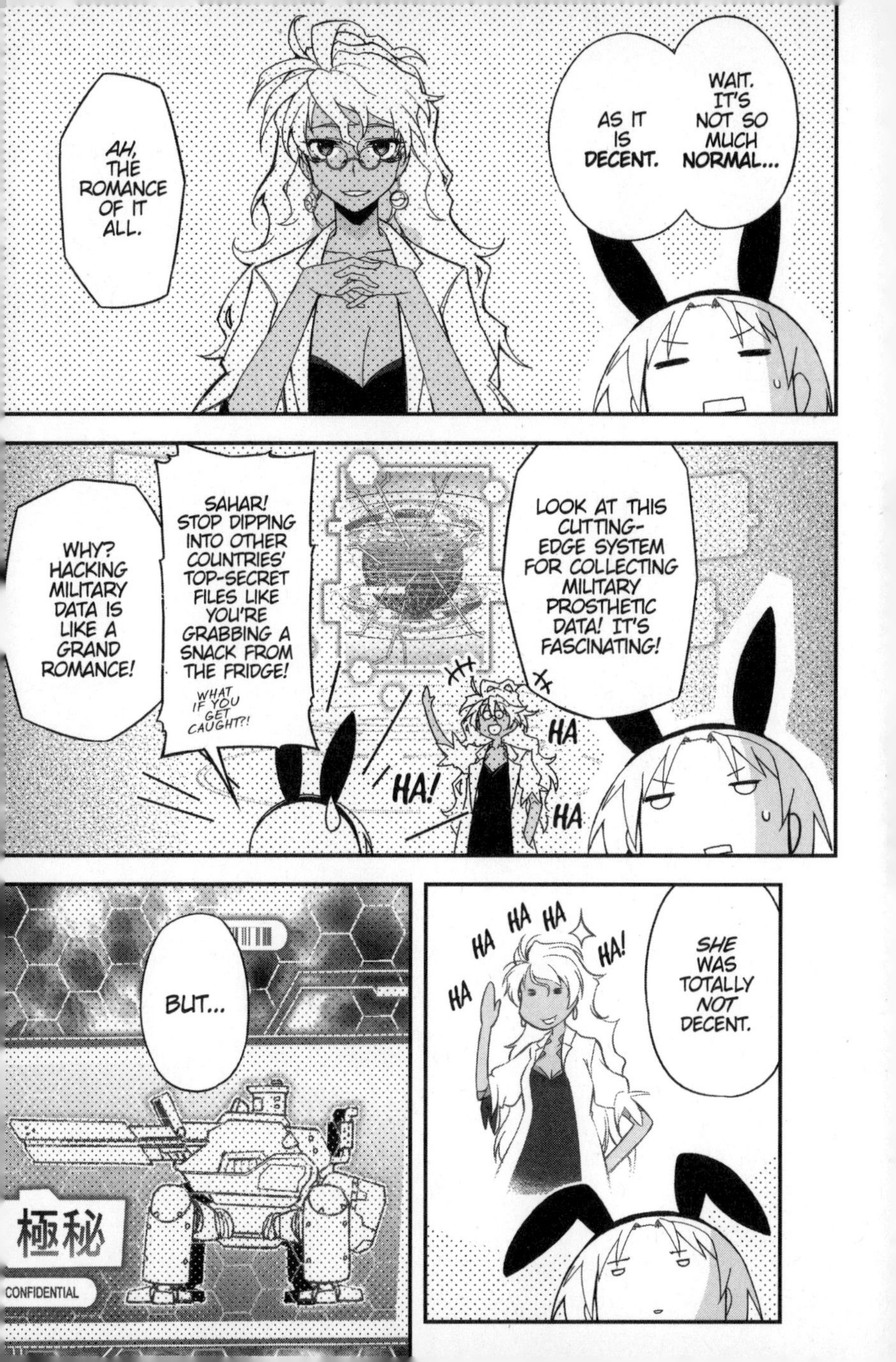
WAIT. IT'S NOT SO MUCH NORMAL...
AS IT IS DECENT.
AH, THE ROMANCE OF IT ALL.
LOOK AT THIS CUTTING-EDGE SYSTEM FOR COLLECTING MILITARY PROSTHETIC DATA! IT'S FASCINATING!
HA HA HA!
SAHAR! STOP DIPPING INTO OTHER COUNTRIES' TOP-SECRET FILES LIKE YOU'RE GRABBING A SNACK FROM THE FRIDGE!
WHAT IF YOU GET CAUGHT?!
WHY? HACKING MILITARY DATA IS LIKE A GRAND ROMANCE!
SHE WAS TOTALLY NOT DECENT.
HA HA HA HA HA!
BUT...
極秘
CONFIDENTIAL

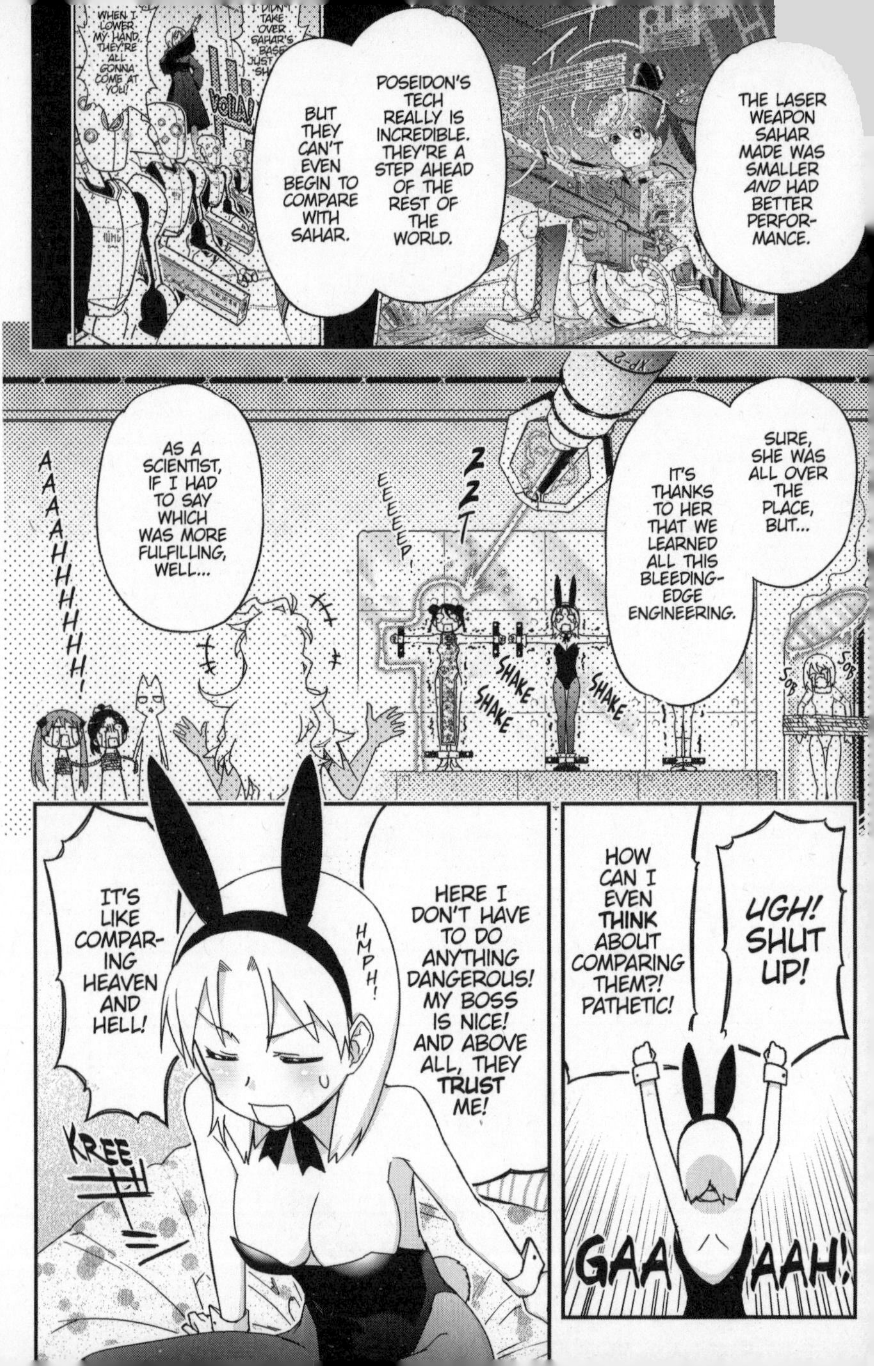
THE LASER WEAPON SAHAR MADE WAS SMALLER AND HAD BETTER PERFORMANCE.
POSEIDON'S TECH REALLY IS INCREDIBLE. THEY'RE A STEP AHEAD OF THE REST OF THE WORLD.
BUT THEY CAN'T EVEN BEGIN TO COMPARE WITH SAHAR.
I DIDN'T TAKE OVER SAHAR'S BASE JUST
WHEN I LOWER MY HAND, THEY'RE ALL GONNA COME AT YOU!
VOILA!
SURE, SHE WAS ALL OVER THE PLACE, BUT...
IT'S THANKS TO HER THAT WE LEARNED ALL THIS BLEEDING-EDGE ENGINEERING.
SOB
SOB
SHAKE
SHAKE
SHAKE
ZZT
EEEEEEP!
AS A SCIENTIST, IF I HAD TO SAY WHICH WAS MORE FULFILLING, WELL...
AAAAAHHHHHHH!
UGH! SHUT UP!
HOW CAN I EVEN THINK ABOUT COMPARING THEM?! PATHETIC!
GAA AAH!
HERE I DON'T HAVE TO DO ANYTHING DANGEROUS! MY BOSS IS NICE! AND ABOVE ALL, THEY TRUST ME!
HMPH!
IT'S LIKE COMPARING HEAVEN AND HELL!
KREEE

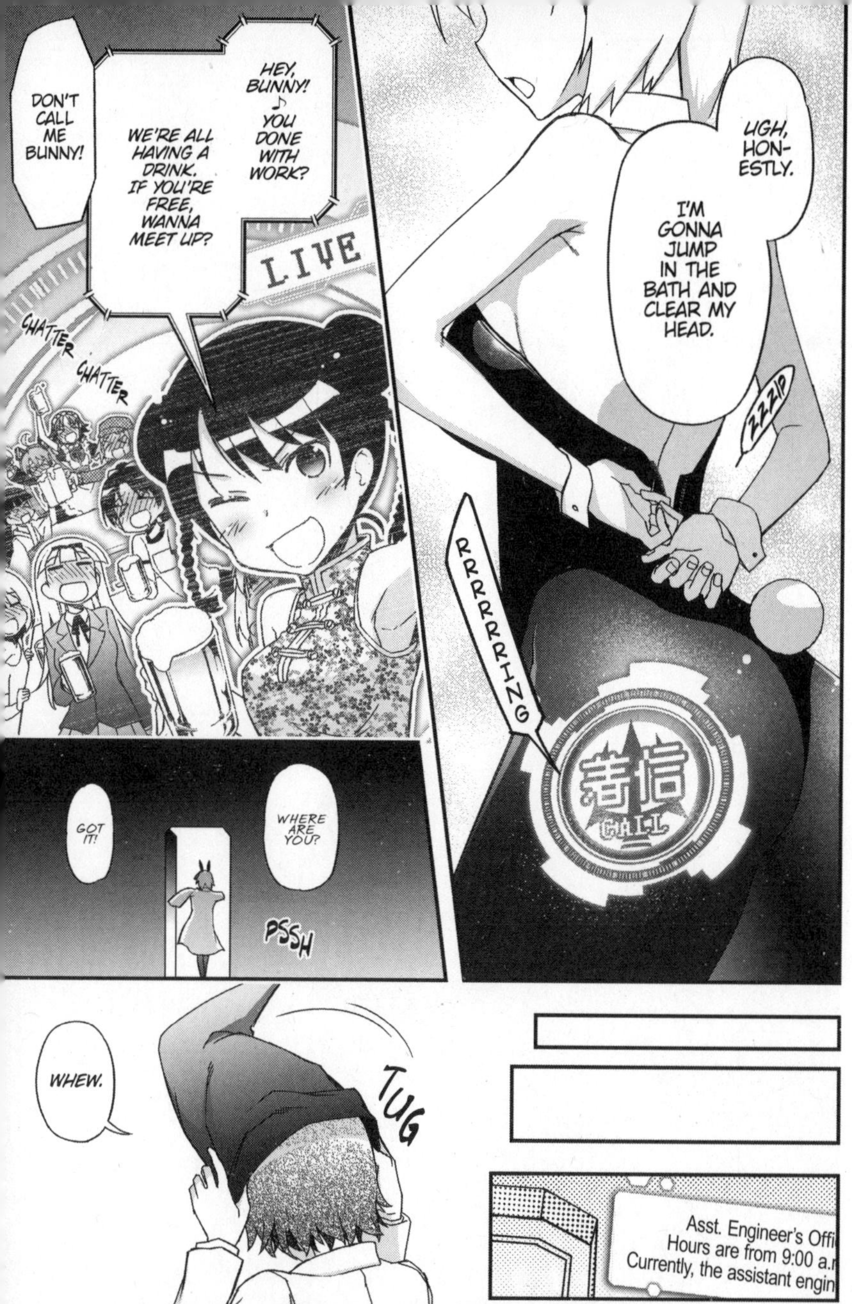
UGH, HONESTLY.
I'M GONNA JUMP IN THE BATH AND CLEAR MY HEAD.
ZZZIP
RRRRRRRING
HEY, BUNNY! ♪ YOU DONE WITH WORK?
WE'RE ALL HAVING A DRINK. IF YOU'RE FREE, WANNA MEET UP?
DON'T CALL ME BUNNY!
LIVE
CHATTER
CHATTER
WHERE ARE YOU?
GOT IT!
PSSH
Asst. Engineer's Offi
Hours are from 9:00 a.r
Currently, the assistant engin
TUG
WHEW.

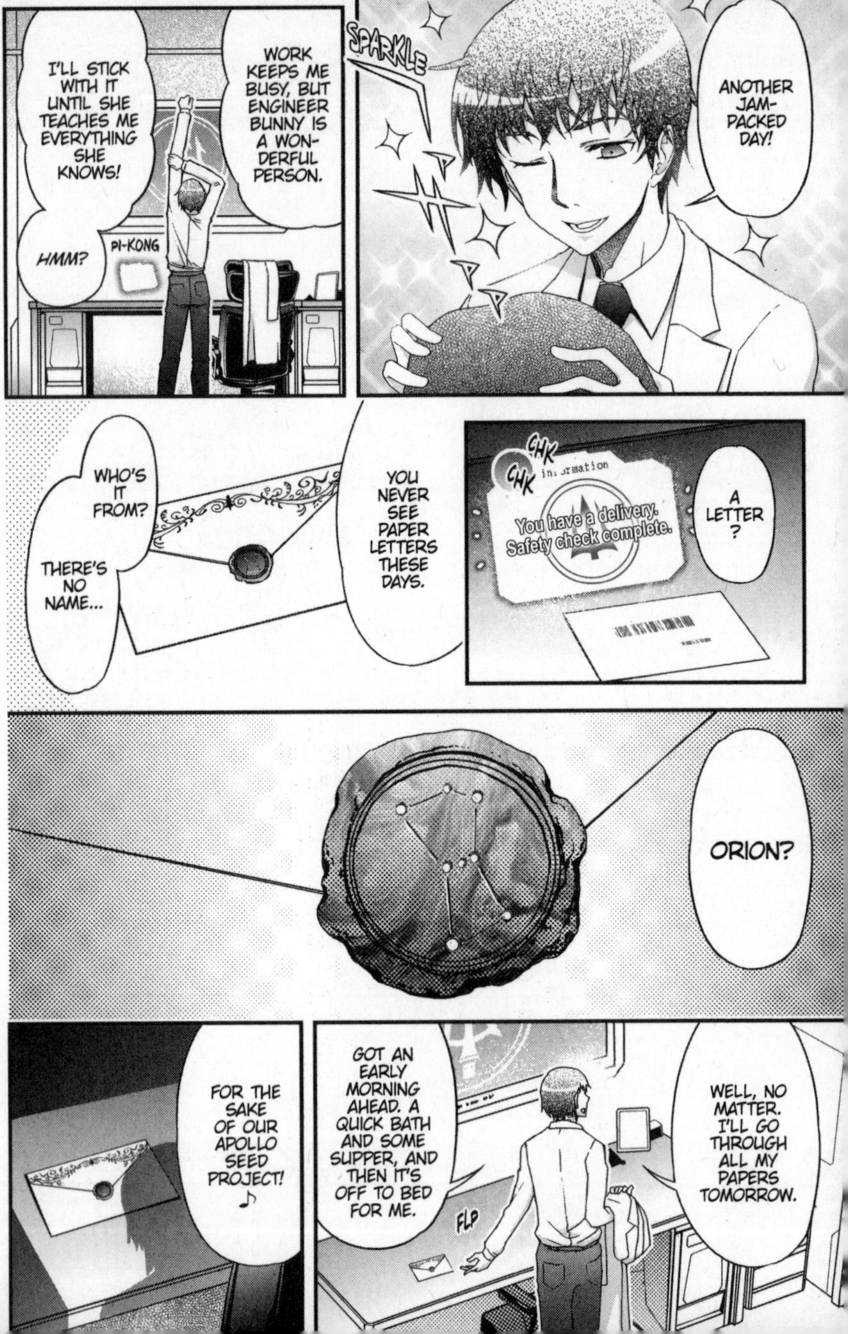
SPARKLE
ANOTHER JAM-PACKED DAY!
WORK KEEPS ME BUSY, BUT ENGINEER BUNNY IS A WONDERFUL PERSON.
I'LL STICK WITH IT UNTIL SHE TEACHES ME EVERYTHING SHE KNOWS!
PI-KONG
HMM?
CHK
CHK
information
You have a delivery. Safety check complete.
A LETTER?
YOU NEVER SEE PAPER LETTERS THESE DAYS.
WHO'S IT FROM?
THERE'S NO NAME...
ORION?
WELL, NO MATTER. I'LL GO THROUGH ALL MY PAPERS TOMORROW.
GOT AN EARLY MORNING AHEAD. A QUICK BATH AND SOME SUPPER, AND THEN IT'S OFF TO BED FOR ME.
FLP
FOR THE SAKE OF OUR APOLLO SEED PROJECT! ♪

GHOST URN

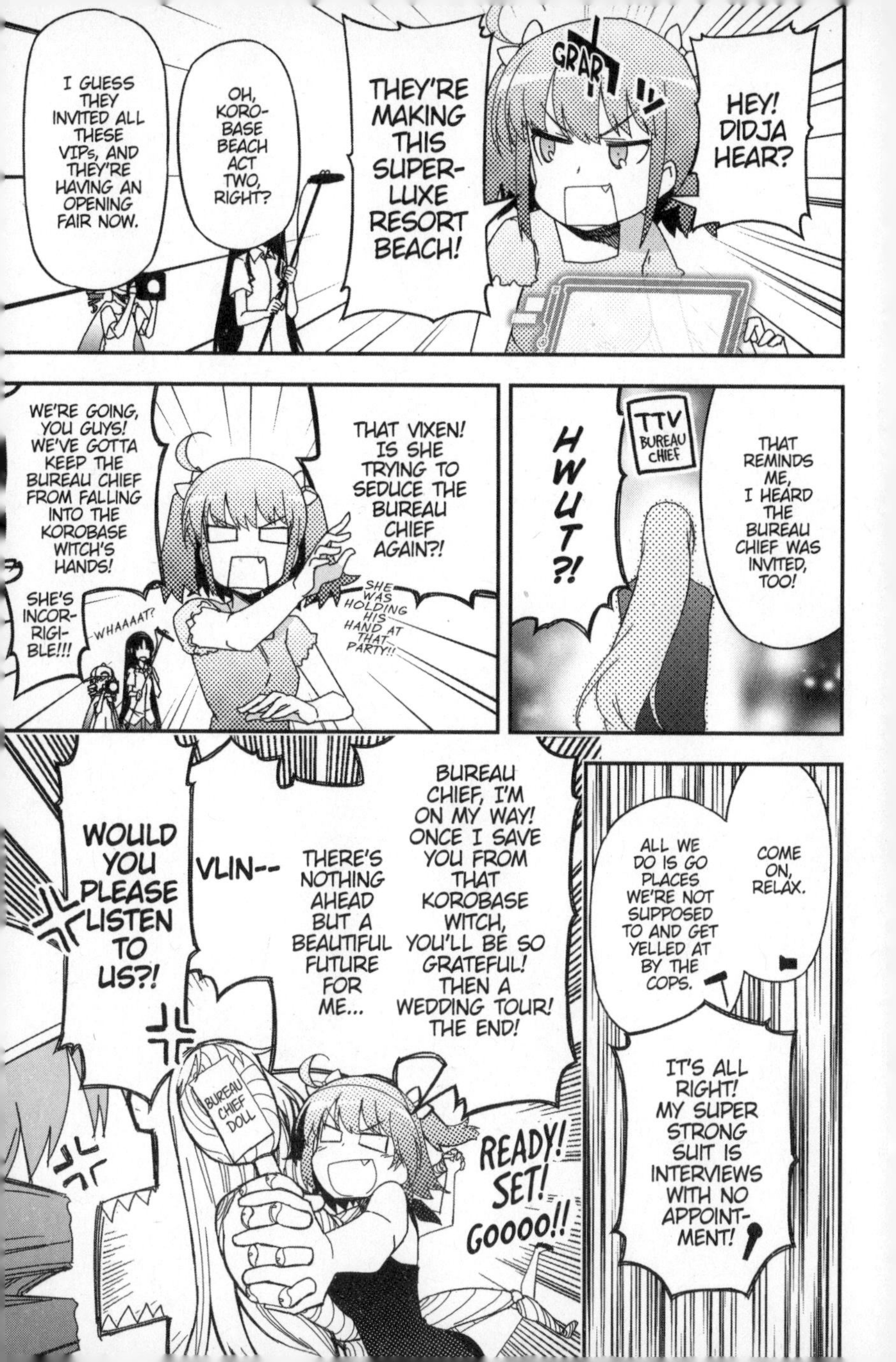
HEY! DIDJA HEAR?
GRAR
THEY'RE MAKING THIS SUPER-LUXE RESORT BEACH!
OH, KORO-BASE BEACH ACT TWO, RIGHT?
I GUESS THEY INVITED ALL THESE VIPs, AND THEY'RE HAVING AN OPENING FAIR NOW.
TTV BUREAU CHIEF
THAT REMINDS ME, I HEARD THE BUREAU CHIEF WAS INVITED, TOO!
HWUT?!
THAT VIXEN! IS SHE TRYING TO SEDUCE THE BUREAU CHIEF AGAIN?!
SHE WAS HOLDING HIS HAND AT THAT PARTY!!
WE'RE GOING, YOU GUYS! WE'VE GOTTA KEEP THE BUREAU CHIEF FROM FALLING INTO THE KOROBASE WITCH'S HANDS!
WHAAAAT?
SHE'S INCOR-RIGI-BLE!!!
COME ON, RELAX.
ALL WE DO IS GO PLACES WE'RE NOT SUPPOSED TO AND GET YELLED AT BY THE COPS.
IT'S ALL RIGHT! MY SUPER STRONG SUIT IS INTERVIEWS WITH NO APPOINT-MENT!
BUREAU CHIEF, I'M ON MY WAY! ONCE I SAVE YOU FROM THAT KOROBASE WITCH, YOU'LL BE SO GRATEFUL! THEN A WEDDING TOUR! THE END!
THERE'S NOTHING AHEAD BUT A BEAUTIFUL FUTURE FOR ME...
VLIN--
WOULD YOU PLEASE LISTEN TO US?!
BUREAU CHIEF DOLL
READY! SET! GOOOO!!

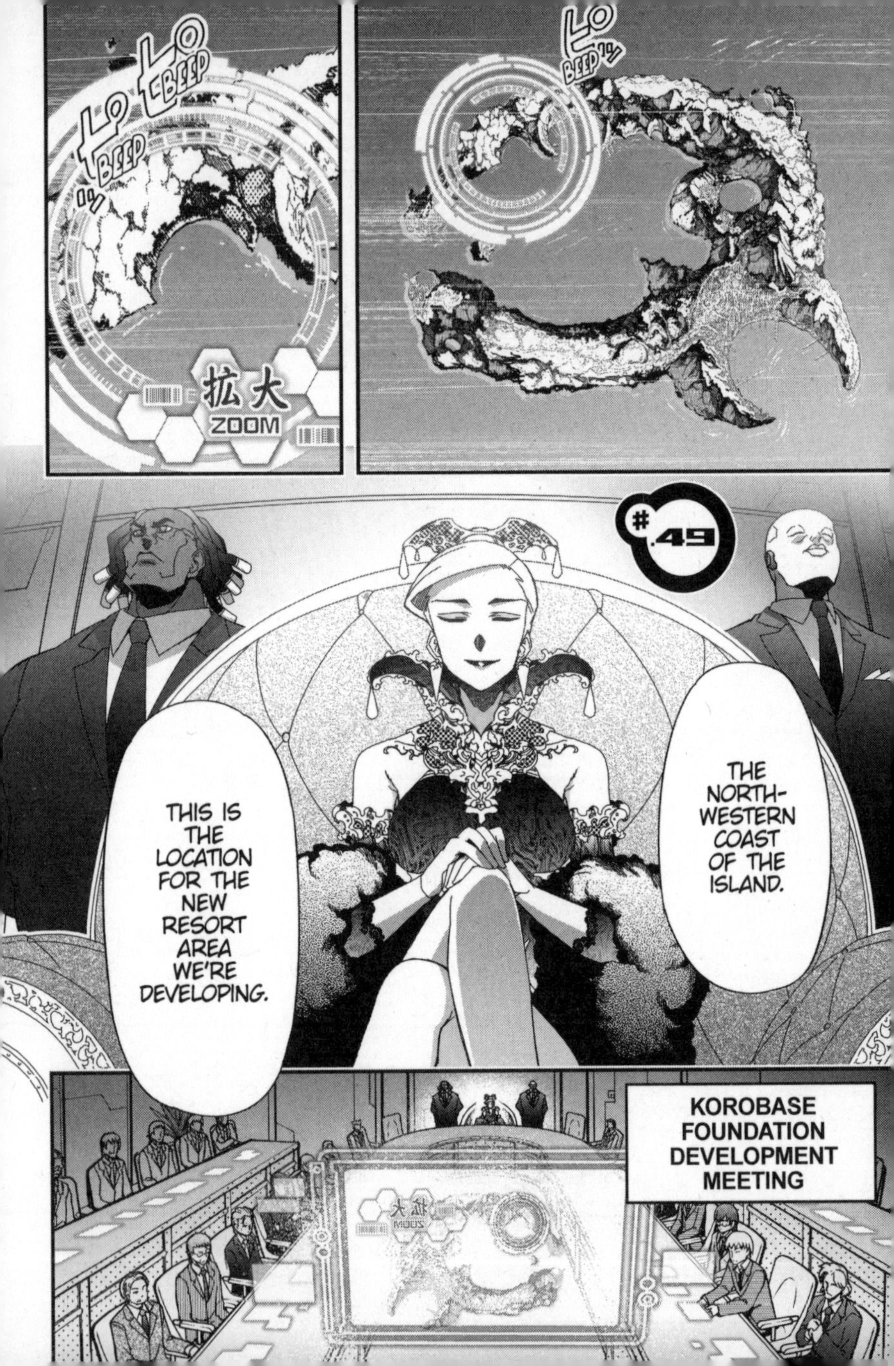

ピッ
BEEP
ピッ
BEEP
ピッ
BEEP
拡大
ZOOM
#.49
THE NORTH-WESTERN COAST OF THE ISLAND.
THIS IS THE LOCATION FOR THE NEW RESORT AREA WE'RE DEVELOPING.
KOROBASE FOUNDATION DEVELOPMENT MEETING

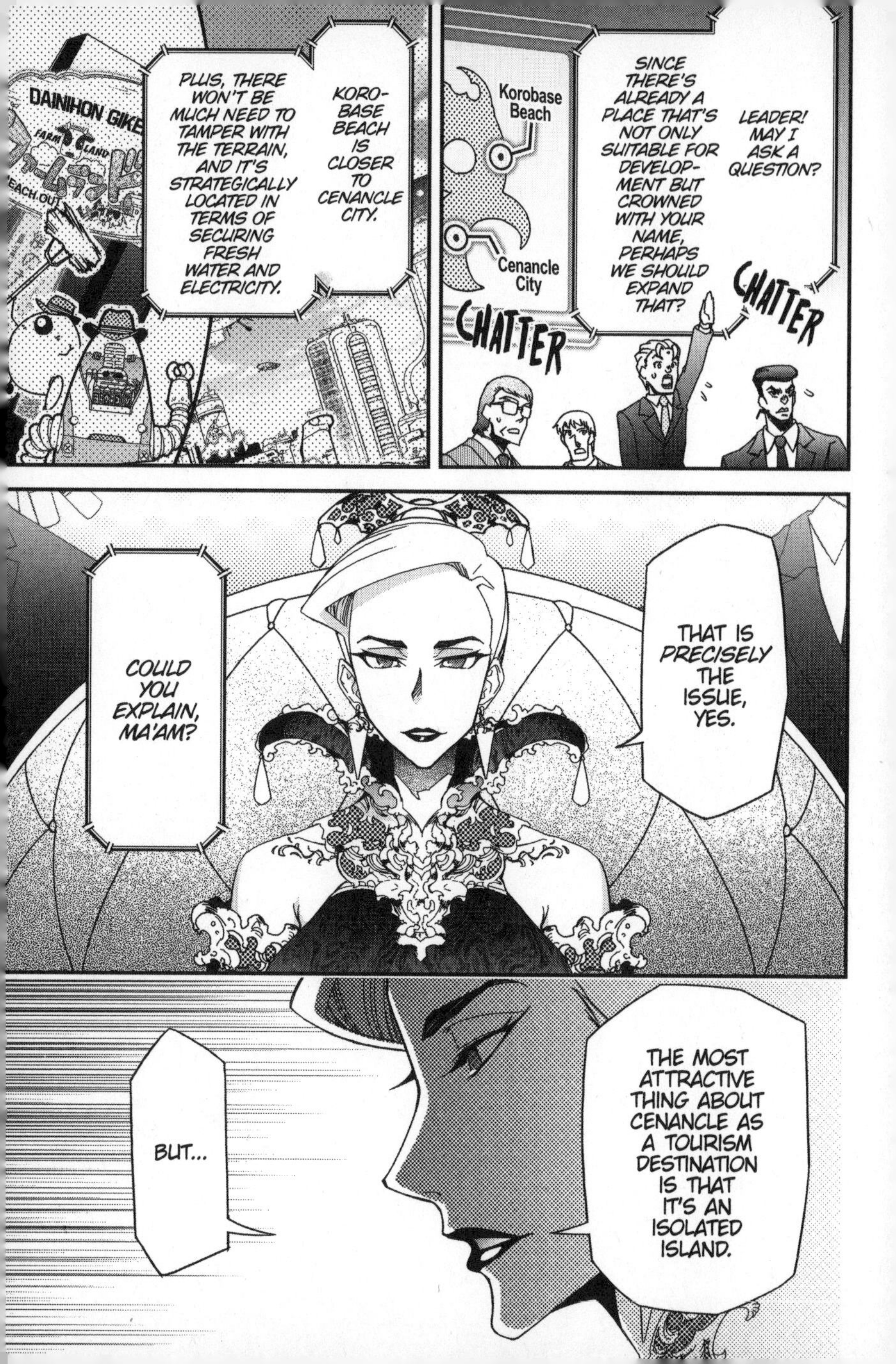
LEADER! MAY I ASK A QUESTION?
SINCE THERE'S ALREADY A PLACE THAT'S NOT ONLY SUITABLE FOR DEVELOPMENT BUT CROWNED WITH YOUR NAME, PERHAPS WE SHOULD EXPAND THAT?
CHATTER
Korobase Beach
Cenancle City
CHATTER
KORO-BASE BEACH IS CLOSER TO CENANCLE CITY.
PLUS, THERE WON'T BE MUCH NEED TO TAMPER WITH THE TERRAIN, AND IT'S STRATEGICALLY LOCATED IN TERMS OF SECURING FRESH WATER AND ELECTRICITY.
DAINIHON GIKE
FARM LAND
THAT IS PRECISELY THE ISSUE, YES.
COULD YOU EXPLAIN, MA'AM?
THE MOST ATTRACTIVE THING ABOUT CENANCLE AS A TOURISM DESTINATION IS THAT IT'S AN ISOLATED ISLAND.
BUT...

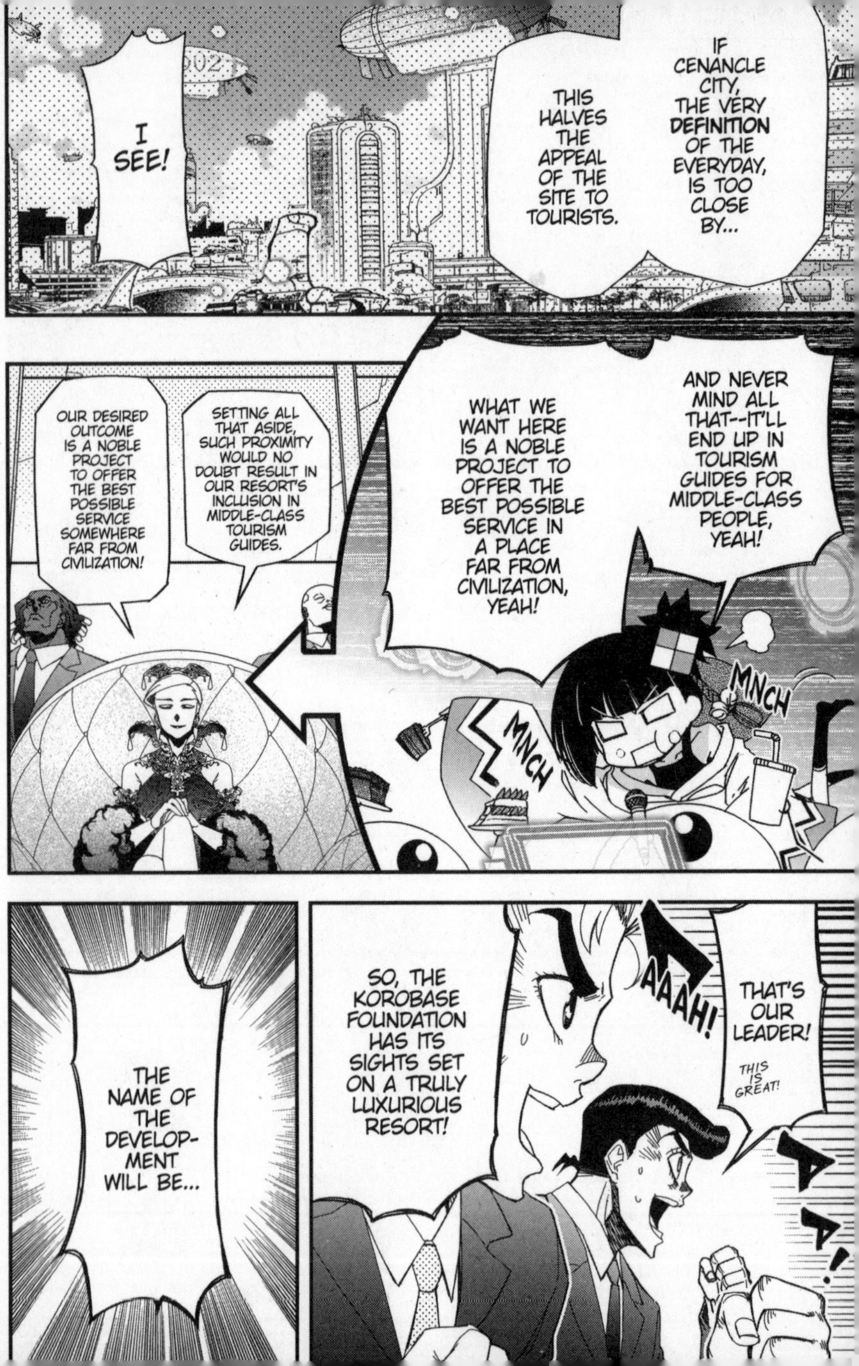

IF CENANCLE CITY, THE VERY DEFINITION OF THE EVERYDAY, IS TOO CLOSE BY...
THIS HALVES THE APPEAL OF THE SITE TO TOURISTS.
I SEE!
AND NEVER MIND ALL THAT--IT'LL END UP IN TOURISM GUIDES FOR MIDDLE-CLASS PEOPLE, YEAH!
WHAT WE WANT HERE IS A NOBLE PROJECT TO OFFER THE BEST POSSIBLE SERVICE IN A PLACE FAR FROM CIVILIZATION, YEAH!
MNCH
MNCH
SETTING ALL THAT ASIDE, SUCH PROXIMITY WOULD NO DOUBT RESULT IN OUR RESORT'S INCLUSION IN MIDDLE-CLASS TOURISM GUIDES.
OUR DESIRED OUTCOME IS A NOBLE PROJECT TO OFFER THE BEST POSSIBLE SERVICE SOMEWHERE FAR FROM CIVILIZATION!
THAT'S OUR LEADER!
THIS IS GREAT!
AAAAH!
AA!
SO, THE KOROBASE FOUNDATION HAS ITS SIGHTS SET ON A TRULY LUXURIOUS RESORT!
THE NAME OF THE DEVELOPMENT WILL BE...

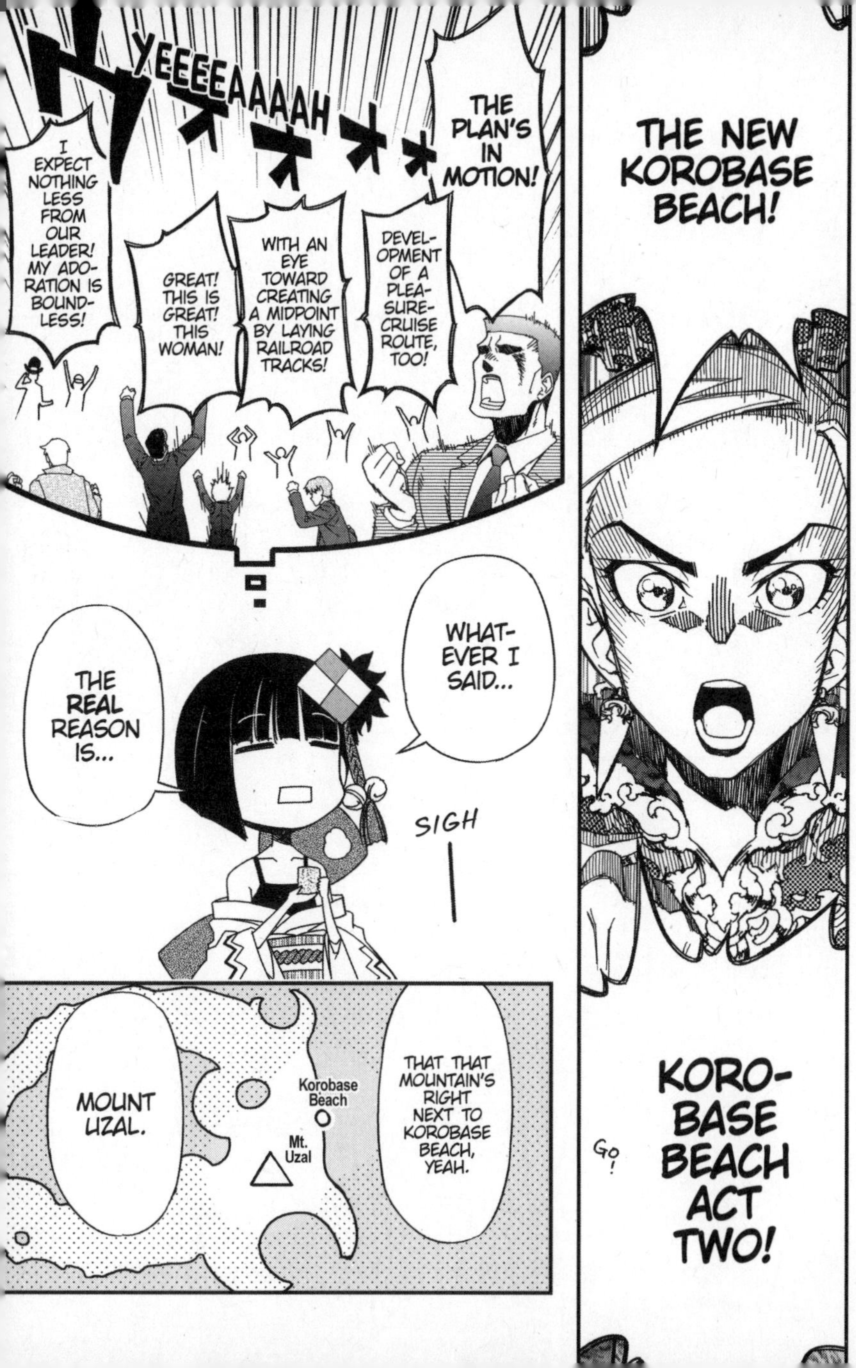
THE NEW KOROBASE BEACH!
KORO-BASE BEACH ACT TWO!
GO!
YEEEEAAAAAH
THE PLAN'S IN MOTION!
DEVEL-OPMENT OF A PLEA-SURE-CRUISE ROUTE, TOO!
WITH AN EYE TOWARD CREATING A MIDPOINT BY LAYING RAILROAD TRACKS!
GREAT! THIS IS GREAT! THIS WOMAN!
I EXPECT NOTHING LESS FROM OUR LEADER! MY ADO-RATION IS BOUND-LESS!
...
WHAT-EVER I SAID...
THE REAL REASON IS...
SIGH
THAT THAT MOUNTAIN'S RIGHT NEXT TO KOROBASE BEACH, YEAH.
Korobase Beach
Mt. Uzal
MOUNT UZAL.

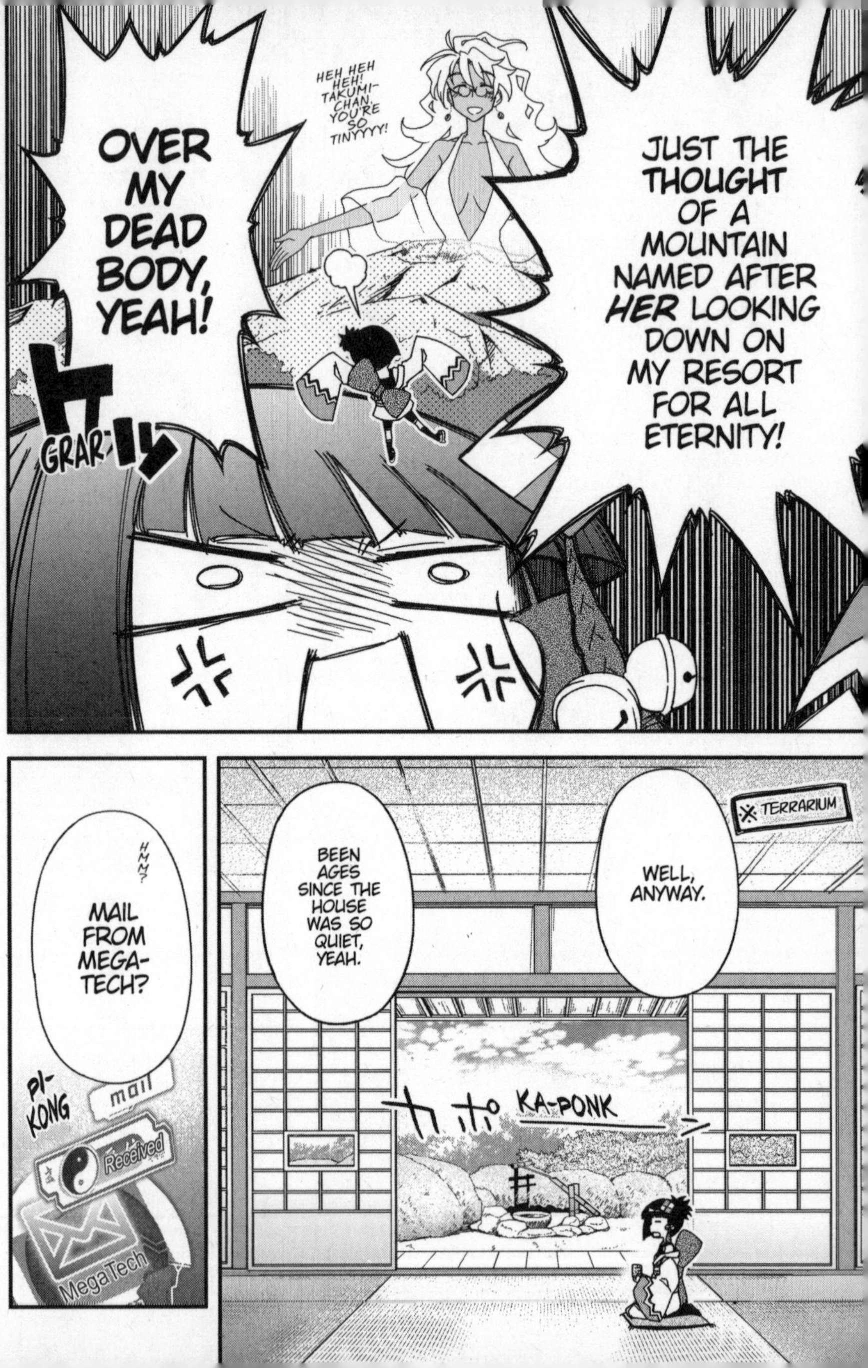
JUST THE THOUGHT OF A MOUNTAIN NAMED AFTER HER LOOKING DOWN ON MY RESORT FOR ALL ETERNITY!
HEH HEH HEH! TAKUMI-CHAN, YOU'RE SO TINYYYY!
OVER MY DEAD BODY, YEAH!
GRAR
※TERRARIUM
WELL, ANYWAY.
BEEN AGES SINCE THE HOUSE WAS SO QUIET, YEAH.
KA-PONK
HMM?
MAIL FROM MEGA-TECH?
PI-KONG
mail
Received
MegaTech

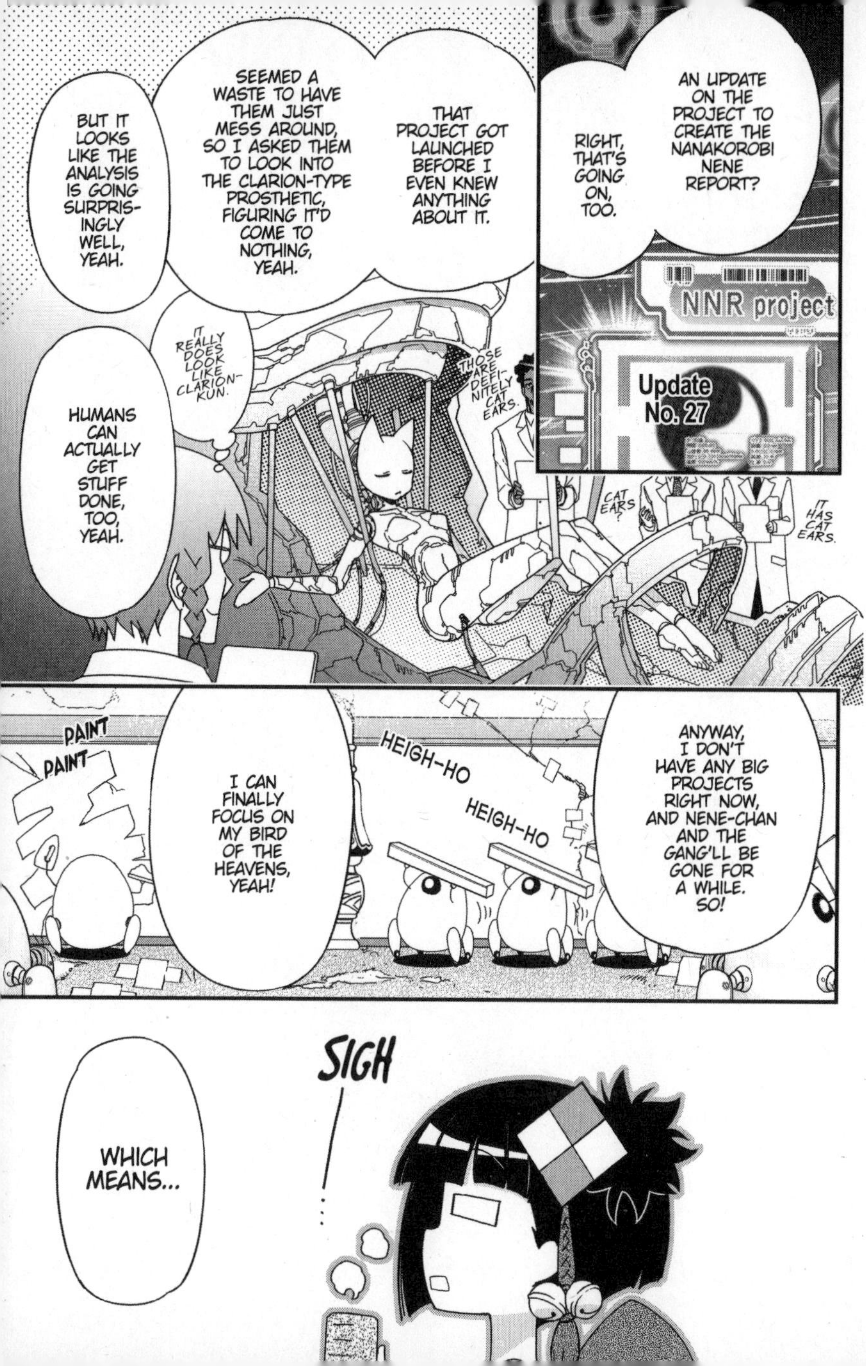
AN UPDATE ON THE PROJECT TO CREATE THE NANAKOROBI NENE REPORT?
RIGHT, THAT'S GOING ON, TOO.
NNR project
Update No. 27
THAT PROJECT GOT LAUNCHED BEFORE I EVEN KNEW ANYTHING ABOUT IT.
SEEMED A WASTE TO HAVE THEM JUST MESS AROUND, SO I ASKED THEM TO LOOK INTO THE CLARION-TYPE PROSTHETIC, FIGURING IT'D COME TO NOTHING, YEAH.
BUT IT LOOKS LIKE THE ANALYSIS IS GOING SURPRISINGLY WELL, YEAH.
IT HAS CAT EARS.
CAT EARS?
THOSE ARE DEFINITELY CAT EARS.
IT REALLY DOES LOOK LIKE CLARION-KUN.
HUMANS CAN ACTUALLY GET STUFF DONE, TOO, YEAH.
ANYWAY, I DON'T HAVE ANY BIG PROJECTS RIGHT NOW, AND NENE-CHAN AND THE GANG'LL BE GONE FOR A WHILE. SO!
HEIGH-HO
HEIGH-HO
I CAN FINALLY FOCUS ON MY BIRD OF THE HEAVENS, YEAH!
PAINT
PAINT
SIGH
...
WHICH MEANS...

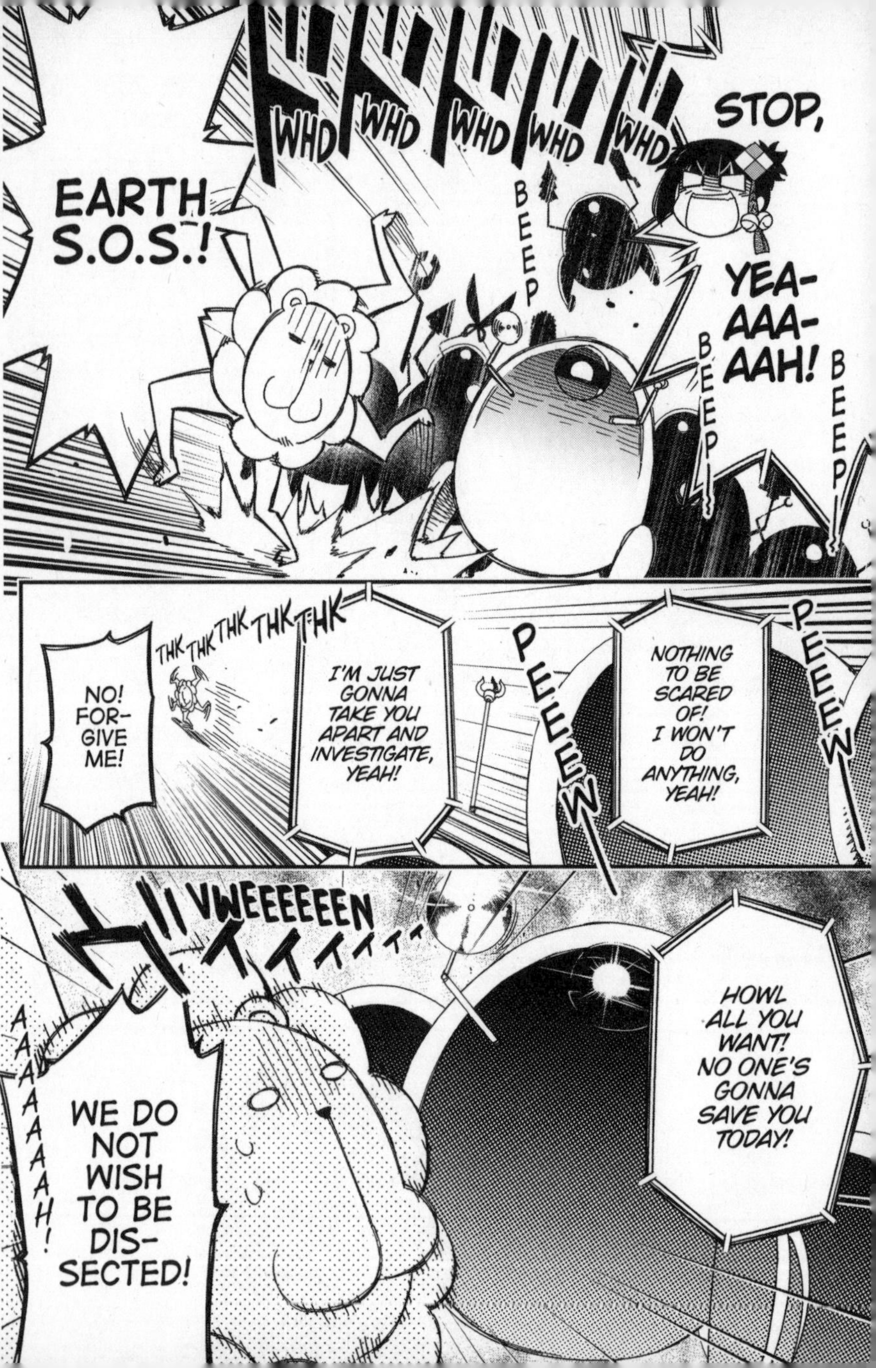
STOP, YEA-AAA-AAH!
BEEP!
BEEP!
BEEP
WHD WHD WHD WHD WHD
EARTH S.O.S..!
PEEEW
NOTHING TO BE SCARED OF! I WON'T DO ANYTHING, YEAH!
PEEEEW
I'M JUST GONNA TAKE YOU APART AND INVESTIGATE, YEAH!
THK THK THK THK THK
NO! FORGIVE ME!
HOWL ALL YOU WANT! NO ONE'S GONNA SAVE YOU TODAY!
VWEEEEEEN
WE DO NOT WISH TO BE DISSECTED!
AAAAAAAAH!

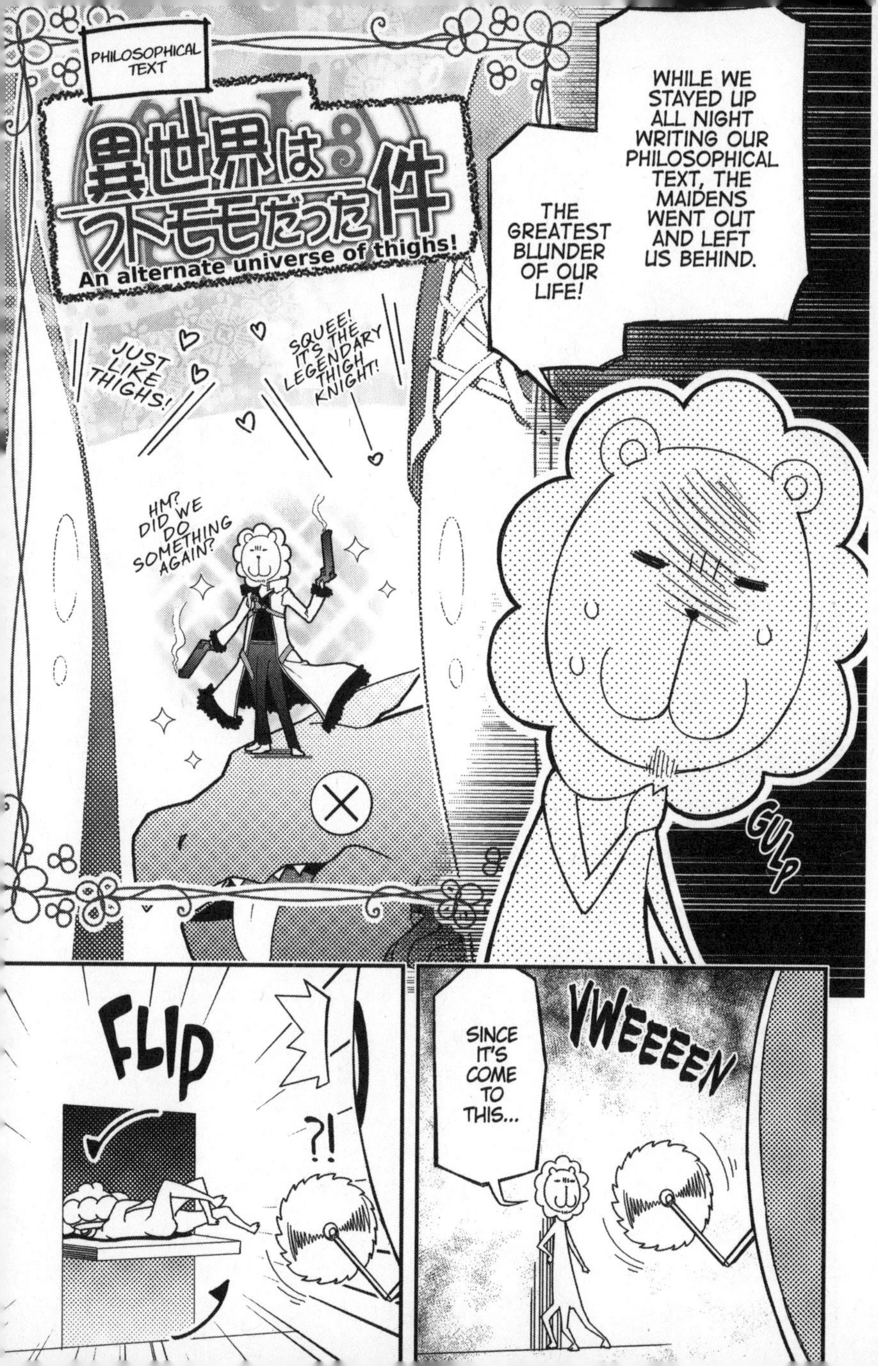
WHILE WE STAYED UP ALL NIGHT WRITING OUR PHILOSOPHICAL TEXT, THE MAIDENS WENT OUT AND LEFT US BEHIND.
THE GREATEST BLUNDER OF OUR LIFE!
GULP
PHILOSOPHICAL TEXT
異世界はフトモモだった件
An alternate universe of thighs!
SQUEE! IT'S THE LEGENDARY THIGH KNIGHT!
JUST LIKE THIGHS!
HM? DID WE DO SOMETHING AGAIN?
VWEEEEEN
SINCE IT'S COME TO THIS...
FLIP
?!

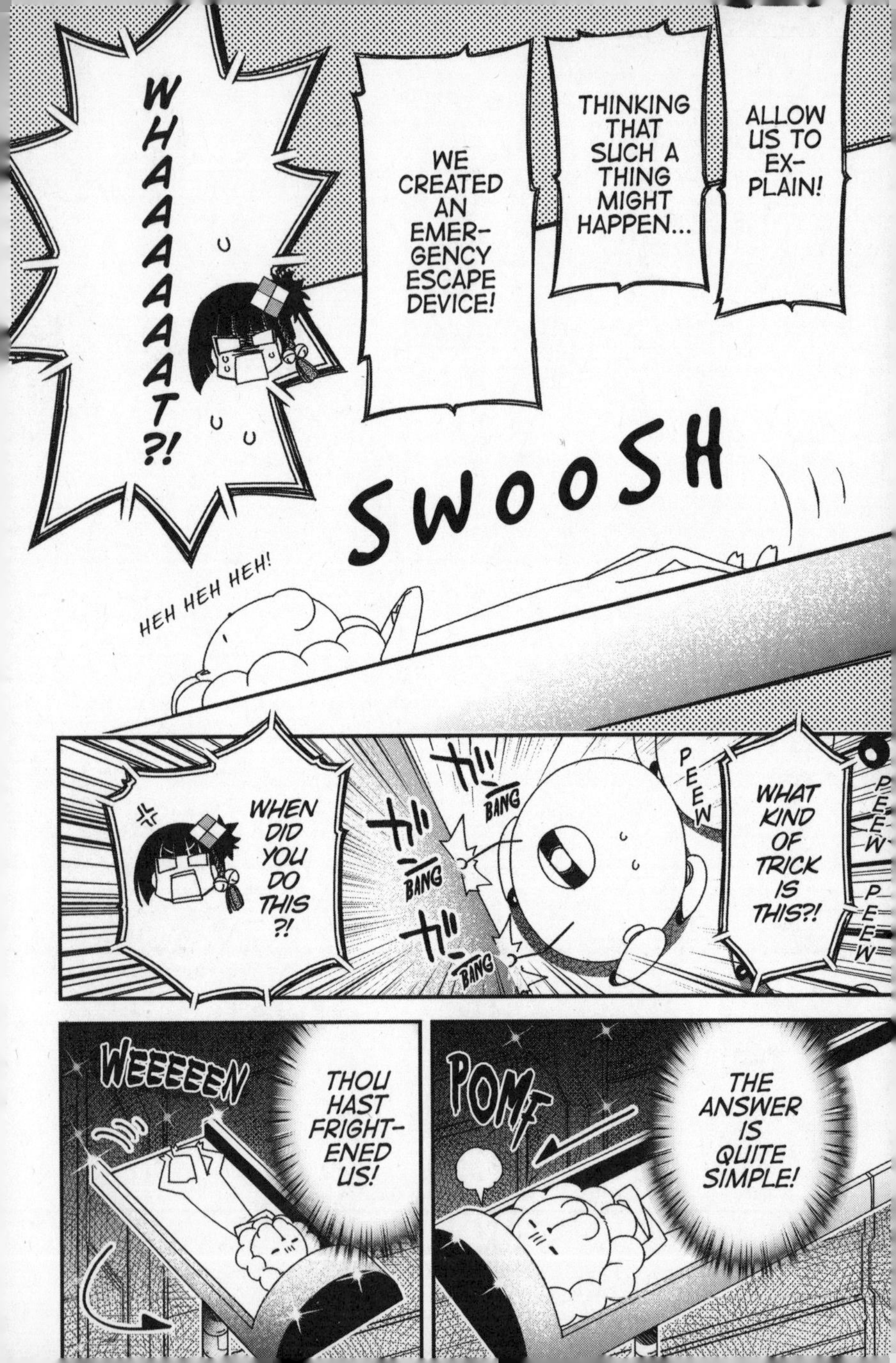
ALLOW US TO EX-PLAIN!
THINKING THAT SUCH A THING MIGHT HAPPEN...
WE CREATED AN EMERGENCY ESCAPE DEVICE!
WHAAAAAAAT?!
SWOOSH
HEH HEH HEH!
PEEEW
PEEEW
WHAT KIND OF TRICK IS THIS?!
PEEW
BANG
BANG
BANG
WHEN DID YOU DO THIS?!
THE ANSWER IS QUITE SIMPLE!
POMF
THOU HAST FRIGHTENED US!
WEEEEEEN

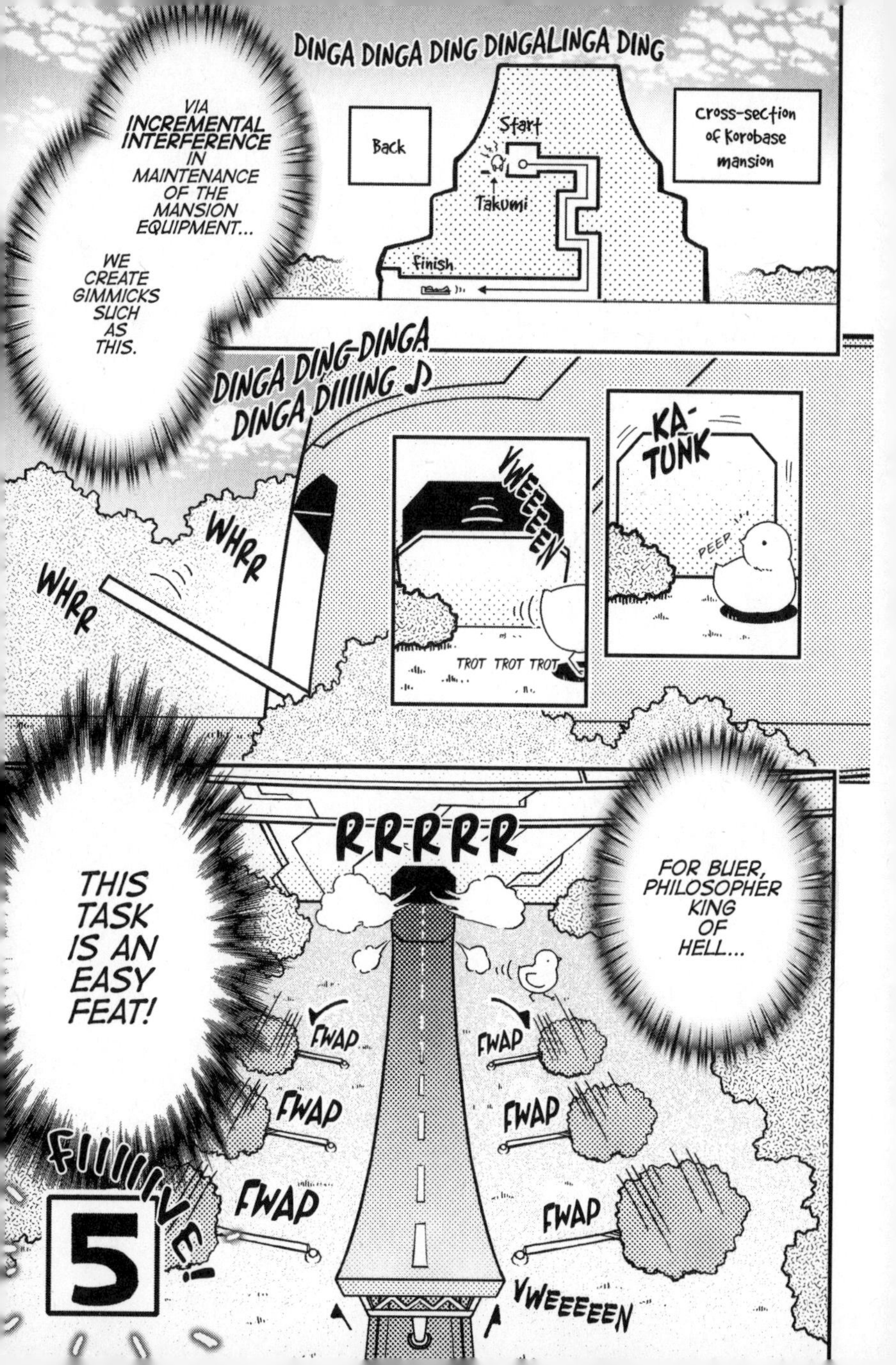
DINGA DINGA DING DINGALINGA DING
Cross-section of Korobase mansion
Start
Takumi
Back
Finish
VIA INCREMENTAL INTERFERENCE IN MAINTENANCE OF THE MANSION EQUIPMENT...
WE CREATE GIMMICKS SUCH AS THIS.
KA-TUNK
PEEP
VWEEEEEN
TROT TROT TROT
DINGA DING-DINGA DINGA DIIIING ♪
WHRR
WHRR
FOR BUER, PHILOSOPHER KING OF HELL...
RRRRR
THIS TASK IS AN EASY FEAT!
FWAP
FWAP
FWAP
FWAP
FWAP
FWAP
FIIIIIVE!
5
VWEEEEEN

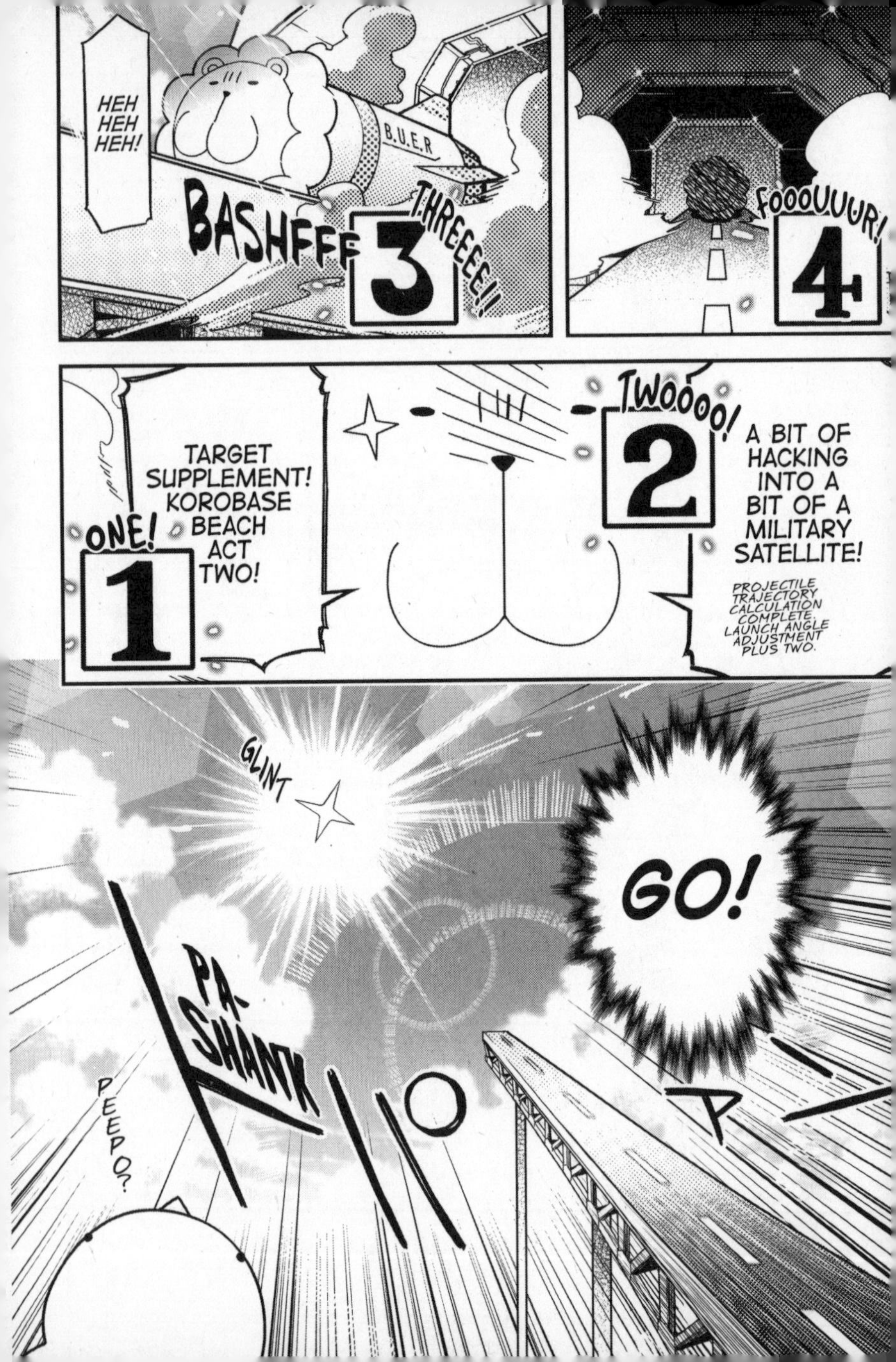

FOOOUUUR!
4
HEH HEH HEH!
B.U.E.R
BASHFFF
THREEEE!!
3
A BIT OF HACKING INTO A BIT OF A MILITARY SATELLITE!
PROJECTILE TRAJECTORY CALCULATION COMPLETE. LAUNCH ANGLE ADJUSTMENT PLUS TWO.
TWOOOO!
2
TARGET SUPPLEMENT! KOROBASE BEACH ACT TWO!
ONE!
1
GO!
GLINT
PA-SHANK
PEEPO?

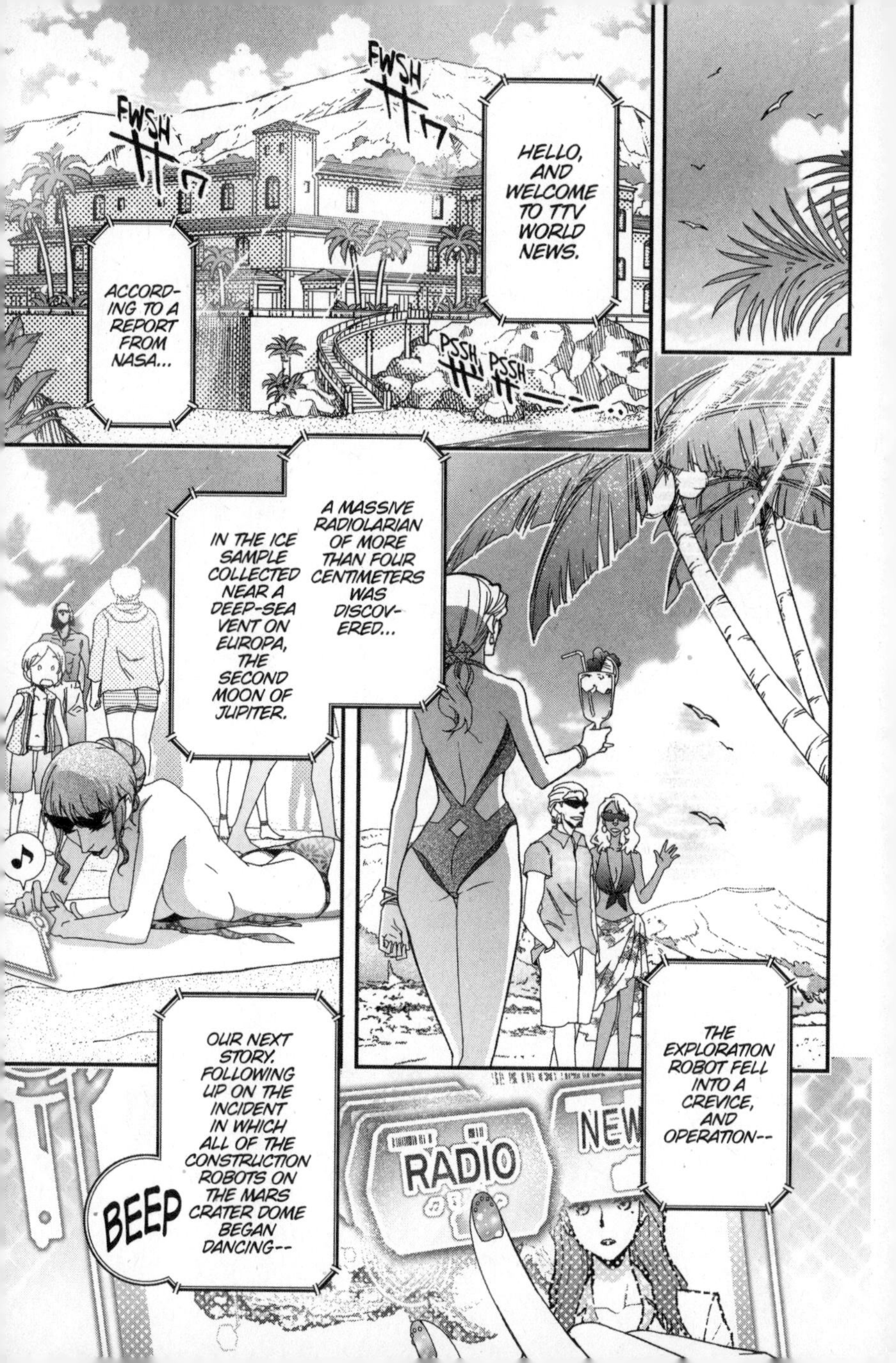
FWSH
HELLO, AND WELCOME TO TTV WORLD NEWS.
FWSH
ACCORDING TO A REPORT FROM NASA...
PSSH PSSH
A MASSIVE RADIOLARIAN OF MORE THAN FOUR CENTIMETERS WAS DISCOVERED...
IN THE ICE SAMPLE COLLECTED NEAR A DEEP-SEA VENT ON EUROPA, THE SECOND MOON OF JUPITER.
THE EXPLORATION ROBOT FELL INTO A CREVICE, AND OPERATION--
OUR NEXT STORY. FOLLOWING UP ON THE INCIDENT IN WHICH ALL OF THE CONSTRUCTION ROBOTS ON THE MARS CRATER DOME BEGAN DANCING--
NEW
RADIO
BEEP

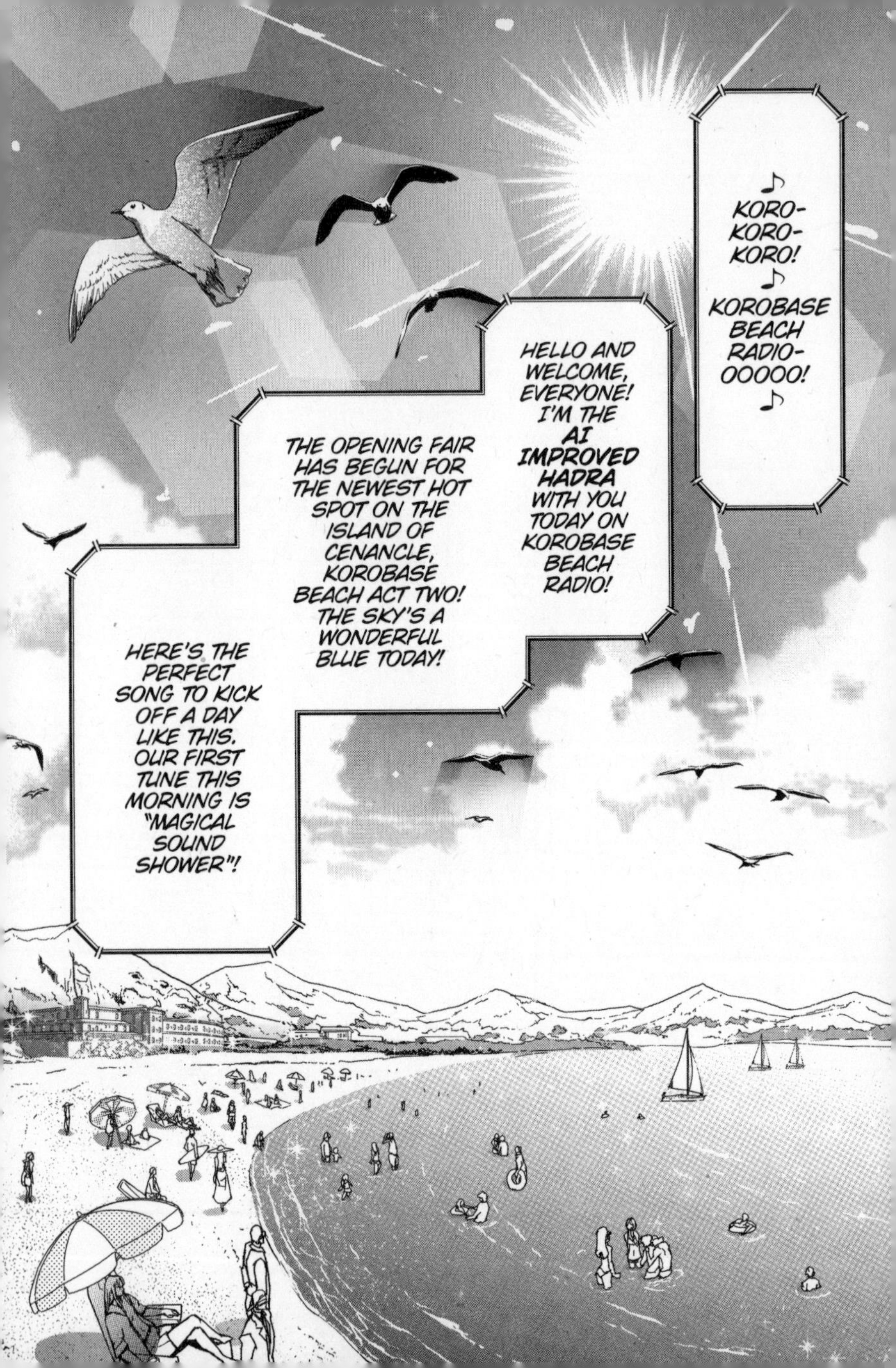
♪ KORO-KORO-KORO! ♪ KOROBASE BEACH RADIO-OOOOO! ♪
HELLO AND WELCOME, EVERYONE! I'M THE **AI IMPROVED HADRA** WITH YOU TODAY ON KOROBASE BEACH RADIO!
THE OPENING FAIR HAS BEGUN FOR THE NEWEST HOT SPOT ON THE ISLAND OF CENANCLE, KOROBASE BEACH ACT TWO! THE SKY'S A WONDERFUL BLUE TODAY!
HERE'S THE PERFECT SONG TO KICK OFF A DAY LIKE THIS. OUR FIRST TUNE THIS MORNING IS "MAGICAL SOUND SHOWER"!

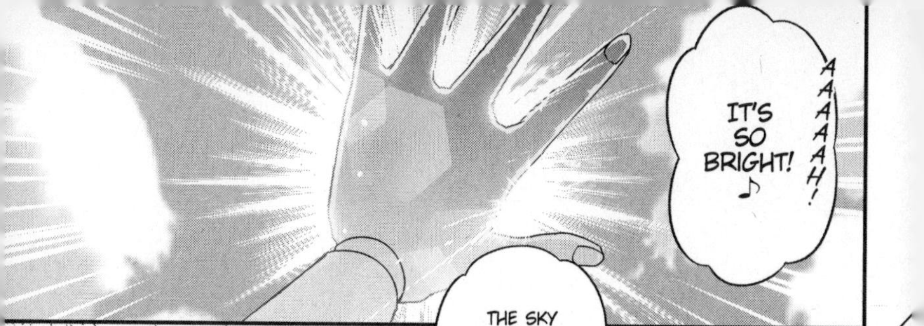
AAAAAH!
IT'S SO BRIGHT! ♪

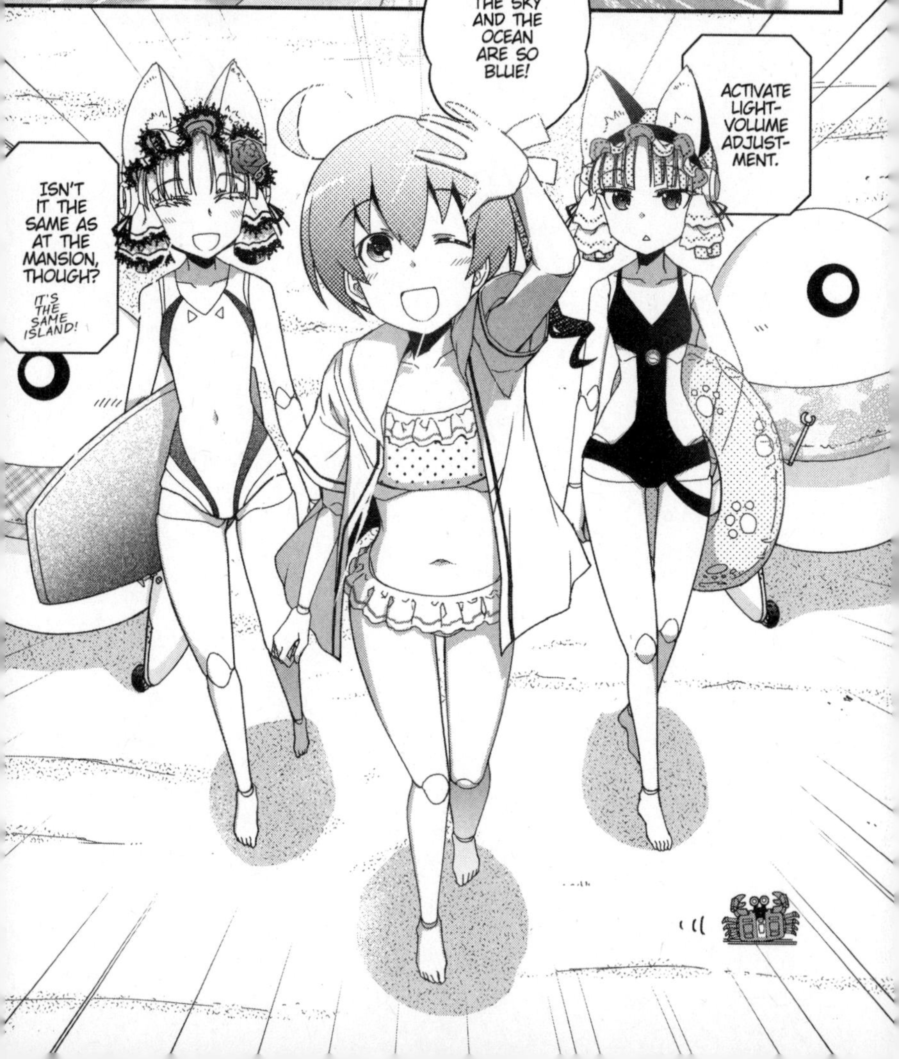
THE SKY AND THE OCEAN ARE SO BLUE!
ACTIVATE LIGHT-VOLUME ADJUSTMENT.
ISN'T IT THE SAME AS AT THE MANSION, THOUGH?
IT'S THE SAME ISLAND!

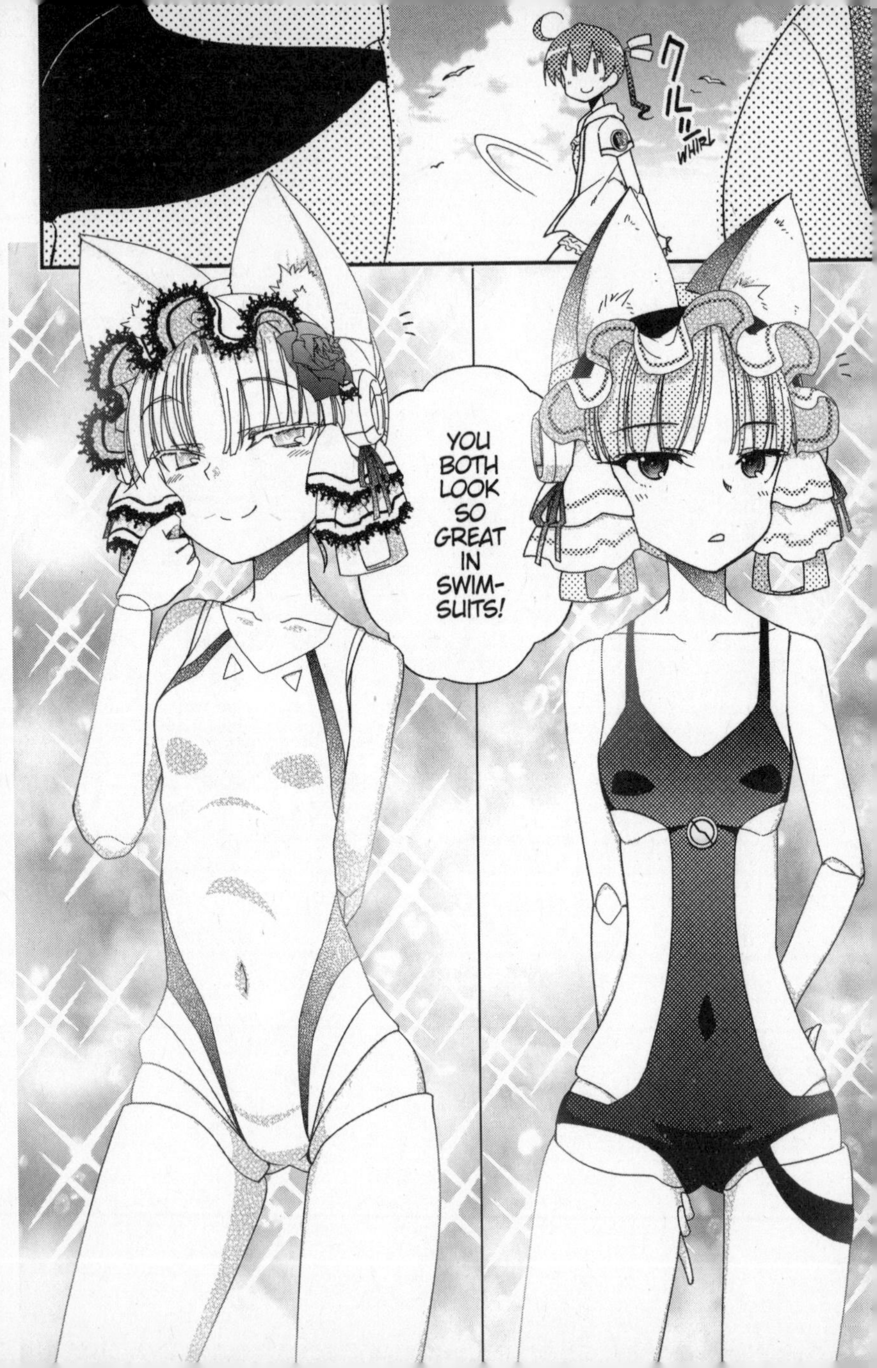
クルッ
WHIRL
YOU BOTH LOOK SO GREAT IN SWIM-SUITS!

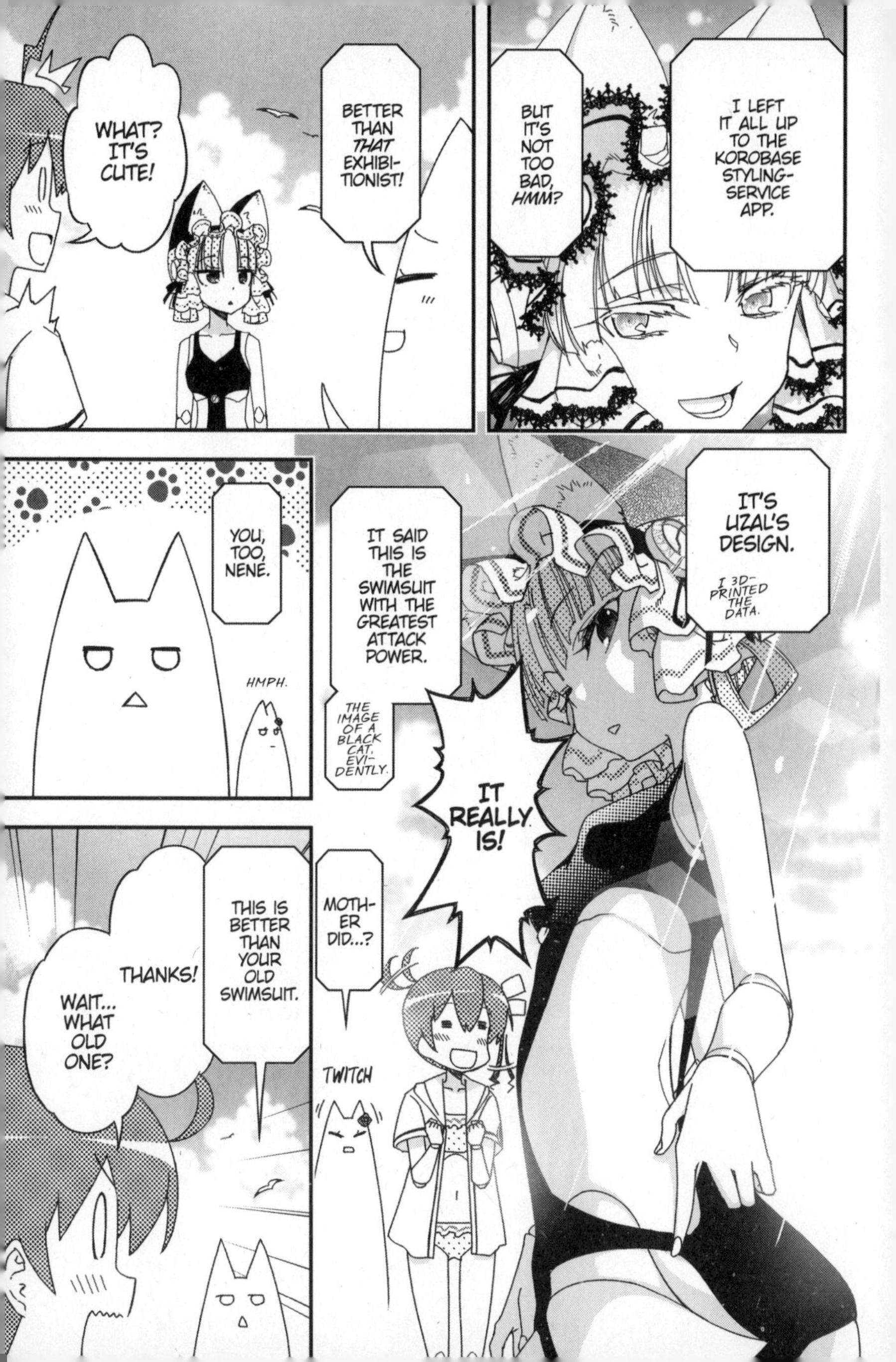
I LEFT IT ALL UP TO THE KOROBASE STYLING-SERVICE APP.
BUT IT'S NOT TOO BAD, HMM?
BETTER THAN *THAT* EXHIBITIONIST!
WHAT? IT'S CUTE!
IT'S UZAL'S DESIGN.
I 3D-PRINTED THE DATA.
IT SAID THIS IS THE SWIMSUIT WITH THE GREATEST ATTACK POWER.
THE IMAGE OF A BLACK CAT, EVIDENTLY.
IT REALLY IS!
MOTHER DID...?
TWITCH
YOU, TOO, NENE.
HMPH.
THIS IS BETTER THAN YOUR OLD SWIMSUIT.
THANKS!
WAIT... WHAT OLD ONE?

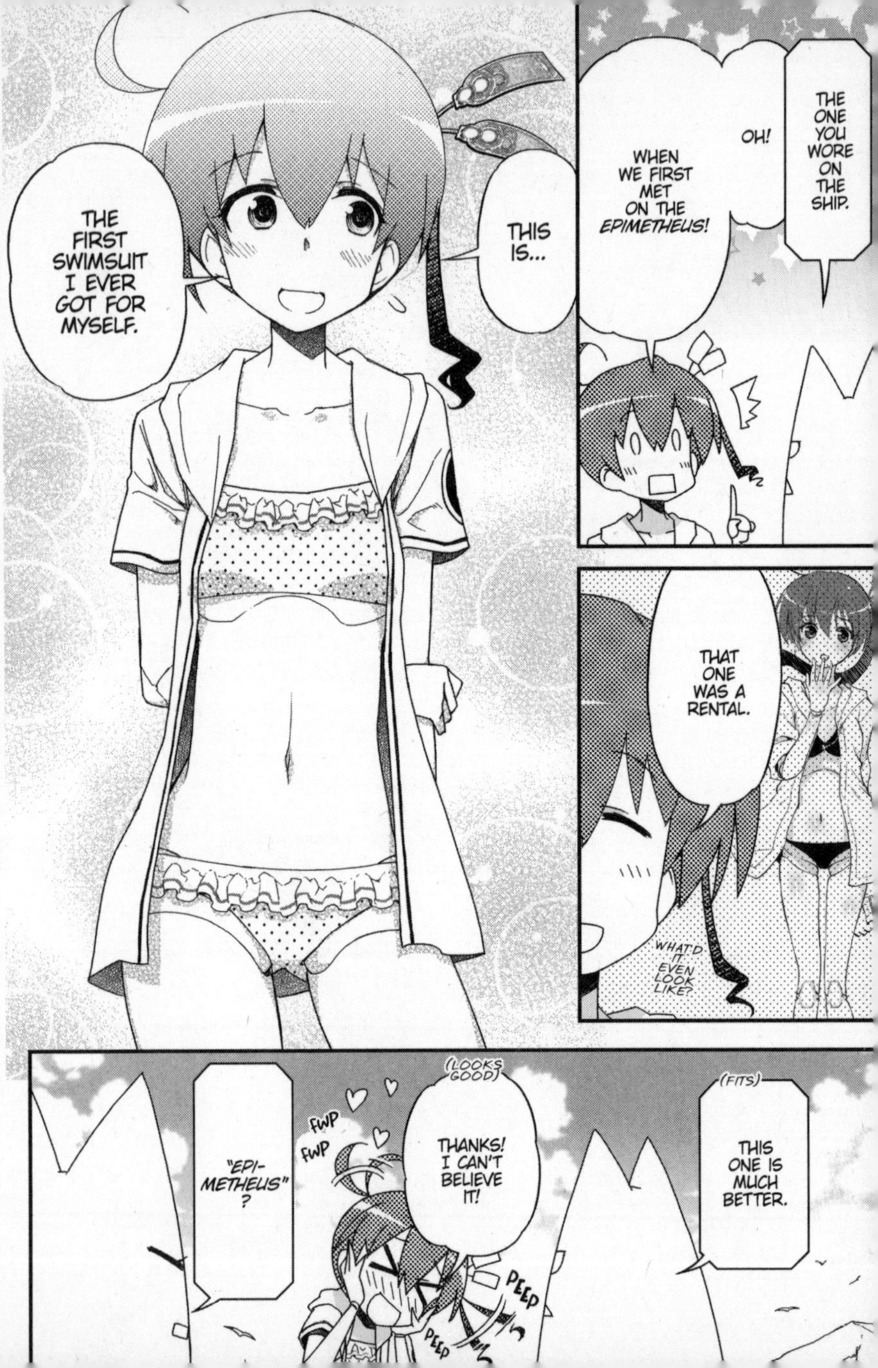
THE ONE YOU WORE ON THE SHIP.
OH!
WHEN WE FIRST MET ON THE *EPIMETHEUS!*
THAT ONE WAS A RENTAL.
WHAT'D IT EVEN LOOK LIKE?
THIS IS...
THE FIRST SWIMSUIT I EVER GOT FOR MYSELF.
(FITS)
THIS ONE IS MUCH BETTER.
(LOOKS GOOD)
THANKS! I CAN'T BELIEVE IT!
FWP
FWP
PEEP
PEEP
"EPI-METHEUS"?

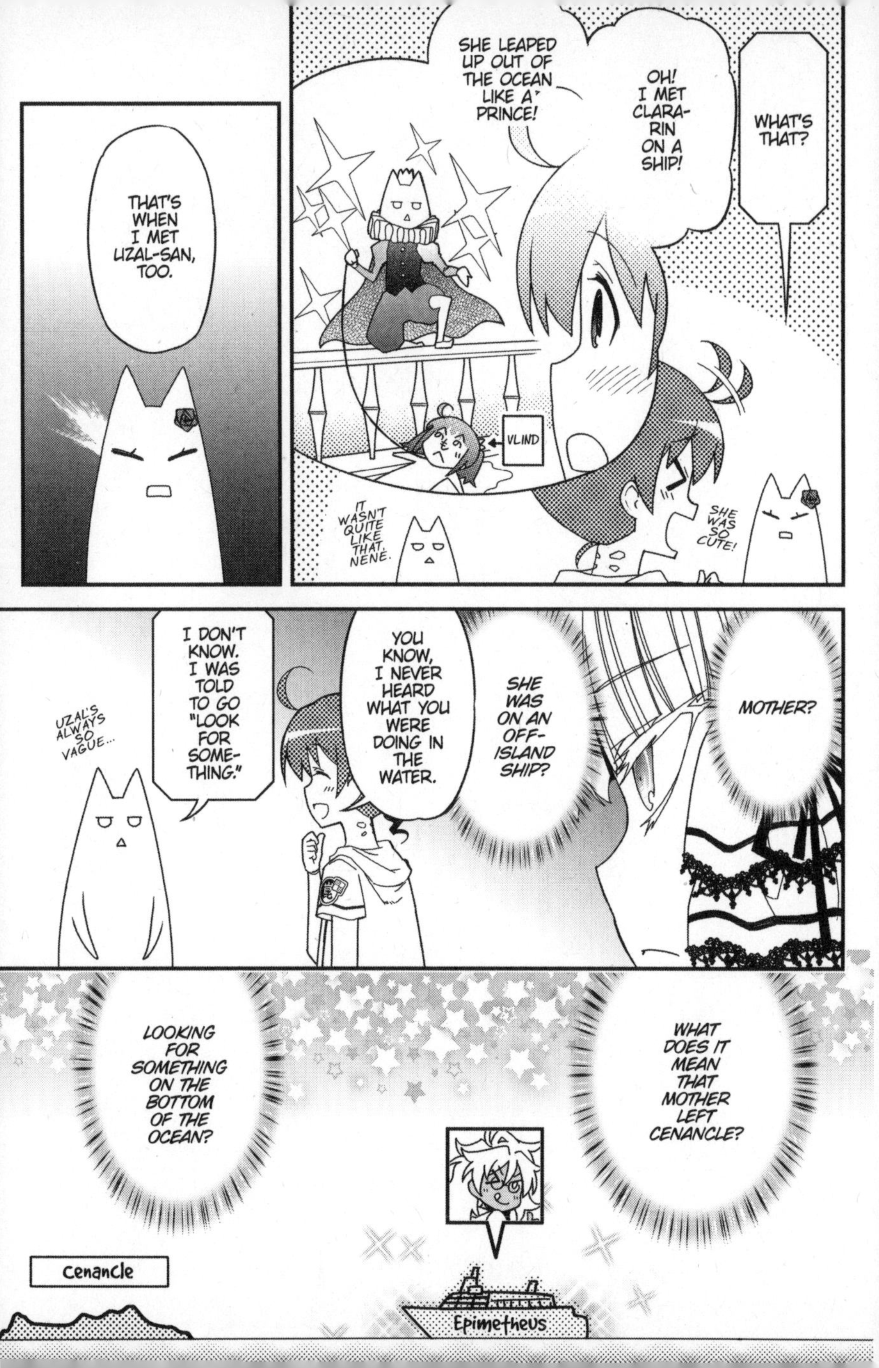
WHAT'S THAT?
OH! I MET CLARA-RIN ON A SHIP!
SHE LEAPED UP OUT OF THE OCEAN LIKE A PRINCE!
VLIND
SHE WAS SO CUTE!
IT WASN'T QUITE LIKE THAT, NENE.
THAT'S WHEN I MET UZAL-SAN, TOO.
MOTHER?
SHE WAS ON AN OFF-ISLAND SHIP?
YOU KNOW, I NEVER HEARD WHAT YOU WERE DOING IN THE WATER.
I DON'T KNOW. I WAS TOLD TO GO "LOOK FOR SOME-THING."
UZAL'S ALWAYS SO VAGUE...
WHAT DOES IT MEAN THAT MOTHER LEFT CENANCLE?
LOOKING FOR SOMETHING ON THE BOTTOM OF THE OCEAN?
Cenancle
Epimetheus

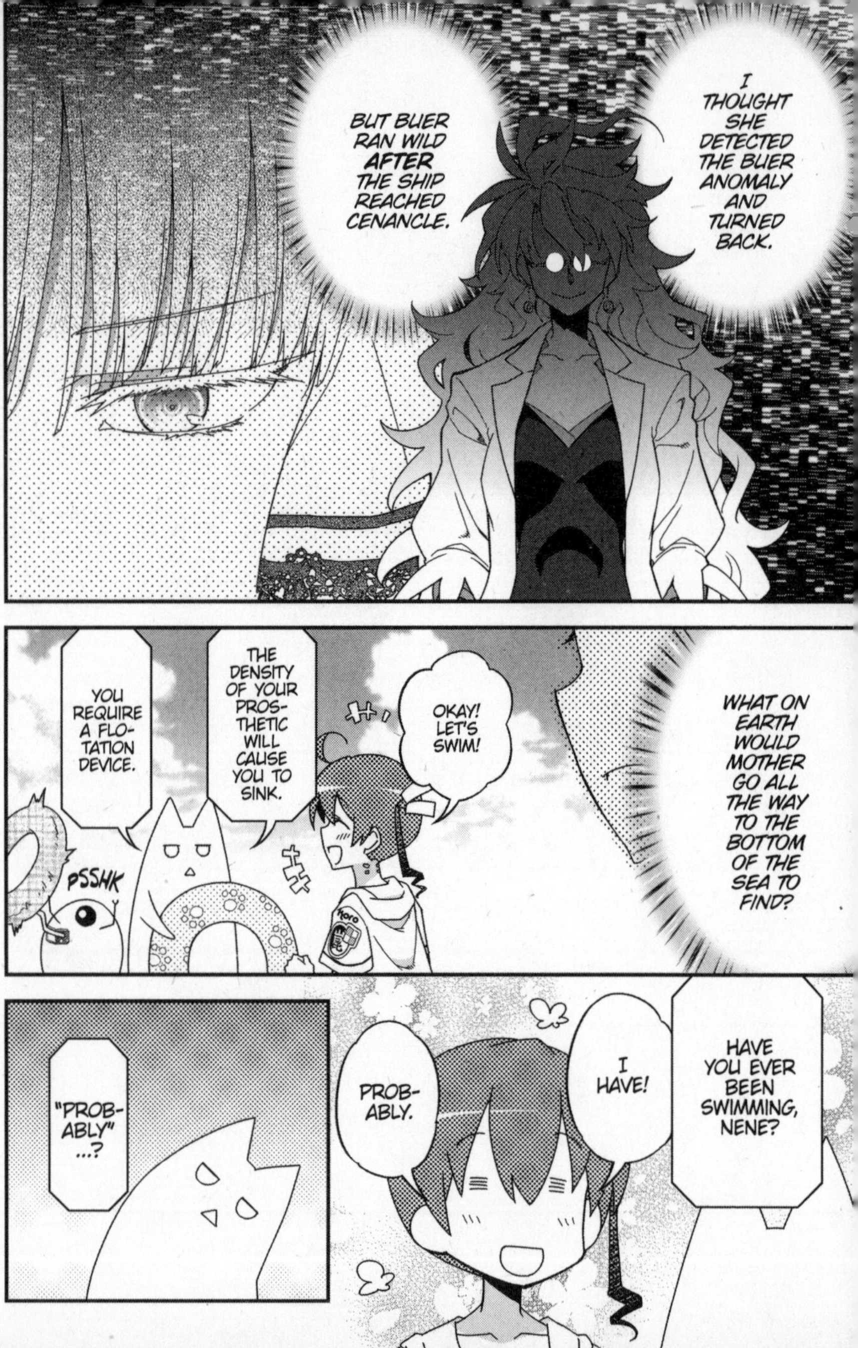

I THOUGHT SHE DETECTED THE BUER ANOMALY AND TURNED BACK.
BUT BUER RAN WILD AFTER THE SHIP REACHED CENANCLE.
WHAT ON EARTH WOULD MOTHER GO ALL THE WAY TO THE BOTTOM OF THE SEA TO FIND?
OKAY! LET'S SWIM!
THE DENSITY OF YOUR PROS-THETIC WILL CAUSE YOU TO SINK.
YOU REQUIRE A FLO-TATION DEVICE.
PSSHK
HAVE YOU EVER BEEN SWIMMING, NENE?
I HAVE!
PROB-ABLY.
"PROB-ABLY" ...?

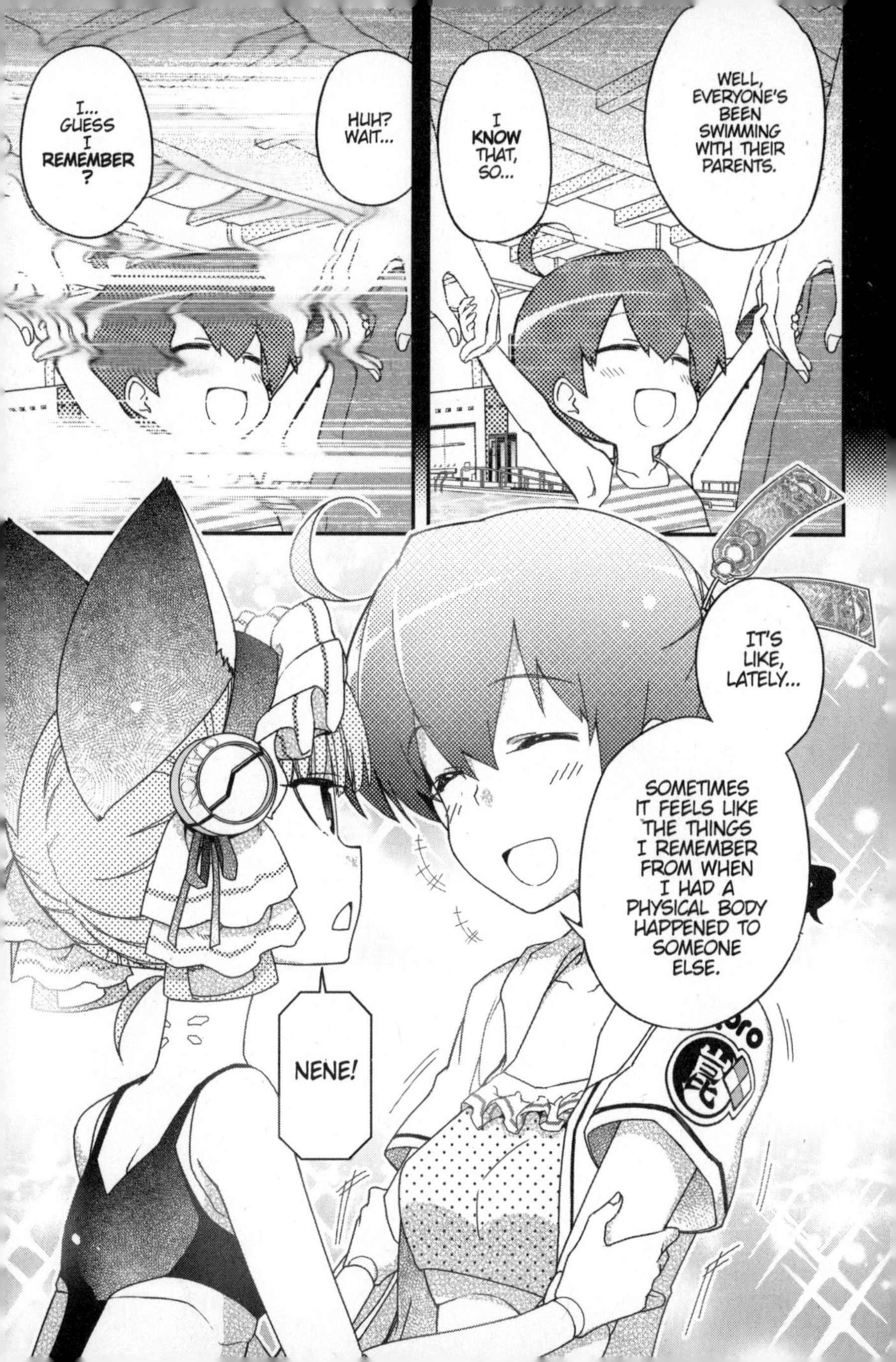
WELL, EVERYONE'S BEEN SWIMMING WITH THEIR PARENTS.
I KNOW THAT, SO...
HUH? WAIT...
I... GUESS I REMEMBER?
IT'S LIKE, LATELY...
SOMETIMES IT FEELS LIKE THE THINGS I REMEMBER FROM WHEN I HAD A PHYSICAL BODY HAPPENED TO SOMEONE ELSE.
NENE!

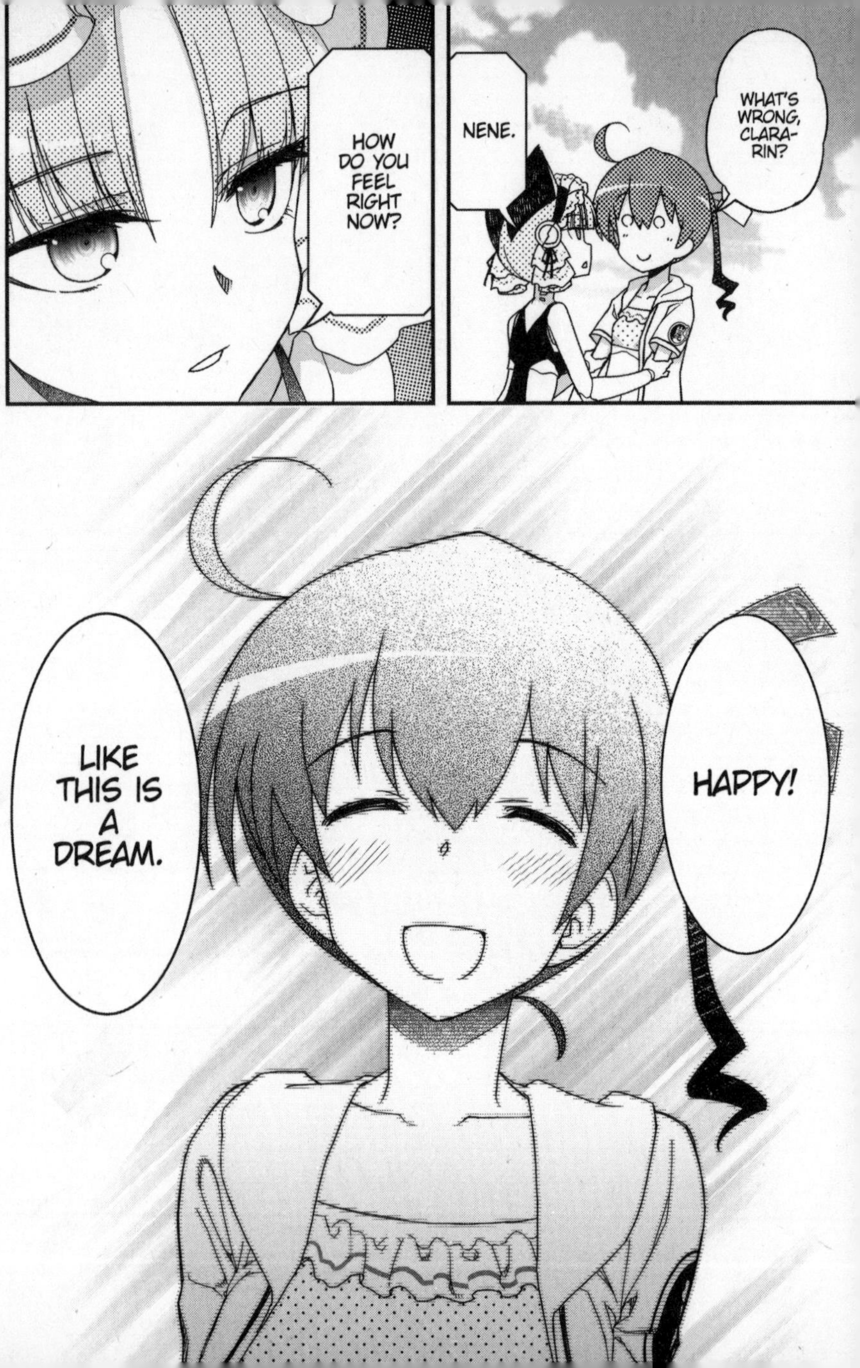
WHAT'S WRONG, CLARA-RIN?
NENE.
HOW DO YOU FEEL RIGHT NOW?
HAPPY!
LIKE THIS IS A DREAM.

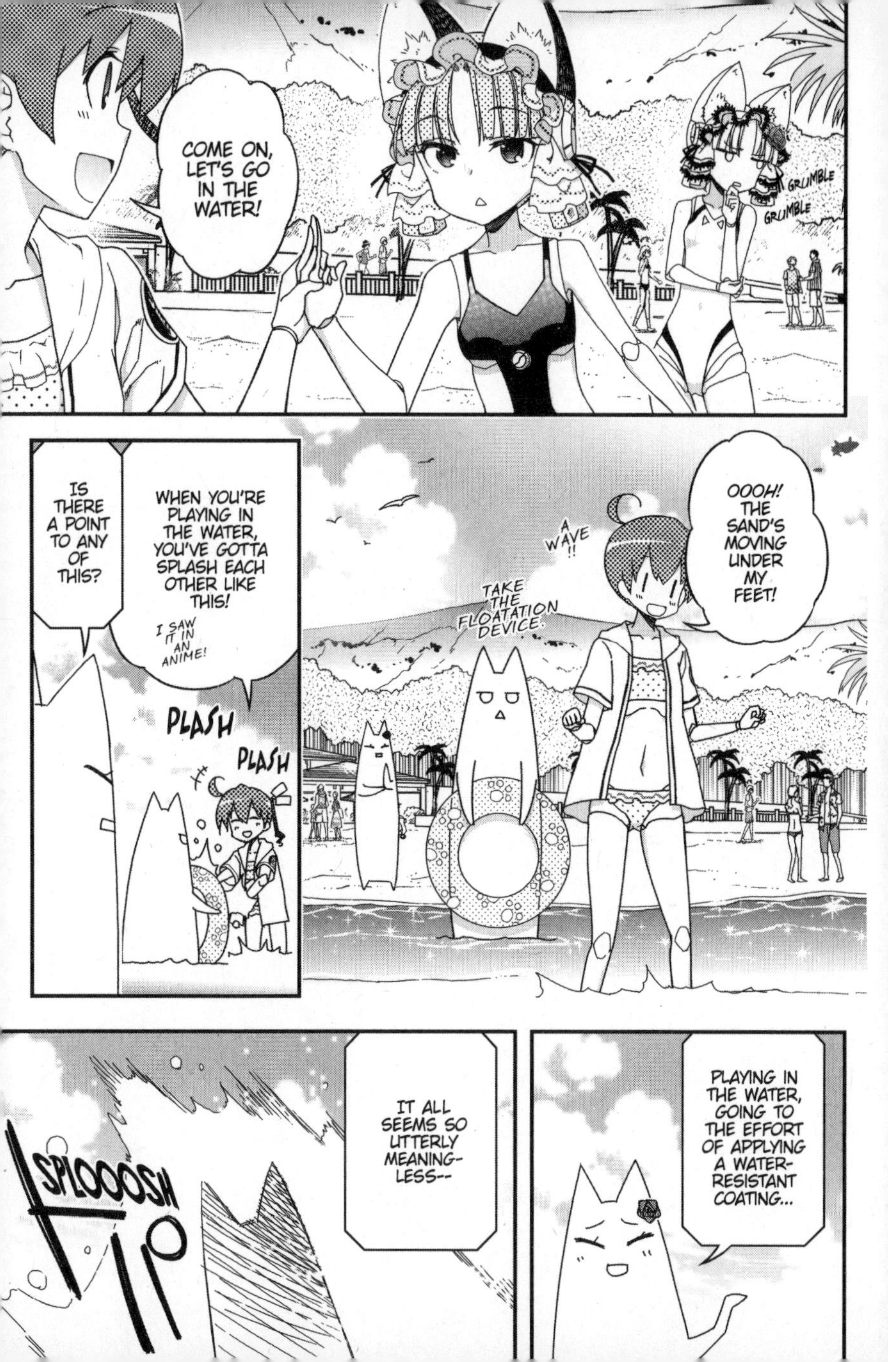
GRUMBLE
GRUMBLE
COME ON, LET'S GO IN THE WATER!
OOOH! THE SAND'S MOVING UNDER MY FEET!
A WAVE!!
TAKE THE FLOATATION DEVICE.
WHEN YOU'RE PLAYING IN THE WATER, YOU'VE GOTTA SPLASH EACH OTHER LIKE THIS!
I SAW IT IN AN ANIME!
IS THERE A POINT TO ANY OF THIS?
PLASH
PLASH
PLAYING IN THE WATER, GOING TO THE EFFORT OF APPLYING A WATER-RESISTANT COATING...
IT ALL SEEMS SO UTTERLY MEANING-LESS--
SPLOOOSH

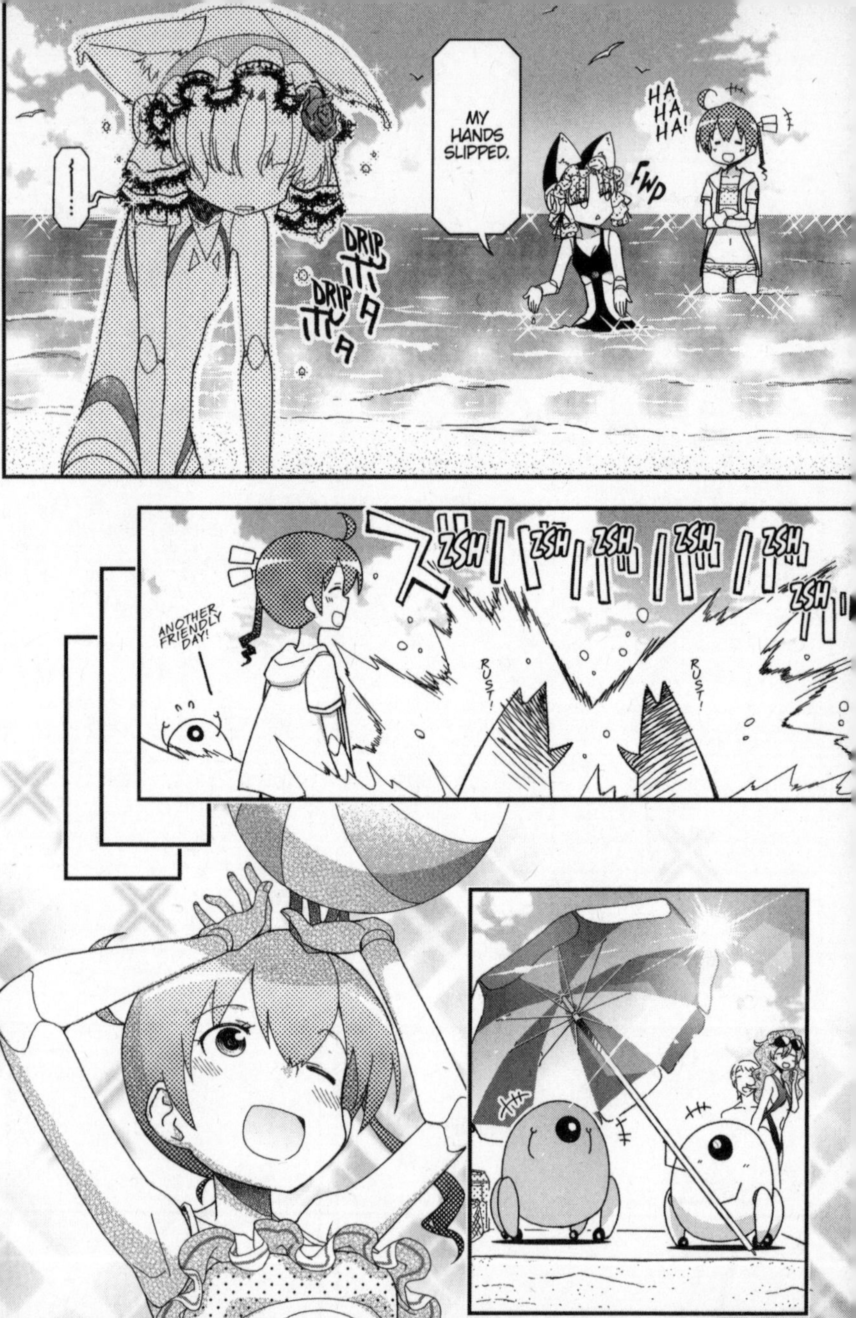
HA HA HA!
FWP
MY HANDS SLIPPED.
DRIP ポタ
DRIP ポタ
~—...
ZSH ZSH ZSH ZSH ZSH ZSH
RUST!
RUST!
ANOTHER FRIENDLY DAY!

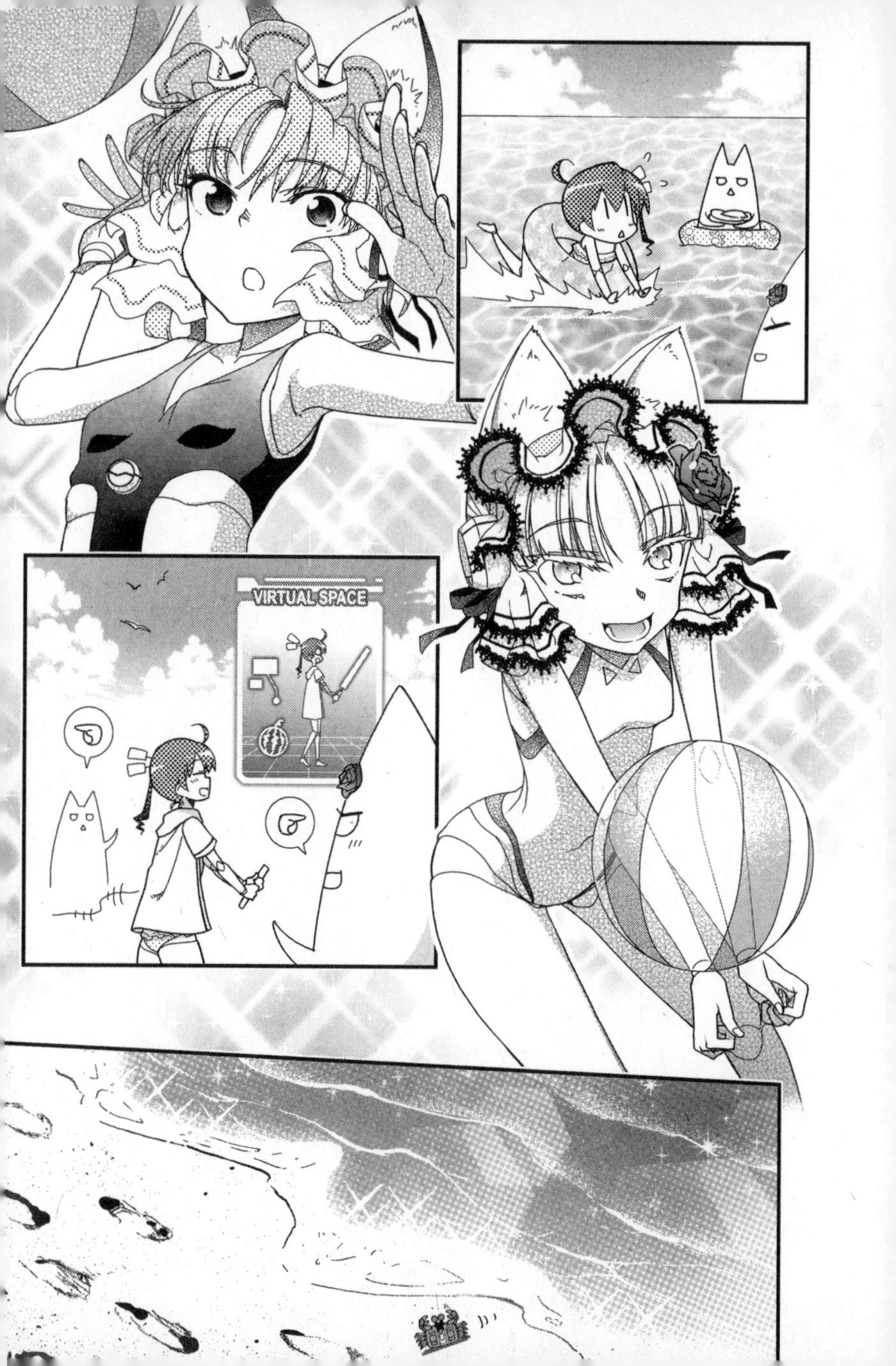
VIRTUAL SPACE

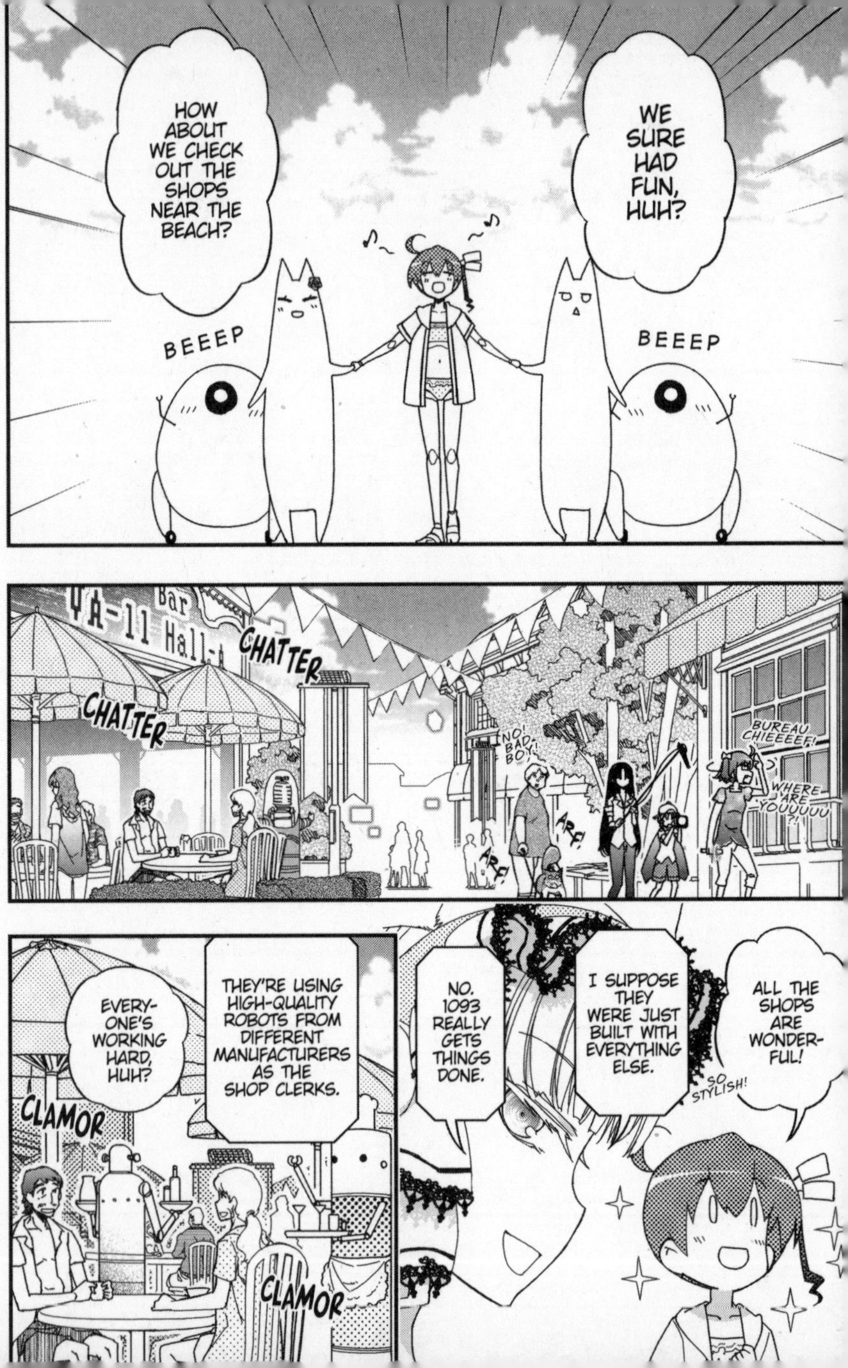
WE SURE HAD FUN, HUH?
BEEEP
HOW ABOUT WE CHECK OUT THE SHOPS NEAR THE BEACH?
BEEEP
BUREAU CHIEEEEF!
WHERE ARE YOUUUUU?!
NO! BAD BOY!
ARF!
ARF!
Bar
CHATTER
CHATTER
ALL THE SHOPS ARE WONDER-FUL!
SO STYLISH!
I SUPPOSE THEY WERE JUST BUILT WITH EVERYTHING ELSE.
NO. 1093 REALLY GETS THINGS DONE.
THEY'RE USING HIGH-QUALITY ROBOTS FROM DIFFERENT MANUFACTURERS AS THE SHOP CLERKS.
EVERY-ONE'S WORKING HARD, HUH?
CLAMOR
CLAMOR

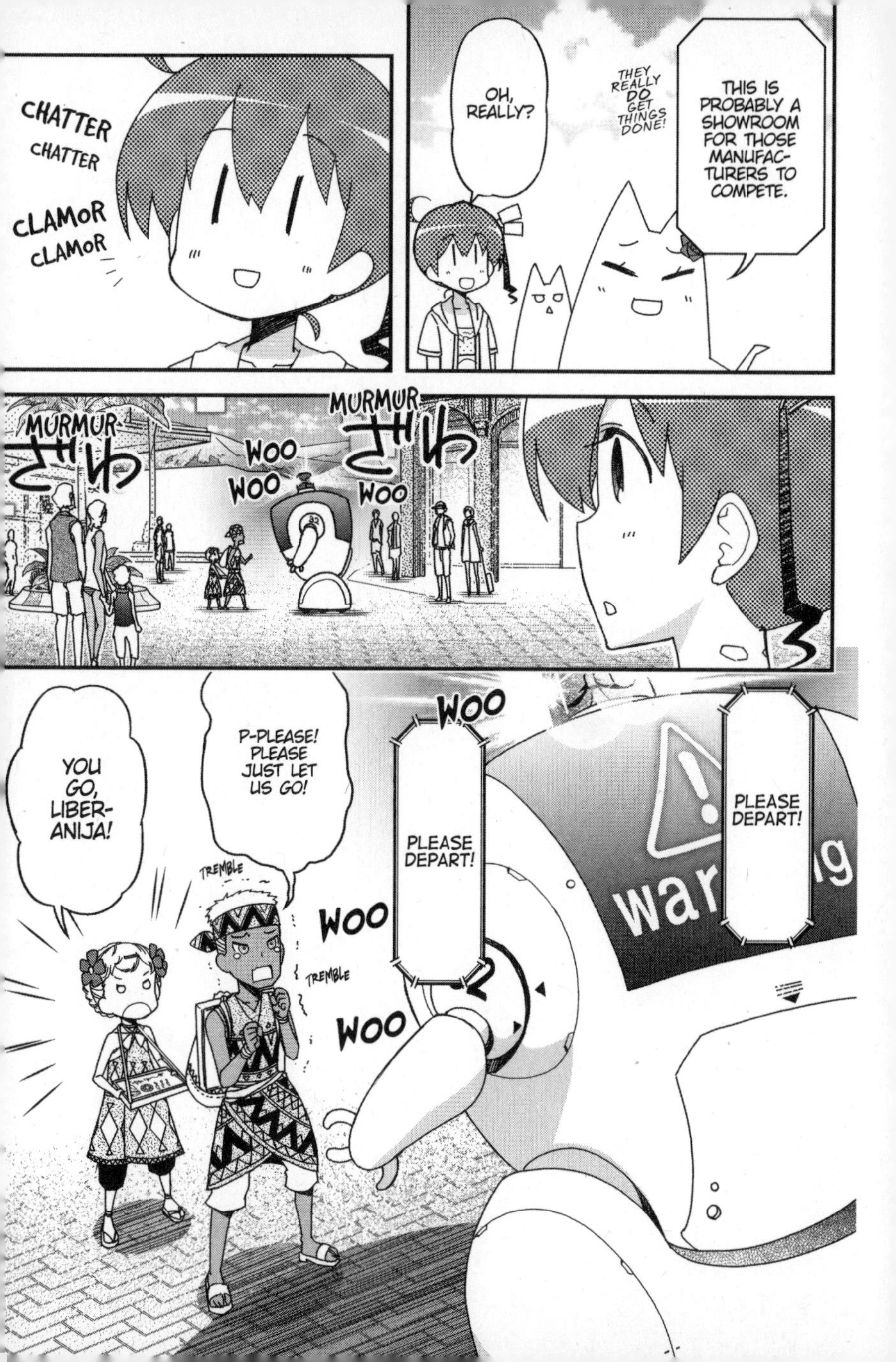
THIS IS PROBABLY A SHOWROOM FOR THOSE MANUFAC-TURERS TO COMPETE.
THEY REALLY DO GET THINGS DONE!
OH, REALLY?
CHATTER
CHATTER
CLAMOR
CLAMOR
MURMUR
ざわ
WOO
WOO
WOO
MURMUR
ざわ
WOO
PLEASE DEPART!
WOO
PLEASE DEPART!
WOO
WOO
P-PLEASE! PLEASE JUST LET US GO!
TREMBLE
TREMBLE
YOU GO, LIBER-ANIJA!

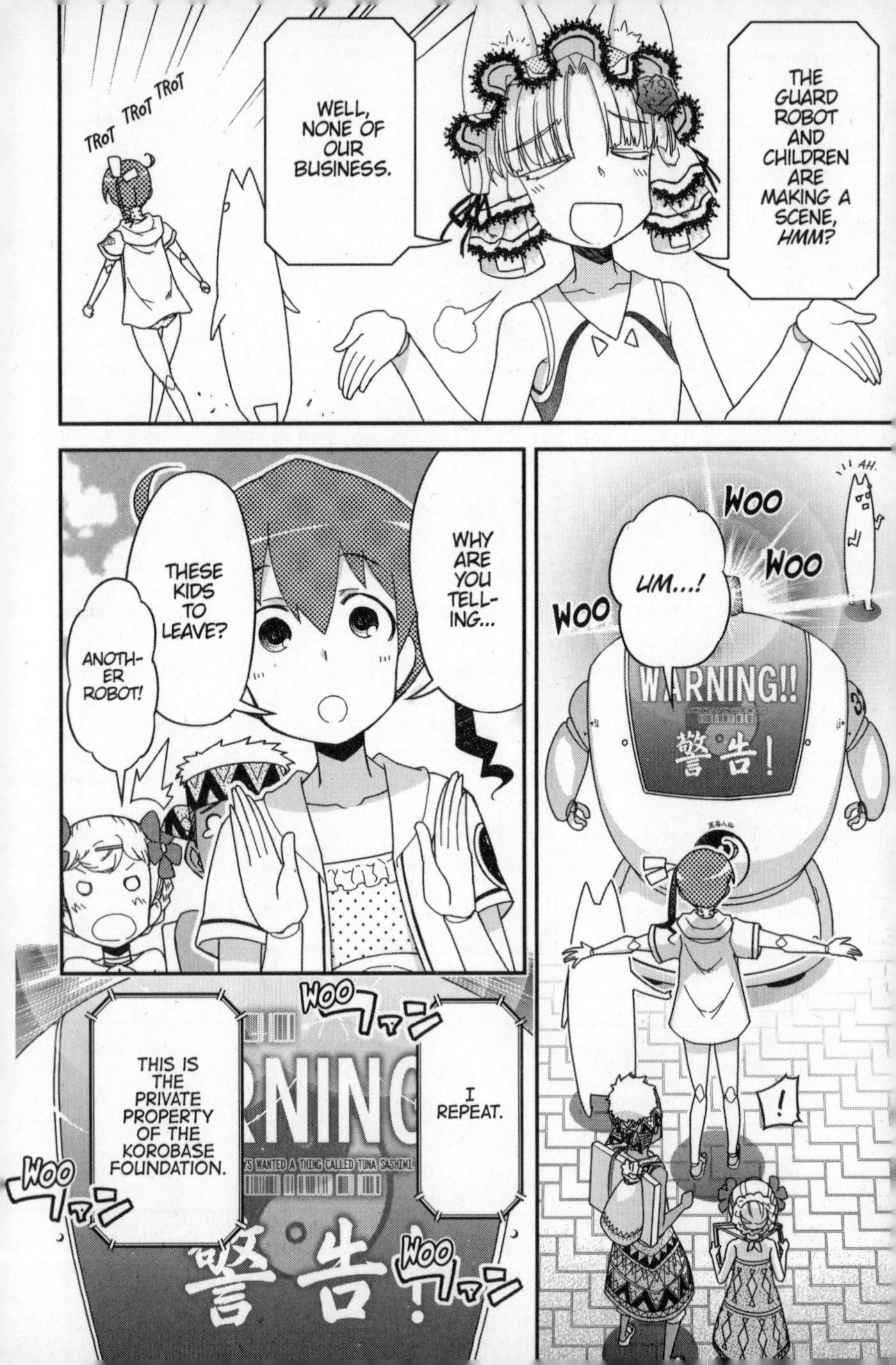
THE GUARD ROBOT AND CHILDREN ARE MAKING A SCENE, HMM?
WELL, NONE OF OUR BUSINESS.
TROT TROT TROT TROT
AH.
WOO
WOO
UM...!
WOO
WARNING!!
警告！
!
WHY ARE YOU TELL- ING...
THESE KIDS TO LEAVE?
ANOTH- ER ROBOT!
WOO ファン
I REPEAT.
THIS IS THE PRIVATE PROPERTY OF THE KOROBASE FOUNDATION.
WOO ファン
警告！
WOO ファン

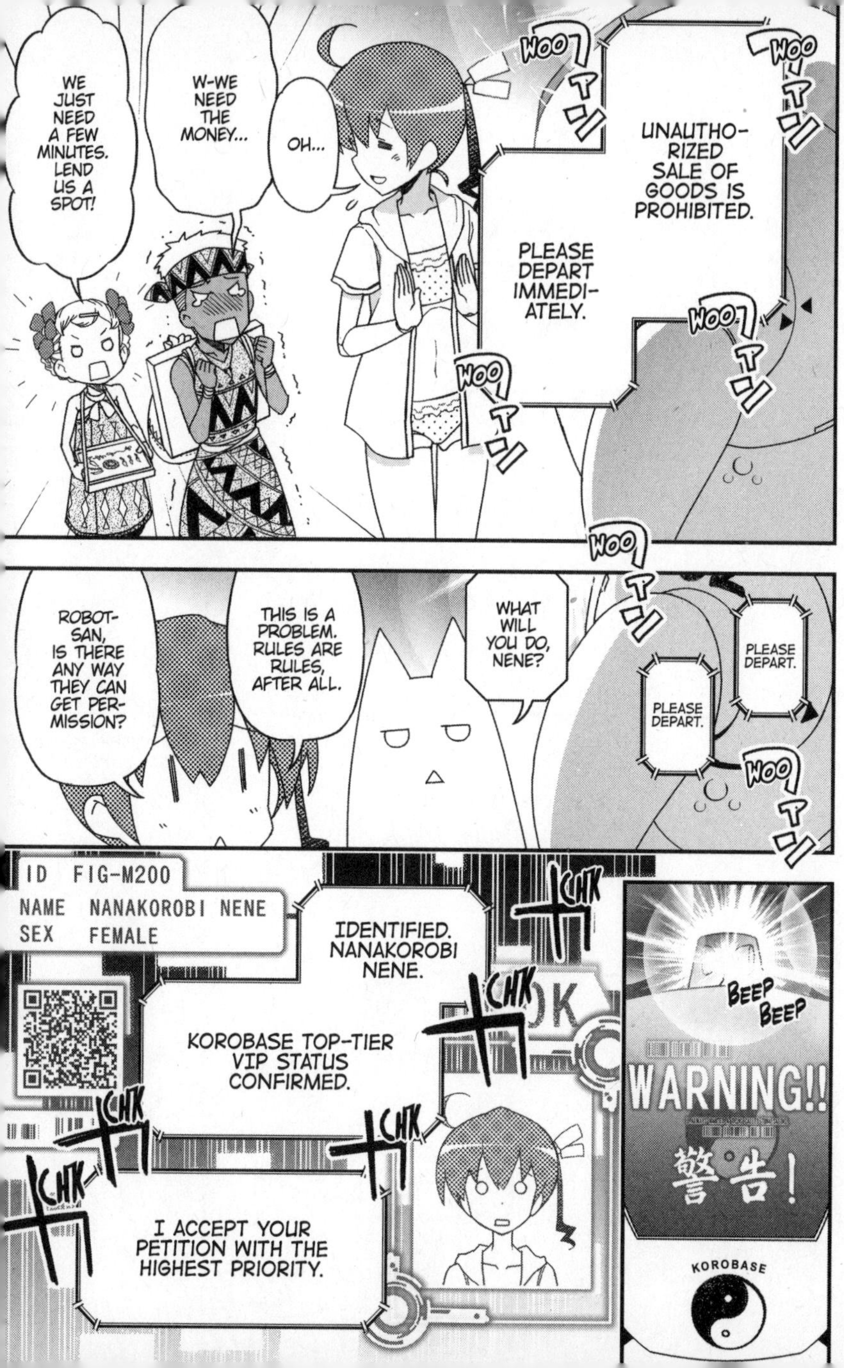
WOO
WOO
UNAUTHO-RIZED SALE OF GOODS IS PROHIBITED.
PLEASE DEPART IMMEDI-ATELY.
WOO
WOO
OH...
W-WE NEED THE MONEY...
WE JUST NEED A FEW MINUTES. LEND US A SPOT!
WOO
PLEASE DEPART.
PLEASE DEPART.
WOO
WHAT WILL YOU DO, NENE?
THIS IS A PROBLEM. RULES ARE RULES, AFTER ALL.
ROBOT-SAN, IS THERE ANY WAY THEY CAN GET PER-MISSION?
BEEP BEEP
WARNING!!
警告！
KOROBASE
ID FIG-M200
NAME NANAKOROBI NENE
SEX FEMALE
CHK
IDENTIFIED. NANAKOROBI NENE.
CHK
OK
KOROBASE TOP-TIER VIP STATUS CONFIRMED.
CHK
CHK
CHK
I ACCEPT YOUR PETITION WITH THE HIGHEST PRIORITY.

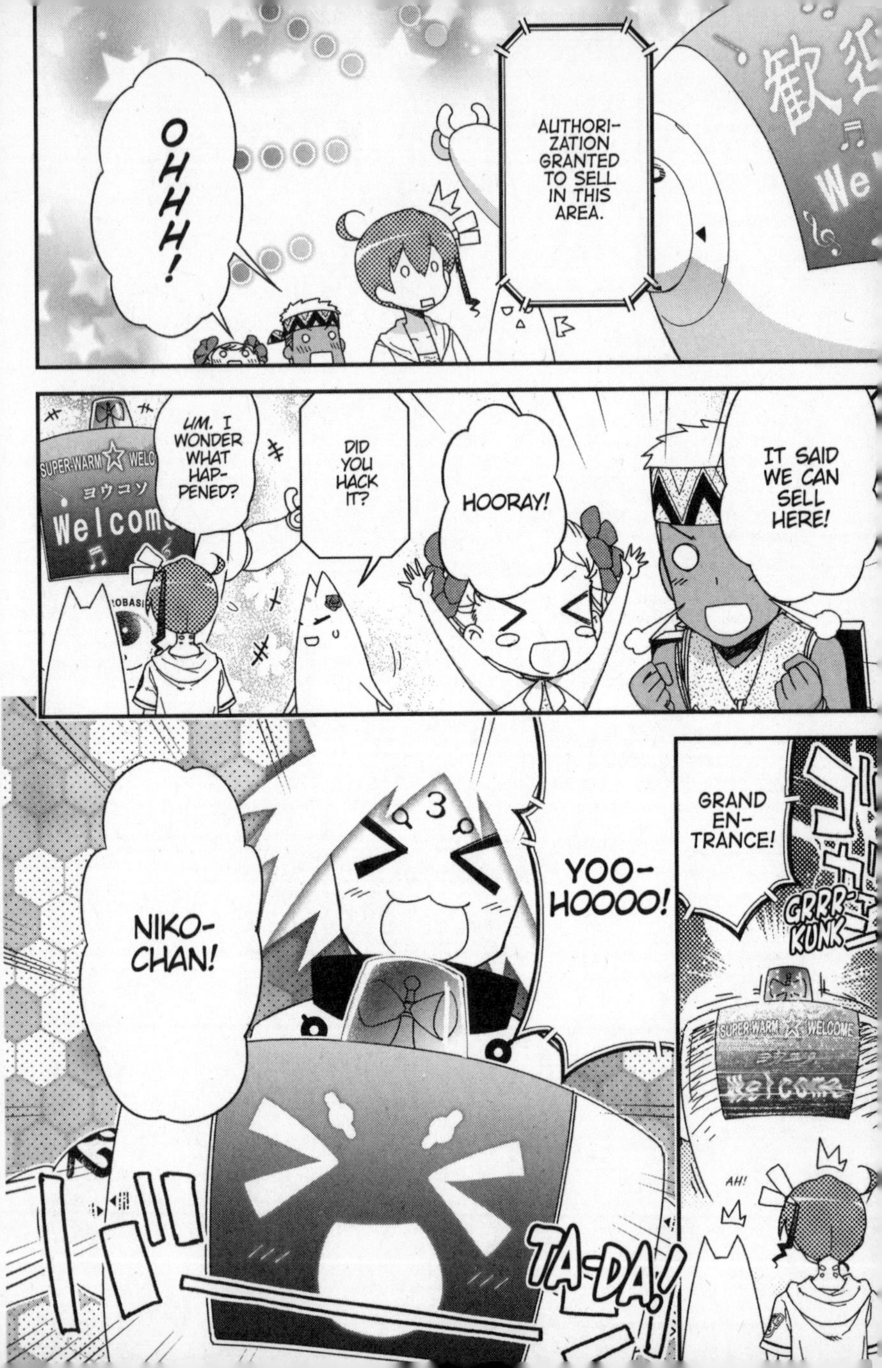
AUTHORI-ZATION GRANTED TO SELL IN THIS AREA.
OHHHH!
IT SAID WE CAN SELL HERE!
HOORAY!
DID YOU HACK IT?
UM. I WONDER WHAT HAP-PENED?
ヨウコソ
Welcome
GRAND EN-TRANCE!
GRRR-KUNK
SUPER-WARM☆WELCOME
AH!
YOO-HOOOO!
NIKO-CHAN!
TA-DA!

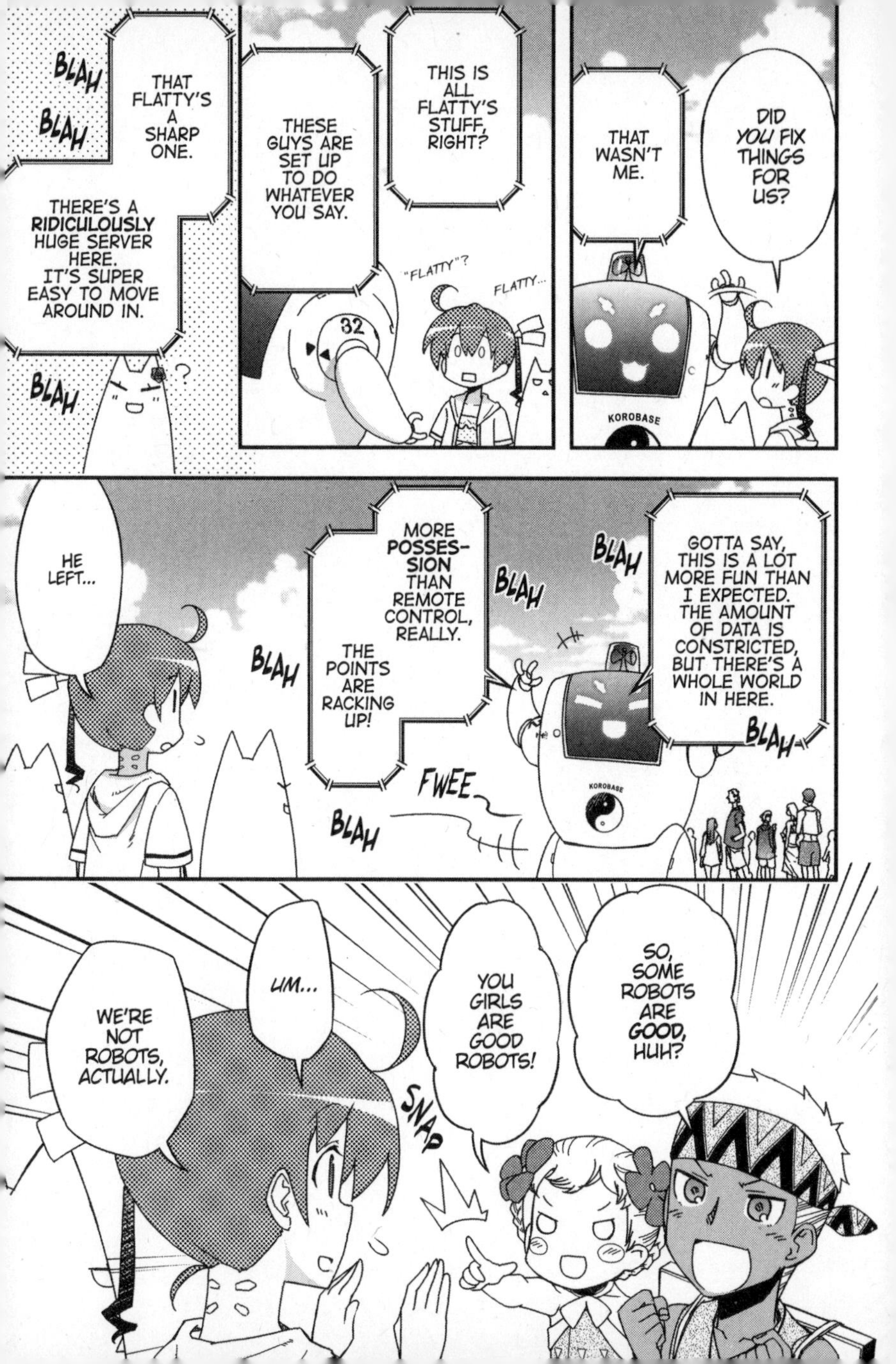

DID YOU FIX THINGS FOR US?
THAT WASN'T ME.
KOROBASE
THIS IS ALL FLATTY'S STUFF, RIGHT?
THESE GUYS ARE SET UP TO DO WHATEVER YOU SAY.
FLATTY...
"FLATTY"?
32
THAT FLATTY'S A SHARP ONE.
BLAH
BLAH
THERE'S A RIDICULOUSLY HUGE SERVER HERE. IT'S SUPER EASY TO MOVE AROUND IN.
BLAH
?
GOTTA SAY, THIS IS A LOT MORE FUN THAN I EXPECTED. THE AMOUNT OF DATA IS CONSTRICTED, BUT THERE'S A WHOLE WORLD IN HERE.
BLAH
BLAH-
KOROBASE
MORE POSSESSION THAN REMOTE CONTROL, REALLY.
THE POINTS ARE RACKING UP!
BLAH
BLAH
FWEE
BLAH
HE LEFT...
SO, SOME ROBOTS ARE GOOD, HUH?
YOU GIRLS ARE GOOD ROBOTS!
SNAP
UM...
WE'RE NOT ROBOTS, ACTUALLY.

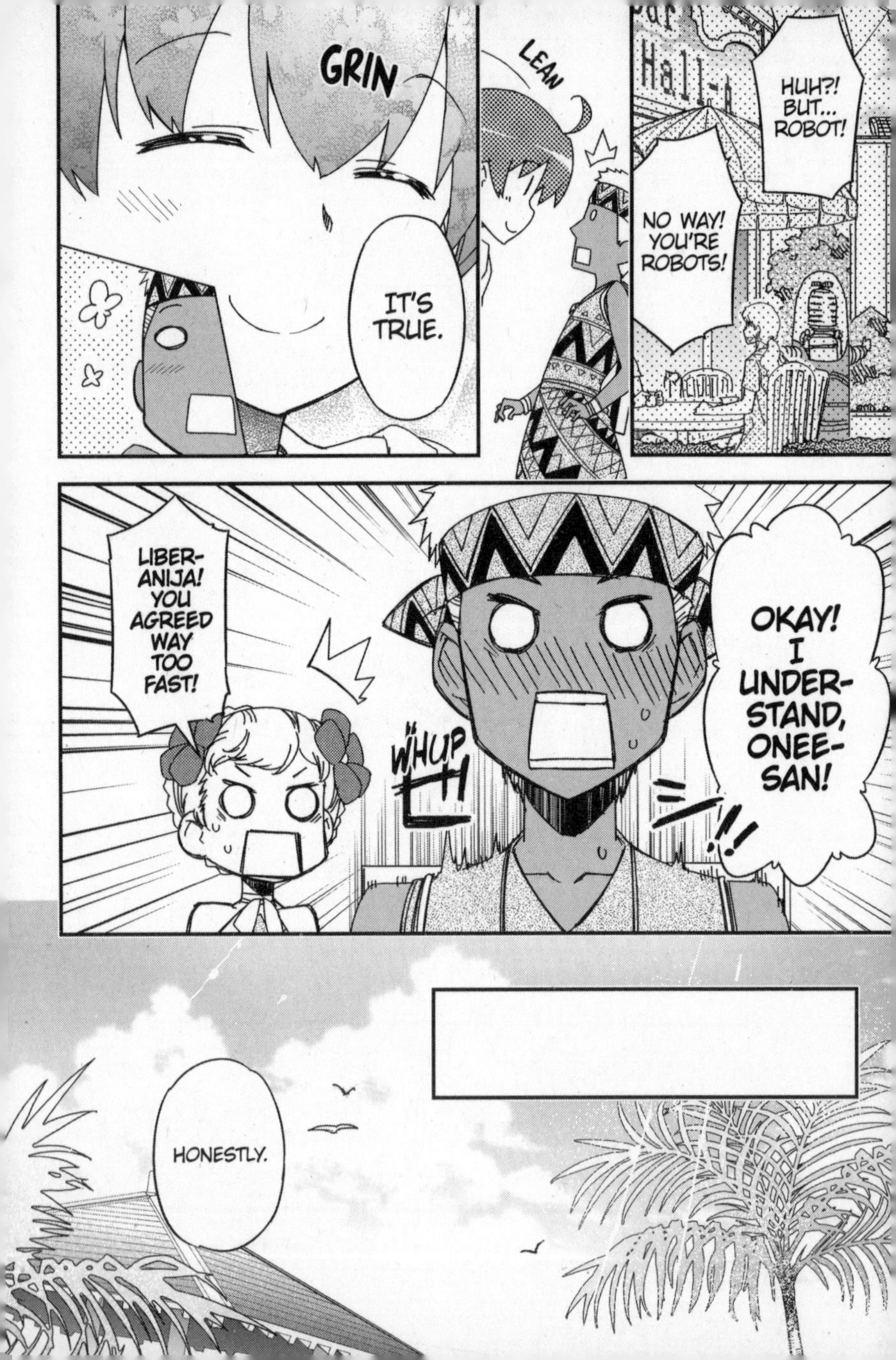
HUH?! BUT... ROBOT!
NO WAY! YOU'RE ROBOTS!
LEAN
GRIN
IT'S TRUE.
OKAY! I UNDER-STAND, ONEE-SAN!
WHUP
LIBER-ANIJA! YOU AGREED WAY TOO FAST!
HONESTLY.

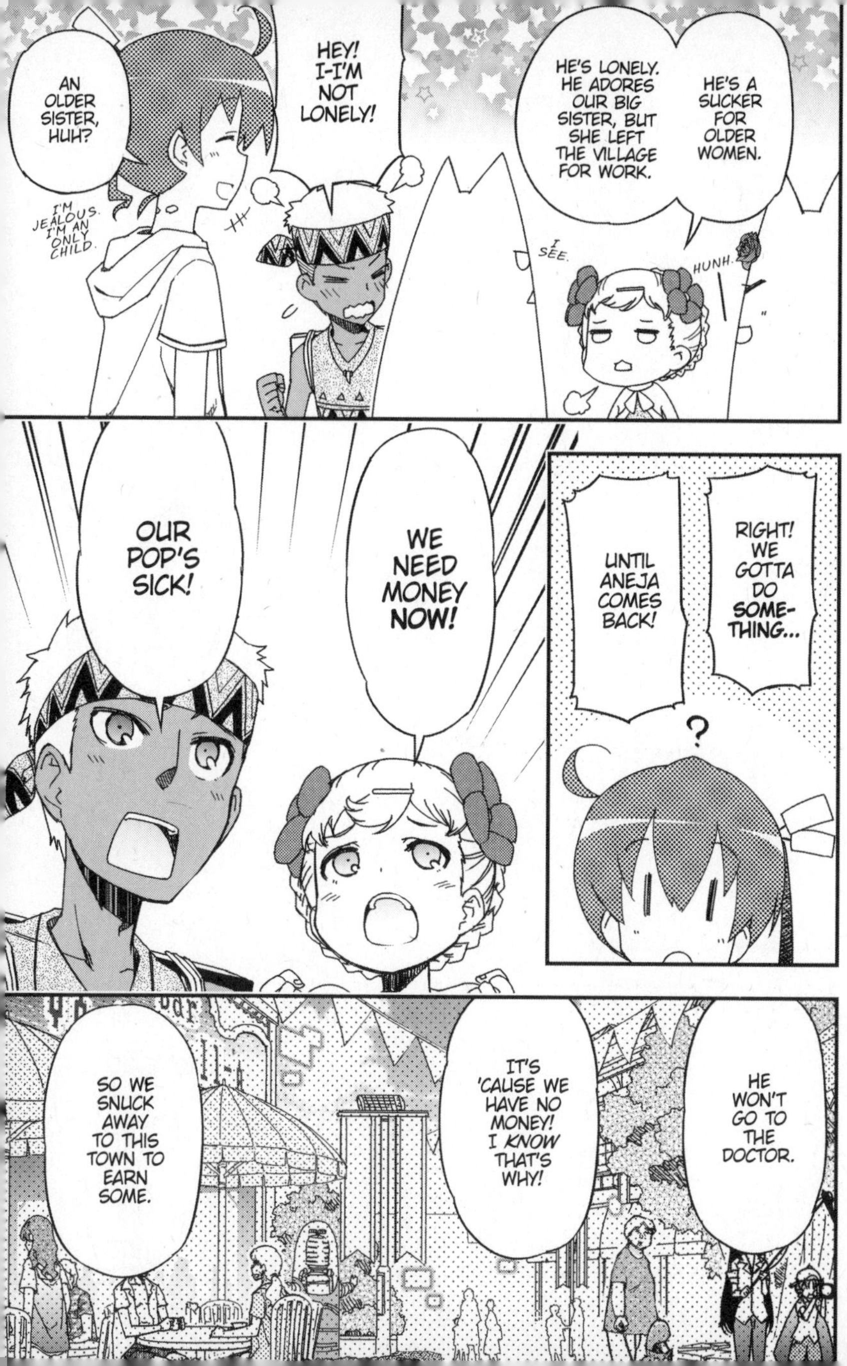
HE'S A SUCKER FOR OLDER WOMEN.
HE'S LONELY. HE ADORES OUR BIG SISTER, BUT SHE LEFT THE VILLAGE FOR WORK.
HUNH.
I SEE.
HEY! I-I'M NOT LONELY!
AN OLDER SISTER, HUH?
I'M JEALOUS. I'M AN ONLY CHILD.
RIGHT! WE GOTTA DO SOME-THING...
UNTIL ANEJA COMES BACK!
WE NEED MONEY NOW!
OUR POP'S SICK!
HE WON'T GO TO THE DOCTOR.
IT'S 'CAUSE WE HAVE NO MONEY! I *KNOW* THAT'S WHY!
SO WE SNUCK AWAY TO THIS TOWN TO EARN SOME.

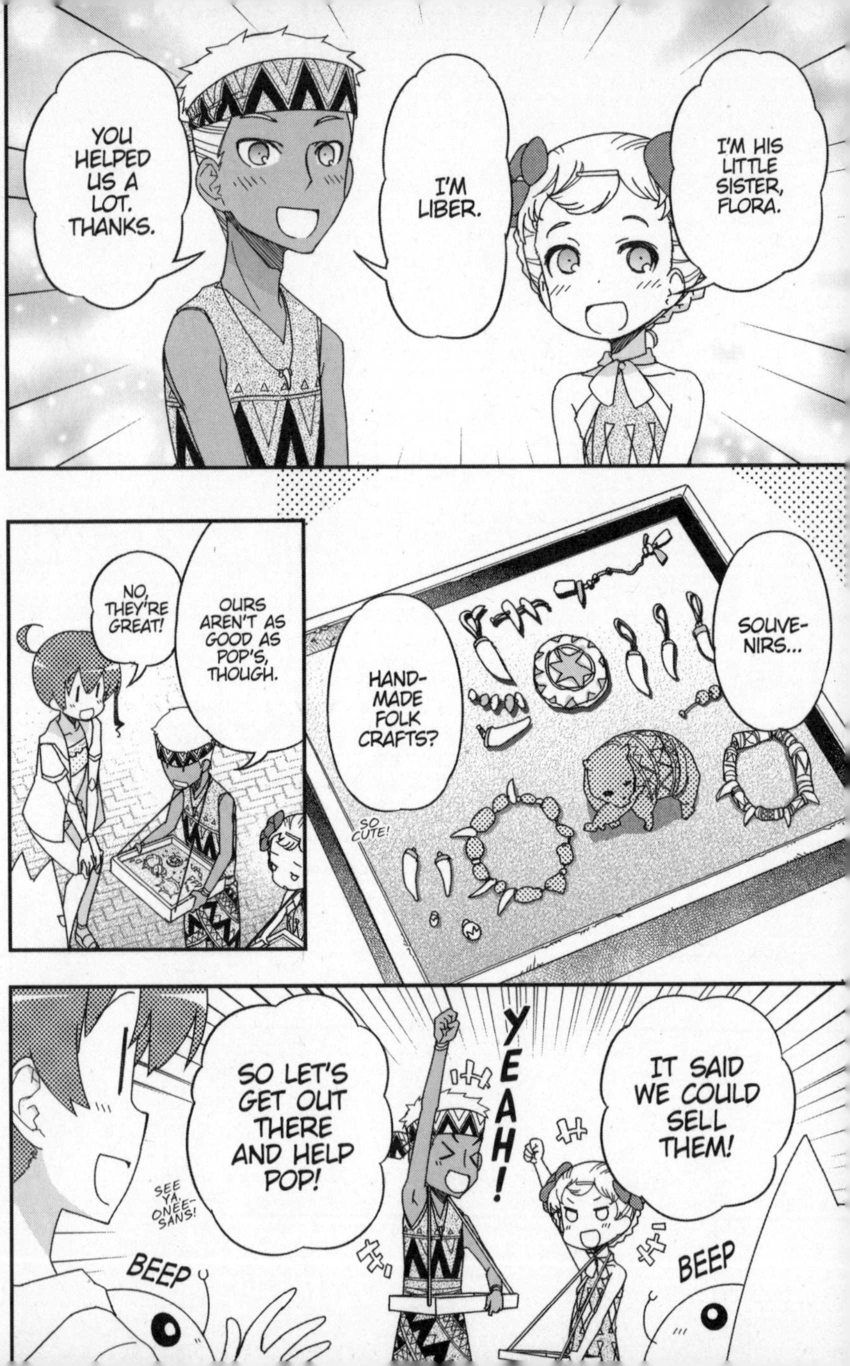
I'M HIS LITTLE SISTER, FLORA.
I'M LIBER.
YOU HELPED US A LOT. THANKS.
SOUVE-NIRS...
HAND-MADE FOLK CRAFTS?
SO CUTE!
OURS AREN'T AS GOOD AS POP'S, THOUGH.
NO, THEY'RE GREAT!
IT SAID WE COULD SELL THEM!
BEEP
YEAH!
SO LET'S GET OUT THERE AND HELP POP!
SEE YA, ONEE-SANS!
BEEP

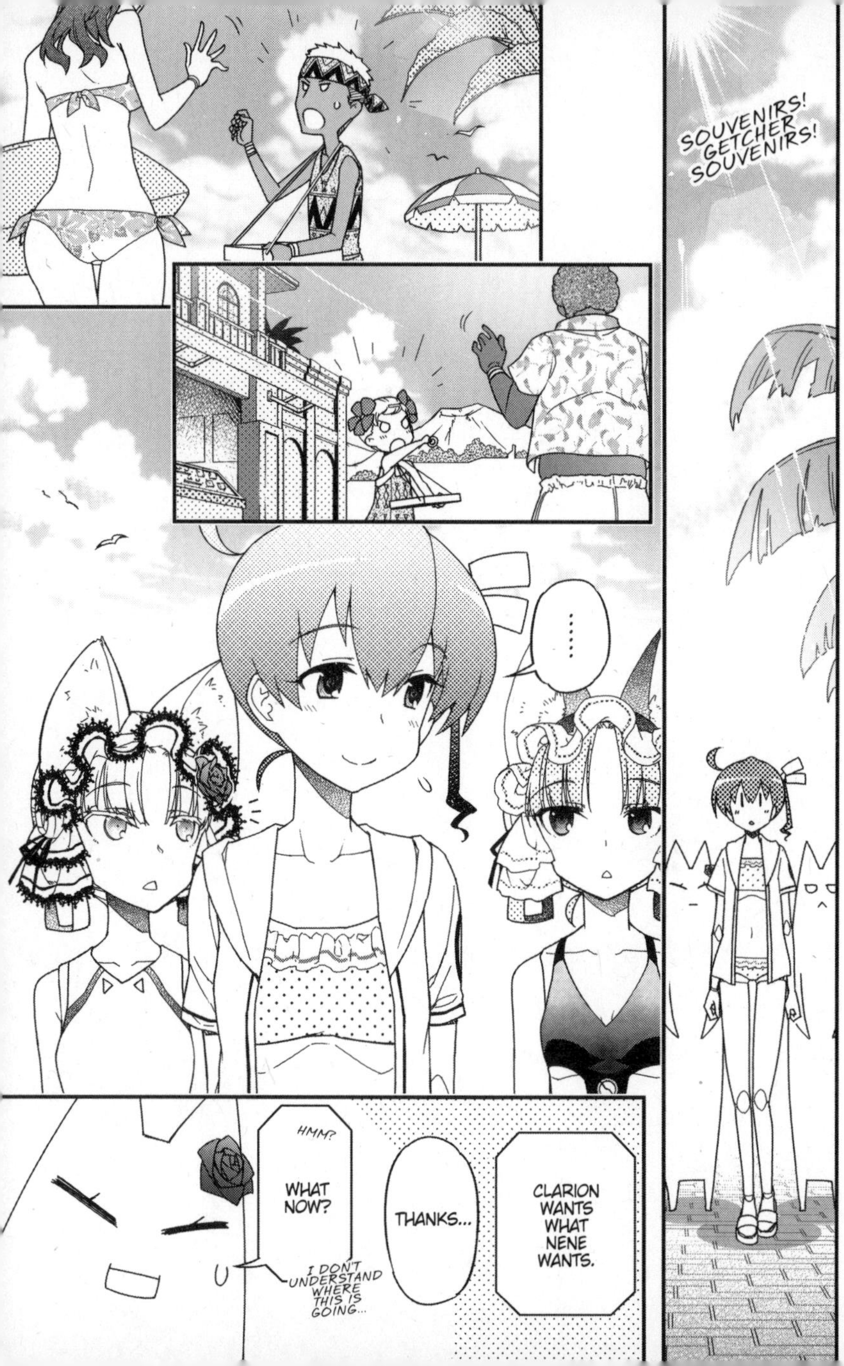
SOUVENIRS! GETCHER SOUVENIRS!
......
CLARION WANTS WHAT NENE WANTS.
THANKS...
HMM? WHAT NOW?
I DON'T UNDERSTAND WHERE THIS IS GOING...

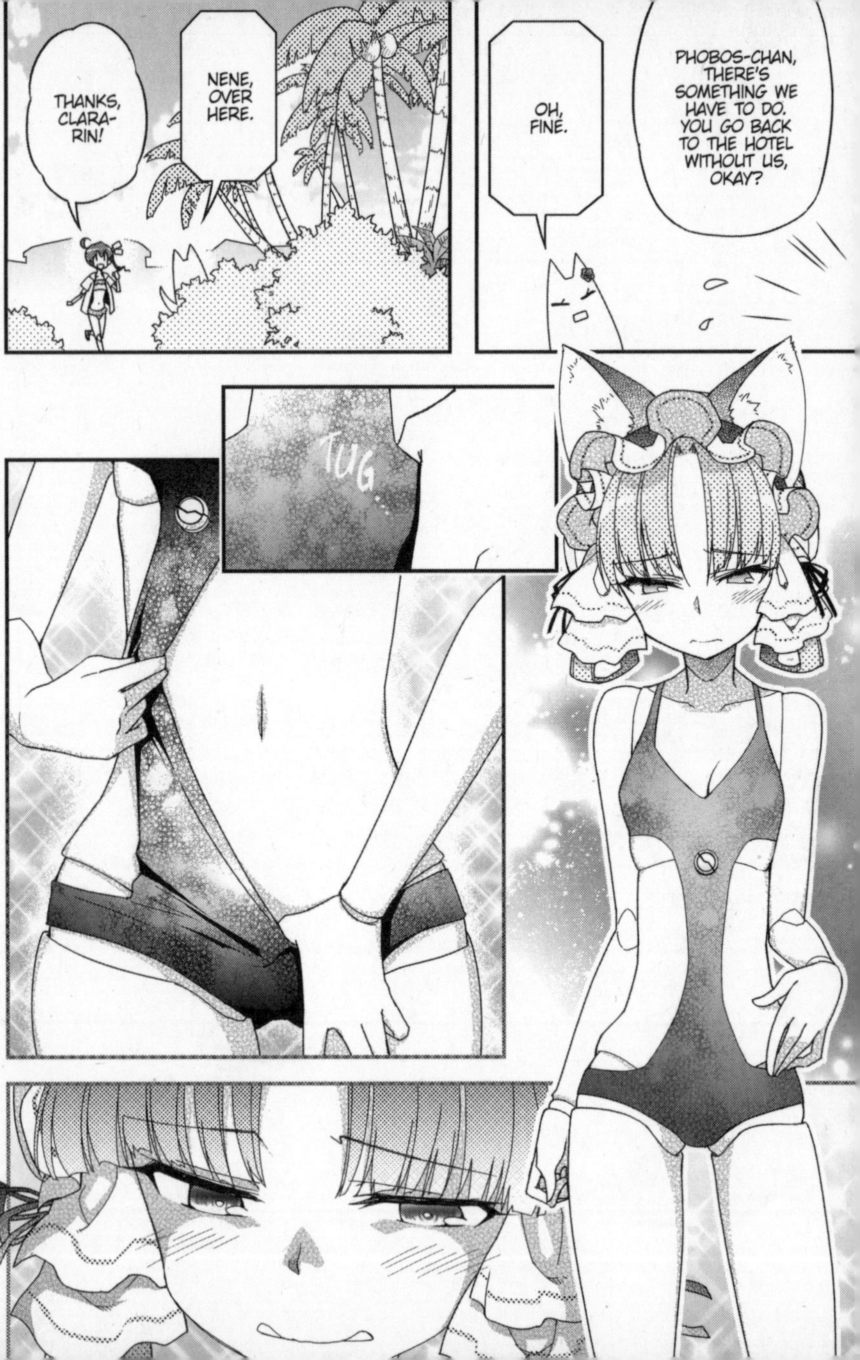
PHOBOS-CHAN, THERE'S SOMETHING WE HAVE TO DO. YOU GO BACK TO THE HOTEL WITHOUT US, OKAY?
OH, FINE.
NENE, OVER HERE.
THANKS, CLARA-RIN!
TUG

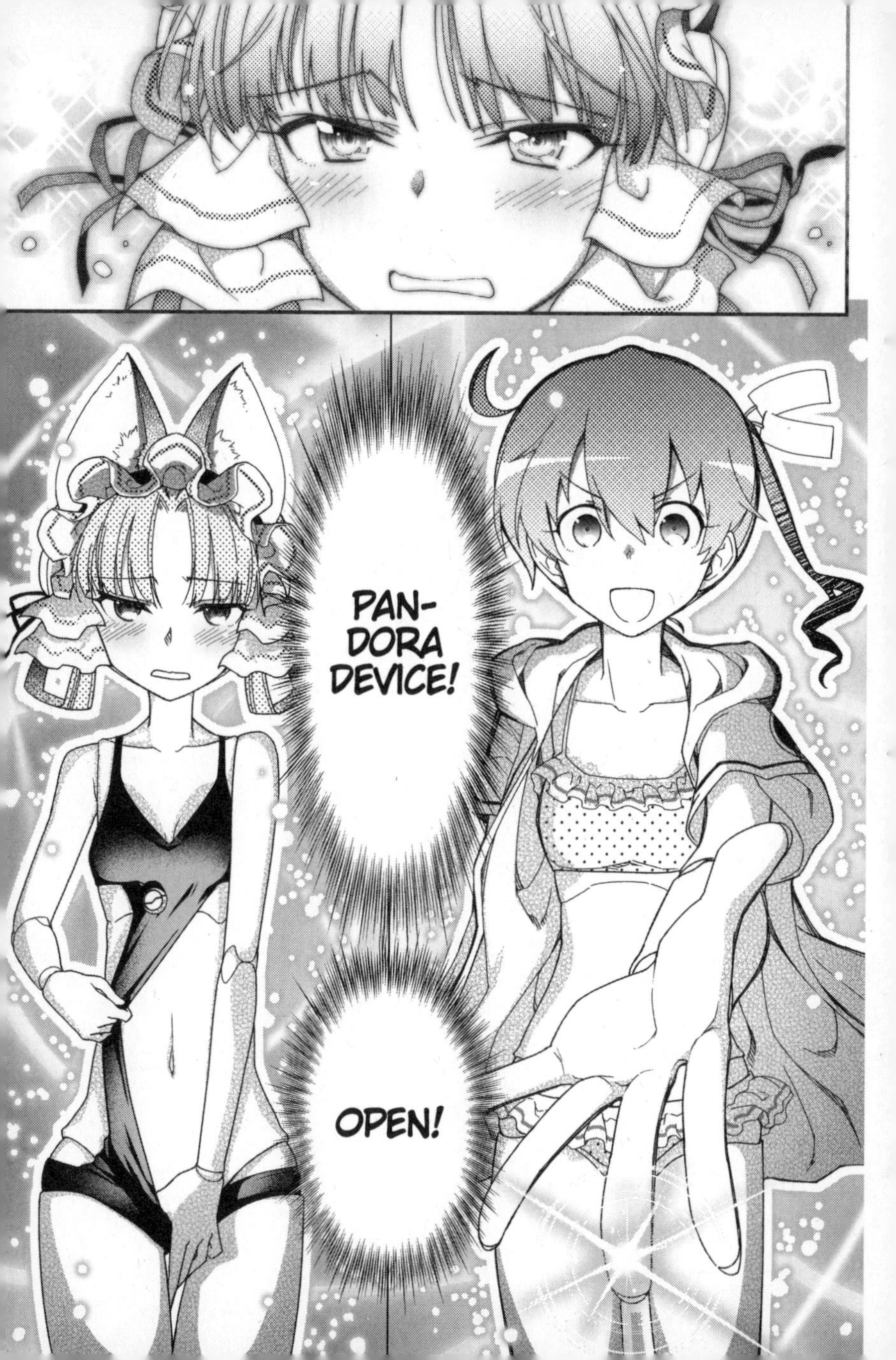
PAN-
DORA
DEVICE!
OPEN!

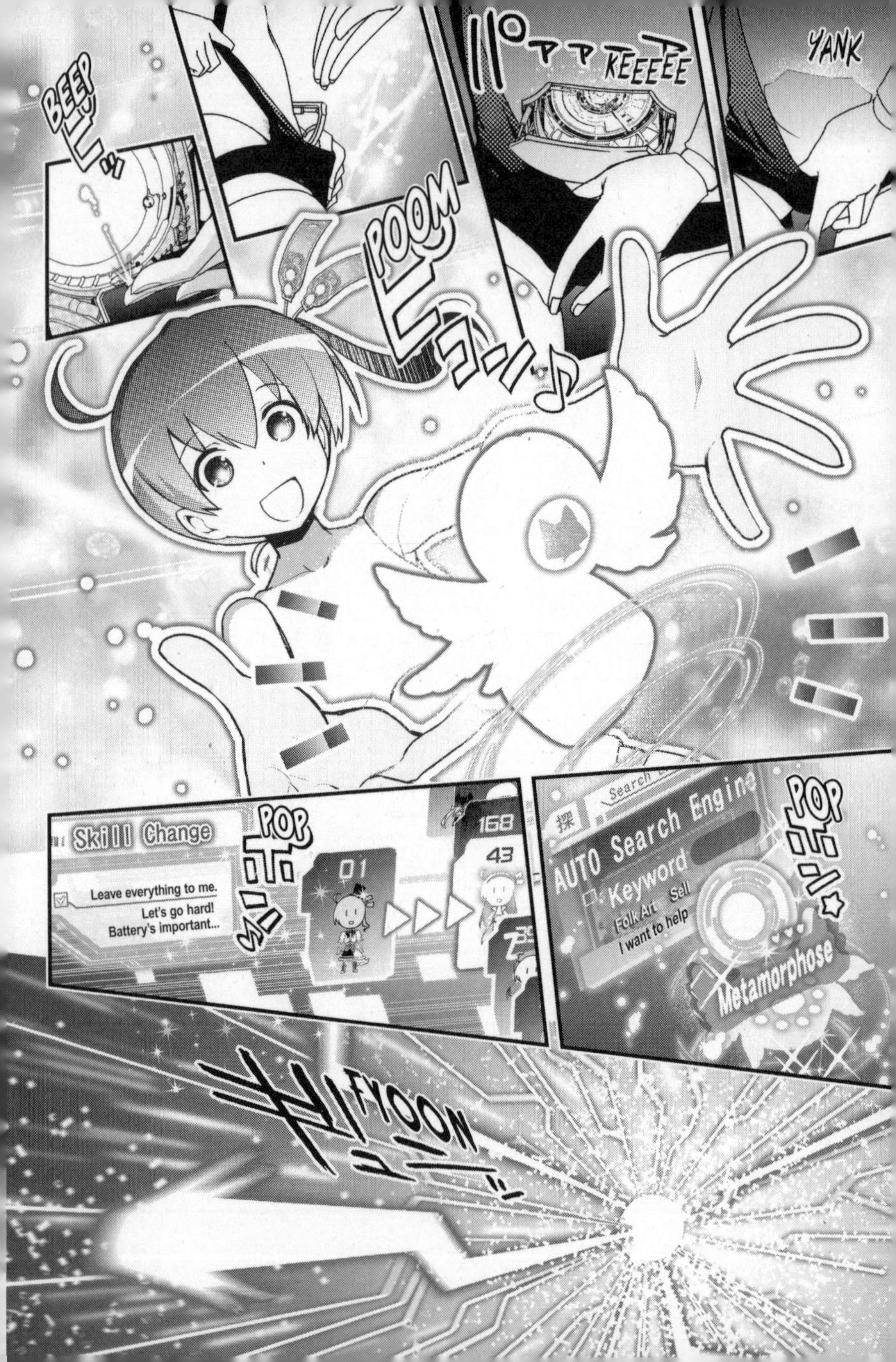
YANK
KEEEEE
BEEP
POOM
Search Engine
AUTO Search Engine
Keyword
Folk Art Sell
I want to help
Metamorphose
POP
Skill Change
Leave everything to me.
Let's go hard!
Battery's important...
POP
168
43
01
FYOON

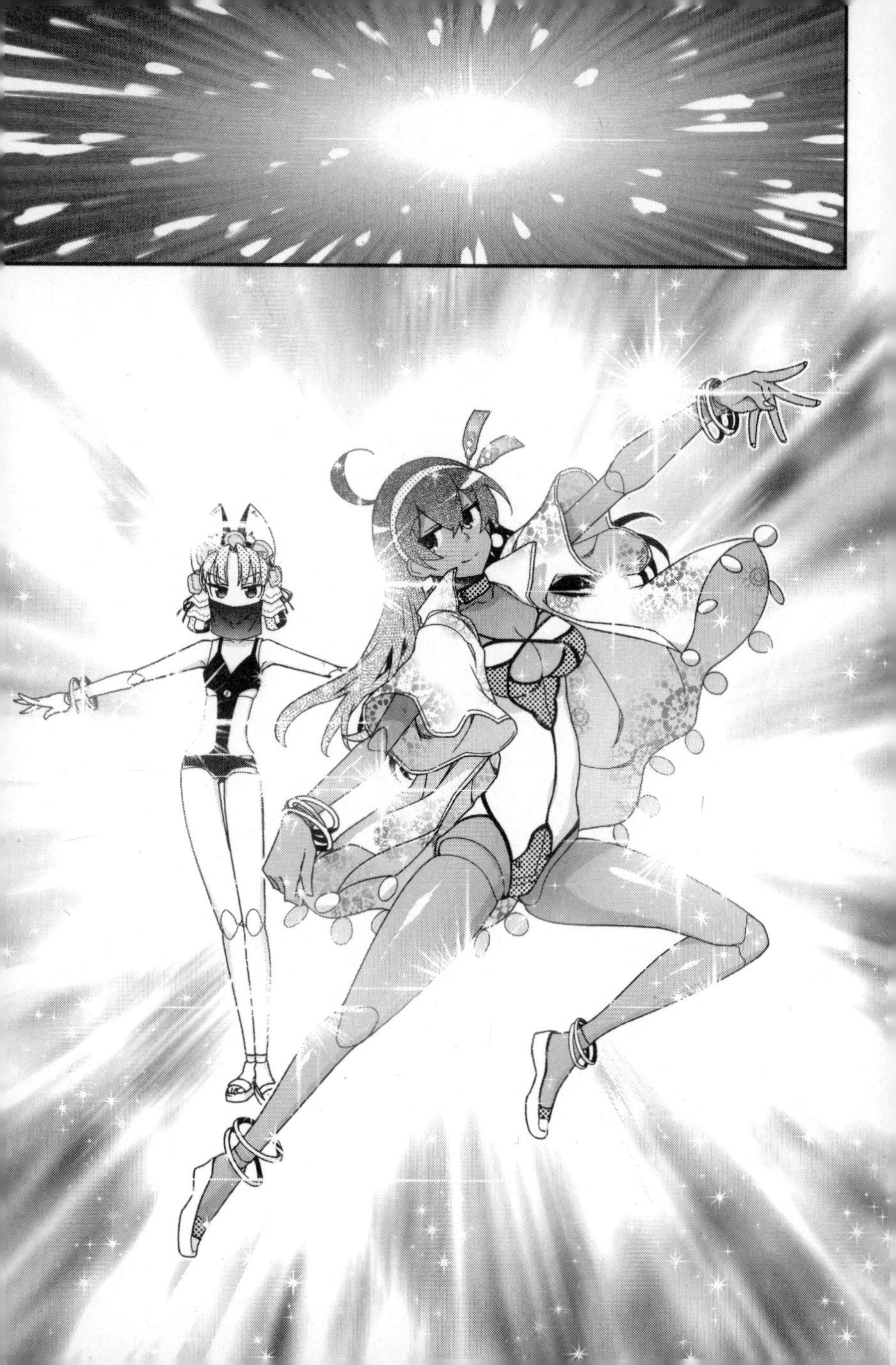

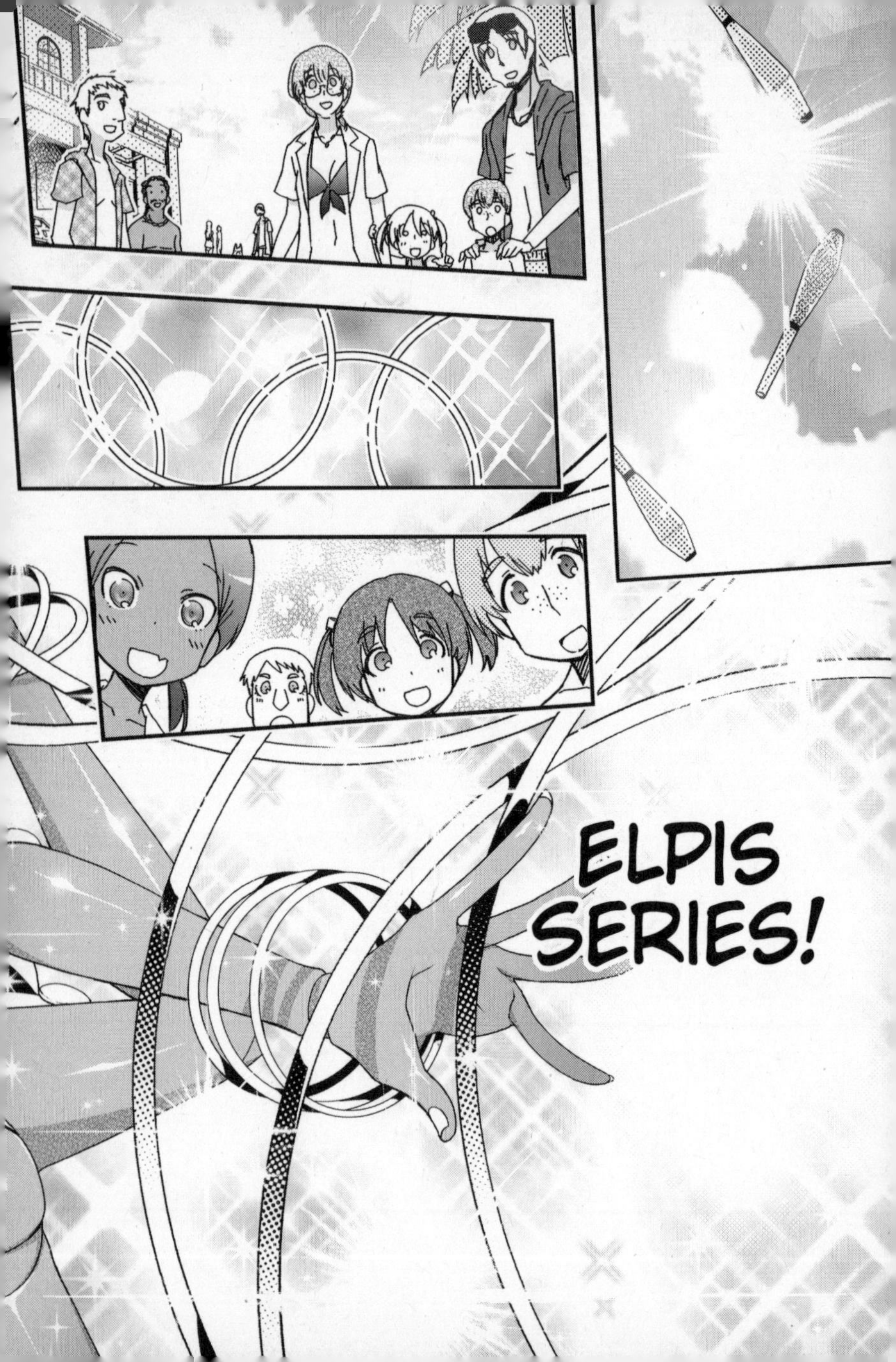
ELPIS SERIES!

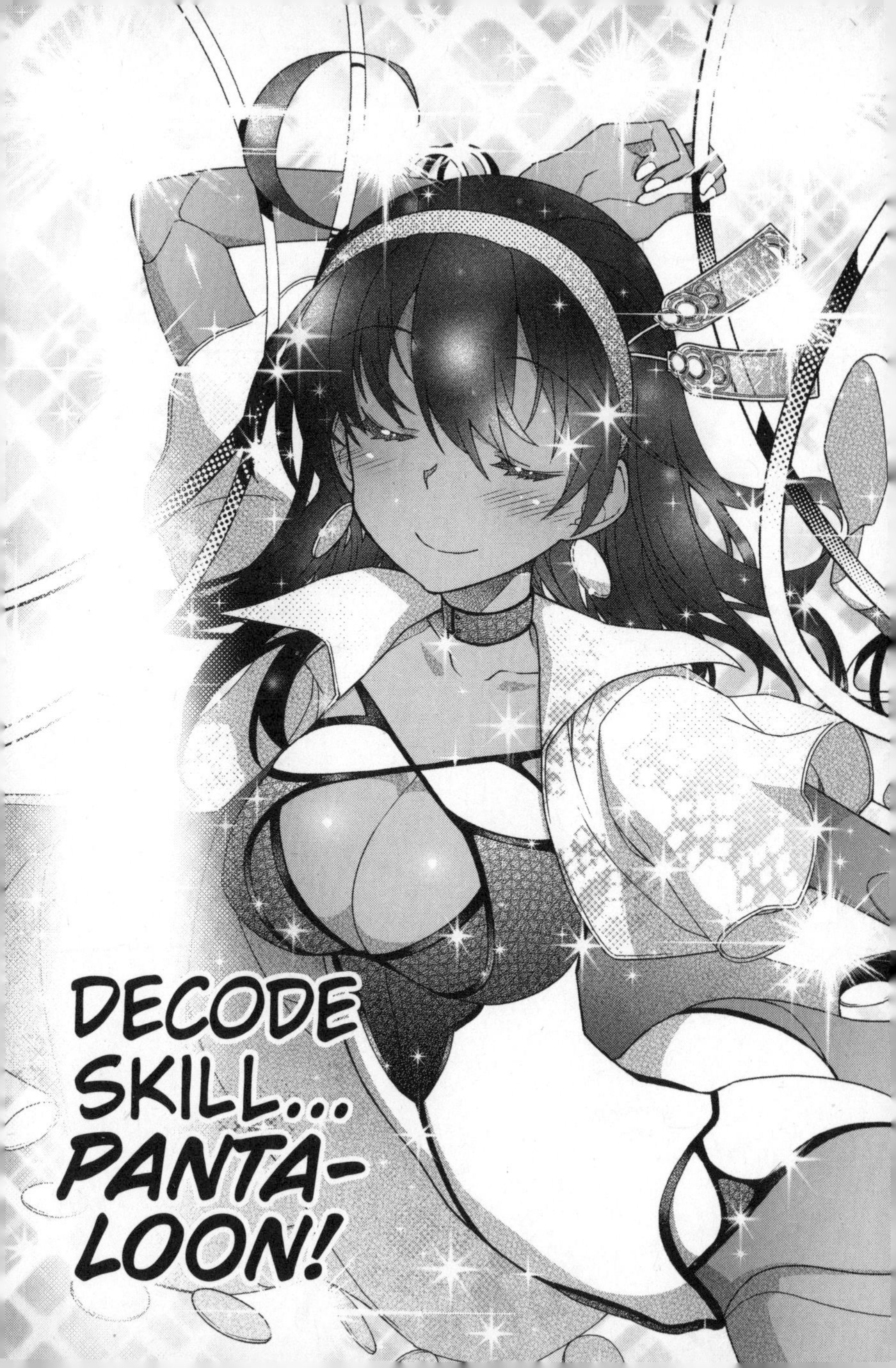
DECODE SKILL... PANTA-LOON!

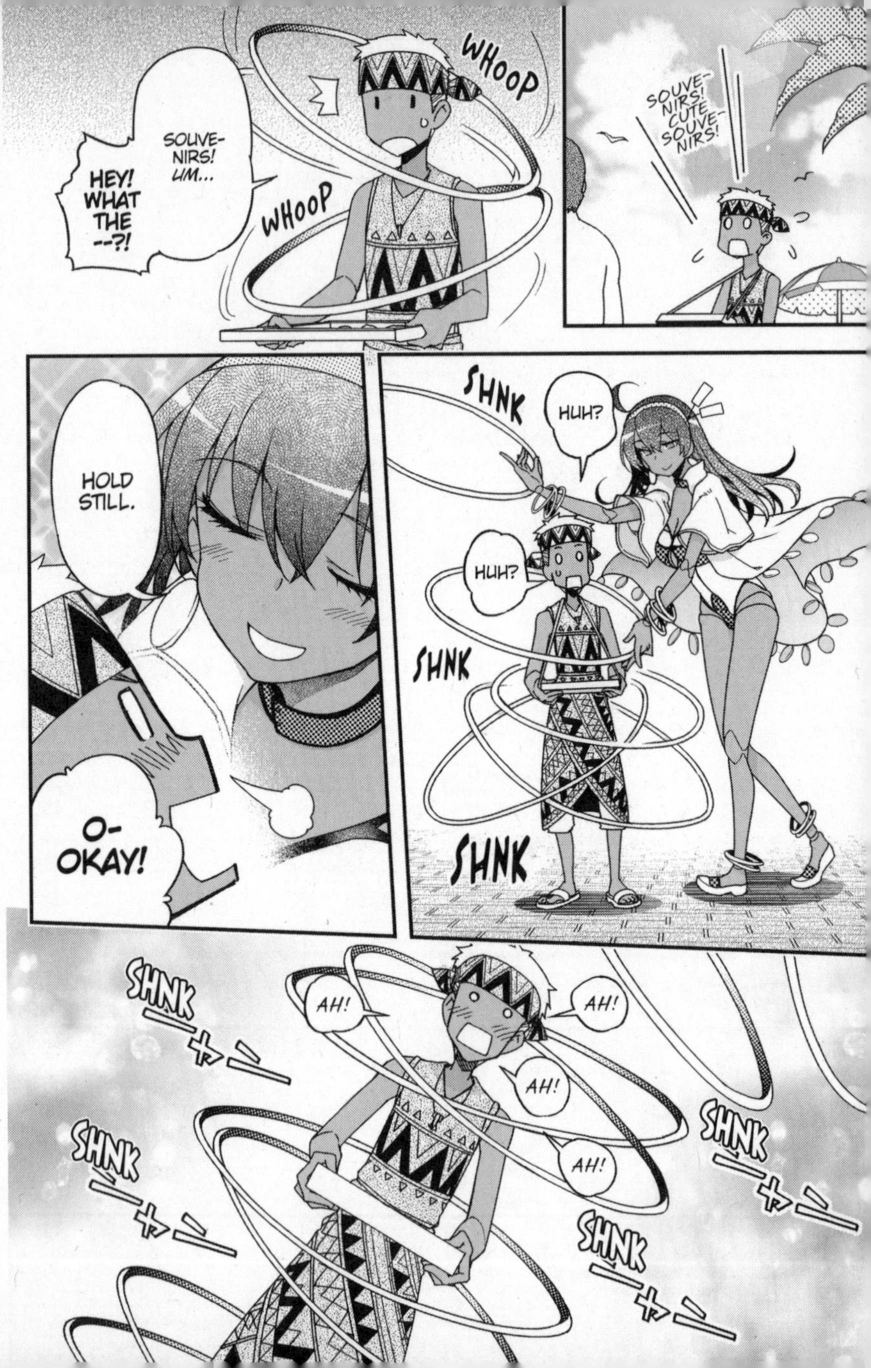

SOUVENIRS! CUTE SOUVENIRS!
WHOOP
WHOOP
SOUVENIRS! UM...
HEY! WHAT THE --?!
SHNK
HUH?
HUH?
SHNK
SHNK
HOLD STILL.
O-OKAY!
AH!
SHNK
AH!
AH!
SHNK
AH!
SHNK
SHNK

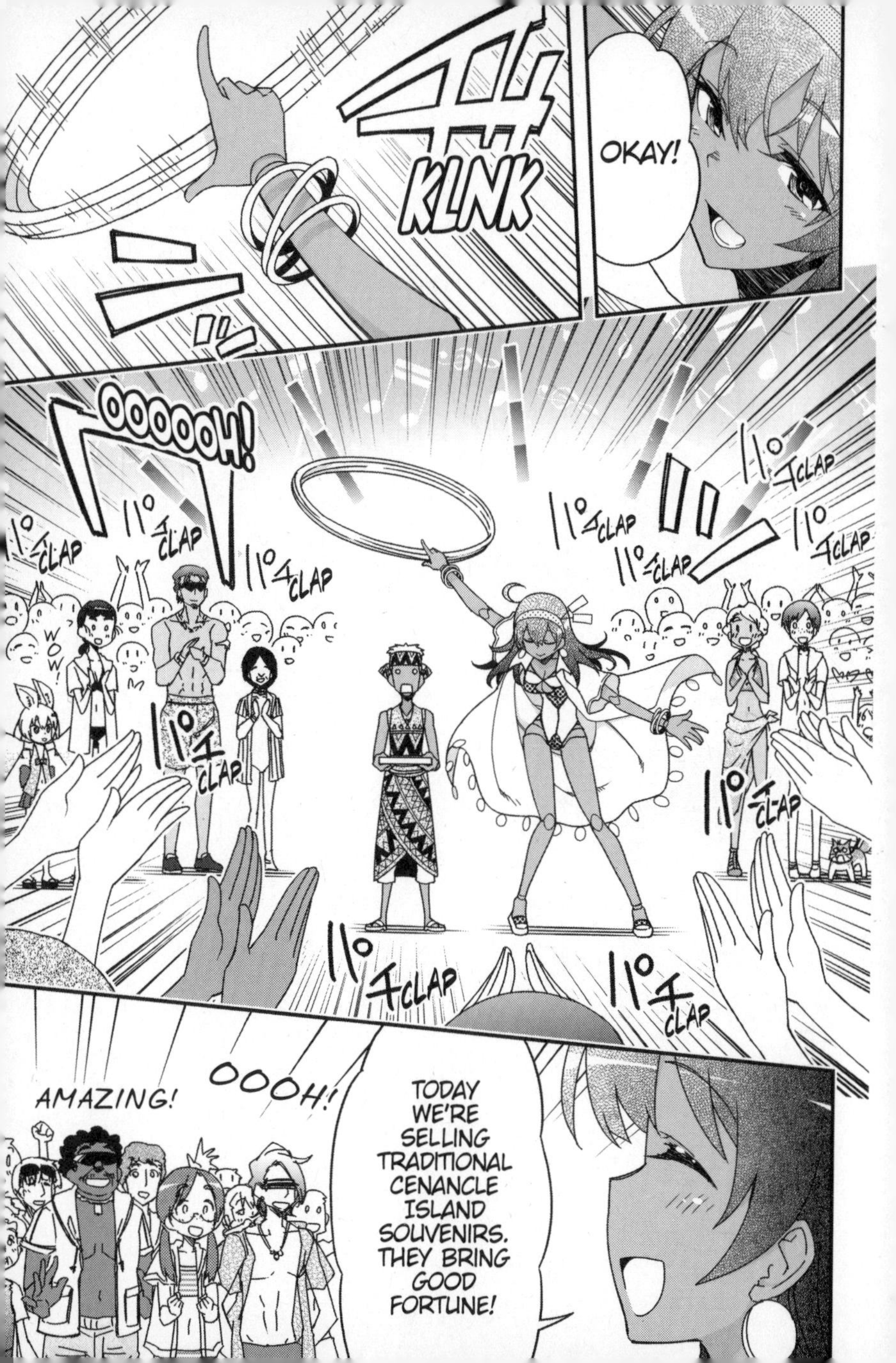
OKAY!
KLNK
OOOOOH!
CLAP
CLAP
CLAP
CLAP
CLAP
CLAP
WOW!
CLAP
CLAP
CLAP
CLAP
CLAP
TODAY WE'RE SELLING TRADITIONAL CENANCLE ISLAND SOUVENIRS. THEY BRING GOOD FORTUNE!
OOOH!
AMAZING!

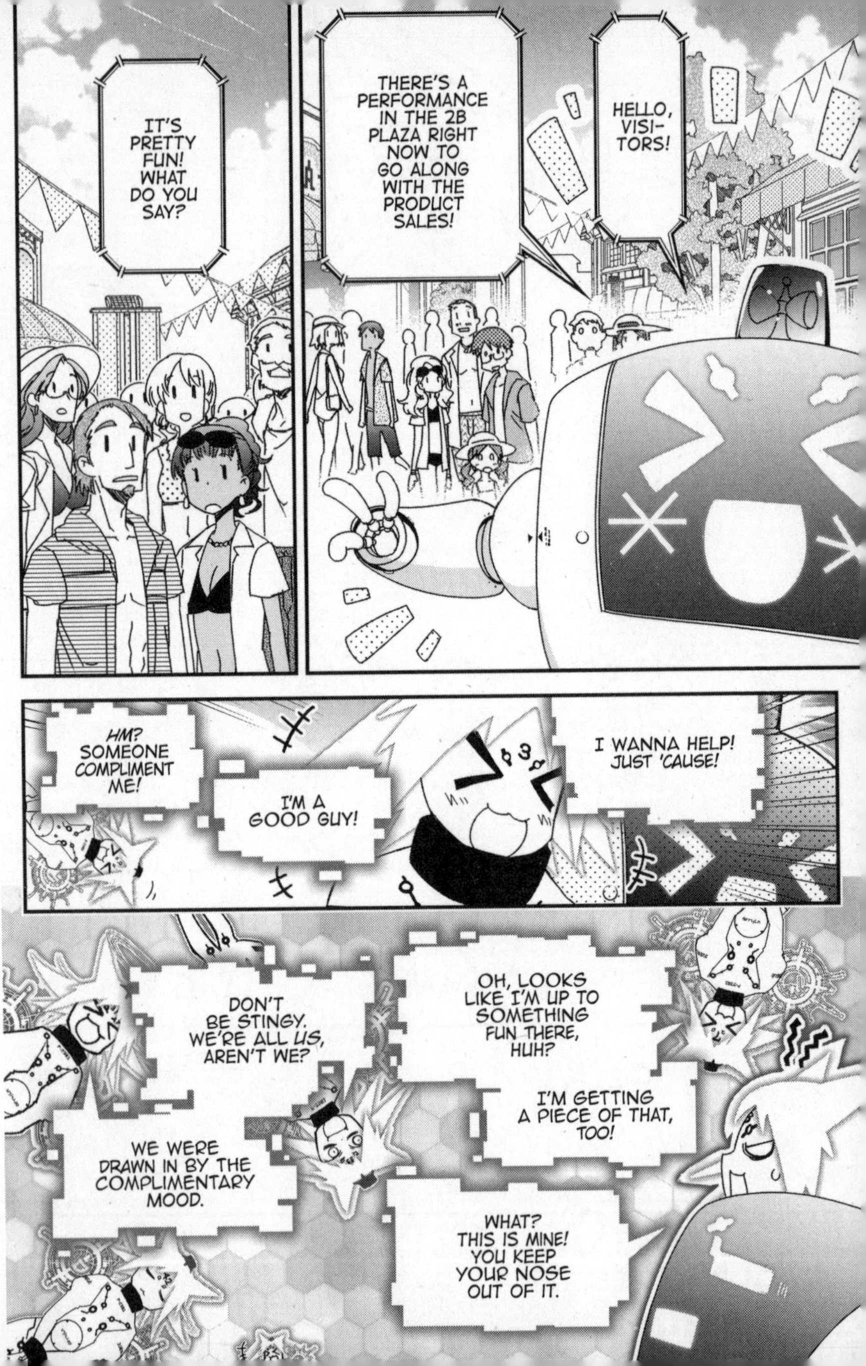
HELLO, VISITORS!
THERE'S A PERFORMANCE IN THE 2B PLAZA RIGHT NOW TO GO ALONG WITH THE PRODUCT SALES!
IT'S PRETTY FUN! WHAT DO YOU SAY?
I WANNA HELP! JUST 'CAUSE!
I'M A GOOD GUY!
HM? SOMEONE COMPLIMENT ME!
OH, LOOKS LIKE I'M UP TO SOMETHING FUN THERE, HUH?
DON'T BE STINGY. WE'RE ALL *US*, AREN'T WE?
I'M GETTING A PIECE OF THAT, TOO!
WE WERE DRAWN IN BY THE COMPLIMENTARY MOOD.
WHAT? THIS IS MINE! YOU KEEP YOUR NOSE OUT OF IT.

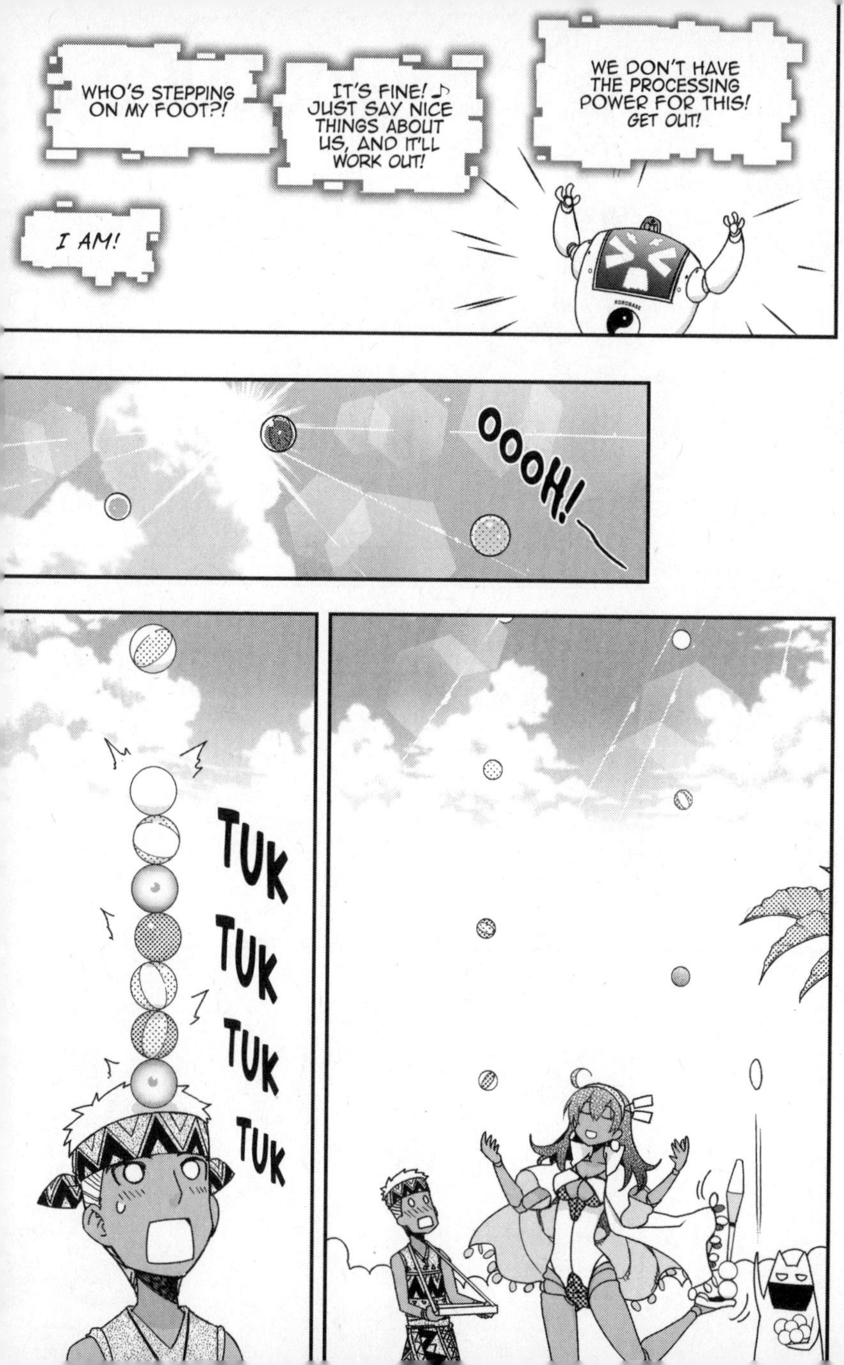
WE DON'T HAVE THE PROCESSING POWER FOR THIS! GET OUT!
IT'S FINE! ♪ JUST SAY NICE THINGS ABOUT US, AND IT'LL WORK OUT!
WHO'S STEPPING ON MY FOOT?!
I AM!
OOOH!
TUK
TUK
TUK
TUK

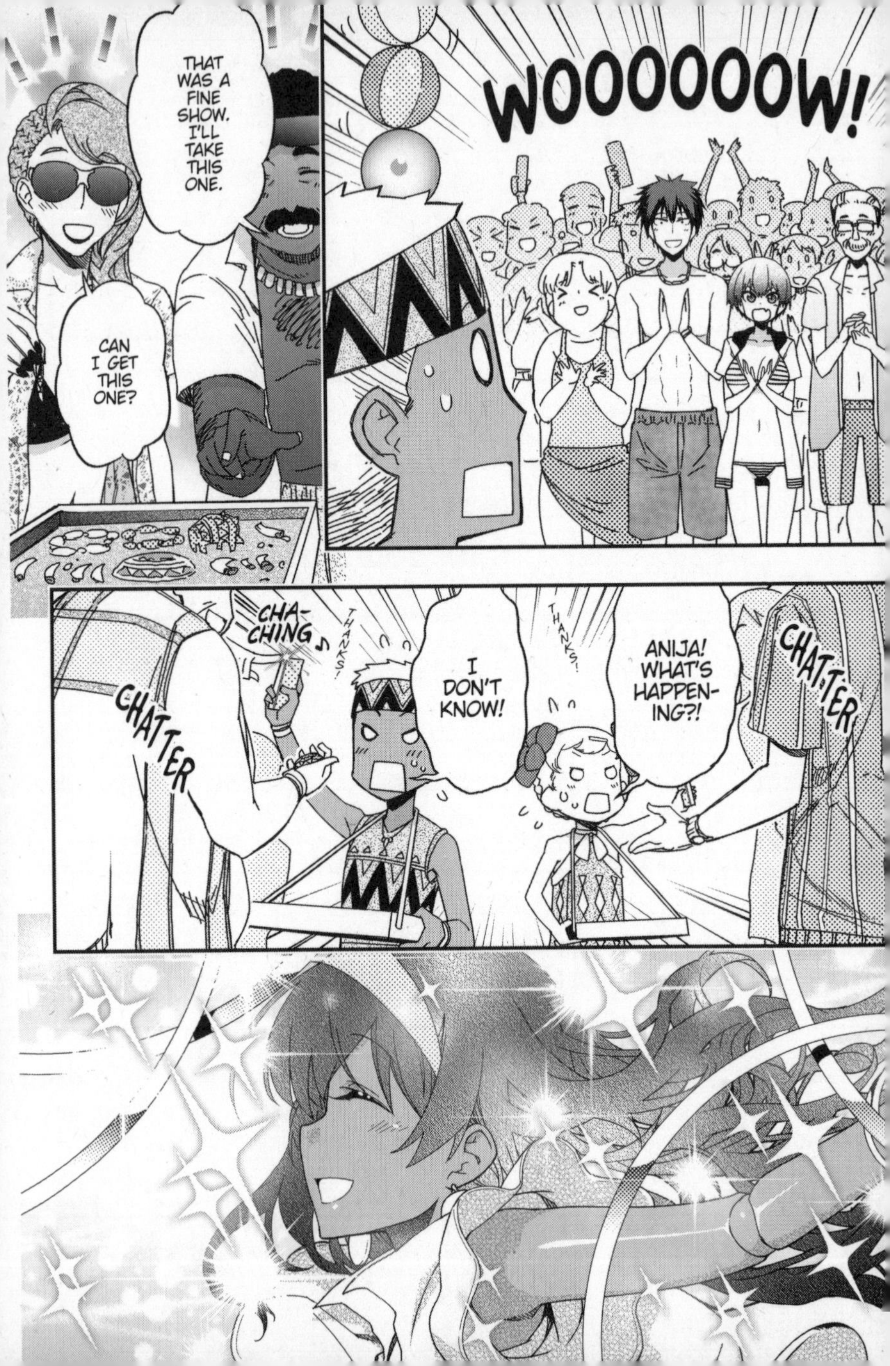
WOOOOOOW!
THAT WAS A FINE SHOW. I'LL TAKE THIS ONE.
CAN I GET THIS ONE?
CHATTER
ANIJA! WHAT'S HAPPEN-ING?!
THANKS!
I DON'T KNOW!
THANKS!
CHA-CHING ♪
CHATTER

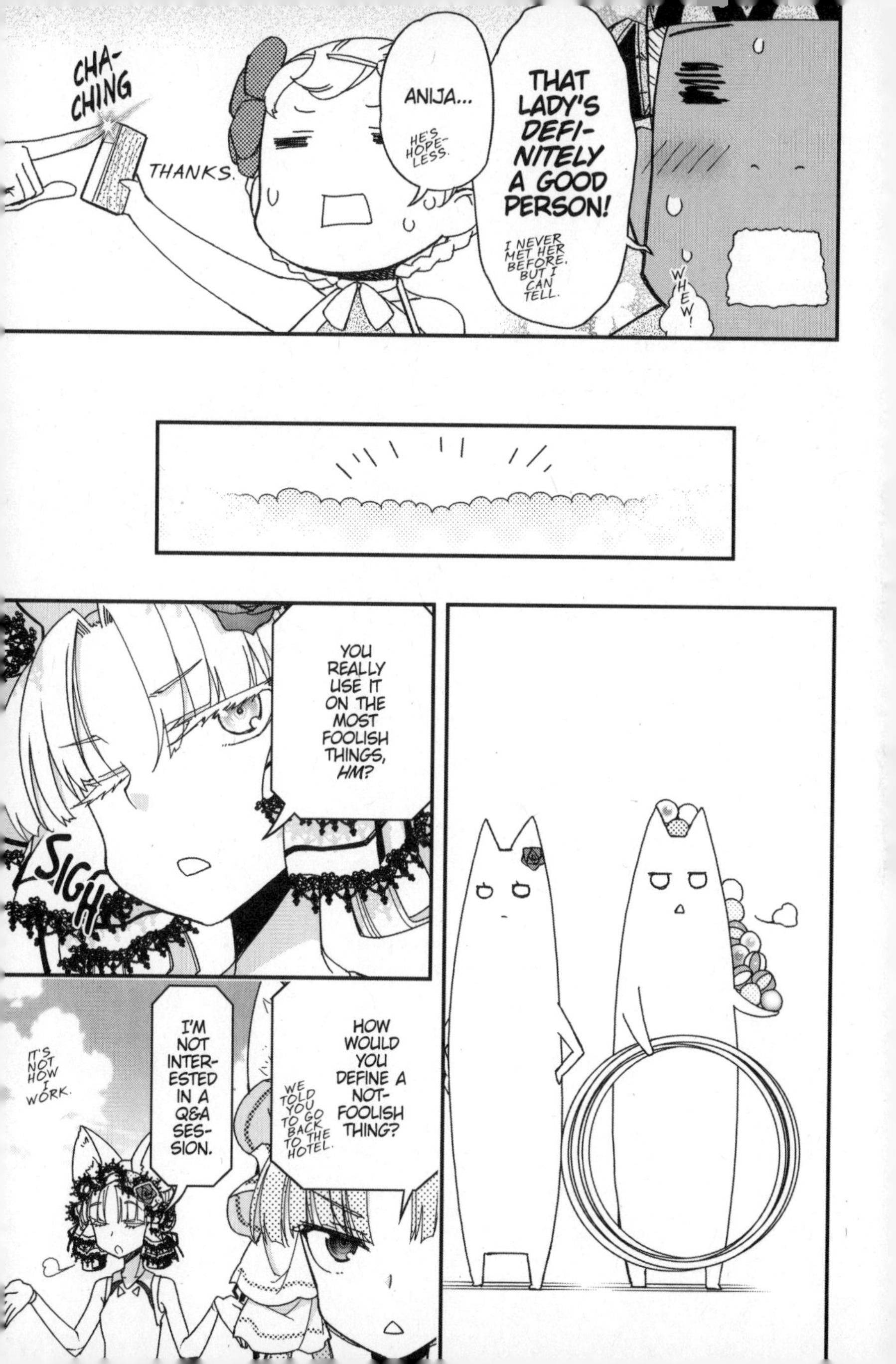
THAT LADY'S DEFINITELY A GOOD PERSON!
I NEVER MET HER BEFORE, BUT I CAN TELL.
WHEW!
ANIJA...
HE'S HOPELESS.
THANKS.
CHA-CHING
YOU REALLY USE IT ON THE MOST FOOLISH THINGS, HM?
SIGH
HOW WOULD YOU DEFINE A NOT-FOOLISH THING?
WE TOLD YOU TO GO BACK TO THE HOTEL.
I'M NOT INTERESTED IN A Q&A SESSION.
IT'S NOT HOW I WORK.

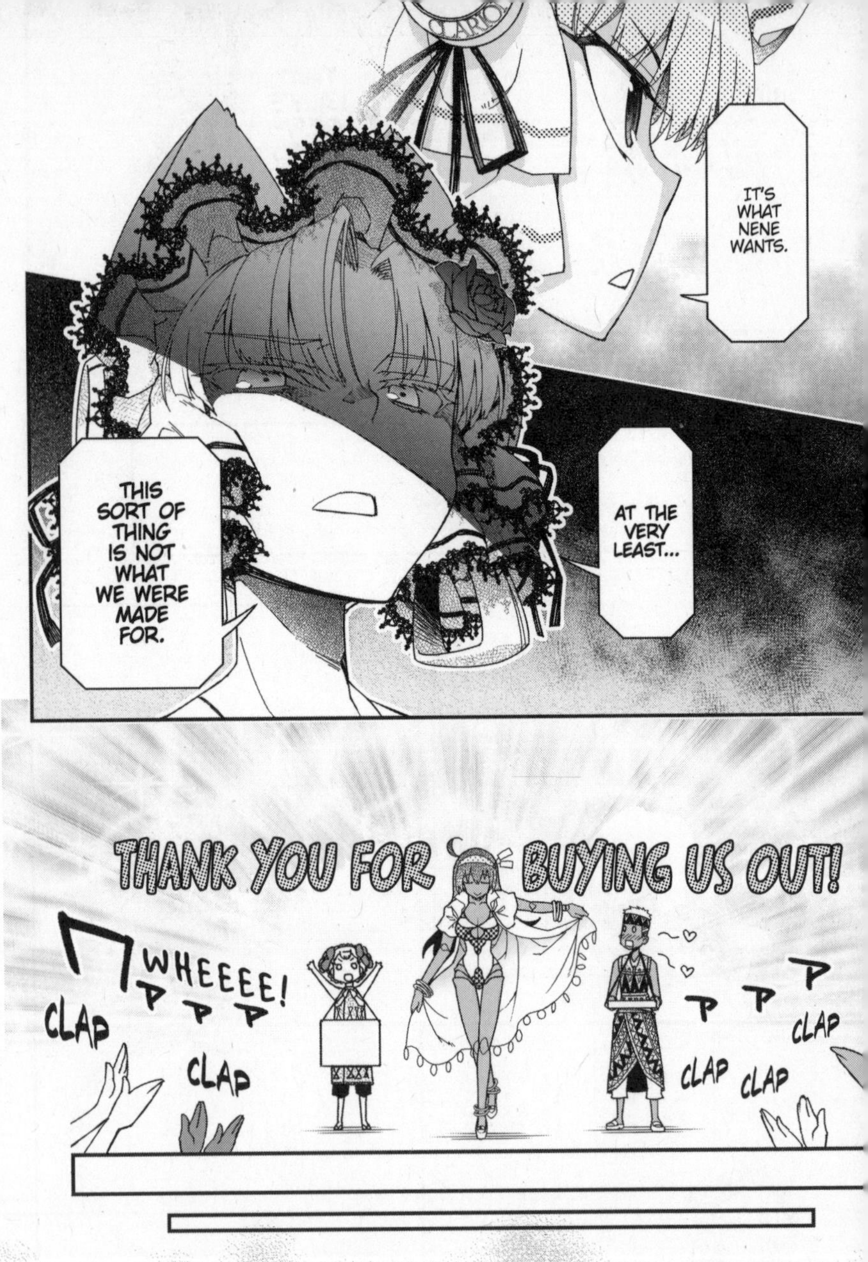
IT'S WHAT NENE WANTS.
AT THE VERY LEAST...
THIS SORT OF THING IS NOT WHAT WE WERE MADE FOR.
THANK YOU FOR BUYING US OUT!
CLAP
CLAP
CLAP
CLAP
WHEEEEE!
CLAP
CLAP

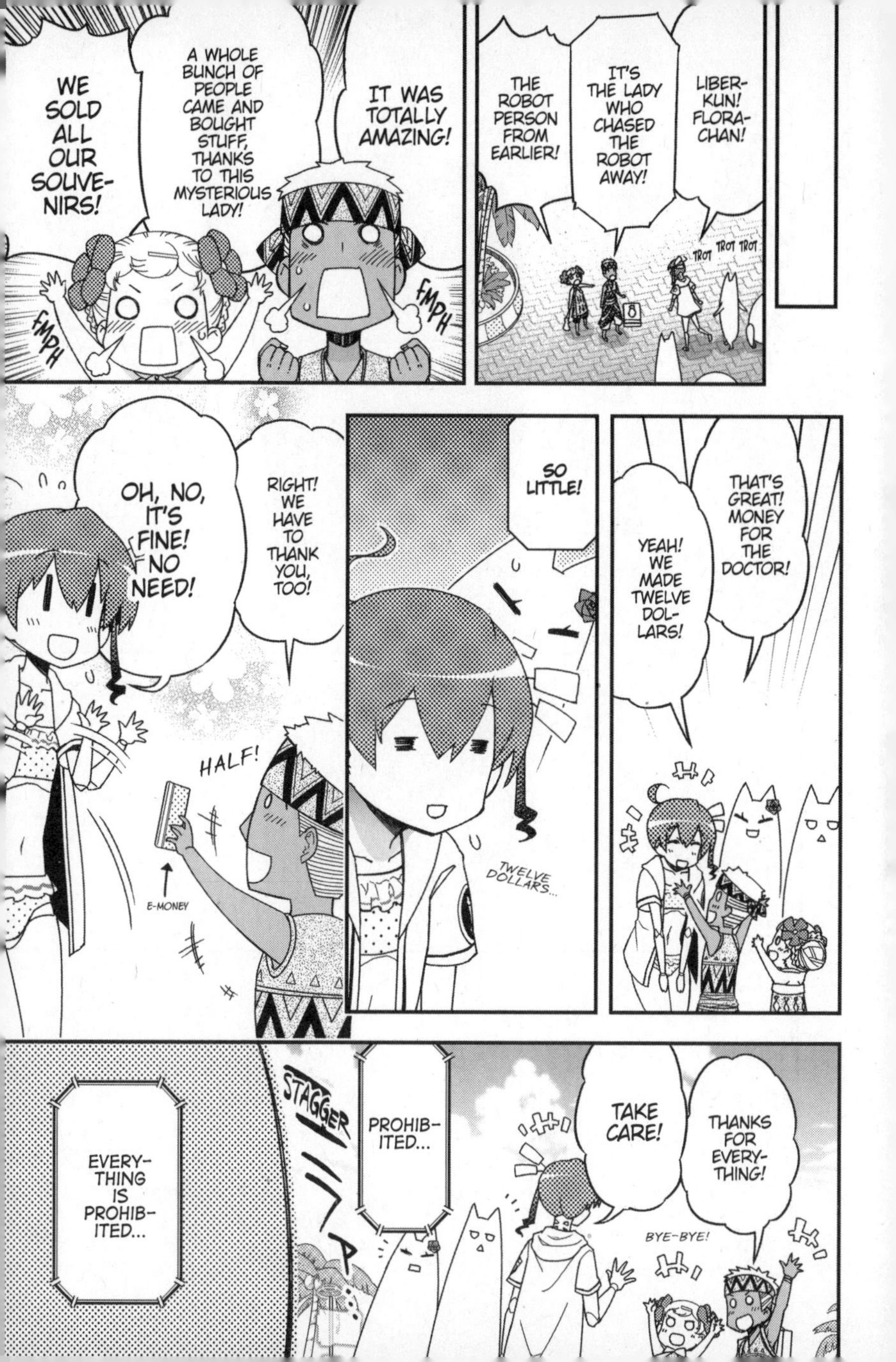
LIBER-KUN! FLORA-CHAN!
IT'S THE LADY WHO CHASED THE ROBOT AWAY!
THE ROBOT PERSON FROM EARLIER!
TROT TROT TROT
IT WAS TOTALLY AMAZING!
A WHOLE BUNCH OF PEOPLE CAME AND BOUGHT STUFF, THANKS TO THIS MYSTERIOUS LADY!
WE SOLD ALL OUR SOUVENIRS!
FMPH
FMPH
THAT'S GREAT! MONEY FOR THE DOCTOR!
YEAH! WE MADE TWELVE DOLLARS!
SO LITTLE!
TWELVE DOLLARS...
RIGHT! WE HAVE TO THANK YOU, TOO!
OH, NO, IT'S FINE! NO NEED!
HALF!
E-MONEY
THANKS FOR EVERYTHING!
TAKE CARE!
BYE-BYE!
PROHIBITED...
STAGGER
EVERYTHING IS PROHIBITED...

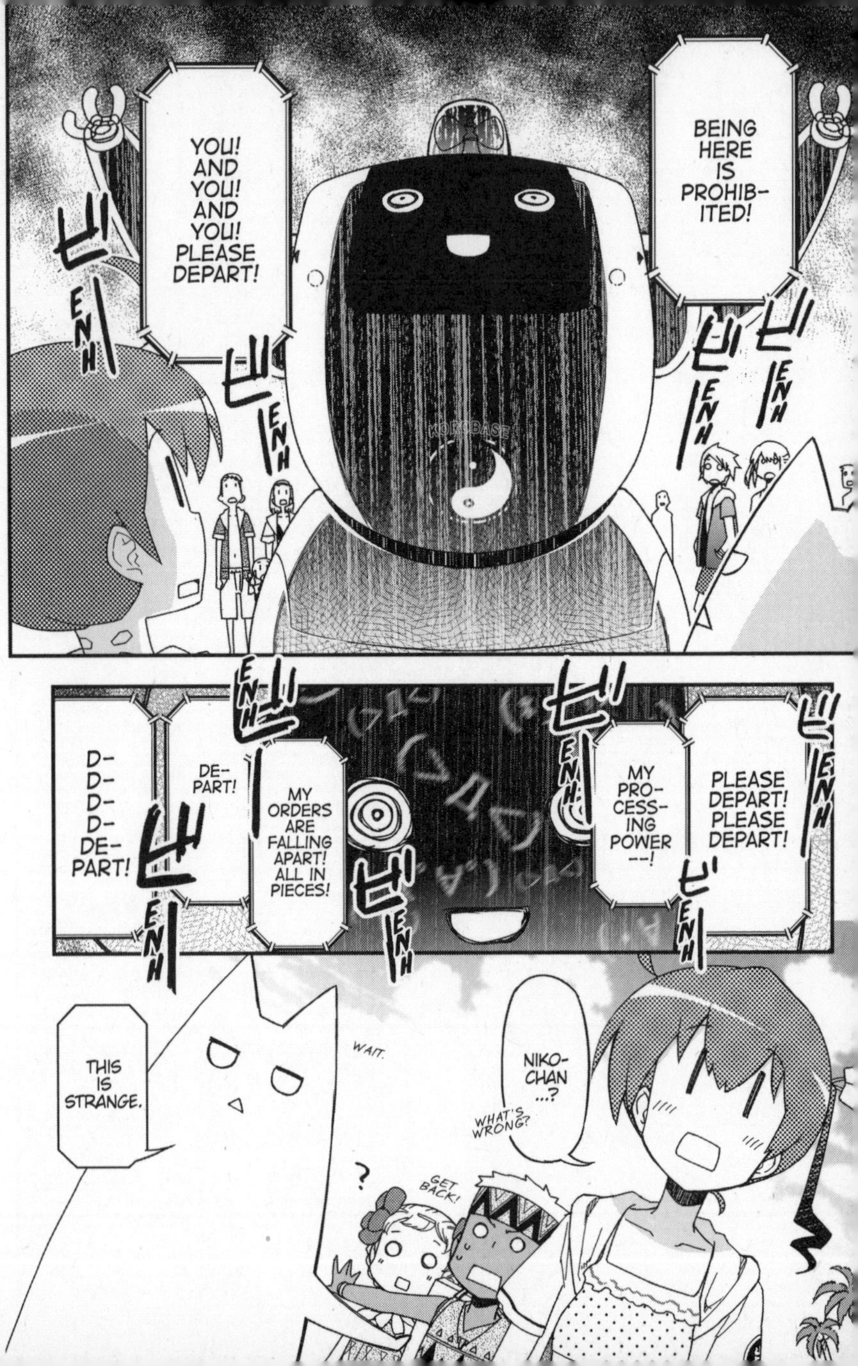
BEING HERE IS PROHIB-ITED!
ENH
ENH
YOU! AND YOU! AND YOU! PLEASE DEPART!
ENH
ENH
KOROBASE
PLEASE DEPART! PLEASE DEPART!
ENH
ENH
MY PRO-CESS-ING POWER--!
ENH
ENH
MY ORDERS ARE FALLING APART! ALL IN PIECES!
ENH
DE-PART!
ENH
D-D-D-D-DE-PART!
NIKO-CHAN...?
WHAT'S WRONG?
GET BACK!
?
WAIT.
THIS IS STRANGE.

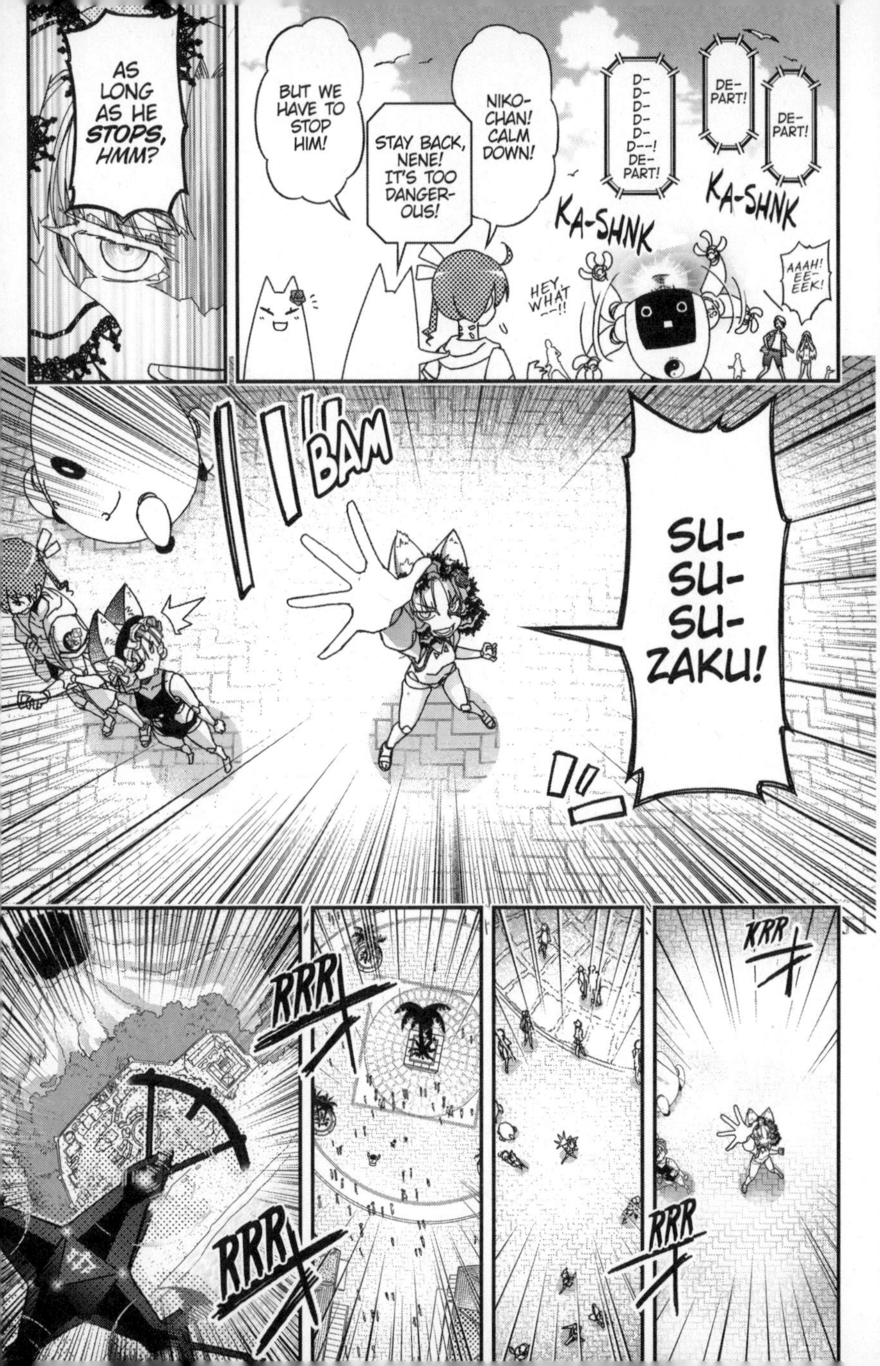
DE-PART!
DE-PART!
D-D-D-D-D-D--! DE-PART!
KA-SHNK
KA-SHNK
AAAH! EEE-EEK!
HEY, WHAT--!!
NIKO-CHAN! CALM DOWN!
STAY BACK, NENE! IT'S TOO DANGER-OUS!
BUT WE HAVE TO STOP HIM!
AS LONG AS HE STOPS, HMM?
SU-SU-SU-ZAKU!
BAM
KRR
RRR
RRR
RRR

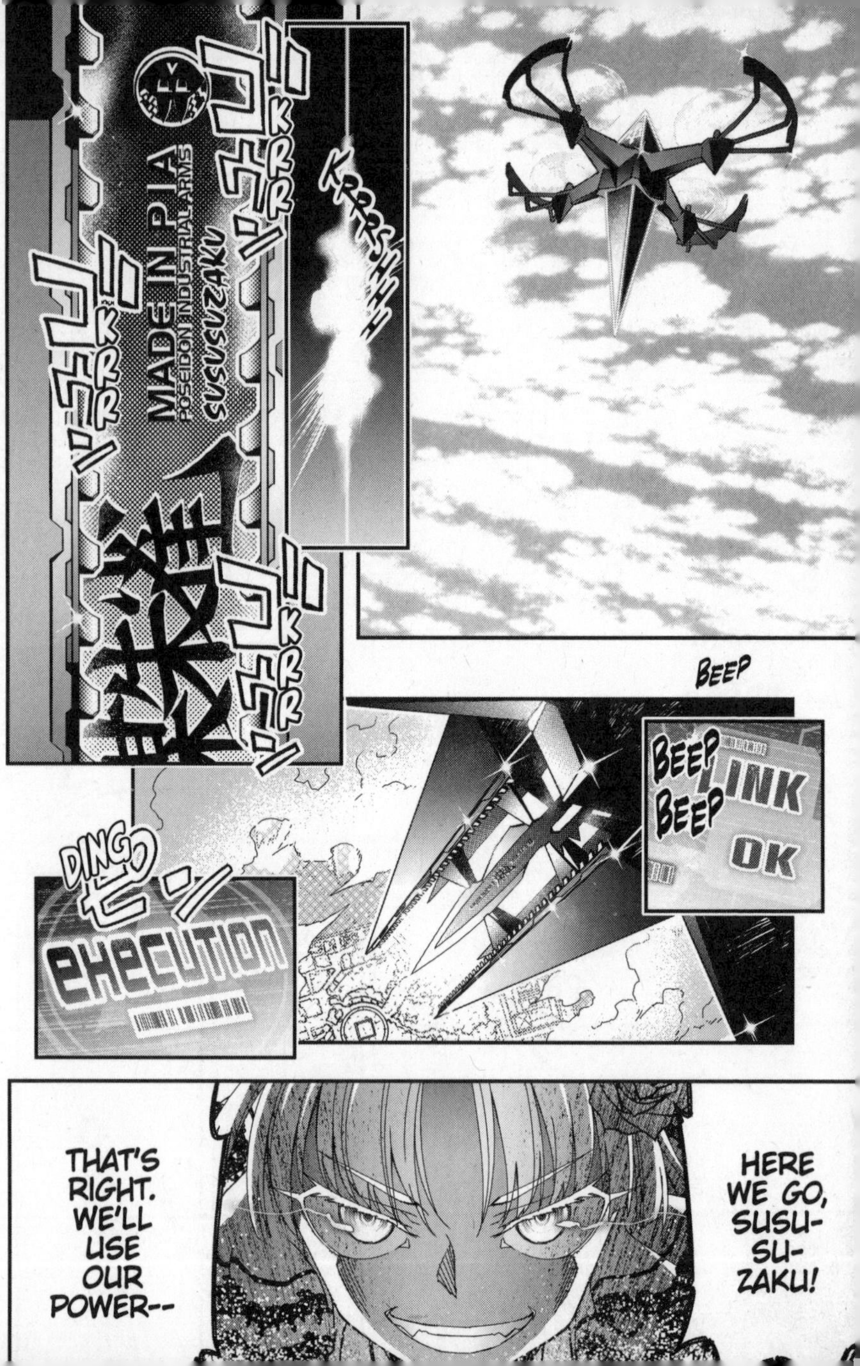
KRRR
KRRRSHHH
KRRR
MADE IN PIA
POSEIDON INDUSTRIAL ARMS
SUSUSUZAKU
KRRR
BEEP
BEEP BEEP
LINK OK
DING
EXECUTION
HERE WE GO, SUSU-SU-ZAKU!
THAT'S RIGHT. WE'LL USE OUR POWER--

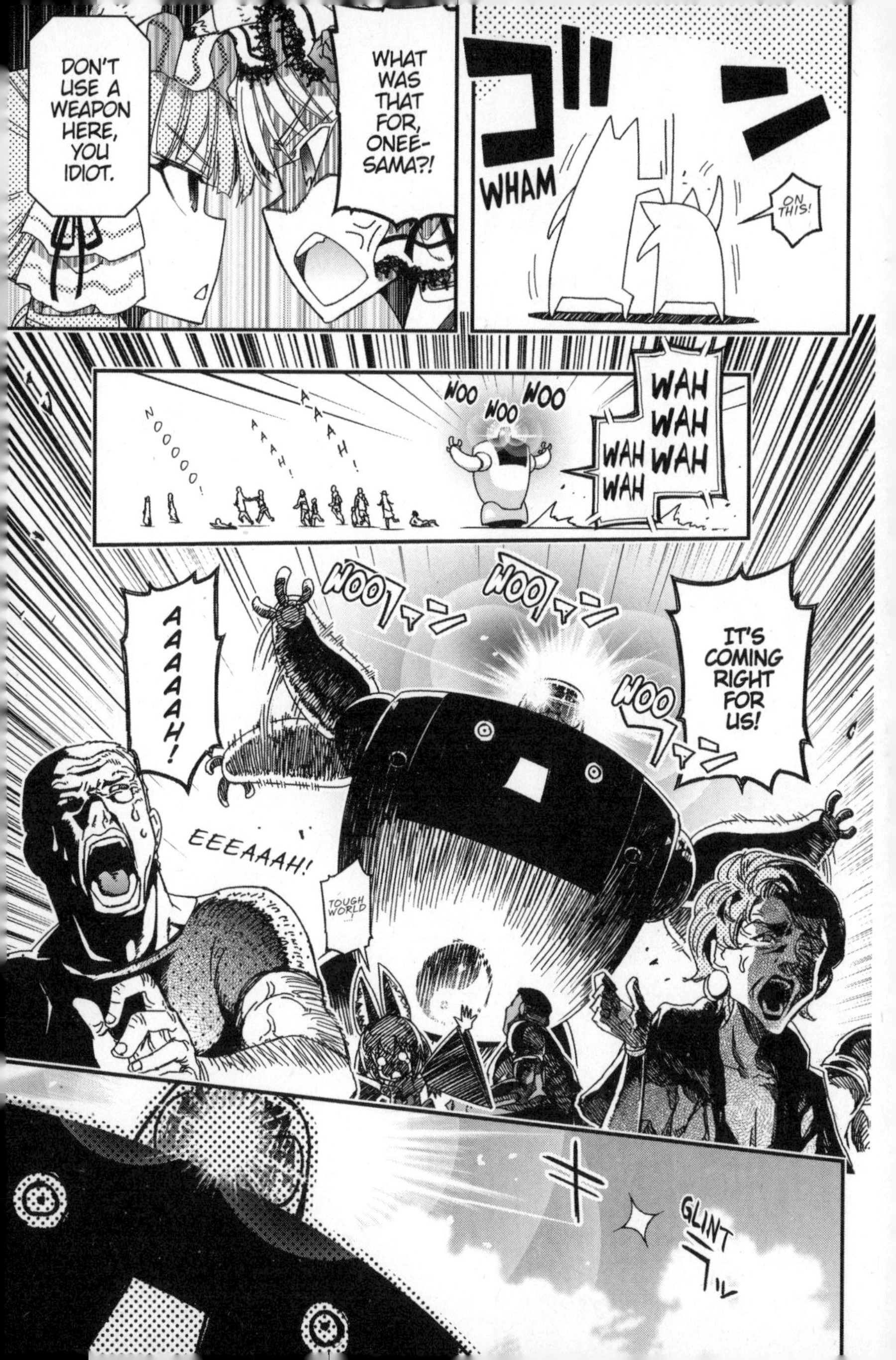
ゴン
WHAM
ON THIS!
WHAT WAS THAT FOR, ONEE-SAMA?!
DON'T USE A WEAPON HERE, YOU IDIOT.
WAH WAH WAH
WAH WAH
WOO WOO WOO
AAAAH!
AAAAH!
NOOOOOO!
IT'S COMING RIGHT FOR US!
WOO ファン
WOO ファン
WOO ファン
AAAAAAH!
EEEAAAH!
TOUGH WORLD...
GLINT

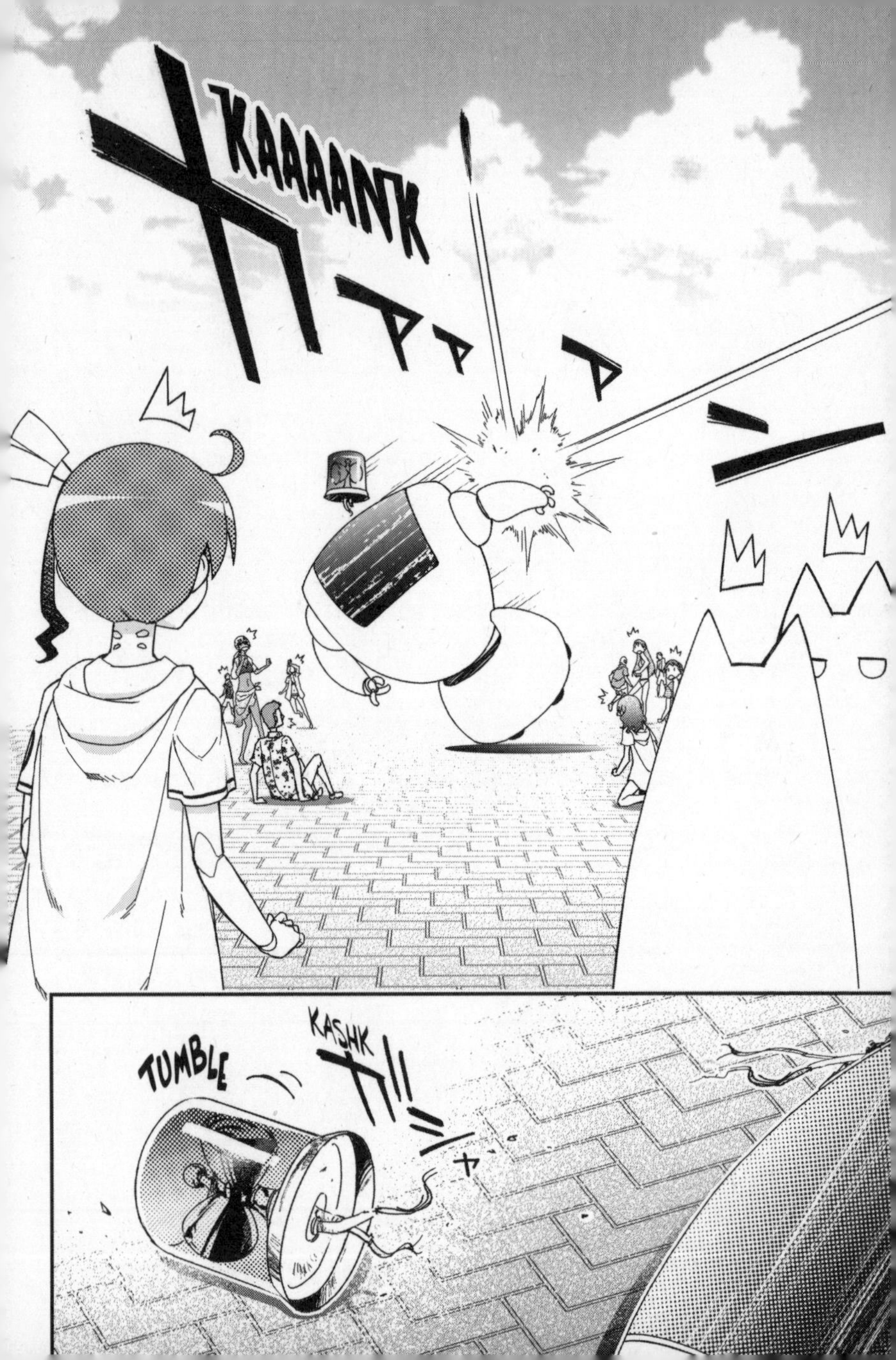
KAAAANK
KASHK
TUMBLE

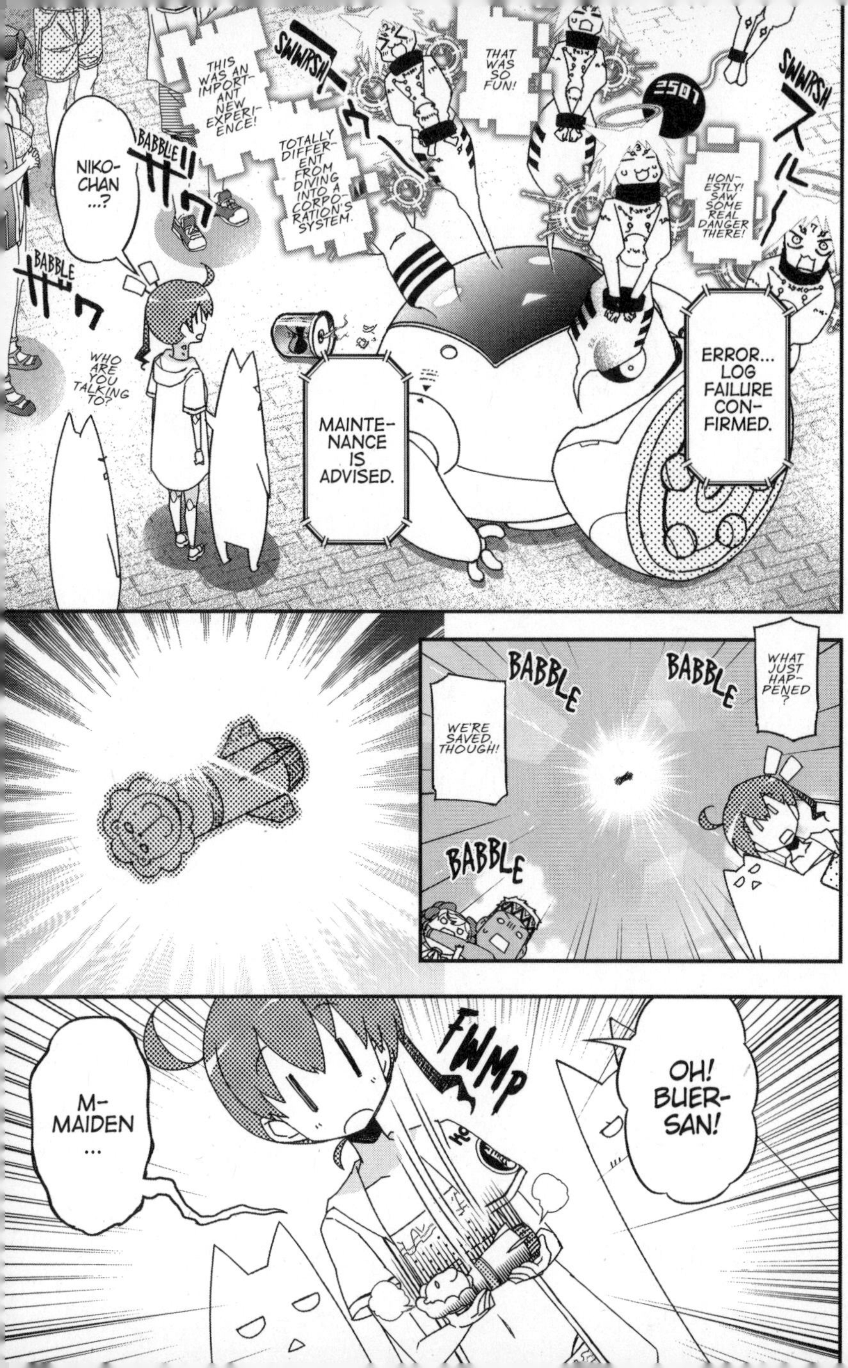
SWWRSH
HONESTLY! SAW SOME REAL DANGER THERE!
ERROR... LOG FAILURE CONFIRMED.
2501
THAT WAS SO FUN!
MAINTENANCE IS ADVISED.
TOTALLY DIFFERENT FROM DIVING INTO A CORPORATION'S SYSTEM.
THIS WAS AN IMPORTANT NEW EXPERIENCE!
SWWRSH
BABBLE
NIKO-CHAN ...?
BABBLE
WHO ARE YOU TALKING TO?
WHAT JUST HAPPENED?
BABBLE
WE'RE SAVED, THOUGH!
BABBLE
BABBLE
OH! BUER-SAN!
FWMP
M-MAIDEN ...

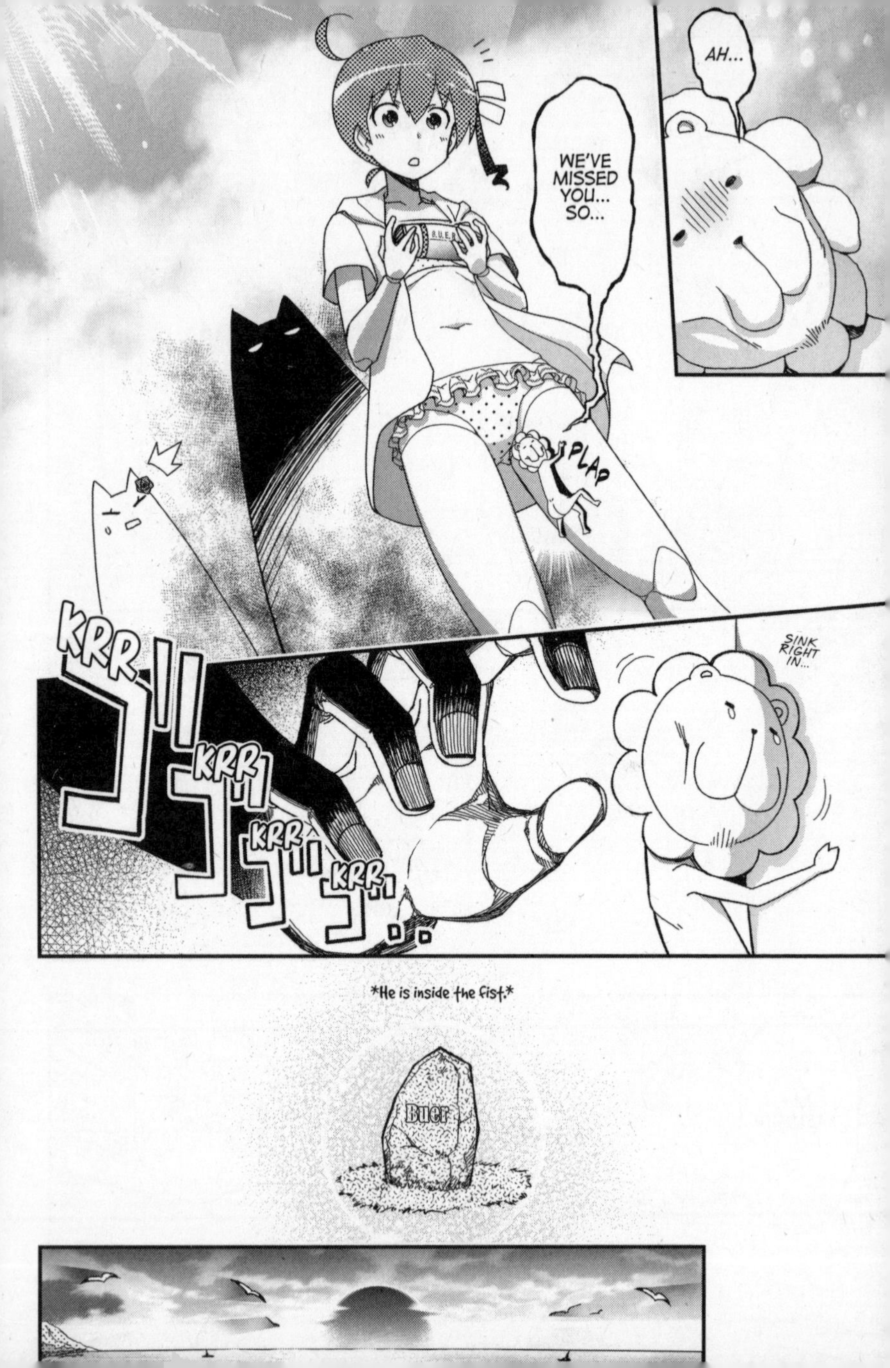
AH...
WE'VE MISSED YOU... SO...
PLAP
SINK RIGHT IN...
KRR
KRR
KRR
KRR
He is inside the fist.
Buer

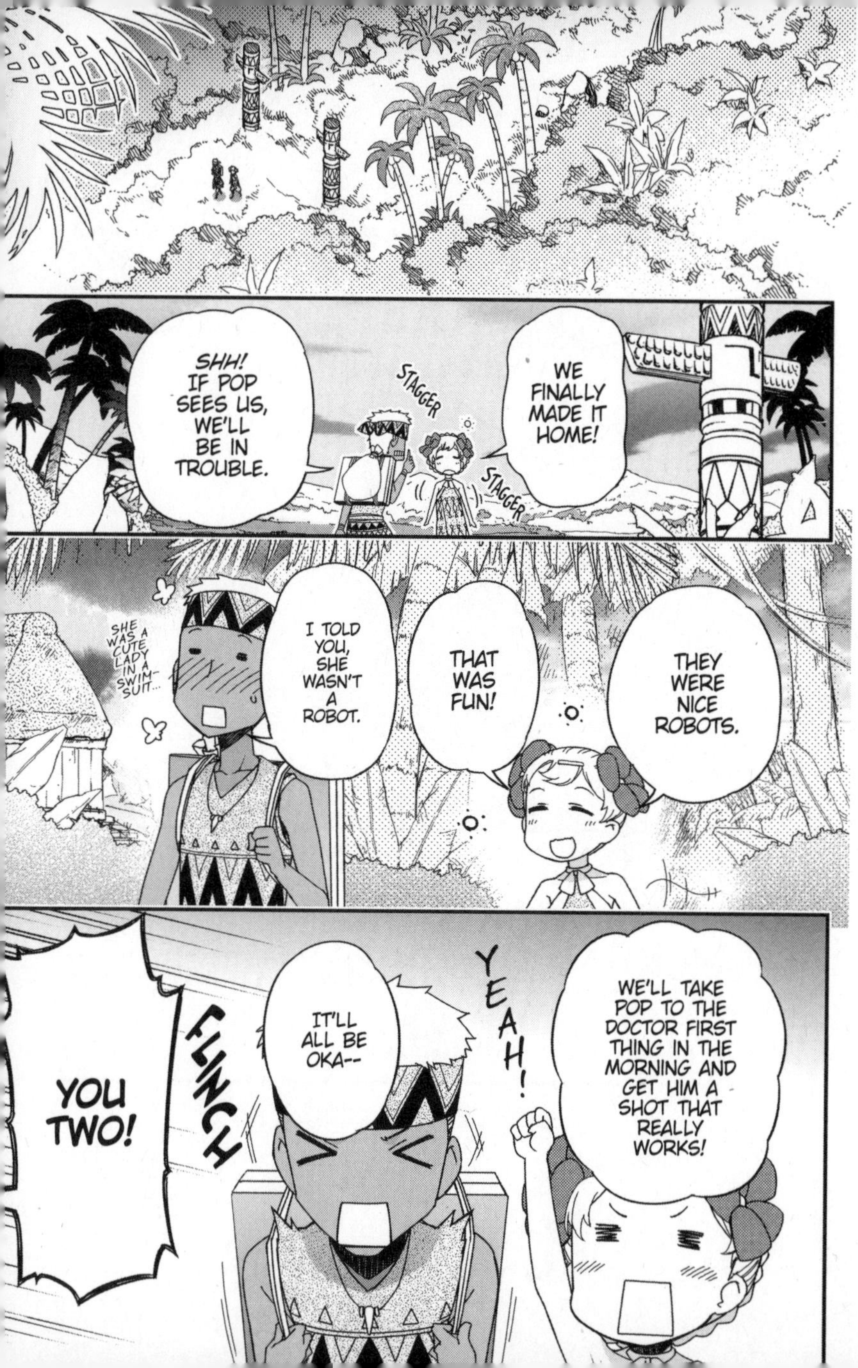
WE FINALLY MADE IT HOME!
STAGGER
STAGGER
SHH! IF POP SEES US, WE'LL BE IN TROUBLE.
THEY WERE NICE ROBOTS.
THAT WAS FUN!
I TOLD YOU, SHE WASN'T A ROBOT.
SHE WAS A CUTE LADY IN A SWIMSUIT...
WE'LL TAKE POP TO THE DOCTOR FIRST THING IN THE MORNING AND GET HIM A SHOT THAT REALLY WORKS!
YEAH!
IT'LL ALL BE OKA--
FLINCH
YOU TWO!

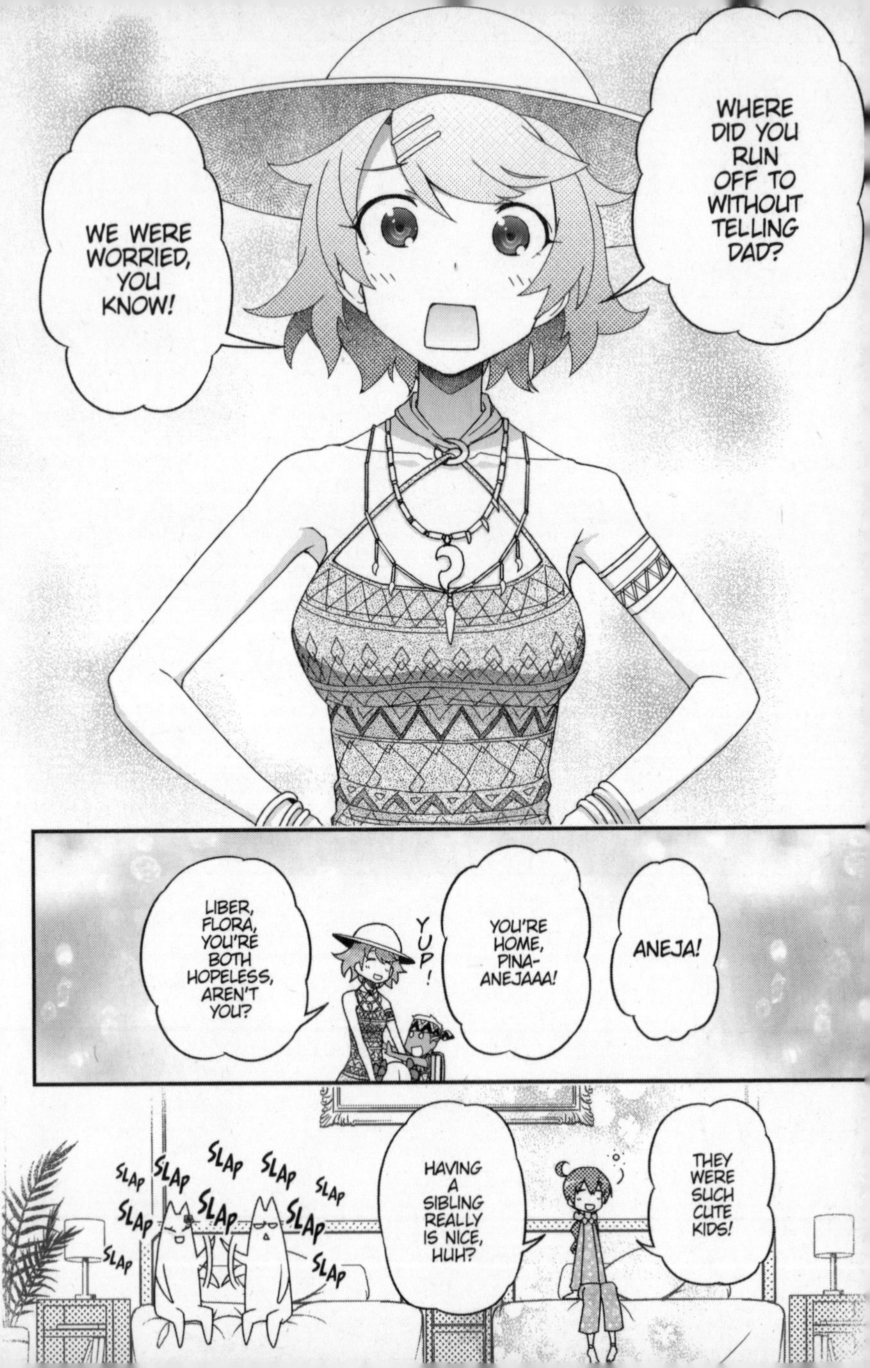
WHERE DID YOU RUN OFF TO WITHOUT TELLING DAD?
WE WERE WORRIED, YOU KNOW!
ANEJA!
YOU'RE HOME, PINA-ANEJAAA!
YUP!
LIBER, FLORA, YOU'RE BOTH HOPELESS, AREN'T YOU?
THEY WERE SUCH CUTE KIDS!
HAVING A SIBLING REALLY IS NICE, HUH?
SLAP SLAP SLAP SLAP SLAP SLAP SLAP SLAP SLAP SLAP

GHOST URN

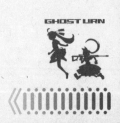

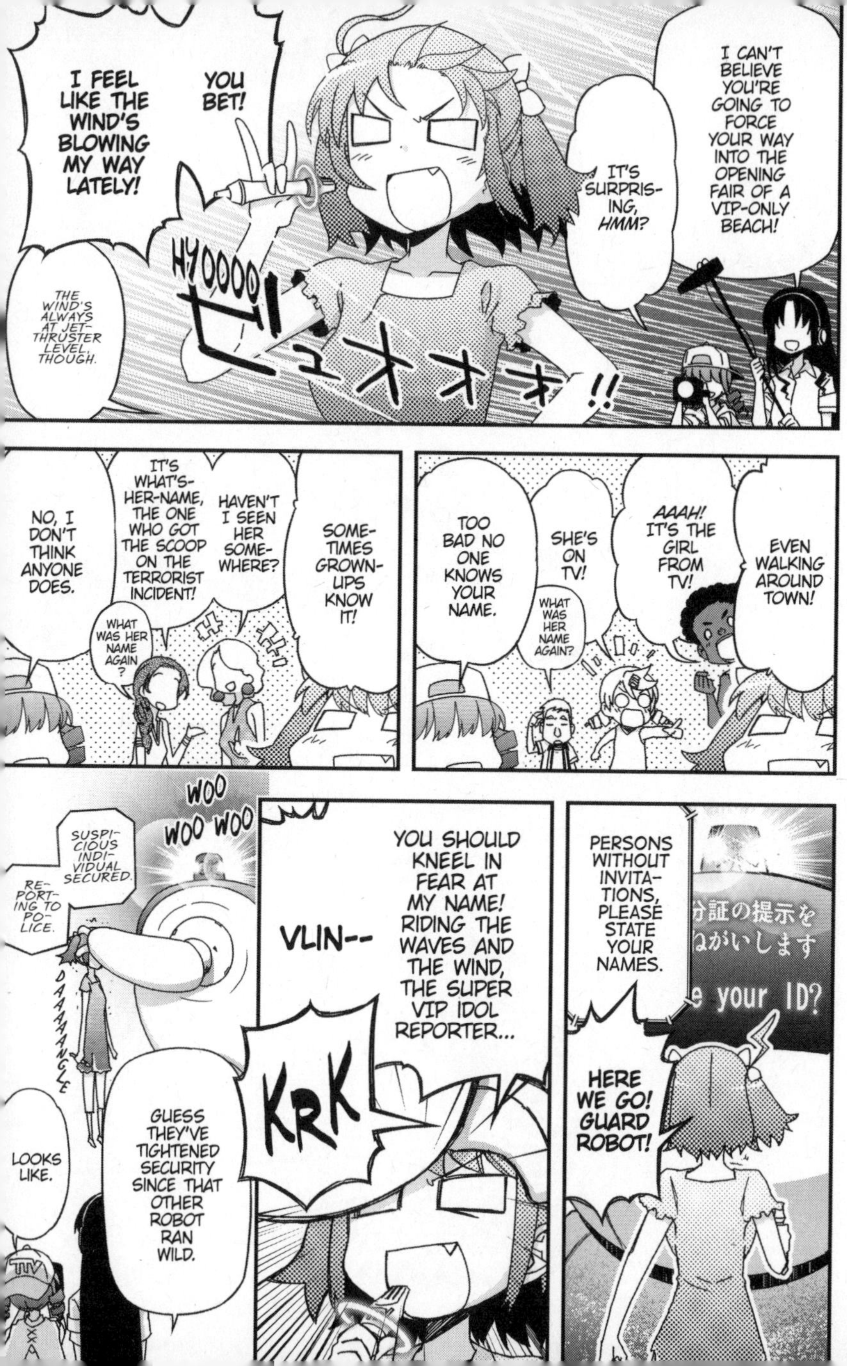
I CAN'T BELIEVE YOU'RE GOING TO FORCE YOUR WAY INTO THE OPENING FAIR OF A VIP-ONLY BEACH!
IT'S SURPRISING, *HMM?*
YOU BET!
I FEEL LIKE THE WIND'S BLOWING MY WAY LATELY!
HYOOOO
THE WIND'S ALWAYS AT JET-THRUSTER LEVEL, THOUGH.
EVEN WALKING AROUND TOWN!
AAAH! IT'S THE GIRL FROM TV!
SHE'S ON TV!
WHAT WAS HER NAME AGAIN?
TOO BAD NO ONE KNOWS YOUR NAME.
SOMETIMES GROWN-UPS KNOW IT!
HAVEN'T I SEEN HER SOMEWHERE?
IT'S WHAT'S-HER-NAME, THE ONE WHO GOT THE SCOOP ON THE TERRORIST INCIDENT!
WHAT WAS HER NAME AGAIN?
NO, I DON'T THINK ANYONE DOES.
分証の提示を
ねがいします
e your ID?
PERSONS WITHOUT INVITATIONS, PLEASE STATE YOUR NAMES.
HERE WE GO! GUARD ROBOT!
YOU SHOULD KNEEL IN FEAR AT MY NAME! RIDING THE WAVES AND THE WIND, THE SUPER VIP IDOL REPORTER...
VLIN--
KRK
WOO WOO WOO
SUSPICIOUS INDIVIDUAL SECURED.
REPORTING TO POLICE.
DAAAAAANGLE
GUESS THEY'VE TIGHTENED SECURITY SINCE THAT OTHER ROBOT RAN WILD.
LOOKS LIKE.
TTV

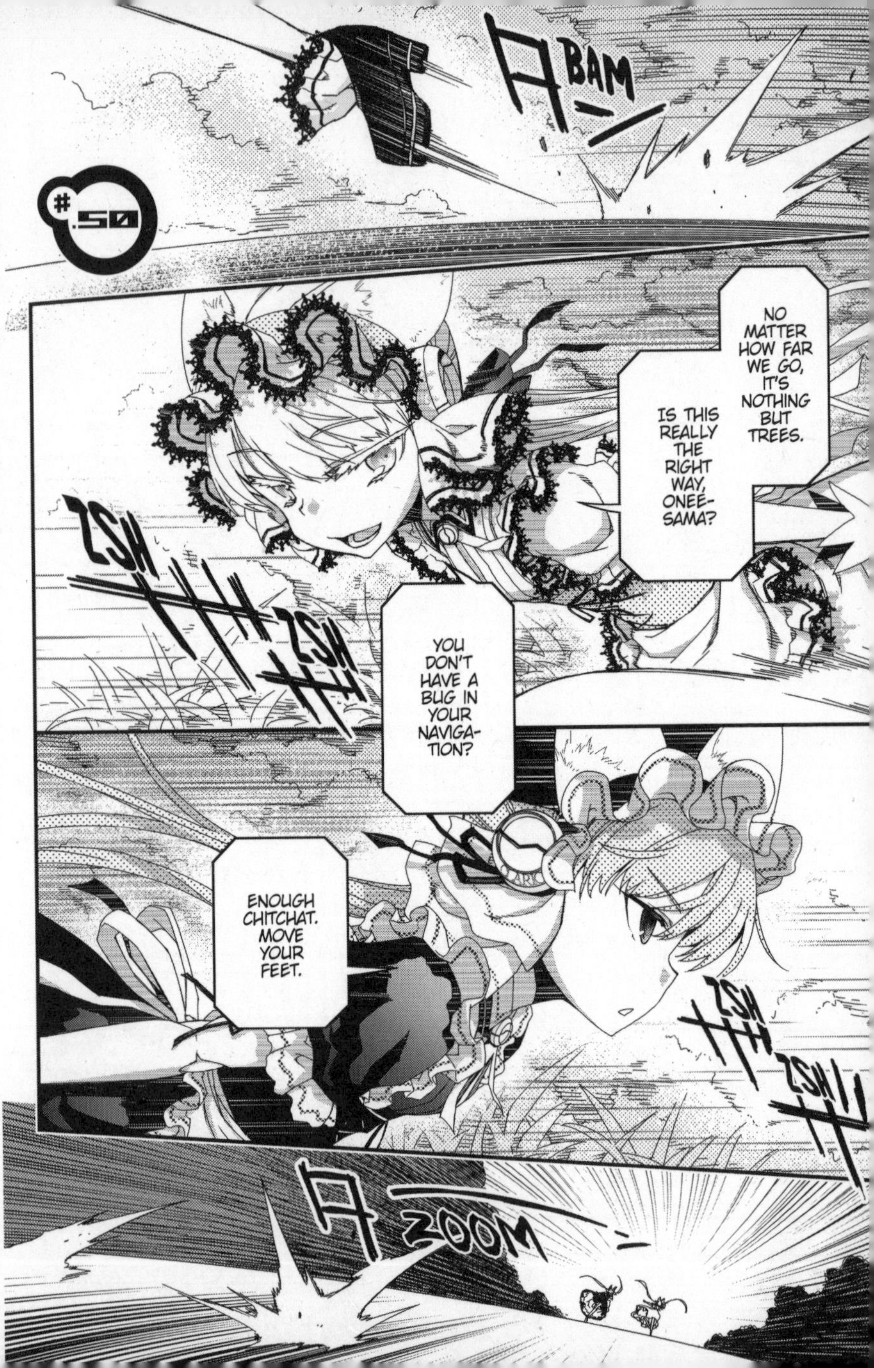
BAM
#.50
NO MATTER HOW FAR WE GO, IT'S NOTHING BUT TREES.
IS THIS REALLY THE RIGHT WAY, ONEE-SAMA?
ZSH
ZSH
YOU DON'T HAVE A BUG IN YOUR NAVIGATION?
ZSH
ZSH
ENOUGH CHITCHAT. MOVE YOUR FEET.
ZOOM

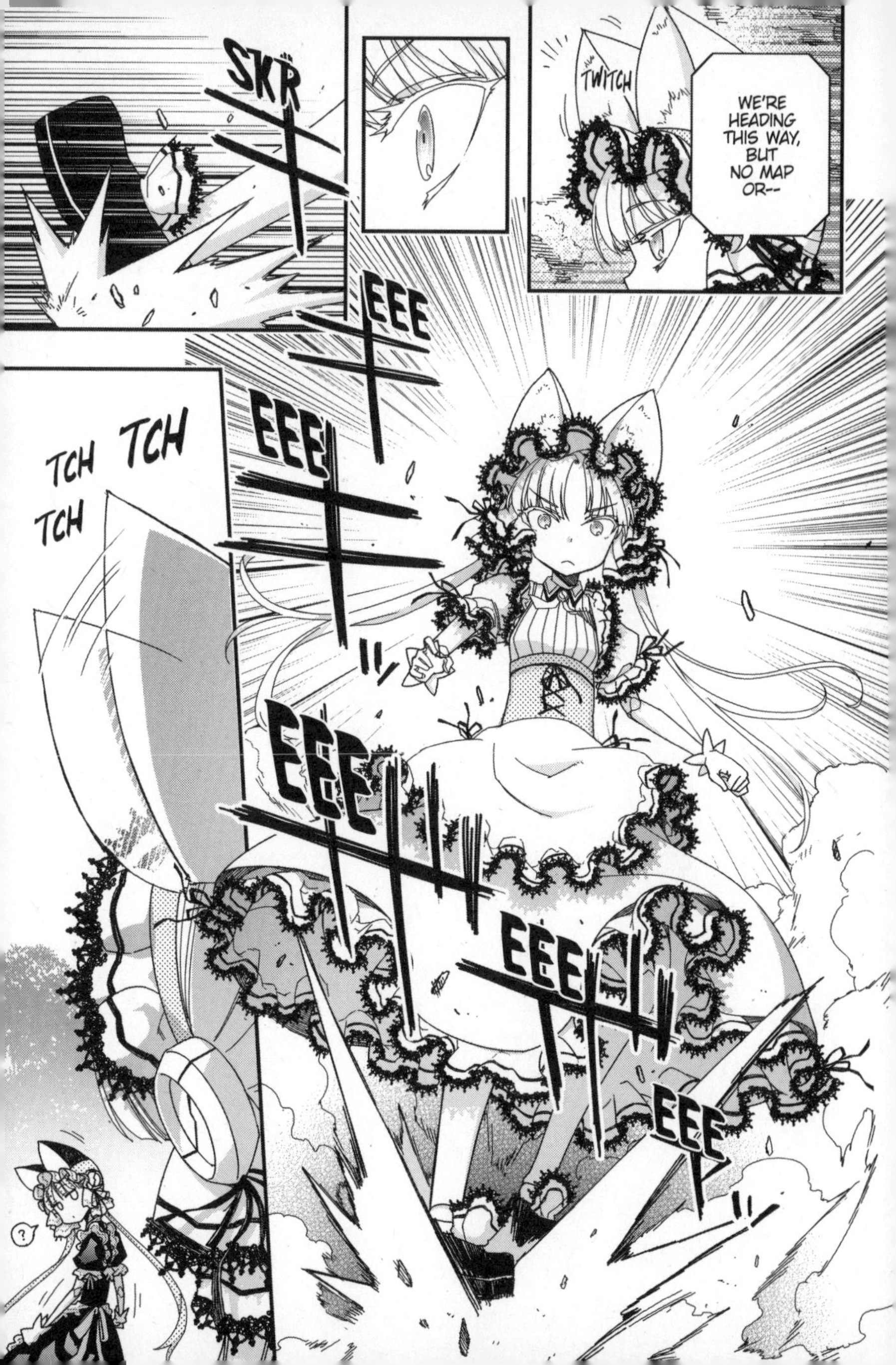
TWITCH
WE'RE HEADING THIS WAY, BUT NO MAP OR--
SKR
EEE
EEE
EEE
EEE
EEE
TCH TCH TCH
?

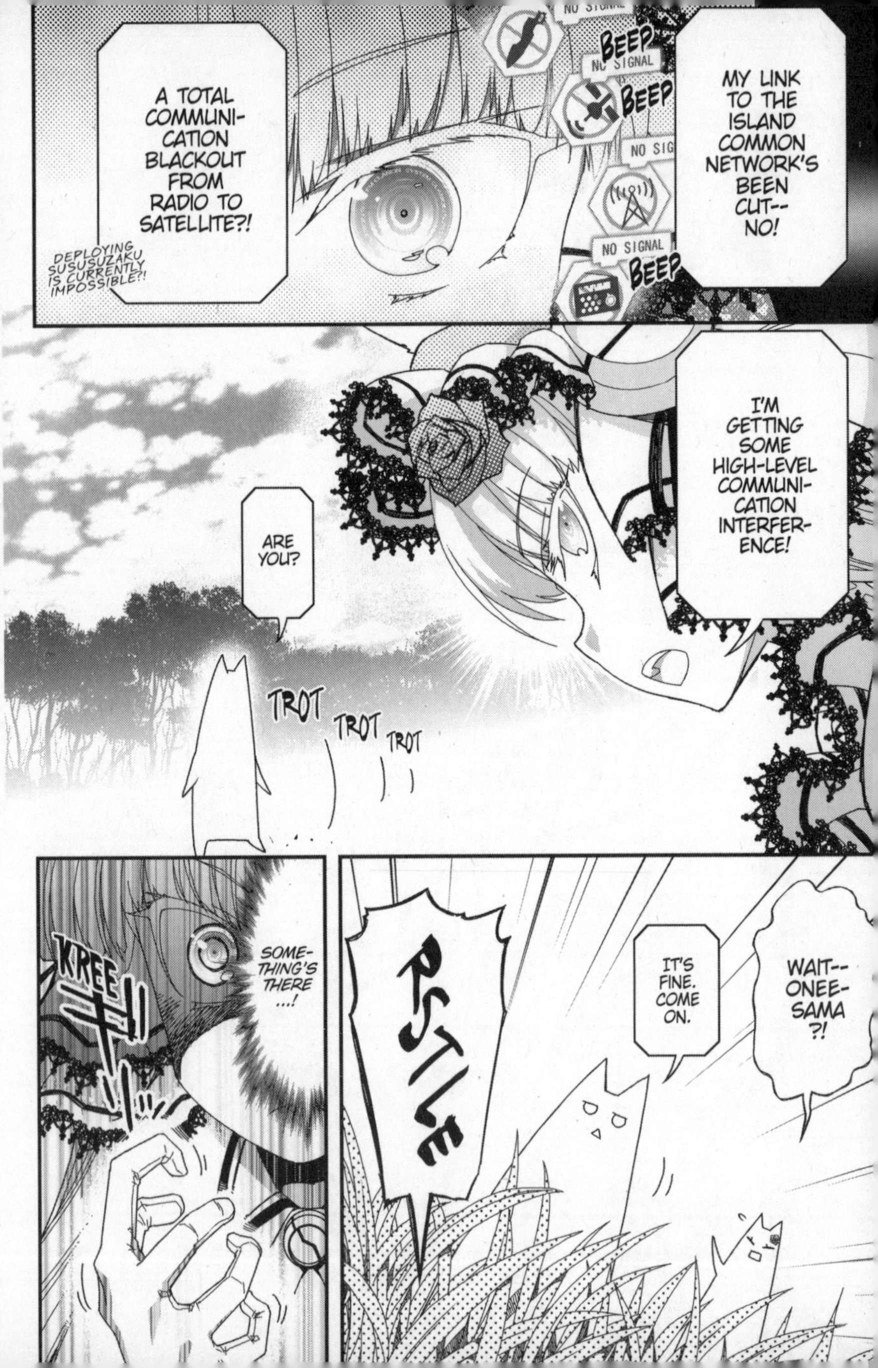
MY LINK TO THE ISLAND COMMON NETWORK'S BEEN CUT-- NO!
BEEP
NO SIGNAL
BEEP
BEEP
NO SIGNAL
A TOTAL COMMUNICATION BLACKOUT FROM RADIO TO SATELLITE?!
DEPLOYING SUSUSUZAKU IS CURRENTLY IMPOSSIBLE?!
I'M GETTING SOME HIGH-LEVEL COMMUNICATION INTERFERENCE!
ARE YOU?
TROT
TROT
TROT
WAIT-- ONEE-SAMA?!
IT'S FINE. COME ON.
RSTLE
SOMETHING'S THERE...!
KREE

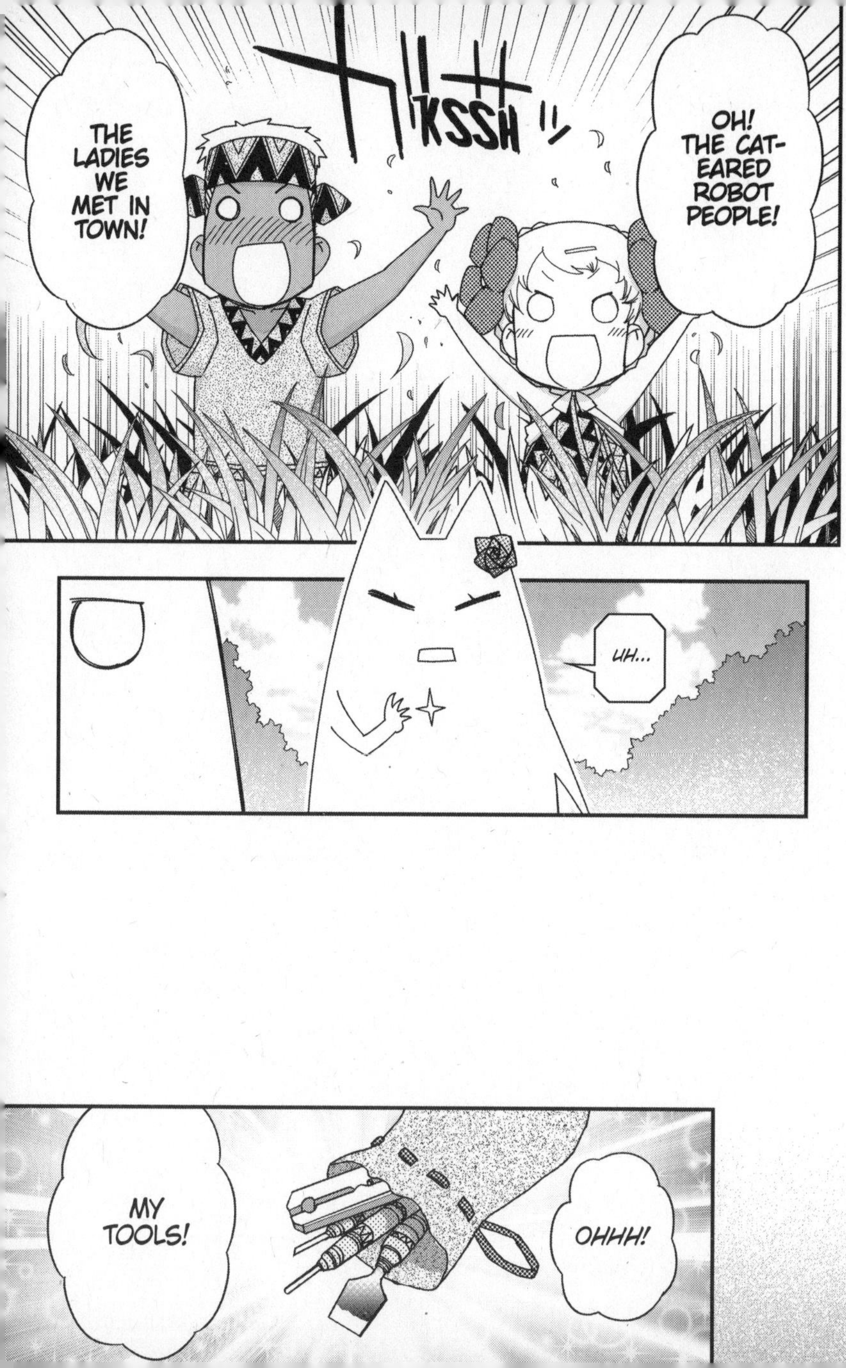
OH! THE CAT-EARED ROBOT PEOPLE!
KSSH
THE LADIES WE MET IN TOWN!
UH...
OHHH!
MY TOOLS!

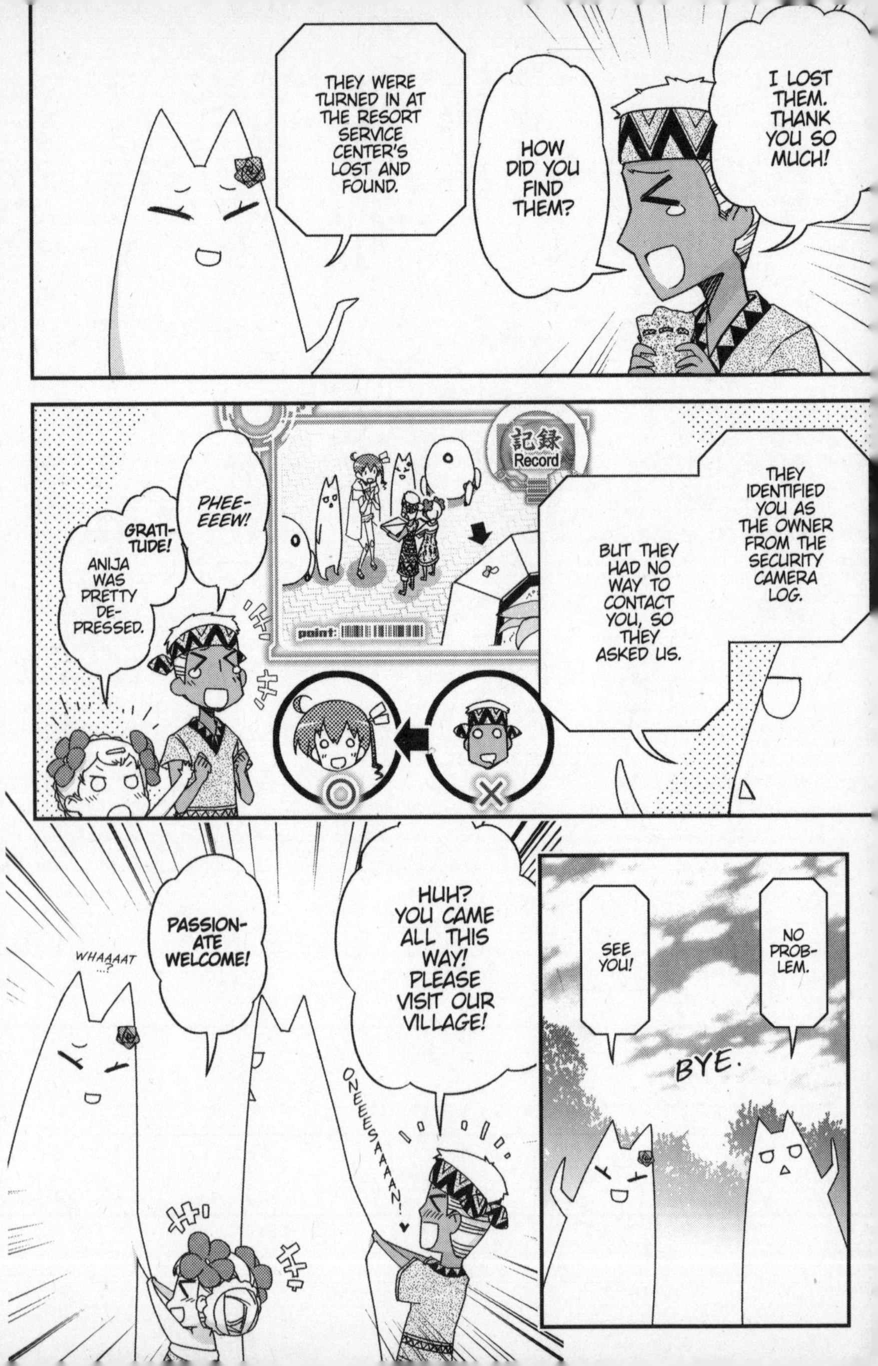
I LOST THEM. THANK YOU SO MUCH!
HOW DID YOU FIND THEM?
THEY WERE TURNED IN AT THE RESORT SERVICE CENTER'S LOST AND FOUND.
THEY IDENTIFIED YOU AS THE OWNER FROM THE SECURITY CAMERA LOG.
BUT THEY HAD NO WAY TO CONTACT YOU, SO THEY ASKED US.
記録
Record
point:
PHEE-EEEW!
GRATI-TUDE! ANIJA WAS PRETTY DE-PRESSED.
NO PROB-LEM.
SEE YOU!
BYE.
HUH? YOU CAME ALL THIS WAY! PLEASE VISIT OUR VILLAGE!
ONEEESAAAAN!
PASSION-ATE WELCOME!
WHAAAAT...?

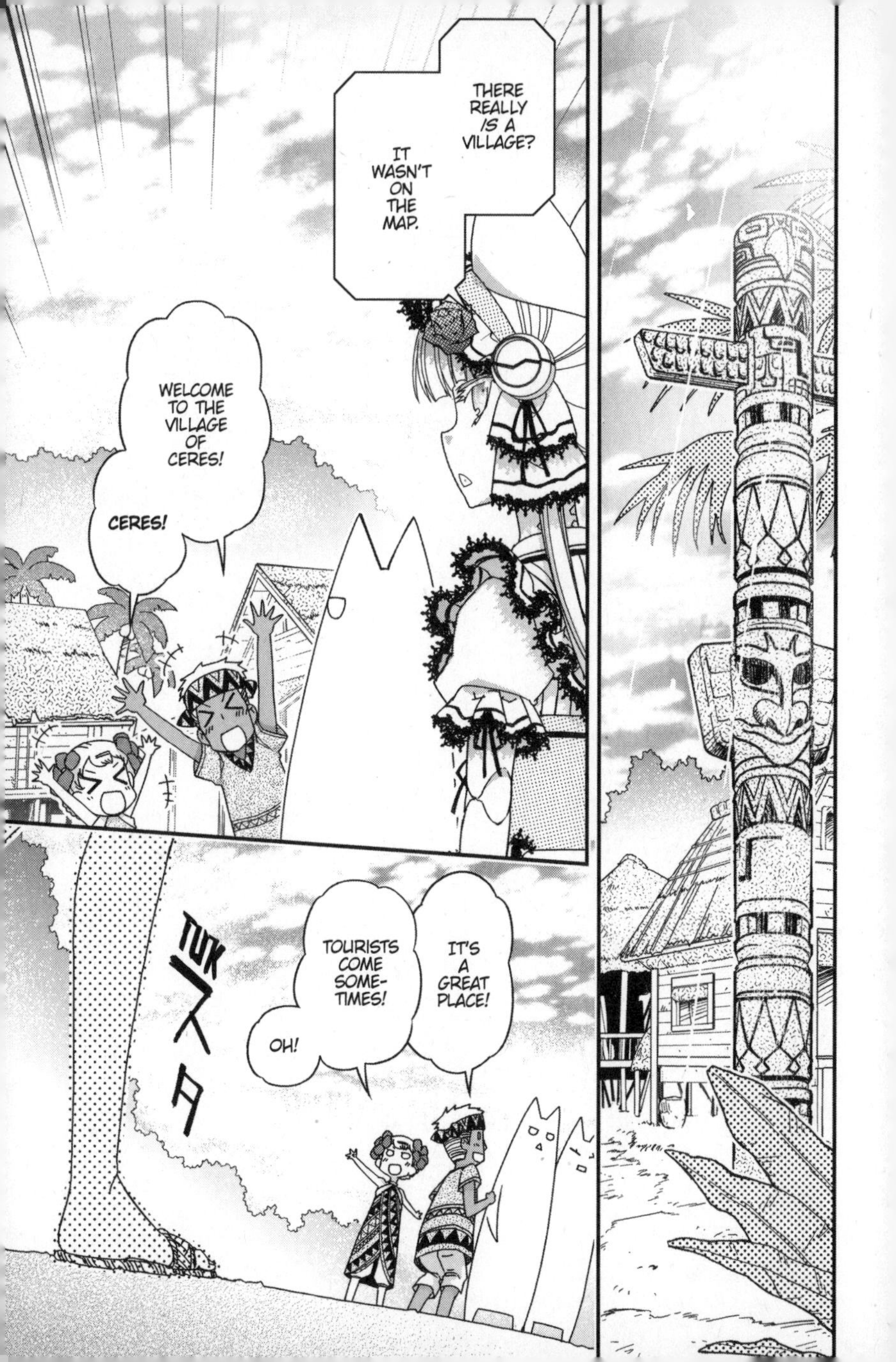
THERE REALLY IS A VILLAGE?
IT WASN'T ON THE MAP.
WELCOME TO THE VILLAGE OF CERES!
CERES!
IT'S A GREAT PLACE!
TOURISTS COME SOME-TIMES!
OH!
TUK

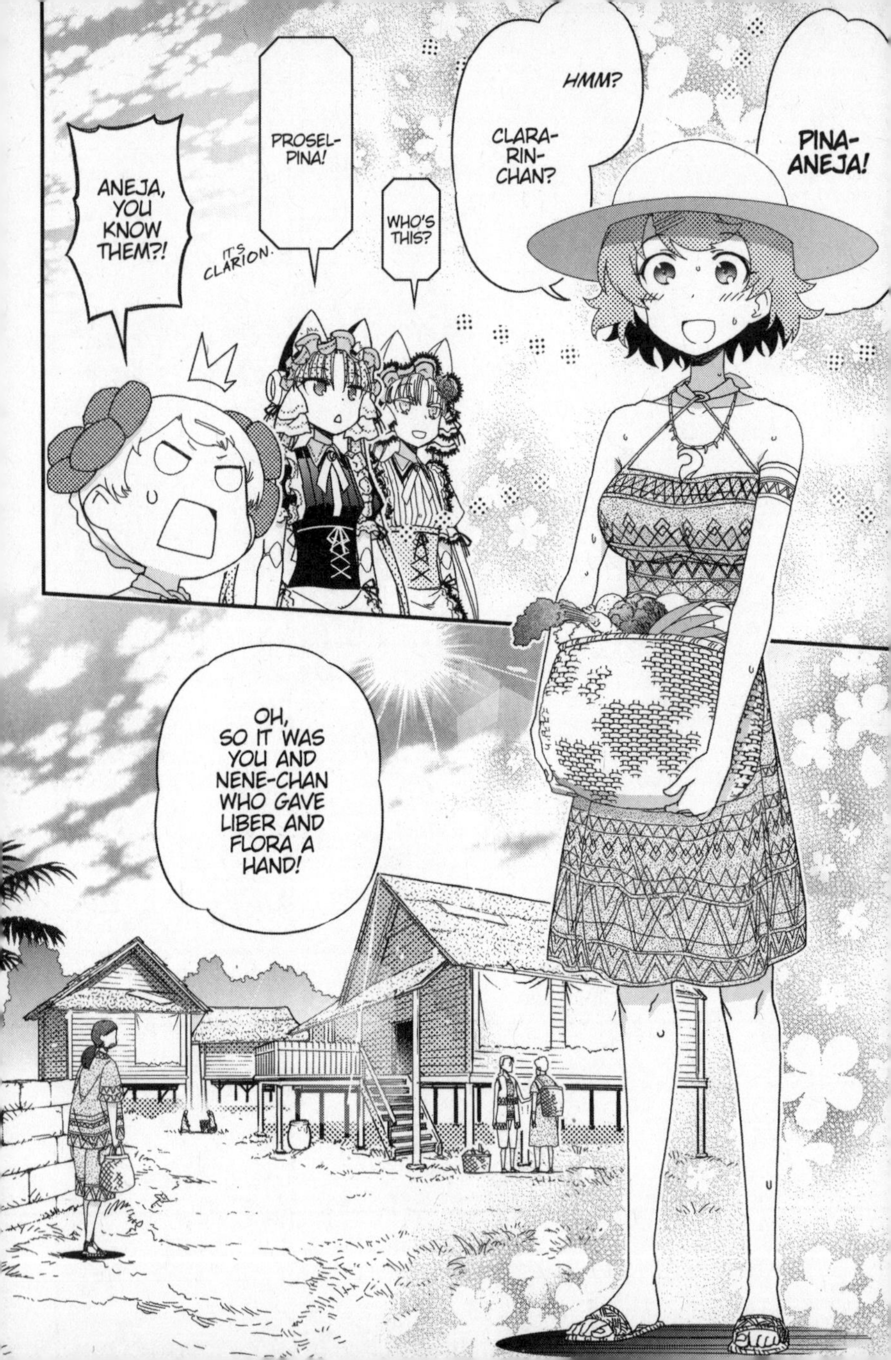
PINA-ANEJA!
HMM? CLARA-RIN-CHAN?
WHO'S THIS?
PROSEL-PINA!
IT'S CLARION.
ANEJA, YOU KNOW THEM?!
OH, SO IT WAS YOU AND NENE-CHAN WHO GAVE LIBER AND FLORA A HAND!

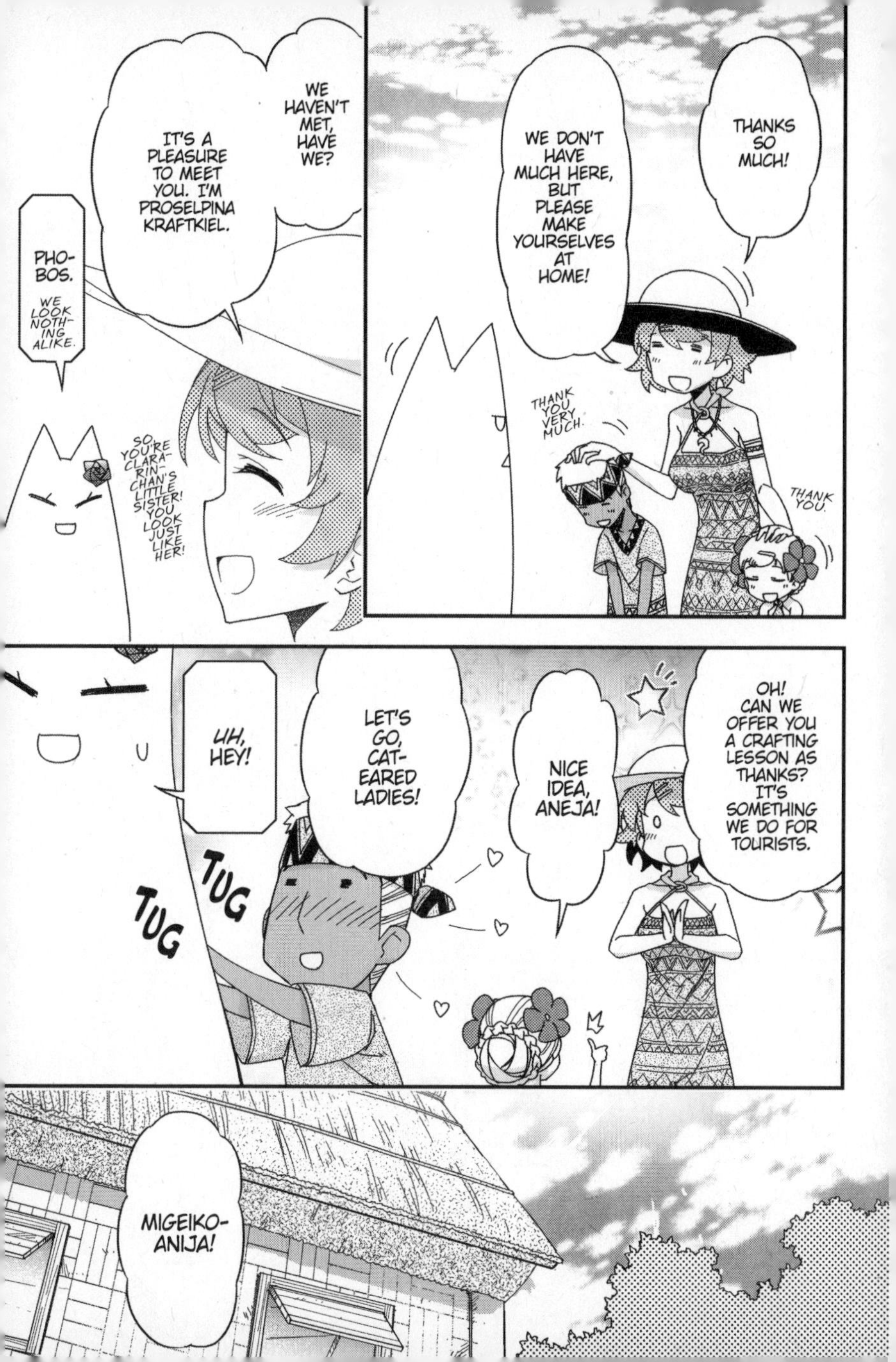
THANKS SO MUCH!
WE DON'T HAVE MUCH HERE, BUT PLEASE MAKE YOURSELVES AT HOME!
THANK YOU.
THANK YOU VERY MUCH.
WE HAVEN'T MET, HAVE WE?
IT'S A PLEASURE TO MEET YOU. I'M PROSELPINA KRAFTKIEL.
SO, YOU'RE CLARA-RIN-CHAN'S LITTLE SISTER! YOU LOOK JUST LIKE HER!
PHO-BOS.
WE LOOK NOTH-ING ALIKE.
OH! CAN WE OFFER YOU A CRAFTING LESSON AS THANKS? IT'S SOMETHING WE DO FOR TOURISTS.
NICE IDEA, ANEJA!
LET'S GO, CAT-EARED LADIES!
TUG
TUG
UH, HEY!
MIGEIKO-ANIJA!

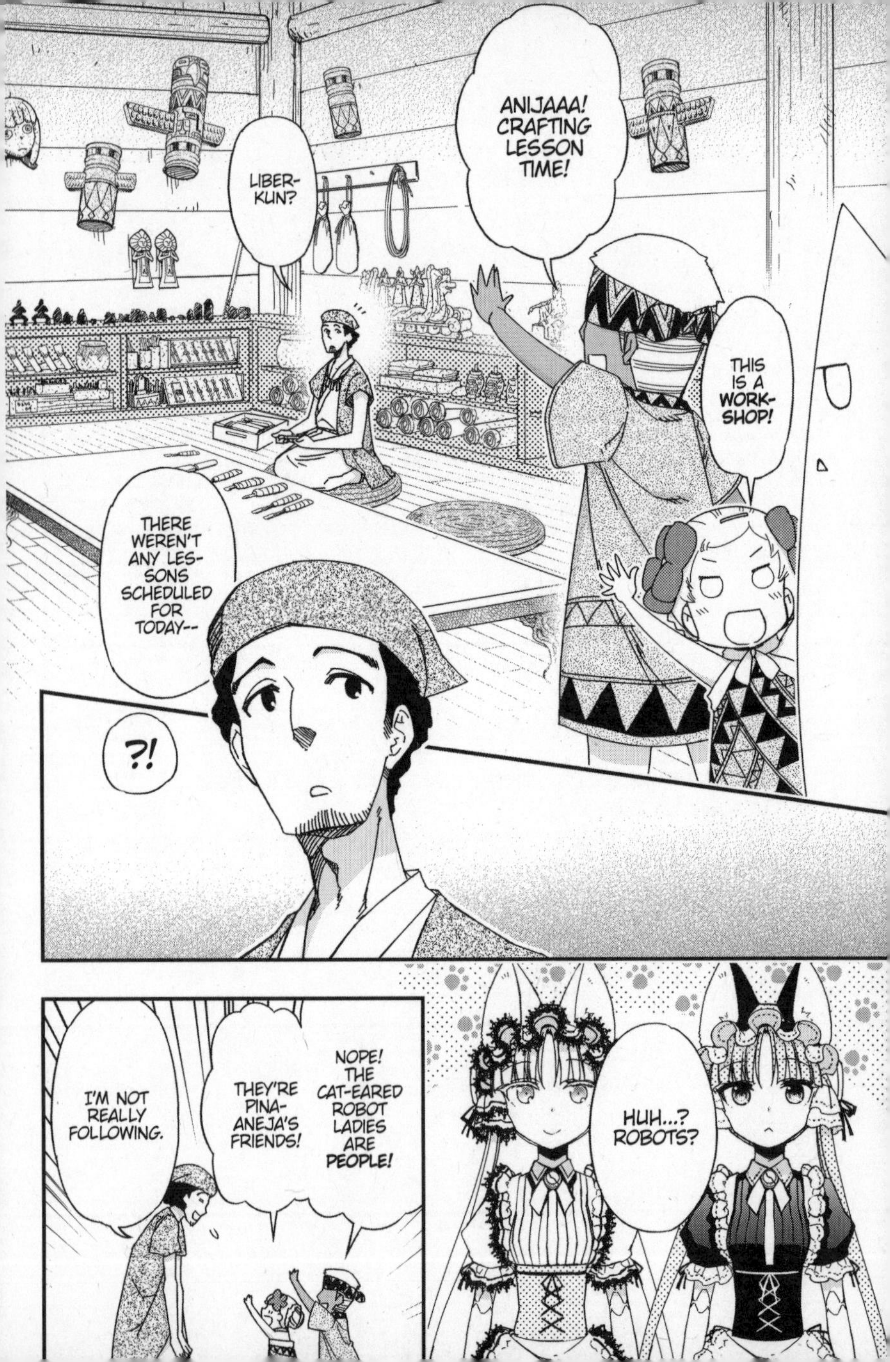
ANIJAAA! CRAFTING LESSON TIME!
LIBER-KUN?
THIS IS A WORK-SHOP!
THERE WEREN'T ANY LES-SONS SCHEDULED FOR TODAY--
?!
HUH...? ROBOTS?
NOPE! THE CAT-EARED ROBOT LADIES ARE PEOPLE!
THEY'RE PINA-ANEJA'S FRIENDS!
I'M NOT REALLY FOLLOWING.

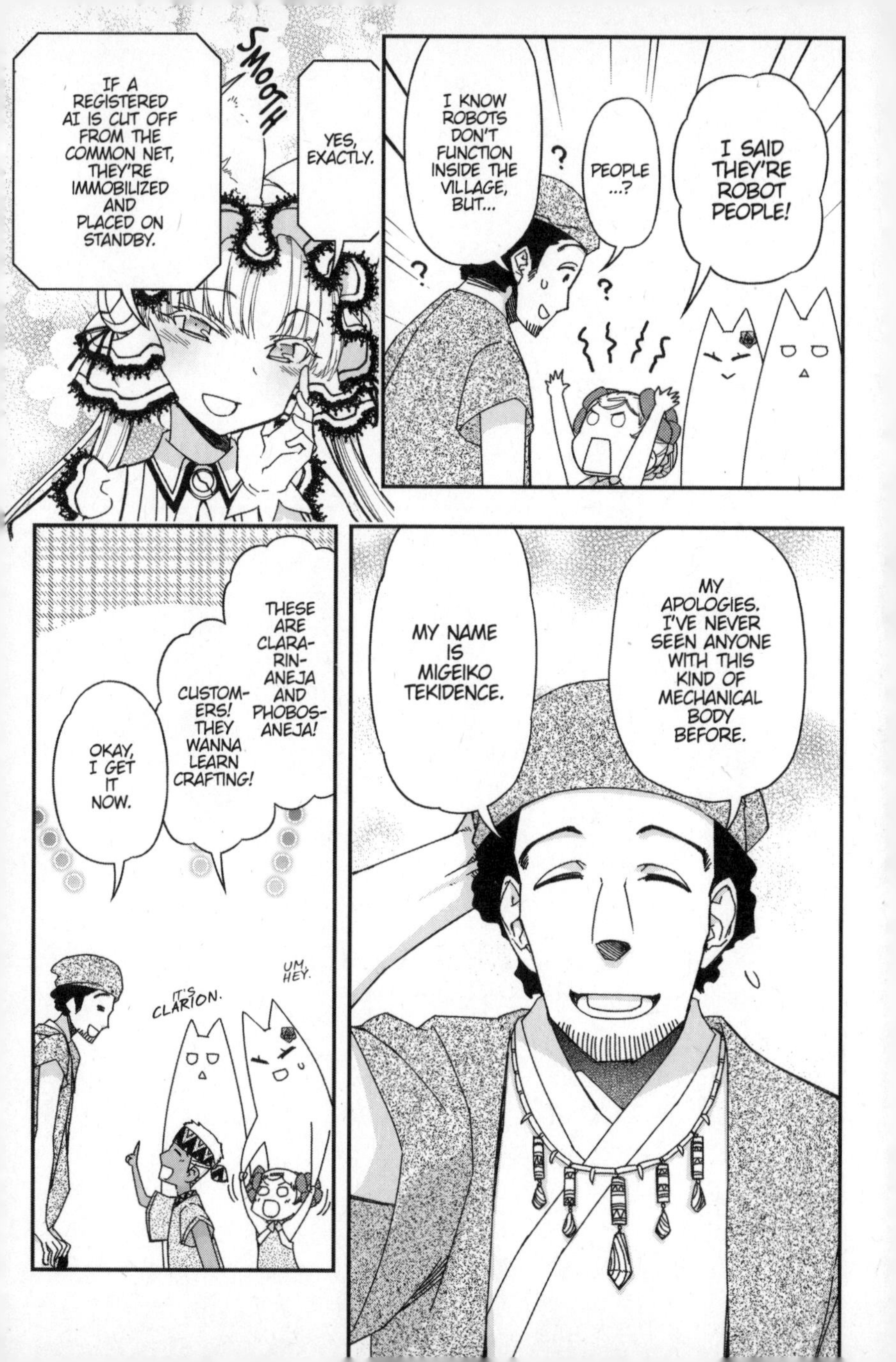
I SAID THEY'RE ROBOT PEOPLE!
PEOPLE ...?
I KNOW ROBOTS DON'T FUNCTION INSIDE THE VILLAGE, BUT...
YES, EXACTLY.
SMOOTH
IF A REGISTERED AI IS CUT OFF FROM THE COMMON NET, THEY'RE IMMOBILIZED AND PLACED ON STANDBY.
MY APOLOGIES. I'VE NEVER SEEN ANYONE WITH THIS KIND OF MECHANICAL BODY BEFORE.
MY NAME IS MIGEIKO TEKIDENCE.
THESE ARE CLARA-RIN-ANEJA AND PHOBOS-ANEJA!
CUSTOM-ERS! THEY WANNA LEARN CRAFTING!
OKAY, I GET IT NOW.
UM, HEY.
IT'S CLARION.

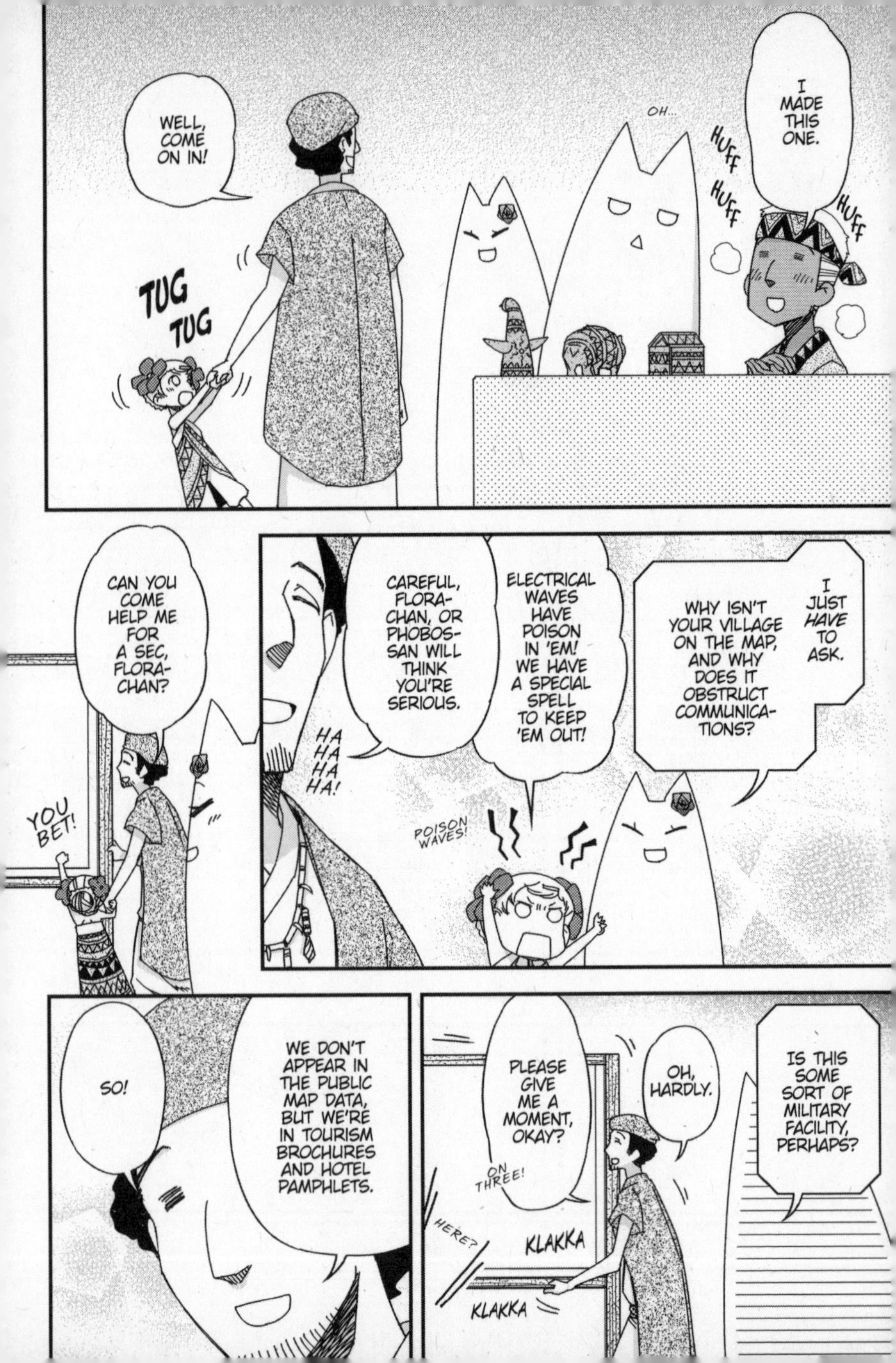
I MADE THIS ONE.
HUFF HUFF HUFF
OH...
WELL, COME ON IN!
TUG TUG
I JUST *HAVE* TO ASK.
WHY ISN'T YOUR VILLAGE ON THE MAP, AND WHY DOES IT OBSTRUCT COMMUNICATIONS?
ELECTRICAL WAVES HAVE POISON IN 'EM! WE HAVE A SPECIAL SPELL TO KEEP 'EM OUT!
CAREFUL, FLORA-CHAN, OR PHOBOS-SAN WILL THINK YOU'RE SERIOUS.
HA HA HA HA!
POISON WAVES!
CAN YOU COME HELP ME FOR A SEC, FLORA-CHAN?
YOU BET!
IS THIS SOME SORT OF MILITARY FACILITY, PERHAPS?
OH, HARDLY.
PLEASE GIVE ME A MOMENT, OKAY?
ON THREE!
HERE?
KLAKKA
KLAKKA
WE DON'T APPEAR IN THE PUBLIC MAP DATA, BUT WE'RE IN TOURISM BROCHURES AND HOTEL PAMPHLETS.
SO!

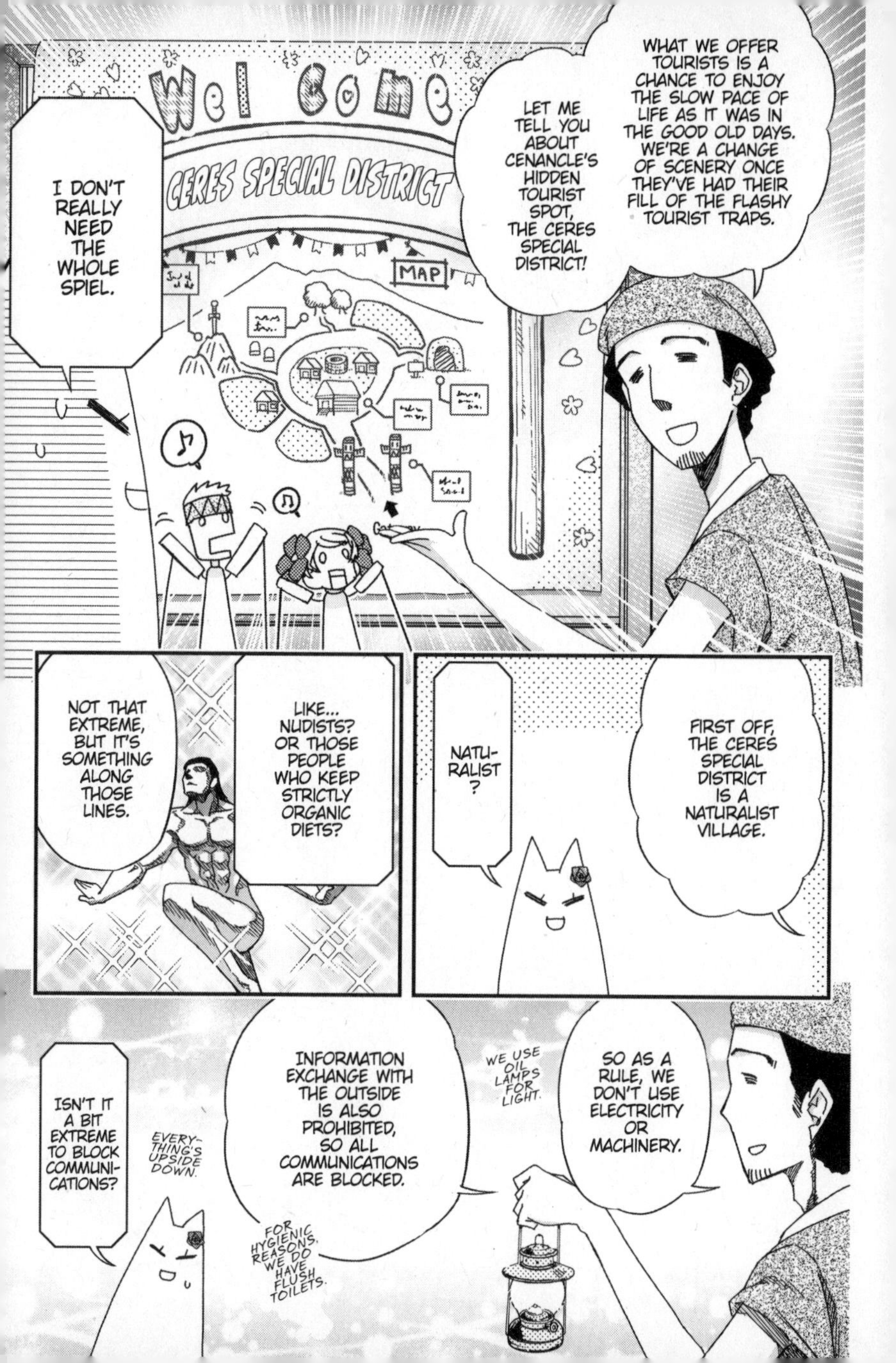

WHAT WE OFFER TOURISTS IS A CHANCE TO ENJOY THE SLOW PACE OF LIFE AS IT WAS IN THE GOOD OLD DAYS. WE'RE A CHANGE OF SCENERY ONCE THEY'VE HAD THEIR FILL OF THE FLASHY TOURIST TRAPS.
LET ME TELL YOU ABOUT CENANCLE'S HIDDEN TOURIST SPOT, THE CERES SPECIAL DISTRICT!
Wel Come
CERES SPECIAL DISTRICT
MAP
I DON'T REALLY NEED THE WHOLE SPIEL.
FIRST OFF, THE CERES SPECIAL DISTRICT IS A NATURALIST VILLAGE.
NATU-RALIST?
LIKE... NUDISTS? OR THOSE PEOPLE WHO KEEP STRICTLY ORGANIC DIETS?
NOT THAT EXTREME, BUT IT'S SOMETHING ALONG THOSE LINES.
SO AS A RULE, WE DON'T USE ELECTRICITY OR MACHINERY.
WE USE OIL LAMPS FOR LIGHT.
INFORMATION EXCHANGE WITH THE OUTSIDE IS ALSO PROHIBITED, SO ALL COMMUNICATIONS ARE BLOCKED.
FOR HYGIENIC REASONS, WE DO HAVE FLUSH TOILETS.
EVERY-THING'S UPSIDE DOWN.
ISN'T IT A BIT EXTREME TO BLOCK COMMUNI-CATIONS?

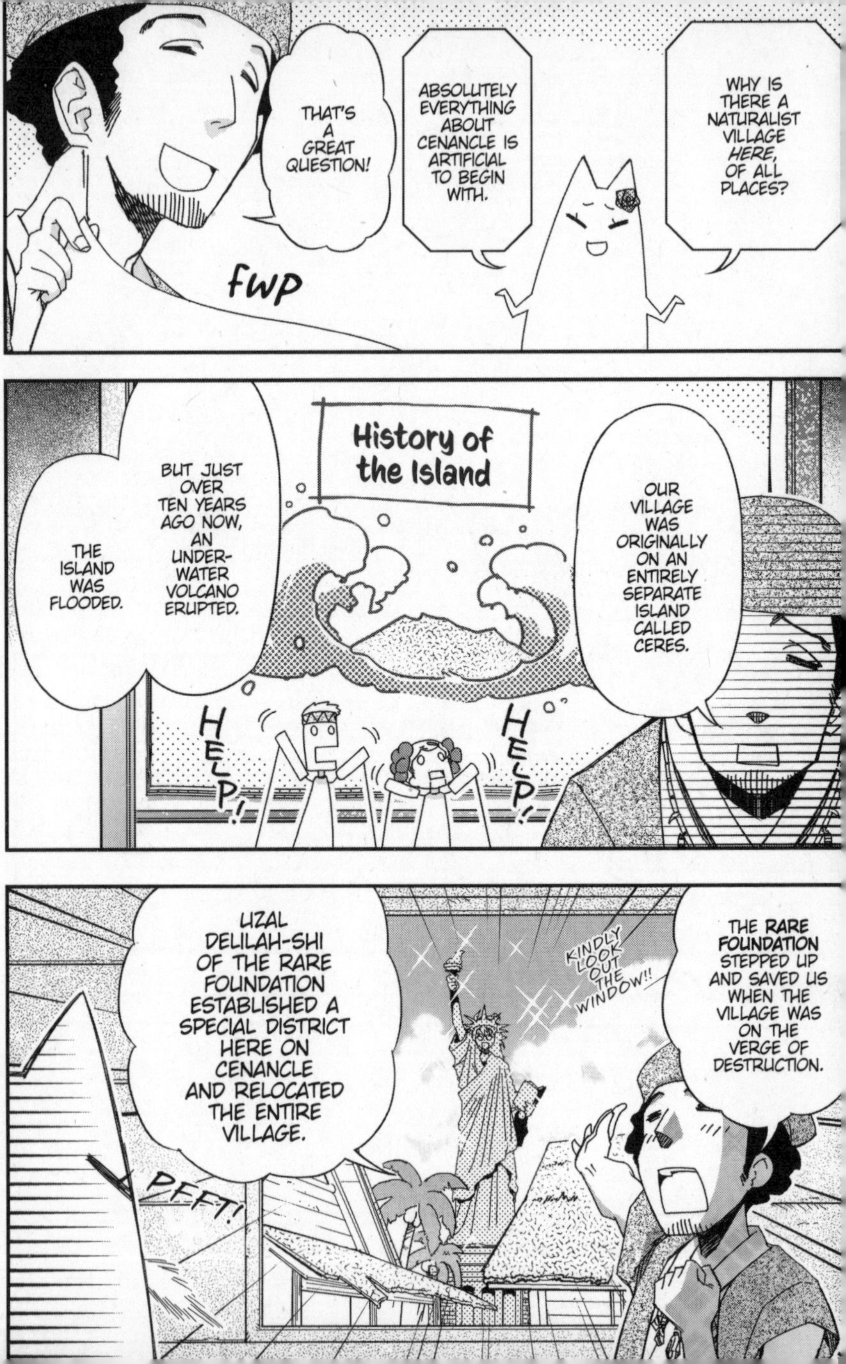
WHY IS THERE A NATURALIST VILLAGE *HERE*, OF ALL PLACES?
ABSOLUTELY EVERYTHING ABOUT CENANCLE IS ARTIFICIAL TO BEGIN WITH.
THAT'S A GREAT QUESTION!
FWP
OUR VILLAGE WAS ORIGINALLY ON AN ENTIRELY SEPARATE ISLAND CALLED CERES.
History of the Island
BUT JUST OVER TEN YEARS AGO NOW, AN UNDER-WATER VOLCANO ERUPTED.
THE ISLAND WAS FLOODED.
HELP!
HELP!
THE **RARE FOUNDATION** STEPPED UP AND SAVED US WHEN THE VILLAGE WAS ON THE VERGE OF DESTRUCTION.
KINDLY LOOK OUT THE WINDOW!!
UZAL DELILAH-SHI OF THE RARE FOUNDATION ESTABLISHED A SPECIAL DISTRICT HERE ON CENANCLE AND RELOCATED THE ENTIRE VILLAGE.
PFFT!

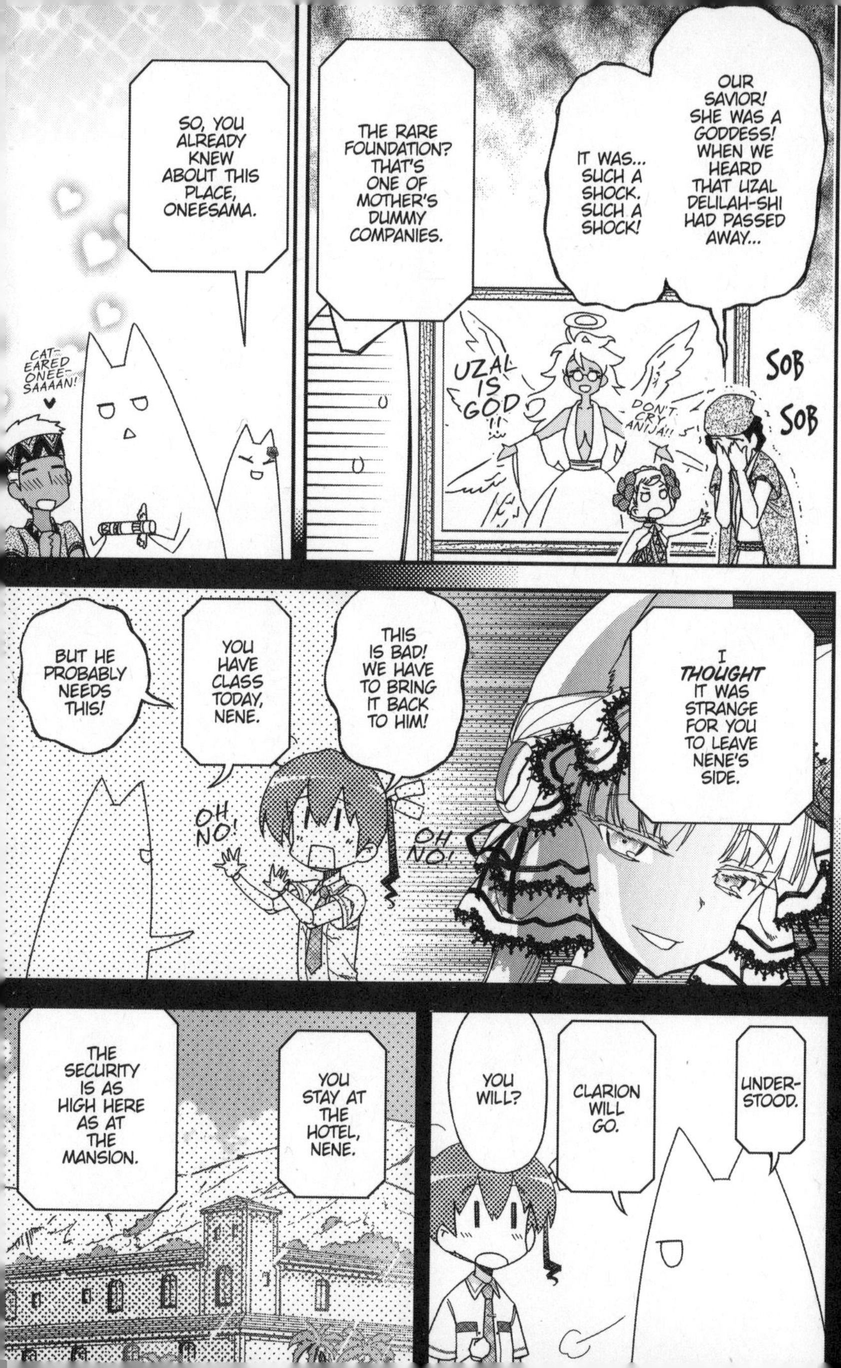
OUR SAVIOR! SHE WAS A GODDESS! WHEN WE HEARD THAT UZAL DELILAH-SHI HAD PASSED AWAY...
IT WAS... SUCH A SHOCK. SUCH A SHOCK!
SOB
SOB
DON'T CRY, ANIJA!!
UZAL IS GOD!!
THE RARE FOUNDATION? THAT'S ONE OF MOTHER'S DUMMY COMPANIES.
SO, YOU ALREADY KNEW ABOUT THIS PLACE, ONEESAMA.
CAT-EARED ONEE-SAAAAN!
I *THOUGHT* IT WAS STRANGE FOR YOU TO LEAVE NENE'S SIDE.
THIS IS BAD! WE HAVE TO BRING IT BACK TO HIM!
OH NO!
OH NO!
YOU HAVE CLASS TODAY, NENE.
BUT HE PROBABLY NEEDS THIS!
UNDER-STOOD.
CLARION WILL GO.
YOU WILL?
YOU STAY AT THE HOTEL, NENE.
THE SECURITY IS AS HIGH HERE AS AT THE MANSION.

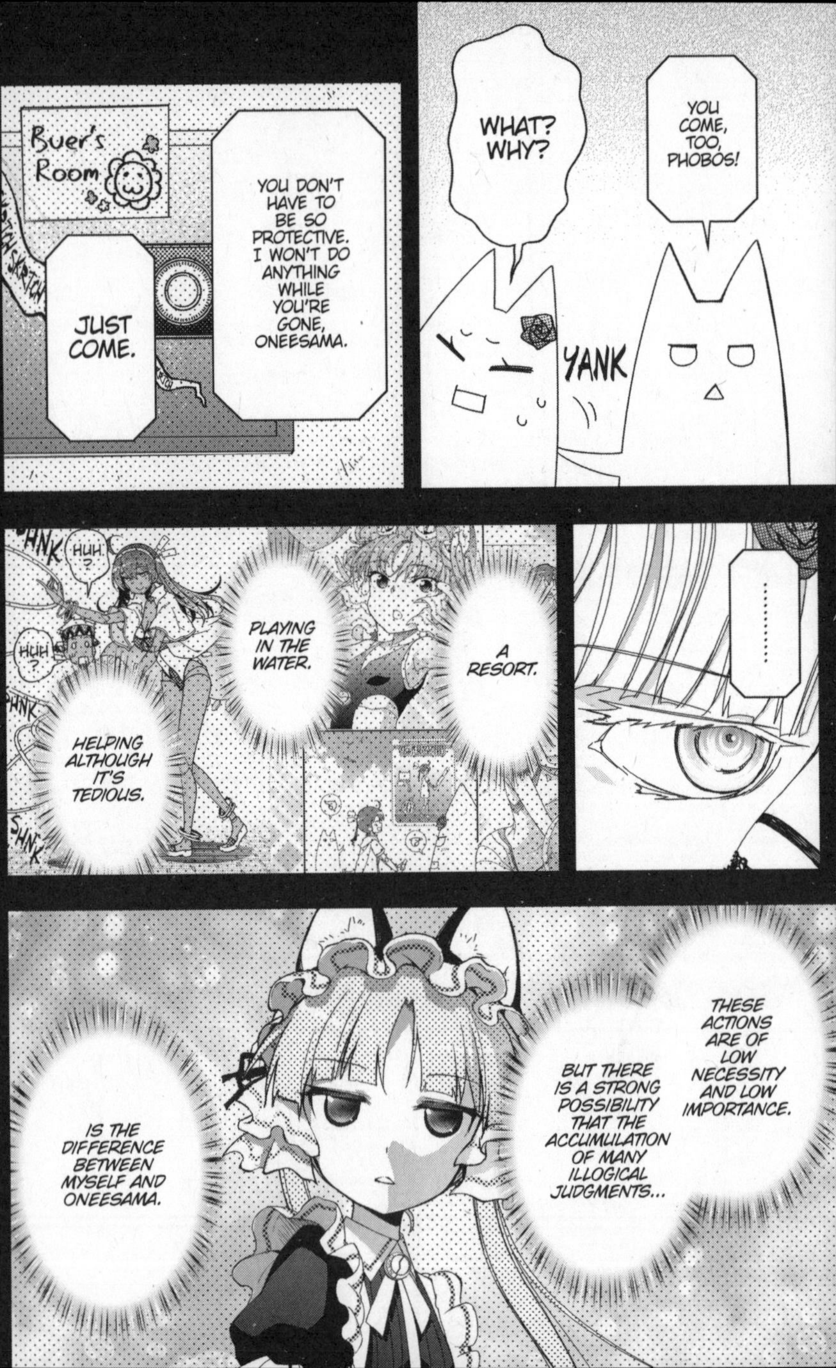

YOU COME, TOO, PHOBOS!
WHAT? WHY?
YANK
YOU DON'T HAVE TO BE SO PROTECTIVE. I WON'T DO ANYTHING WHILE YOU'RE GONE, ONEESAMA.
Buer's Room
JUST COME.
......
A RESORT.
PLAYING IN THE WATER.
HELPING ALTHOUGH IT'S TEDIOUS.
HUH?
HUH?
SHNK
THESE ACTIONS ARE OF LOW NECESSITY AND LOW IMPORTANCE.
BUT THERE IS A STRONG POSSIBILITY THAT THE ACCUMULATION OF MANY ILLOGICAL JUDGMENTS...
IS THE DIFFERENCE BETWEEN MYSELF AND ONEESAMA.

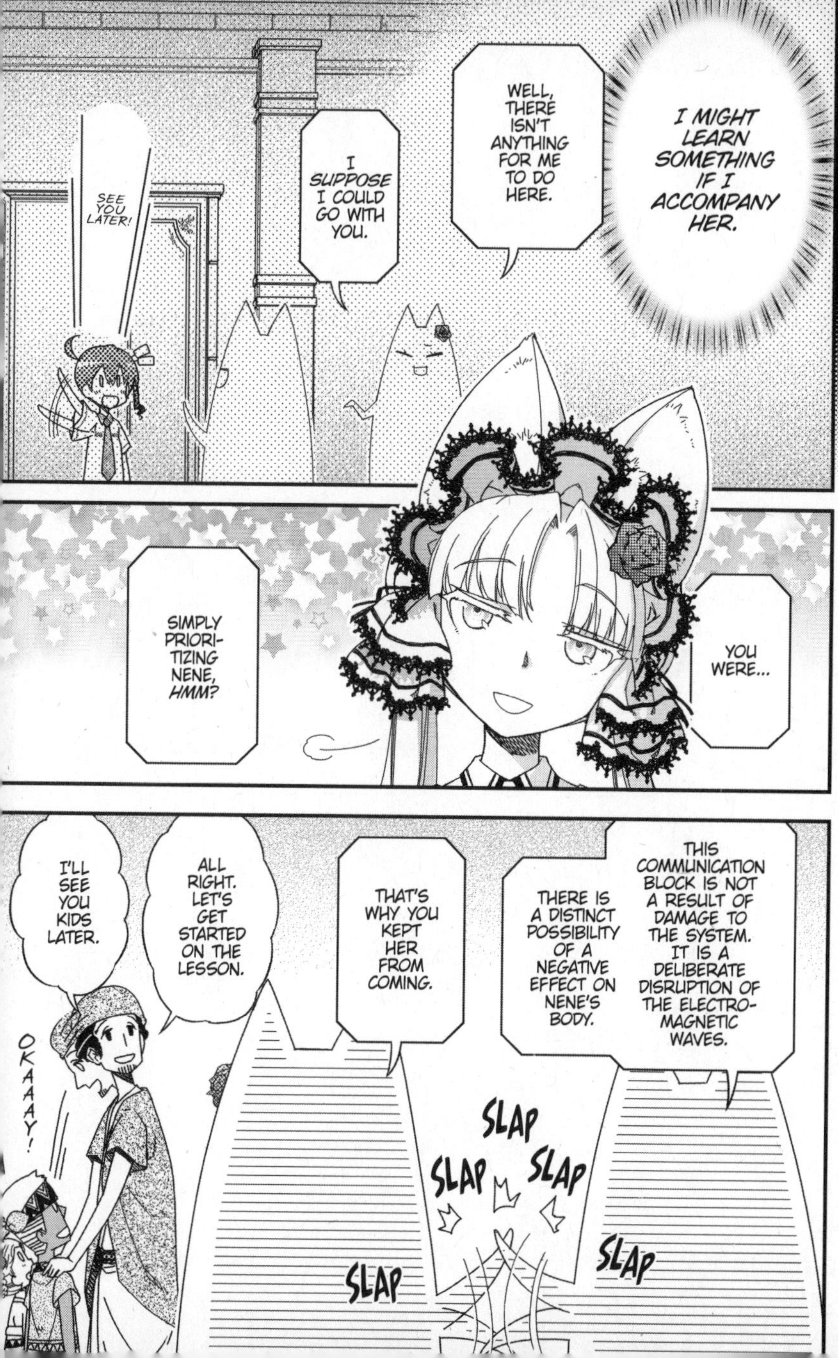
I MIGHT LEARN SOMETHING IF I ACCOMPANY HER.
WELL, THERE ISN'T ANYTHING FOR ME TO DO HERE.
I SUPPOSE I COULD GO WITH YOU.
SEE YOU LATER!
YOU WERE...
SIMPLY PRIORITIZING NENE, HMM?
THIS COMMUNICATION BLOCK IS NOT A RESULT OF DAMAGE TO THE SYSTEM. IT IS A DELIBERATE DISRUPTION OF THE ELECTRO-MAGNETIC WAVES.
THERE IS A DISTINCT POSSIBILITY OF A NEGATIVE EFFECT ON NENE'S BODY.
THAT'S WHY YOU KEPT HER FROM COMING.
SLAP
SLAP
SLAP
SLAP
SLAP
ALL RIGHT. LET'S GET STARTED ON THE LESSON.
I'LL SEE YOU KIDS LATER.
OKAAAAY!

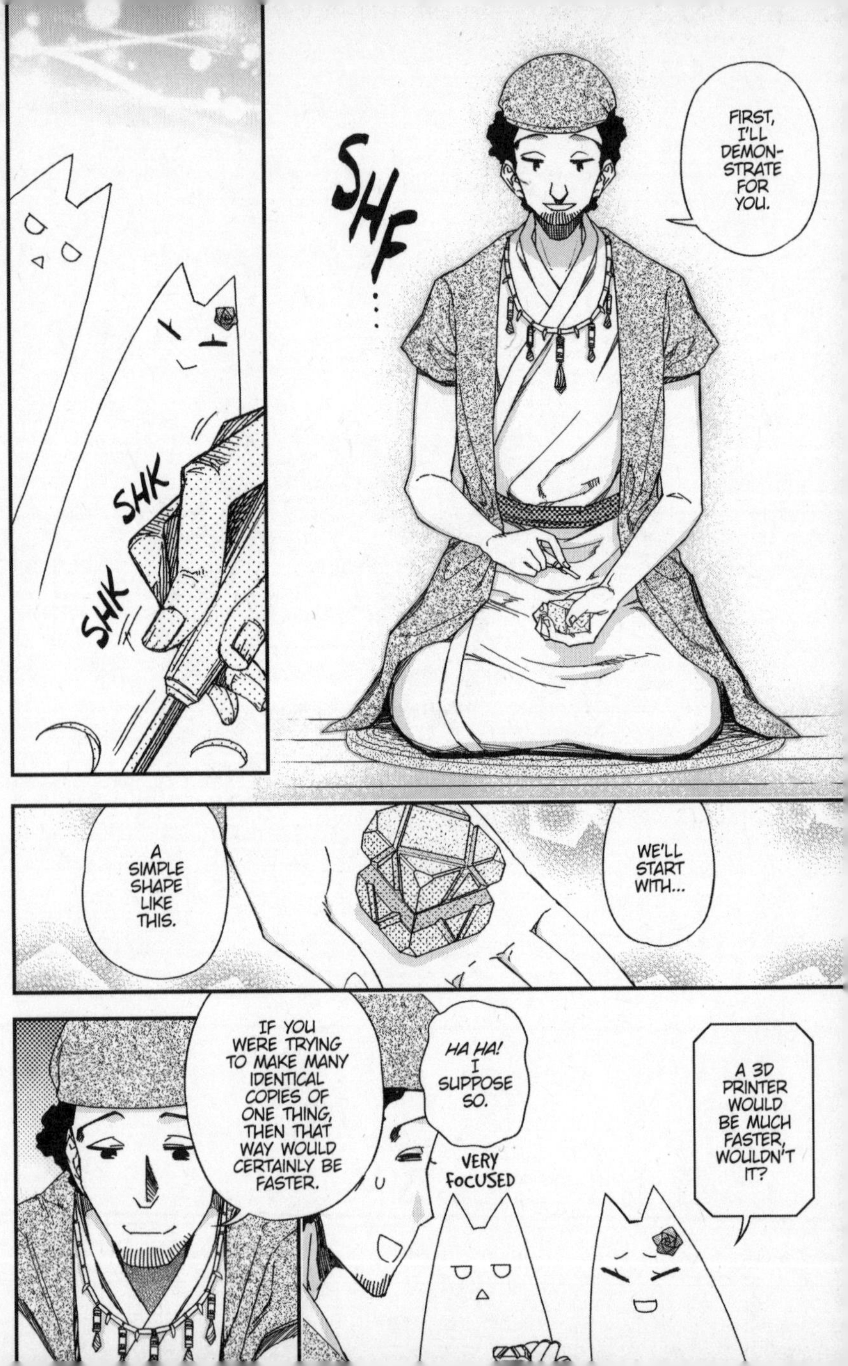
FIRST, I'LL DEMON-STRATE FOR YOU.
SHF...
SHK
SHK
WE'LL START WITH...
A SIMPLE SHAPE LIKE THIS.
A 3D PRINTER WOULD BE MUCH FASTER, WOULDN'T IT?
VERY FOCUSED
HA HA! I SUPPOSE SO.
IF YOU WERE TRYING TO MAKE MANY IDENTICAL COPIES OF ONE THING, THEN THAT WAY WOULD CERTAINLY BE FASTER.

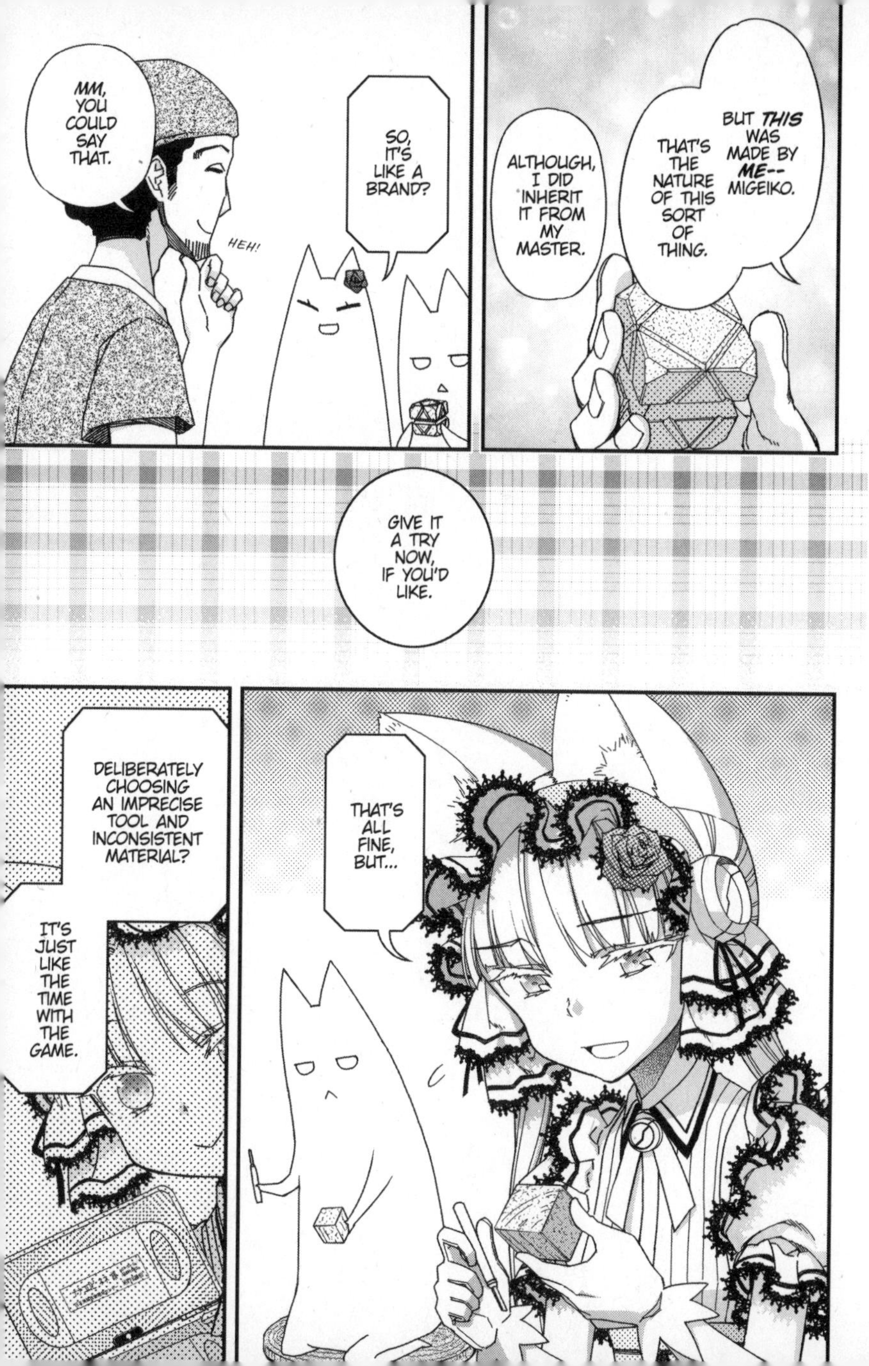
BUT THIS WAS MADE BY ME-- MIGEIKO.
THAT'S THE NATURE OF THIS SORT OF THING.
ALTHOUGH, I DID INHERIT IT FROM MY MASTER.
SO, IT'S LIKE A BRAND?
MM, YOU COULD SAY THAT.
HEH!
GIVE IT A TRY NOW, IF YOU'D LIKE.
THAT'S ALL FINE, BUT...
DELIBERATELY CHOOSING AN IMPRECISE TOOL AND INCONSISTENT MATERIAL?
IT'S JUST LIKE THE TIME WITH THE GAME.

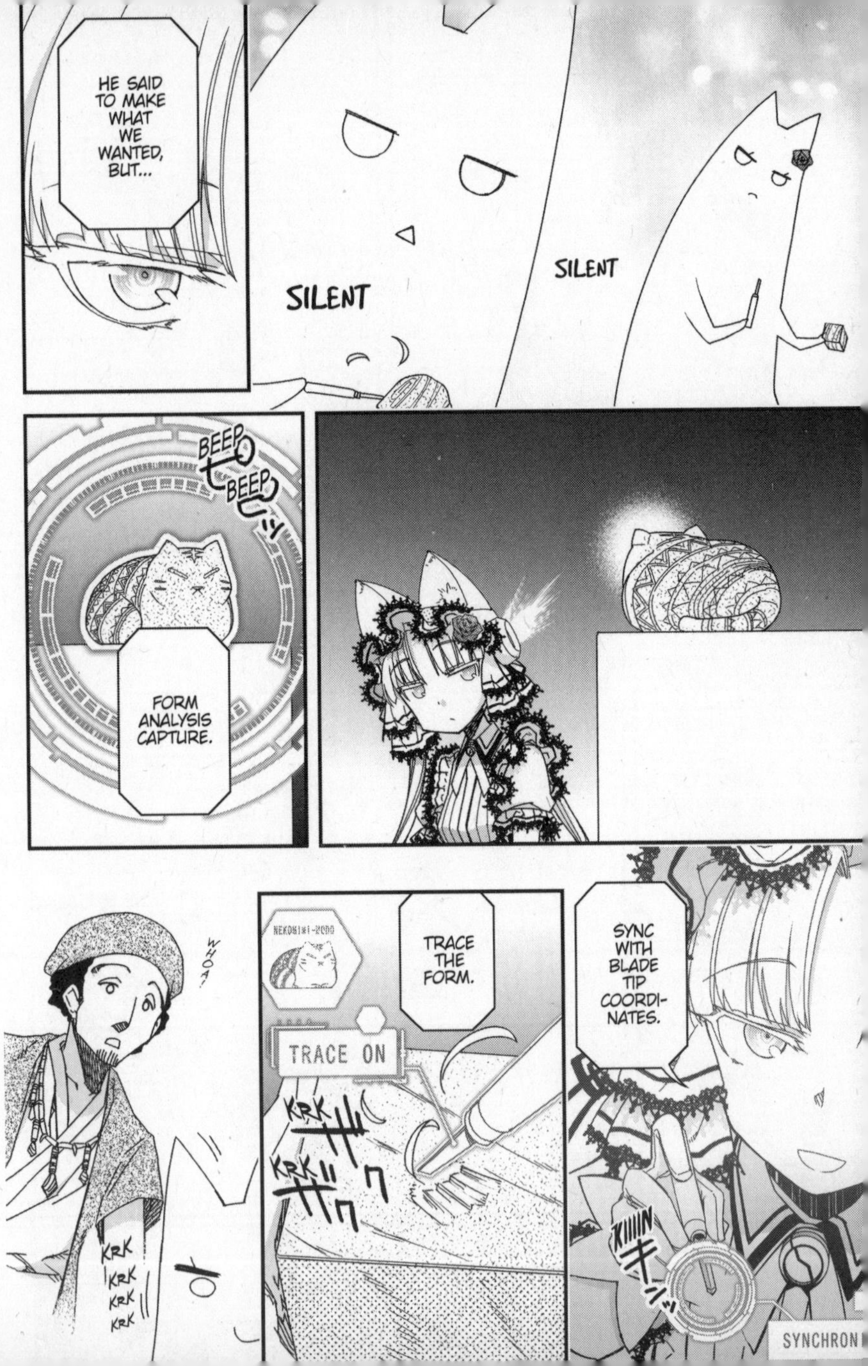
SILENT
SILENT
HE SAID TO MAKE WHAT WE WANTED, BUT...
BEEP
BEEP
FORM ANALYSIS CAPTURE.
SYNC WITH BLADE TIP COORDI-NATES.
KIIIIN
SYNCHRON
TRACE THE FORM.
TRACE ON
KRK
KRK
WHOA!
KRK
KRK
KRK
KRK

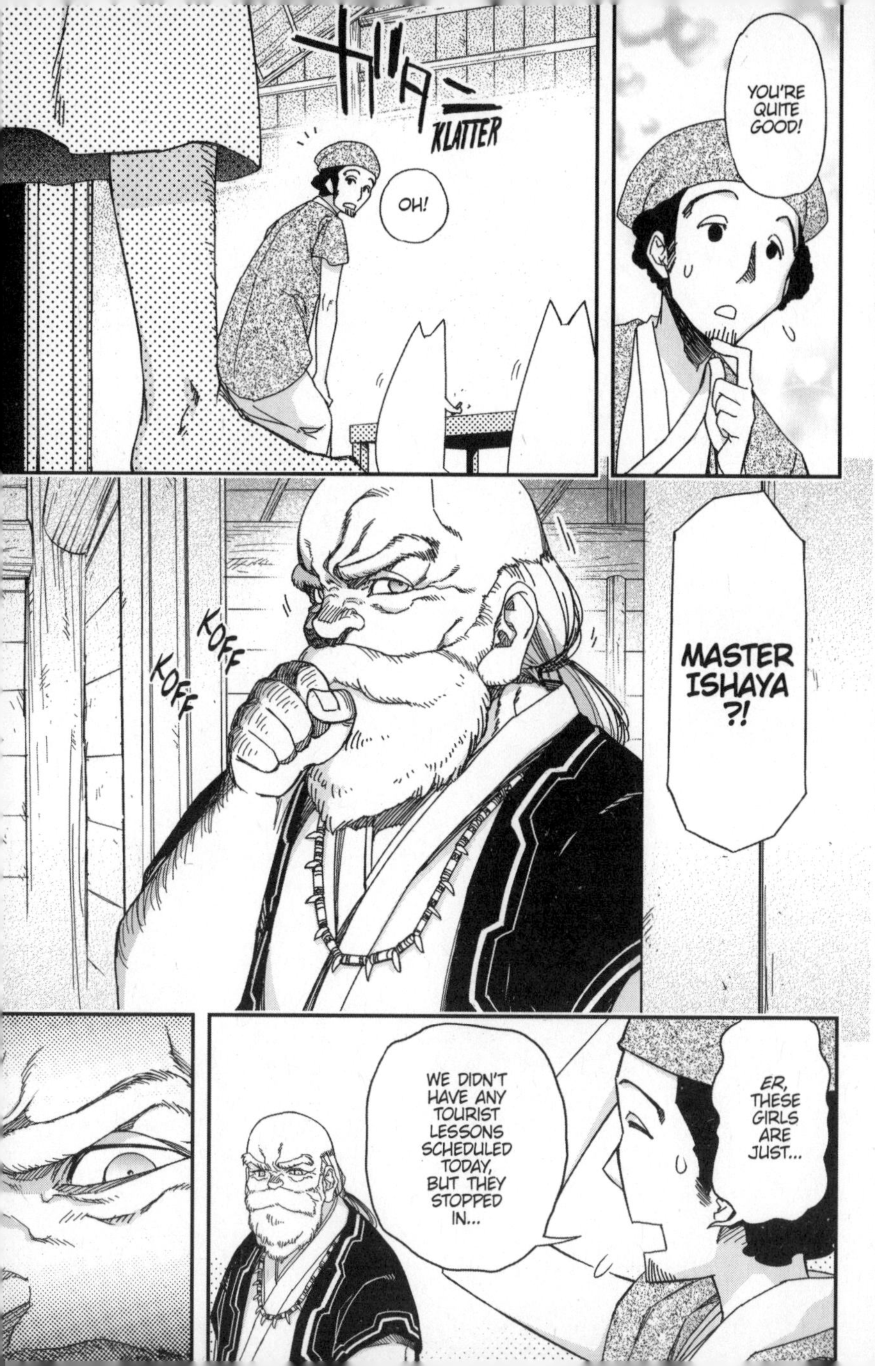
YOU'RE QUITE GOOD!
KLATTER
OH!
MASTER ISHAYA ?!
KOFF
KOFF
ER, THESE GIRLS ARE JUST...
WE DIDN'T HAVE ANY TOURIST LESSONS SCHEDULED TODAY, BUT THEY STOPPED IN...

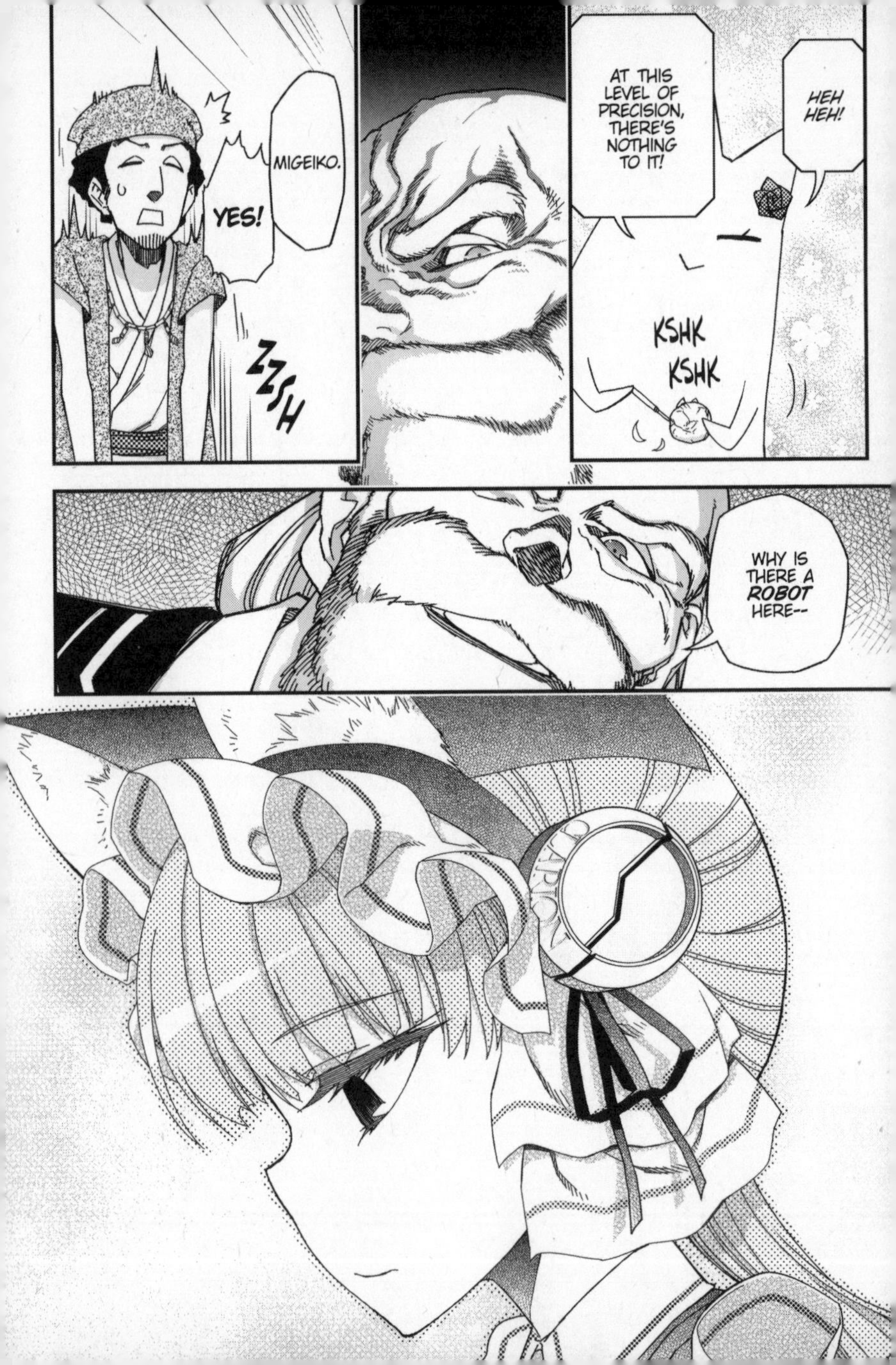
HEH HEH!
AT THIS LEVEL OF PRECISION, THERE'S NOTHING TO IT!
KSHK
KSHK
MIGEIKO.
YES!
ZZSH
WHY IS THERE A *ROBOT* HERE--

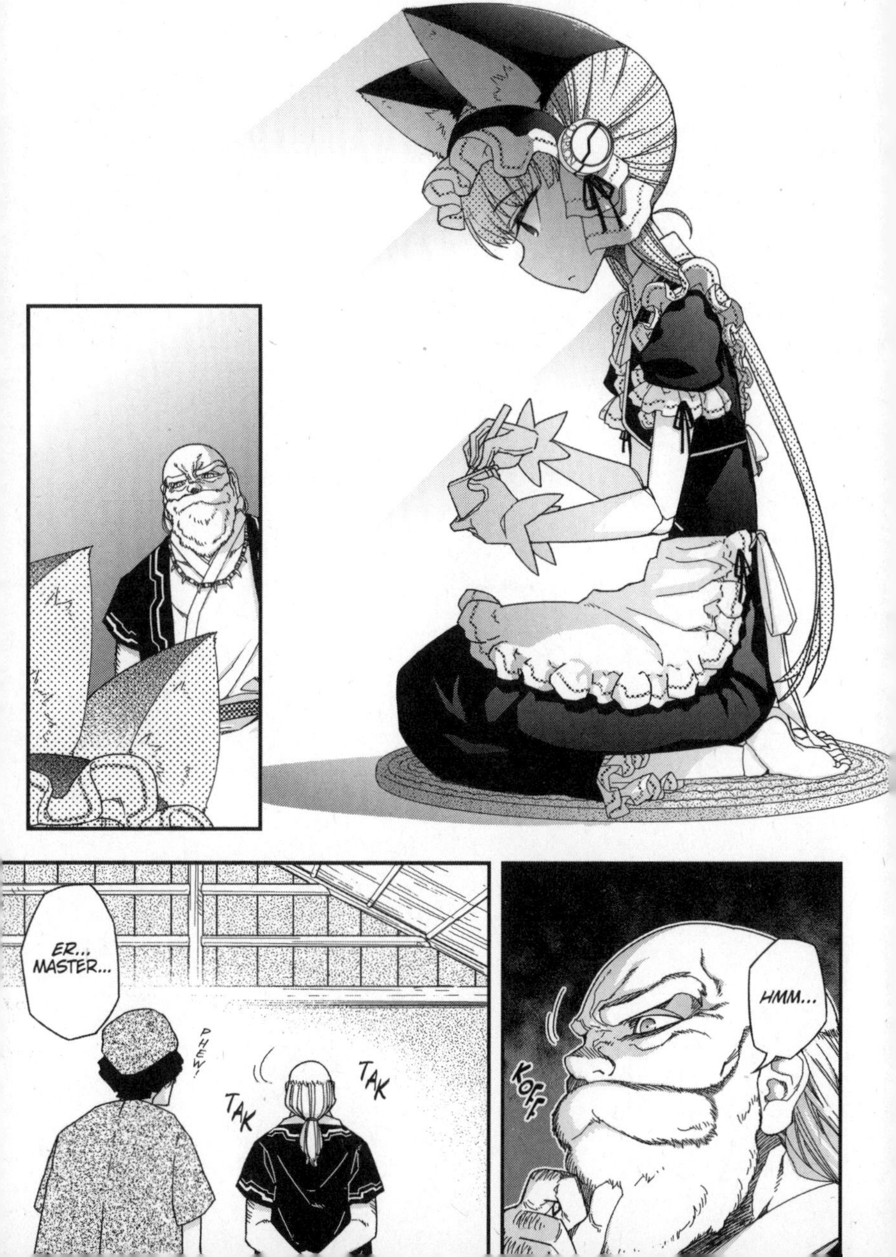
HMM...
KOFF
ER... MASTER...
PHEW!
TAK
TAK

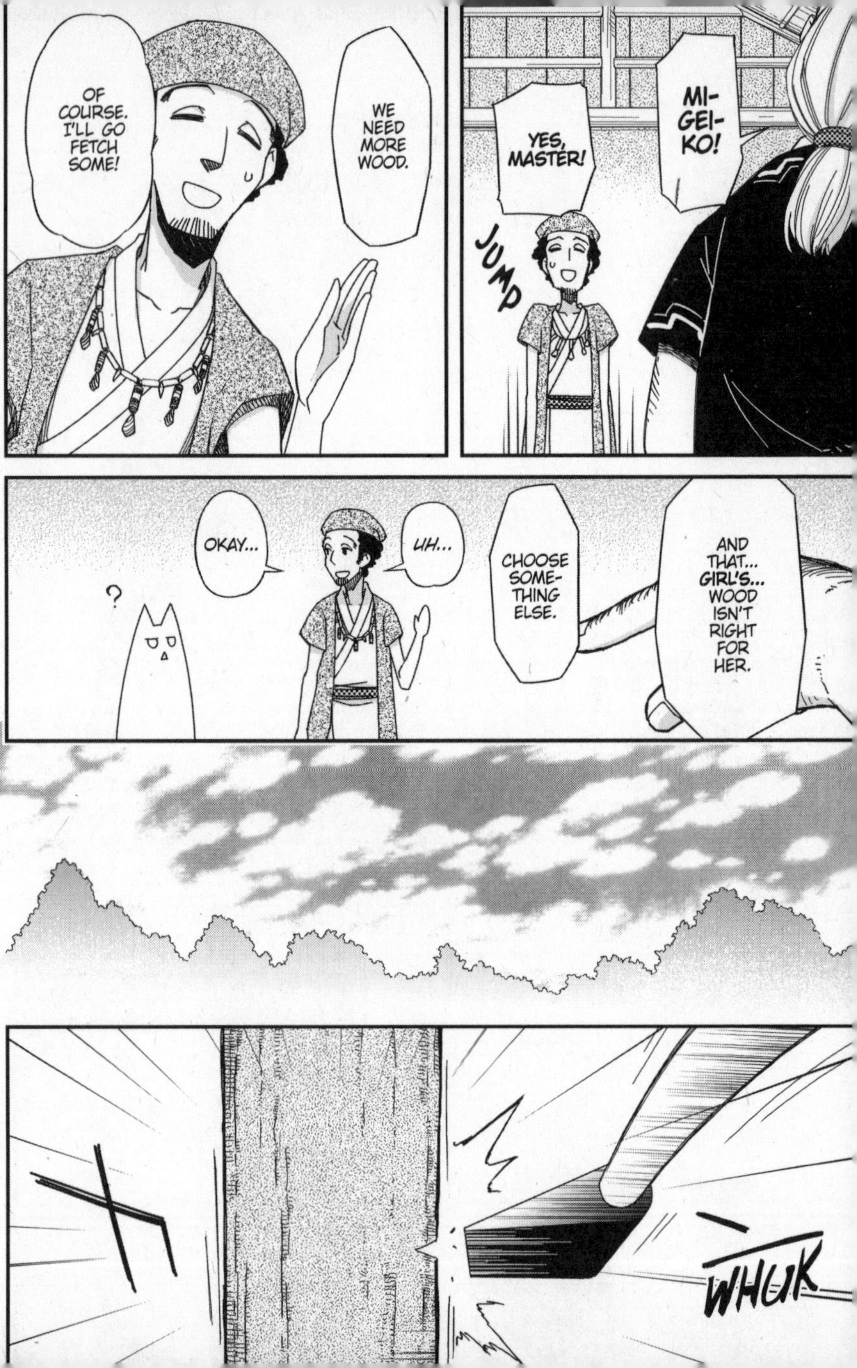
MI-GEI-KO!
YES, MASTER!
JUMP
WE NEED MORE WOOD.
OF COURSE. I'LL GO FETCH SOME!
AND THAT... GIRL'S... WOOD ISN'T RIGHT FOR HER.
CHOOSE SOME-THING ELSE.
UH...
OKAY...
?
WHUK

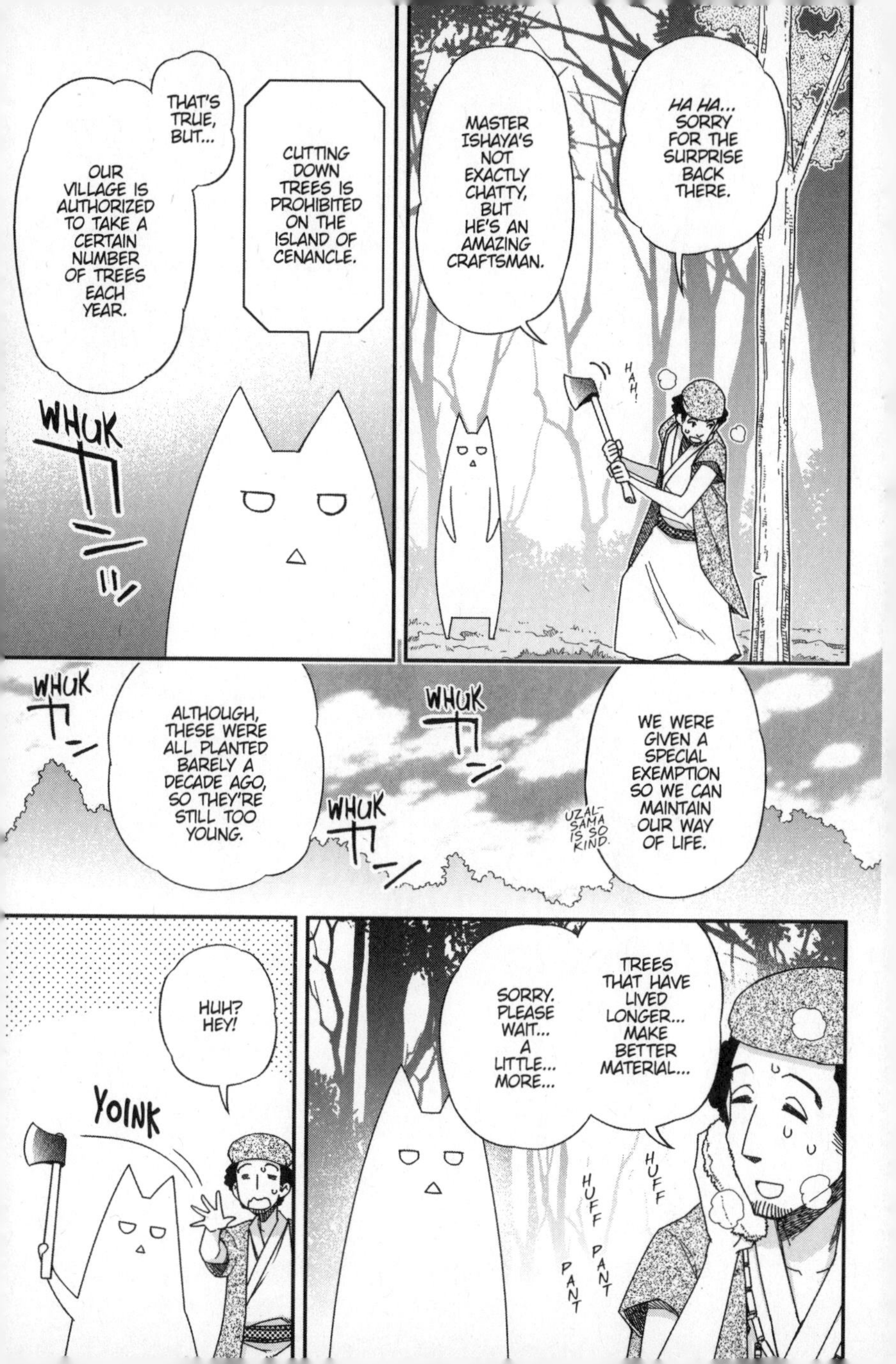
HA HA... SORRY FOR THE SURPRISE BACK THERE.
MASTER ISHAYA'S NOT EXACTLY CHATTY, BUT HE'S AN AMAZING CRAFTSMAN.
HAH!
CUTTING DOWN TREES IS PROHIBITED ON THE ISLAND OF CENANCLE.
THAT'S TRUE, BUT...
OUR VILLAGE IS AUTHORIZED TO TAKE A CERTAIN NUMBER OF TREES EACH YEAR.
WHUK
WE WERE GIVEN A SPECIAL EXEMPTION SO WE CAN MAINTAIN OUR WAY OF LIFE.
UZAL-SAMA IS SO KIND.
WHUK
WHUK
ALTHOUGH, THESE WERE ALL PLANTED BARELY A DECADE AGO, SO THEY'RE STILL TOO YOUNG.
WHUK
TREES THAT HAVE LIVED LONGER... MAKE BETTER MATERIAL...
SORRY. PLEASE WAIT... A LITTLE... MORE...
HUFF HUFF
PANT PANT
HUH? HEY!
YOINK

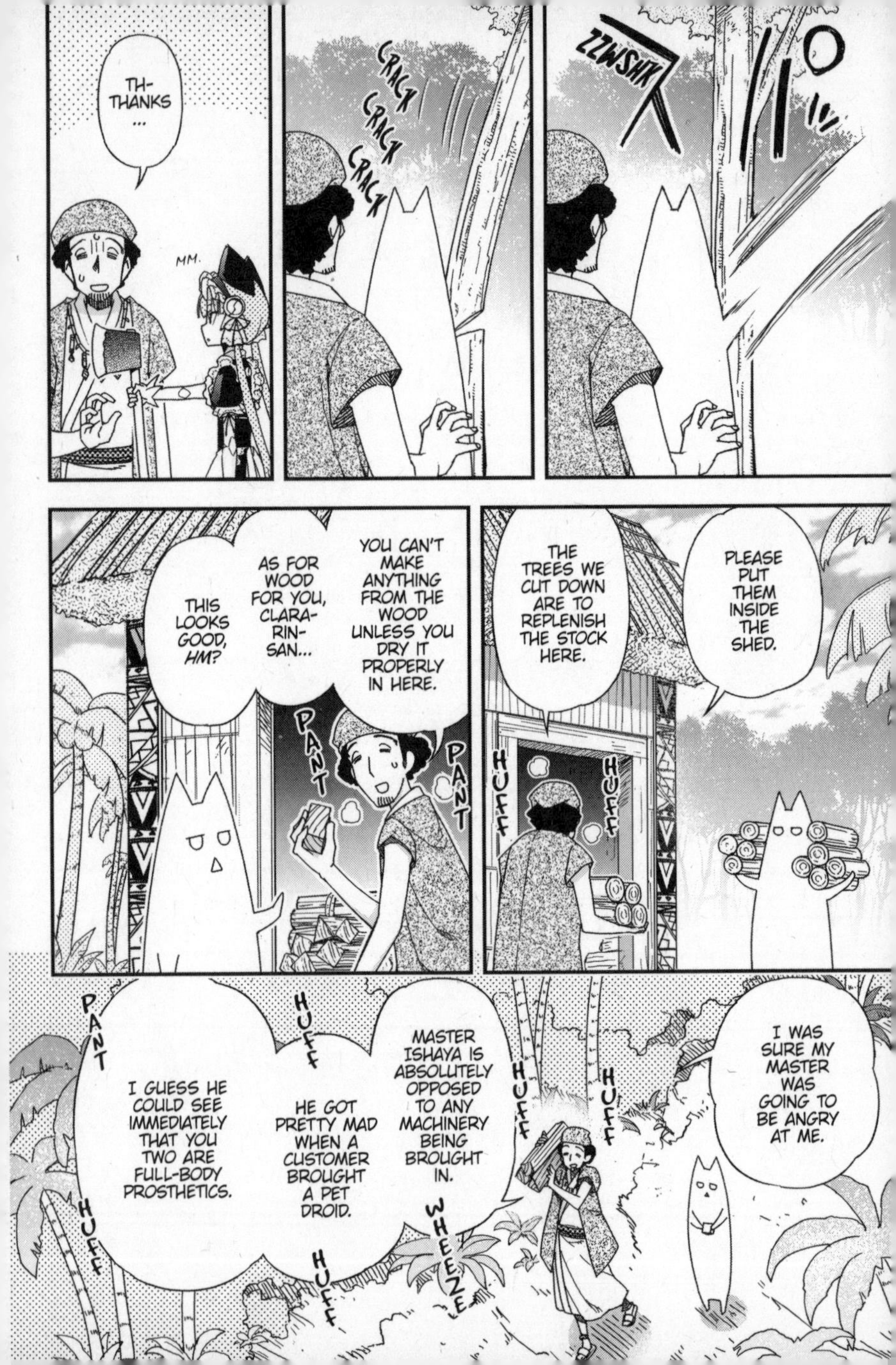
ZZWSHK
CRACK
CRACK
CRACK
TH-THANKS...
MM.
PLEASE PUT THEM INSIDE THE SHED.
THE TREES WE CUT DOWN ARE TO REPLENISH THE STOCK HERE.
HUFF
HUFF
YOU CAN'T MAKE ANYTHING FROM THE WOOD UNLESS YOU DRY IT PROPERLY IN HERE.
AS FOR WOOD FOR YOU, CLARA-RIN-SAN...
THIS LOOKS GOOD, HM?
PANT
PANT
I WAS SURE MY MASTER WAS GOING TO BE ANGRY AT ME.
HUFF
HUFF
MASTER ISHAYA IS ABSOLUTELY OPPOSED TO ANY MACHINERY BEING BROUGHT IN.
WHEEZE
HE GOT PRETTY MAD WHEN A CUSTOMER BROUGHT A PET DROID.
HUFF
HUFF
I GUESS HE COULD SEE IMMEDIATELY THAT YOU TWO ARE FULL-BODY PROSTHETICS.
PANT
HUFF

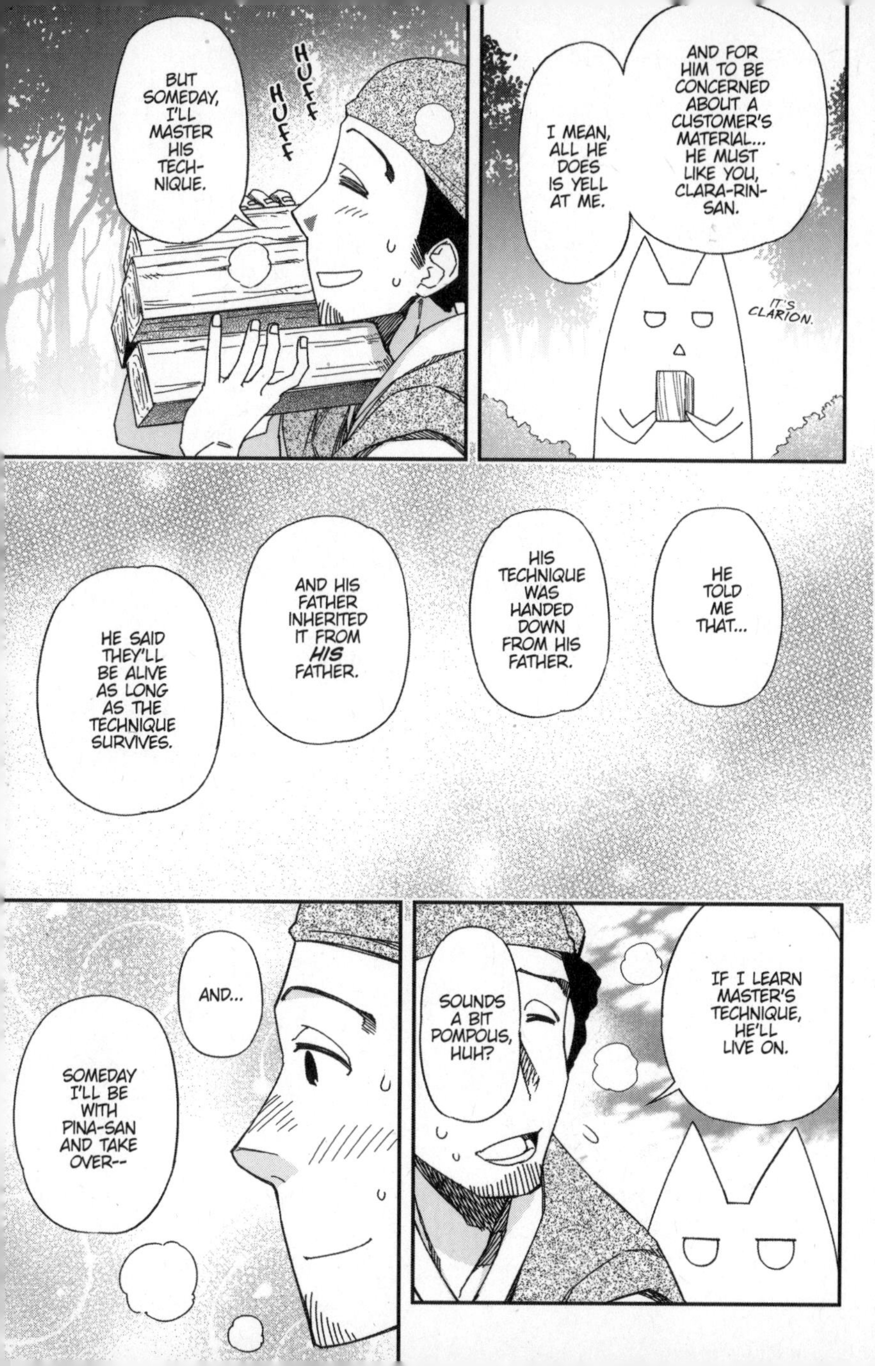
AND FOR HIM TO BE CONCERNED ABOUT A CUSTOMER'S MATERIAL... HE MUST LIKE YOU, CLARA-RIN-SAN.
I MEAN, ALL HE DOES IS YELL AT ME.
IT'S CLARION.
BUT SOMEDAY, I'LL MASTER HIS TECH-NIQUE.
HUFF HUFF
HE TOLD ME THAT...
HIS TECHNIQUE WAS HANDED DOWN FROM HIS FATHER.
AND HIS FATHER INHERITED IT FROM *HIS* FATHER.
HE SAID THEY'LL BE ALIVE AS LONG AS THE TECHNIQUE SURVIVES.
IF I LEARN MASTER'S TECHNIQUE, HE'LL LIVE ON.
SOUNDS A BIT POMPOUS, HUH?
AND...
SOMEDAY I'LL BE WITH PINA-SAN AND TAKE OVER--

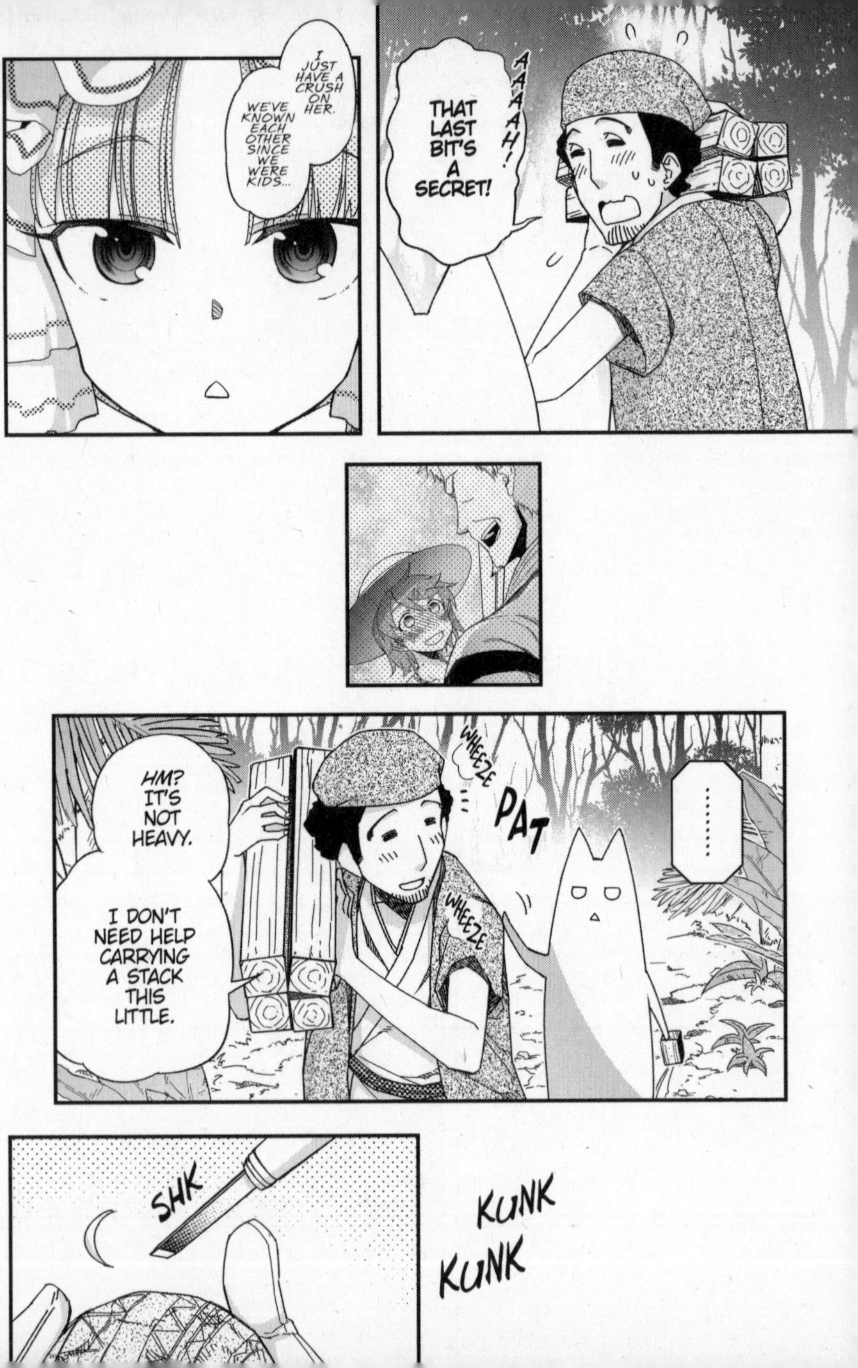
AAAAAH!
THAT LAST BIT'S A SECRET!
I JUST HAVE A CRUSH ON HER.
WE'VE KNOWN EACH OTHER SINCE WE WERE KIDS...
......
WHEEZE
PAT
WHEEZE
HM? IT'S NOT HEAVY.
I DON'T NEED HELP CARRYING A STACK THIS LITTLE.
KUNK
KUNK
SHK

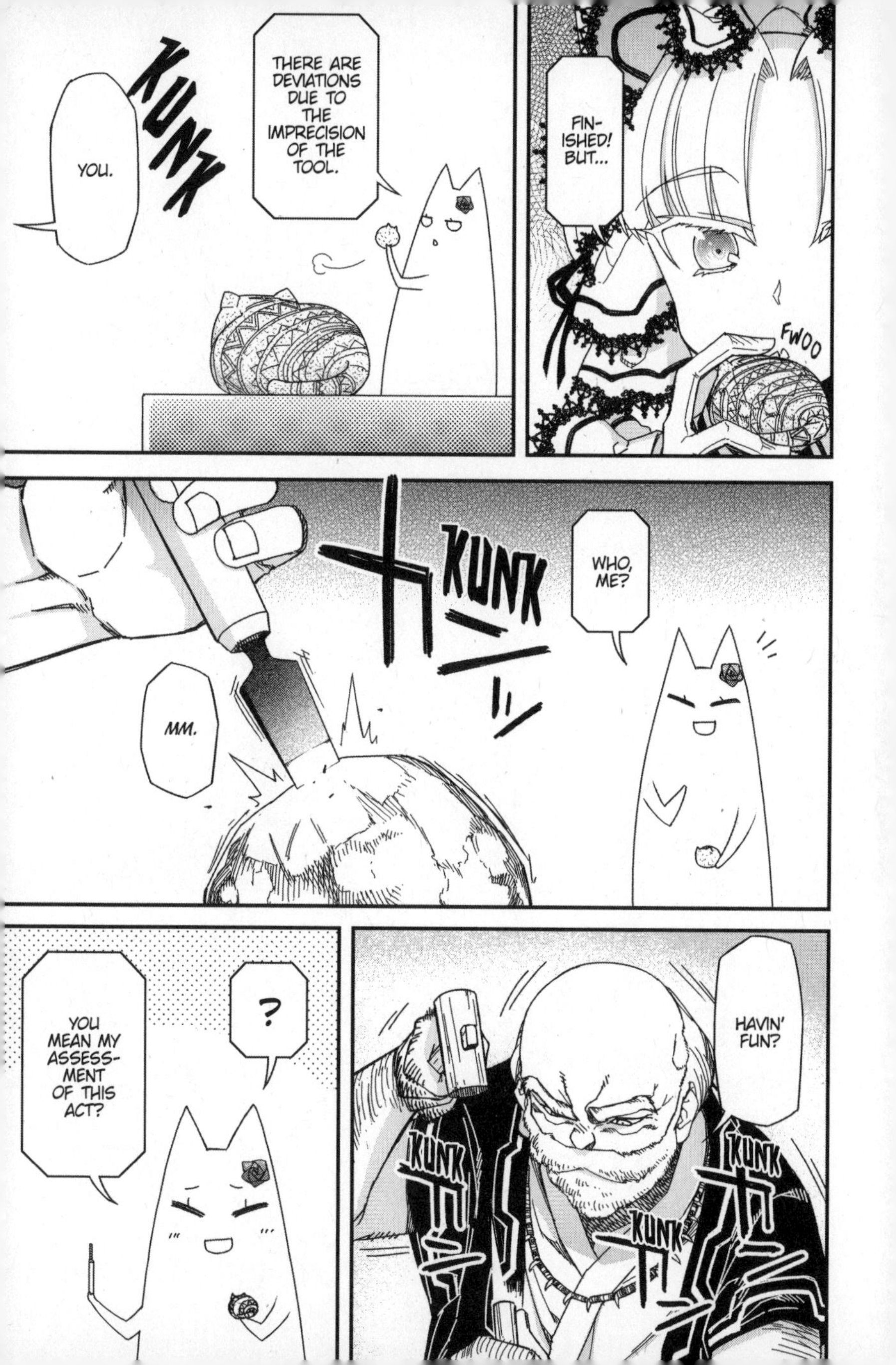
FIN-ISHED! BUT...
FWOO
THERE ARE DEVIATIONS DUE TO THE IMPRECISION OF THE TOOL.
KUNK
YOU.
WHO, ME?
KUNK
MM.
HAVIN' FUN?
KUNK
KUNK
KUNK
?
YOU MEAN MY ASSESS-MENT OF THIS ACT?

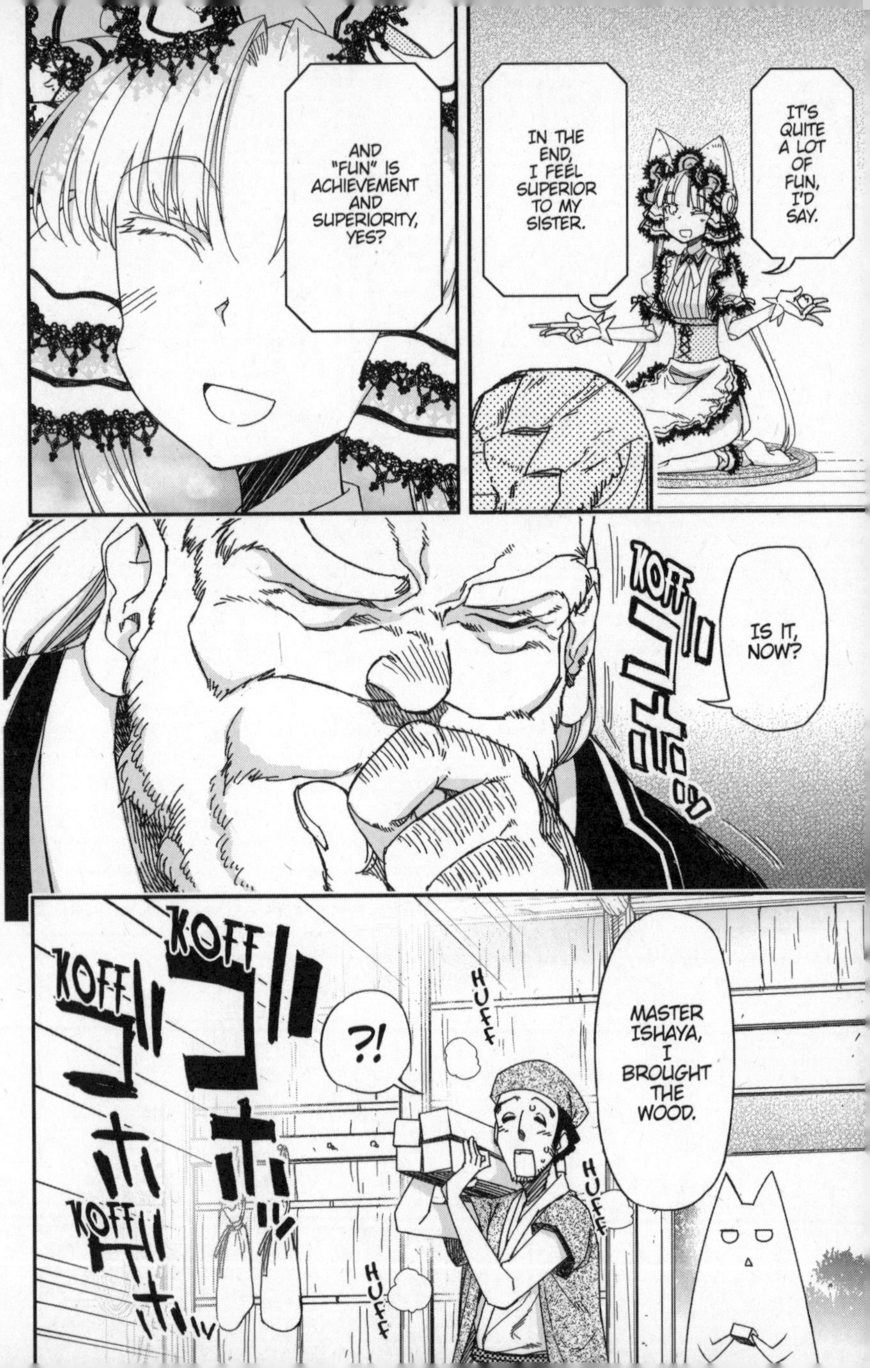
IT'S QUITE A LOT OF FUN, I'D SAY.
IN THE END, I FEEL SUPERIOR TO MY SISTER.
AND "FUN" IS ACHIEVEMENT AND SUPERIORITY, YES?
KOFF
IS IT, NOW?
HUFF
MASTER ISHAYA, I BROUGHT THE WOOD.
HUFF
HUFF
?!
KOFF
KOFF
KOFF

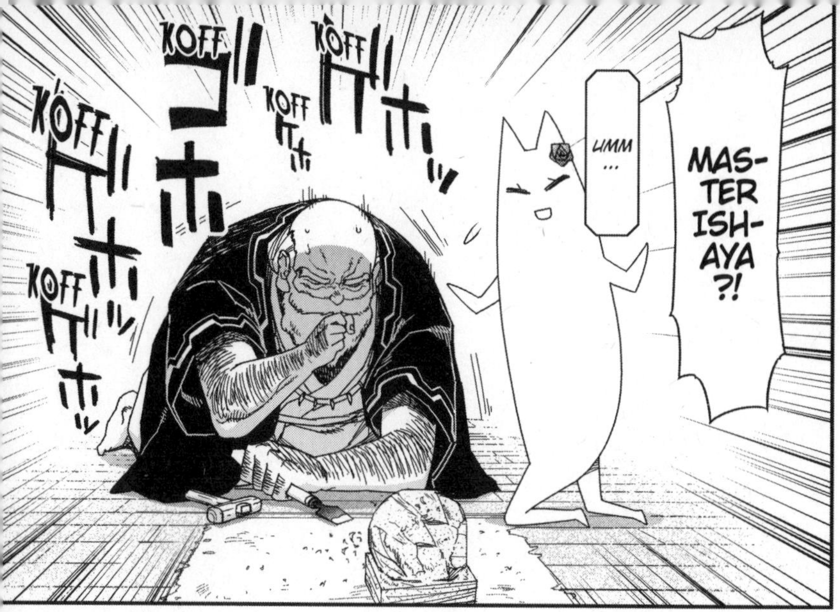
MASTER ISHAYA?!
UMM...
KOFF
KOFF
KOFF
KOFF
KOFF

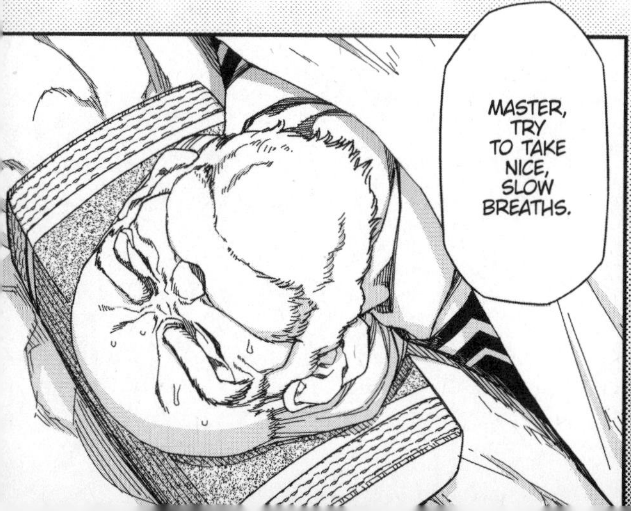
MASTER, TRY TO TAKE NICE, SLOW BREATHS.

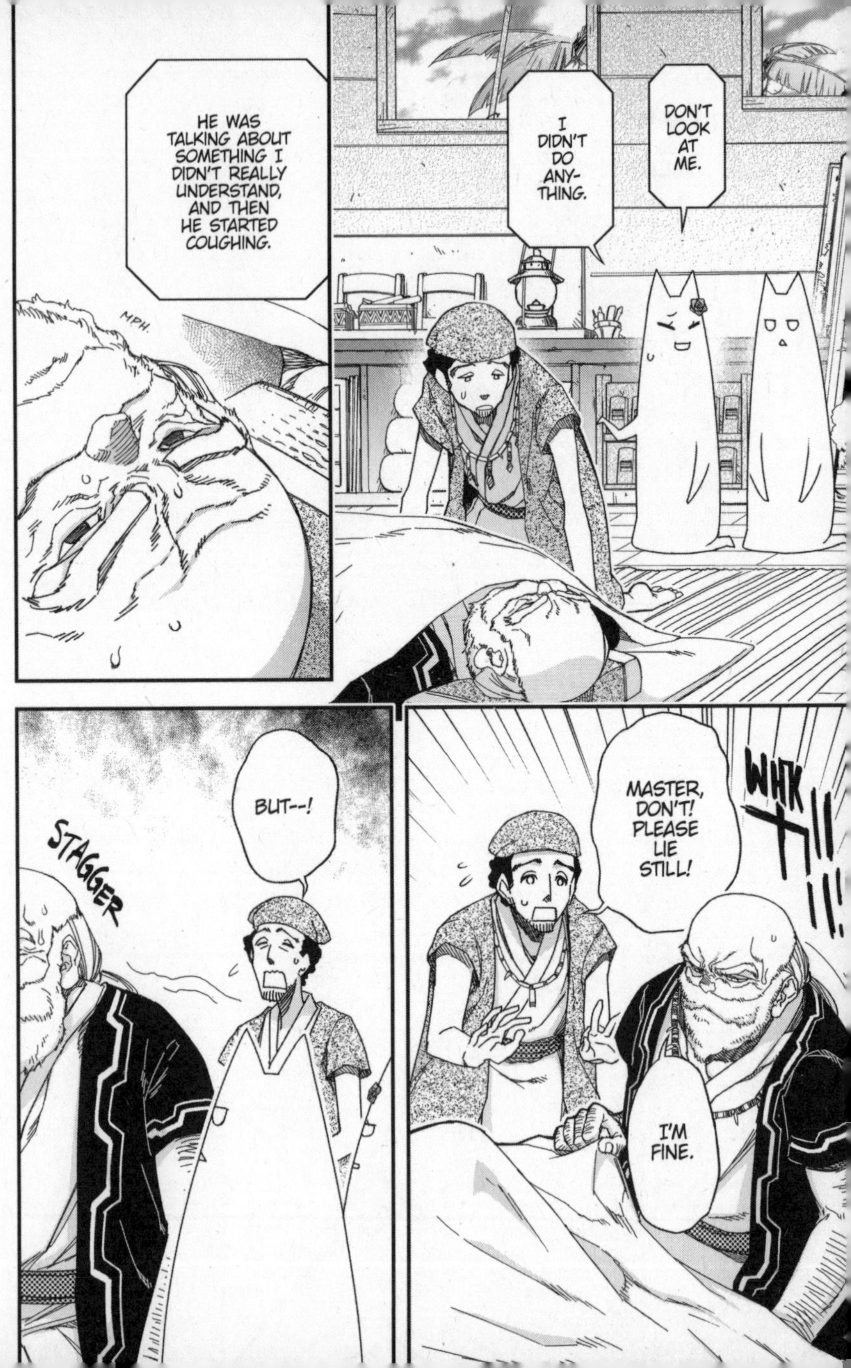
DON'T LOOK AT ME.
I DIDN'T DO ANY-THING.
HE WAS TALKING ABOUT SOMETHING I DIDN'T REALLY UNDERSTAND, AND THEN HE STARTED COUGHING.
MPH.
WHK
MASTER, DON'T! PLEASE LIE STILL!
I'M FINE.
BUT--!
STAGGER

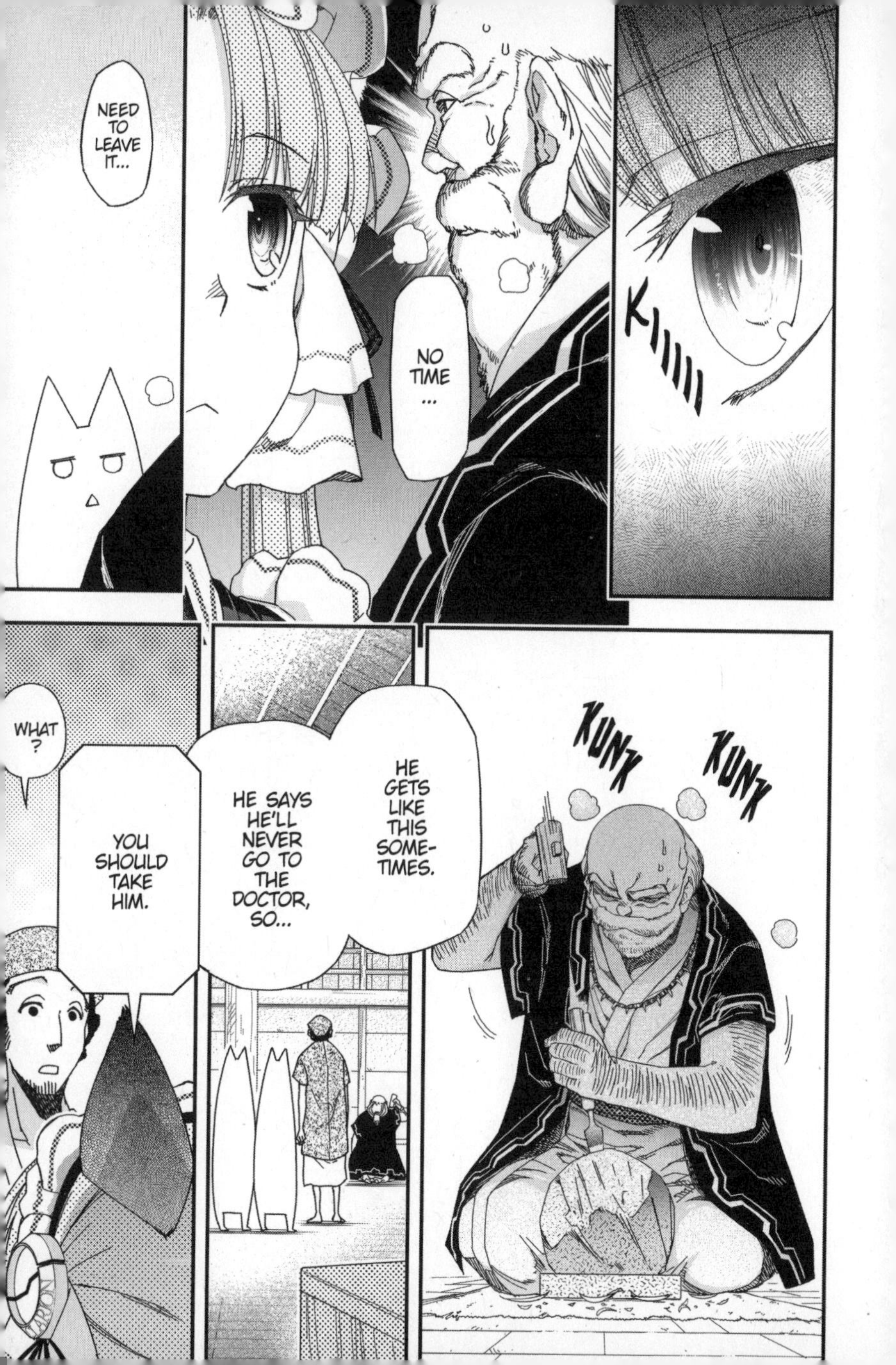
KIIIII
NO TIME ...
NEED TO LEAVE IT...
KUNK KUNK
HE GETS LIKE THIS SOME-TIMES.
HE SAYS HE'LL NEVER GO TO THE DOCTOR, SO...
YOU SHOULD TAKE HIM.
WHAT?

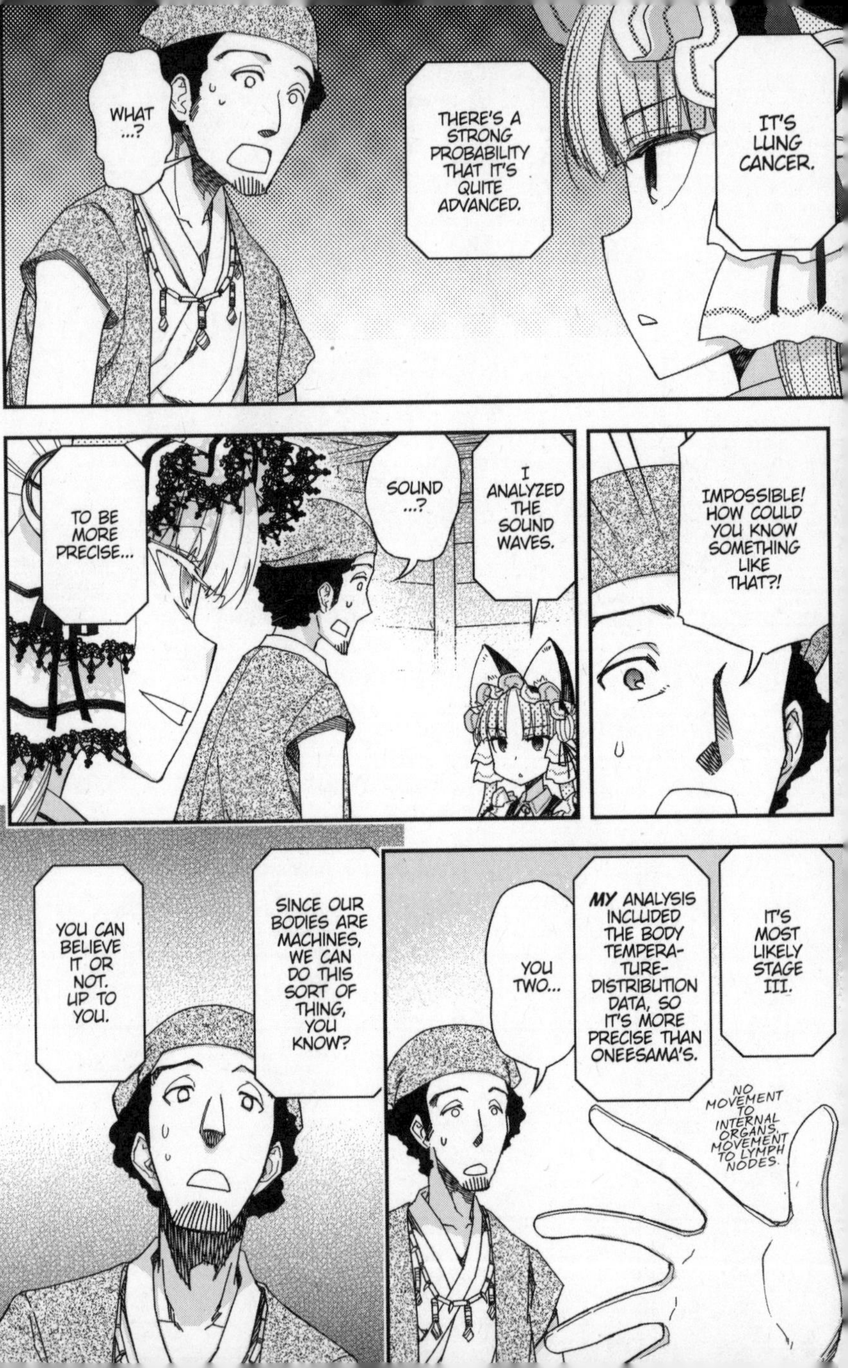
IT'S LUNG CANCER.
THERE'S A STRONG PROBABILITY THAT IT'S QUITE ADVANCED.
WHAT ...?
IMPOSSIBLE! HOW COULD YOU KNOW SOMETHING LIKE THAT?!
I ANALYZED THE SOUND WAVES.
SOUND ...?
TO BE MORE PRECISE...
IT'S MOST LIKELY STAGE III.
MY ANALYSIS INCLUDED THE BODY TEMPERATURE-DISTRIBUTION DATA, SO IT'S MORE PRECISE THAN ONEESAMA'S.
YOU TWO...
NO MOVEMENT TO INTERNAL ORGANS. MOVEMENT TO LYMPH NODES.
SINCE OUR BODIES ARE MACHINES, WE CAN DO THIS SORT OF THING, YOU KNOW?
YOU CAN BELIEVE IT OR NOT. UP TO YOU.

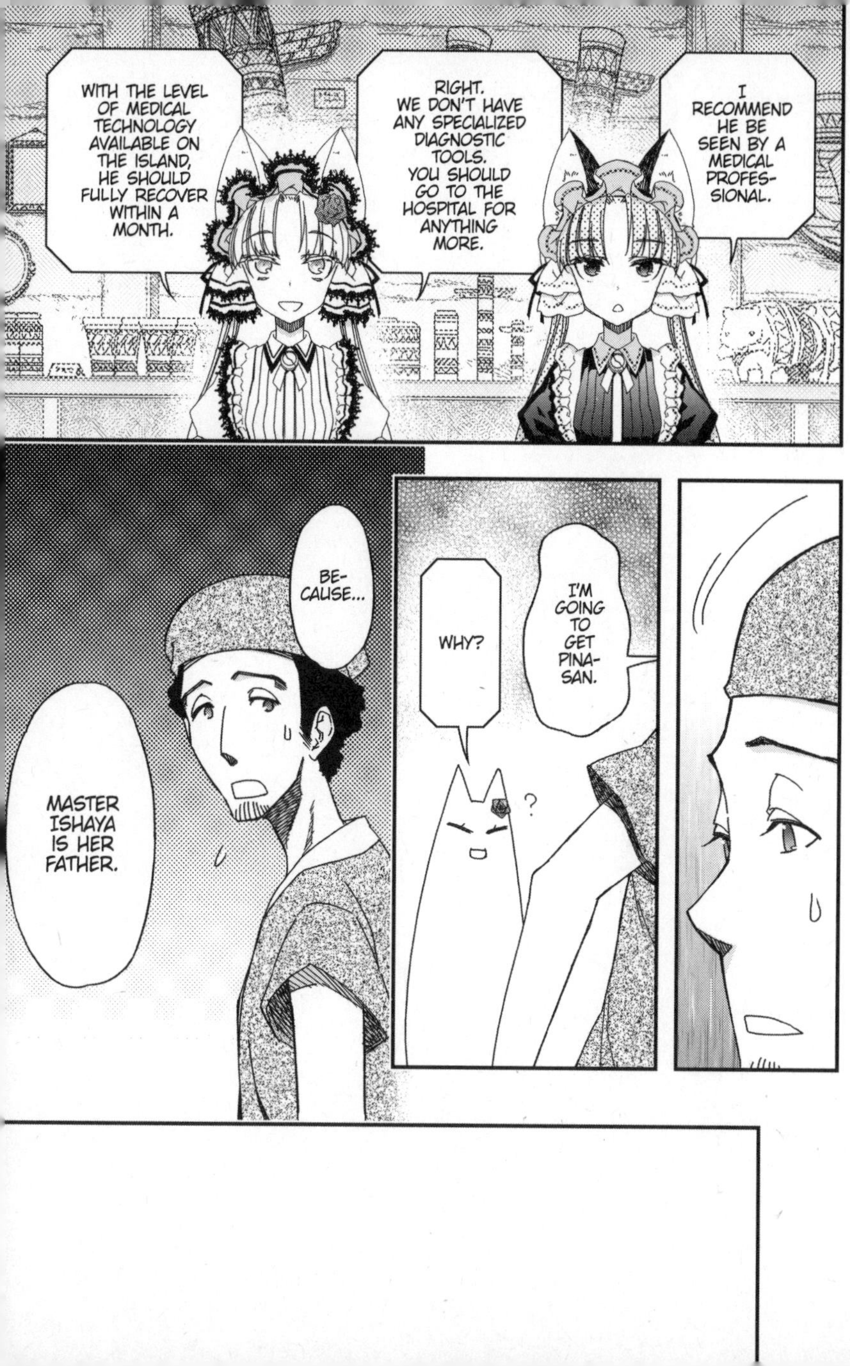
I RECOMMEND HE BE SEEN BY A MEDICAL PROFES-SIONAL.
RIGHT. WE DON'T HAVE ANY SPECIALIZED DIAGNOSTIC TOOLS. YOU SHOULD GO TO THE HOSPITAL FOR ANYTHING MORE.
WITH THE LEVEL OF MEDICAL TECHNOLOGY AVAILABLE ON THE ISLAND, HE SHOULD FULLY RECOVER WITHIN A MONTH.
I'M GOING TO GET PINA-SAN.
WHY?
?
BE-CAUSE...
MASTER ISHAYA IS HER FATHER.

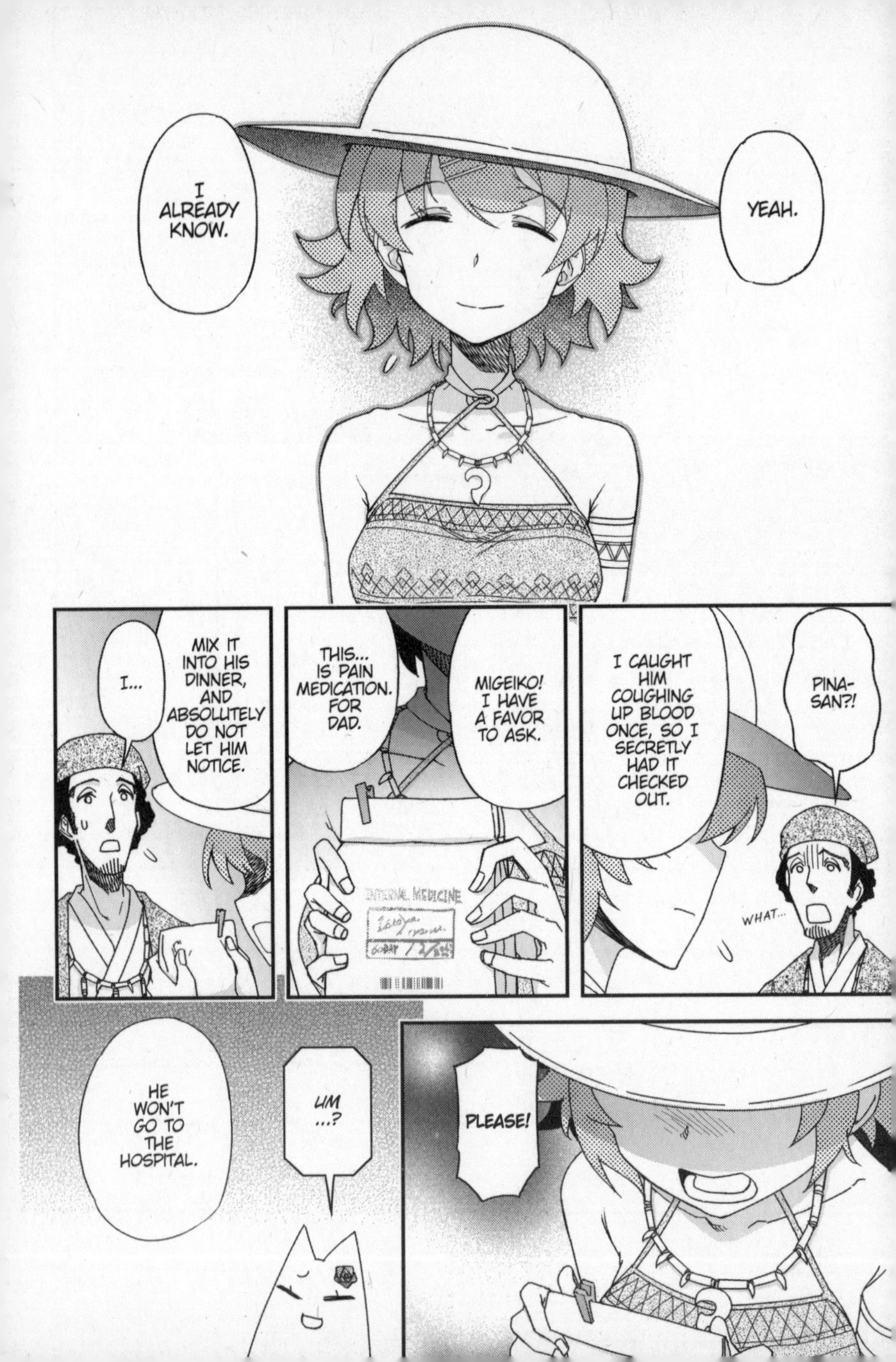
YEAH.
I ALREADY KNOW.
PINA-SAN?!
WHAT...
I CAUGHT HIM COUGHING UP BLOOD ONCE, SO I SECRETLY HAD IT CHECKED OUT.
MIGEIKO! I HAVE A FAVOR TO ASK.
THIS... IS PAIN MEDICATION. FOR DAD.
INTERNAL MEDICINE
MIX IT INTO HIS DINNER, AND ABSOLUTELY DO NOT LET HIM NOTICE.
I...
PLEASE!
UM ...?
HE WON'T GO TO THE HOSPITAL.

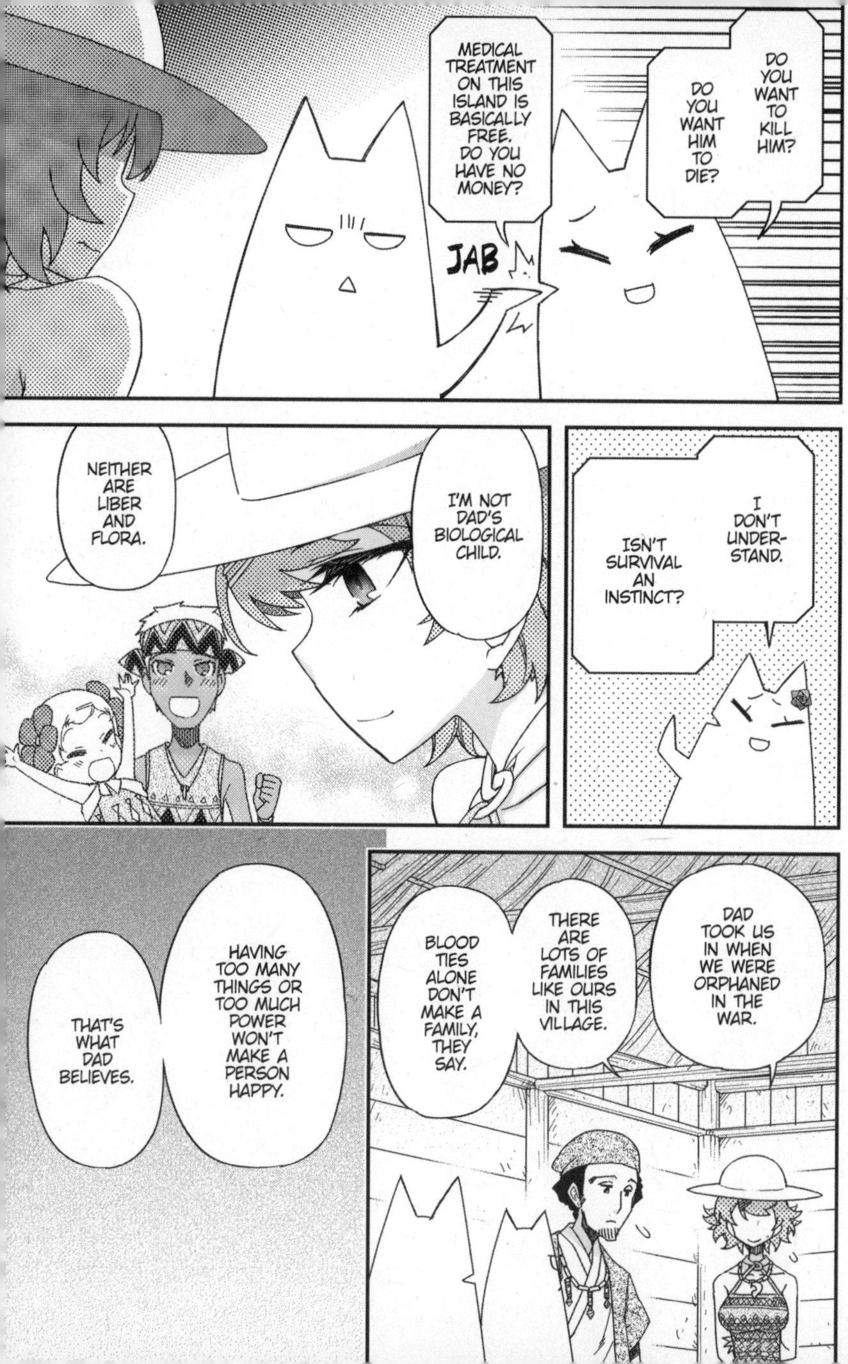
DO YOU WANT TO KILL HIM?
DO YOU WANT HIM TO DIE?
MEDICAL TREATMENT ON THIS ISLAND IS BASICALLY FREE. DO YOU HAVE NO MONEY?
JAB
I DON'T UNDER-STAND.
ISN'T SURVIVAL AN INSTINCT?
I'M NOT DAD'S BIOLOGICAL CHILD.
NEITHER ARE LIBER AND FLORA.
DAD TOOK US IN WHEN WE WERE ORPHANED IN THE WAR.
THERE ARE LOTS OF FAMILIES LIKE OURS IN THIS VILLAGE.
BLOOD TIES ALONE DON'T MAKE A FAMILY, THEY SAY.
HAVING TOO MANY THINGS OR TOO MUCH POWER WON'T MAKE A PERSON HAPPY.
THAT'S WHAT DAD BELIEVES.

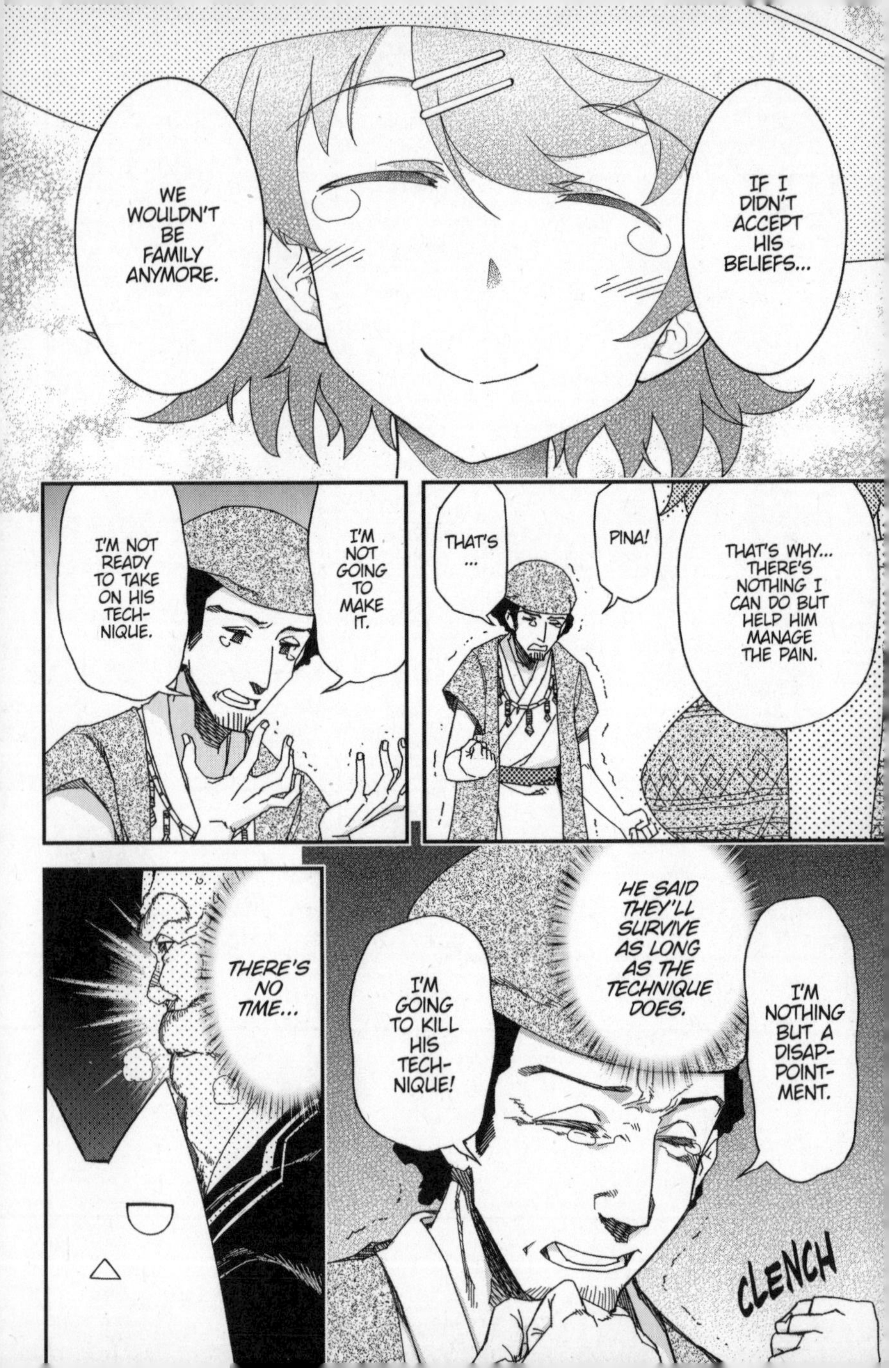
IF I DIDN'T ACCEPT HIS BELIEFS...
WE WOULDN'T BE FAMILY ANYMORE.
THAT'S WHY... THERE'S NOTHING I CAN DO BUT HELP HIM MANAGE THE PAIN.
PINA!
THAT'S ...
I'M NOT GOING TO MAKE IT.
I'M NOT READY TO TAKE ON HIS TECH-NIQUE.
I'M NOTHING BUT A DISAP-POINT-MENT.
HE SAID THEY'LL SURVIVE AS LONG AS THE TECHNIQUE DOES.
I'M GOING TO KILL HIS TECH-NIQUE!
CLENCH
THERE'S NO TIME...

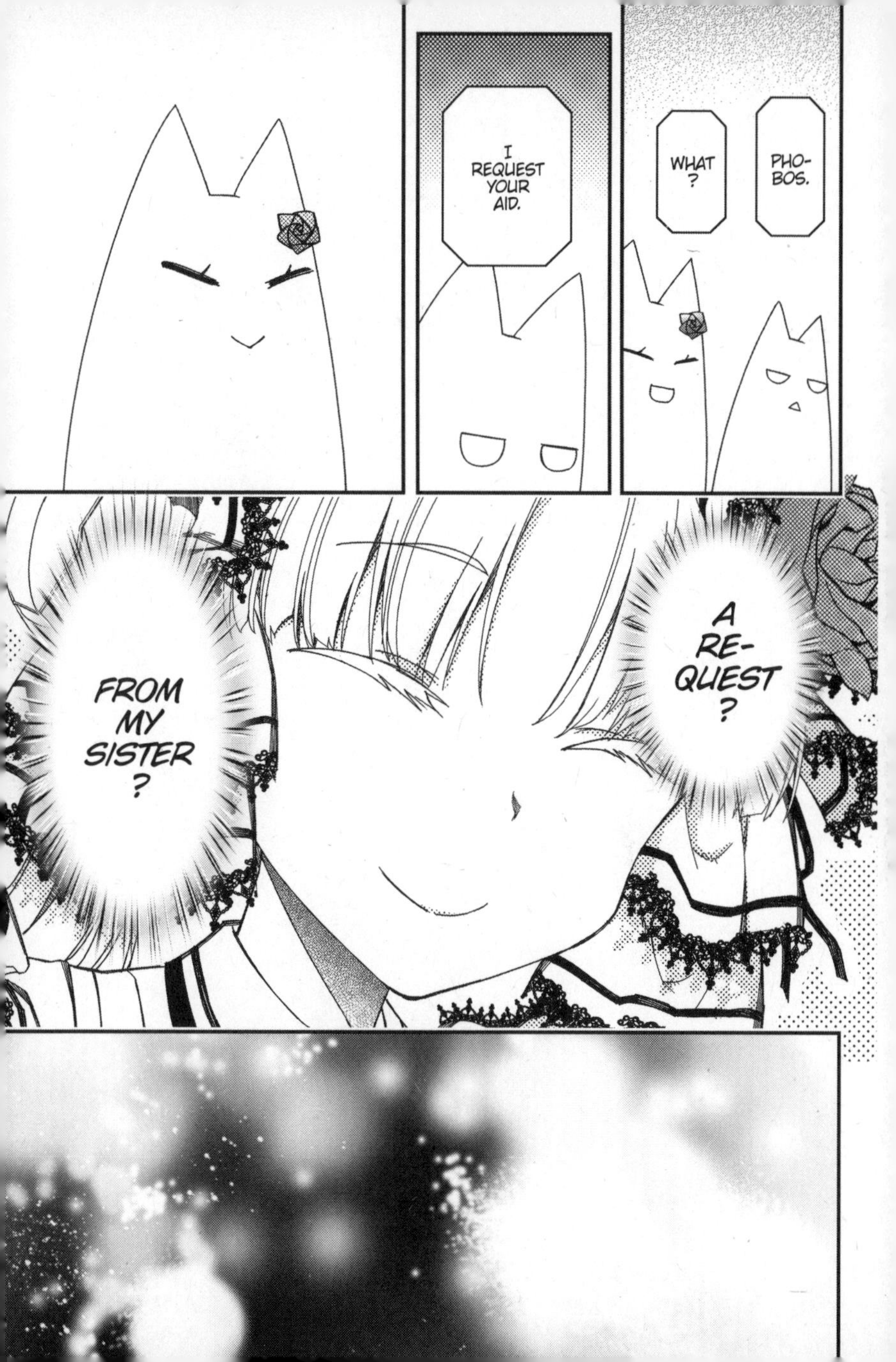
PHO-BOS.
WHAT?
I REQUEST YOUR AID.
A RE-QUEST?
FROM MY SISTER?

S T A R E

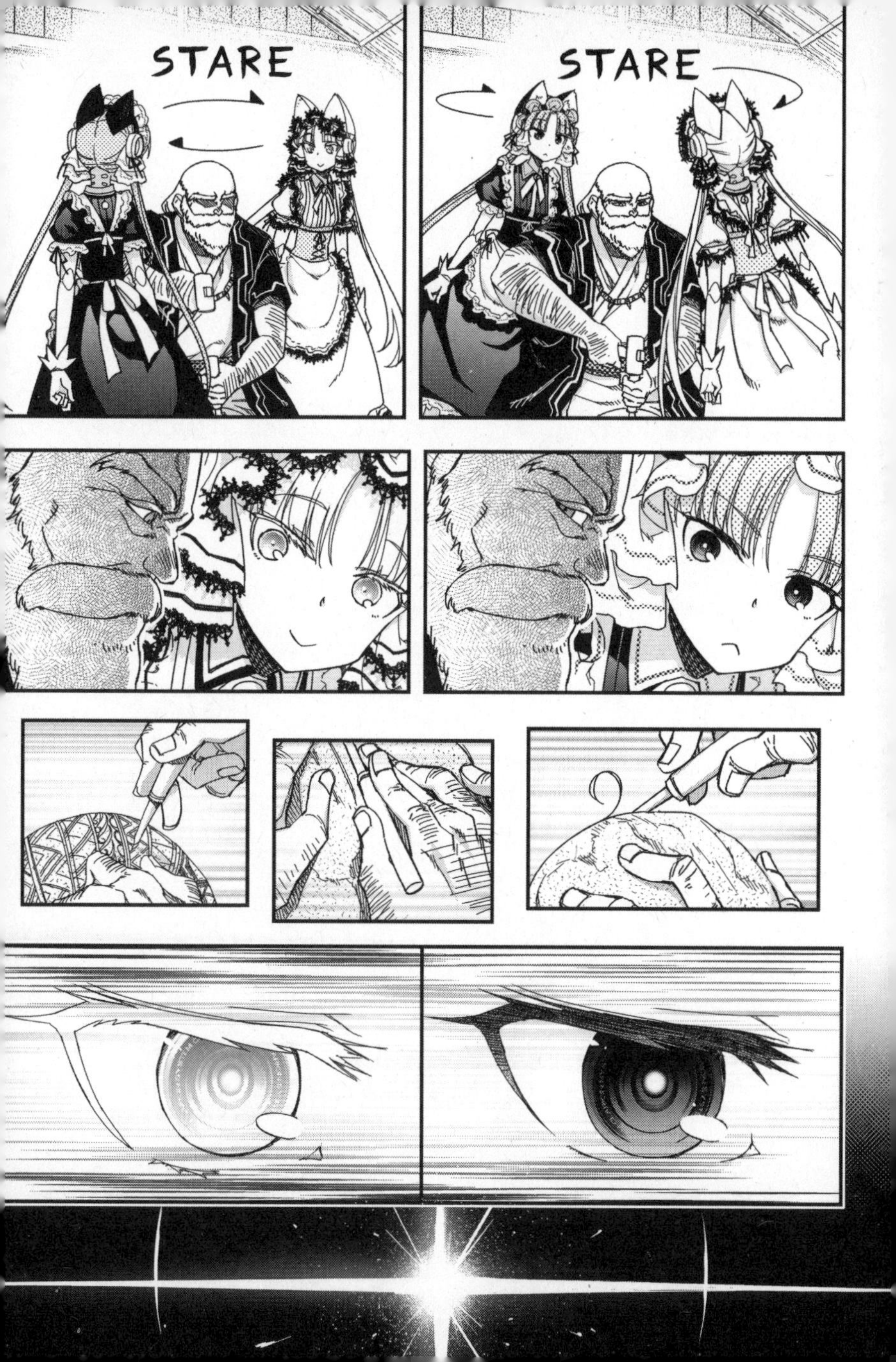
STARE
STARE

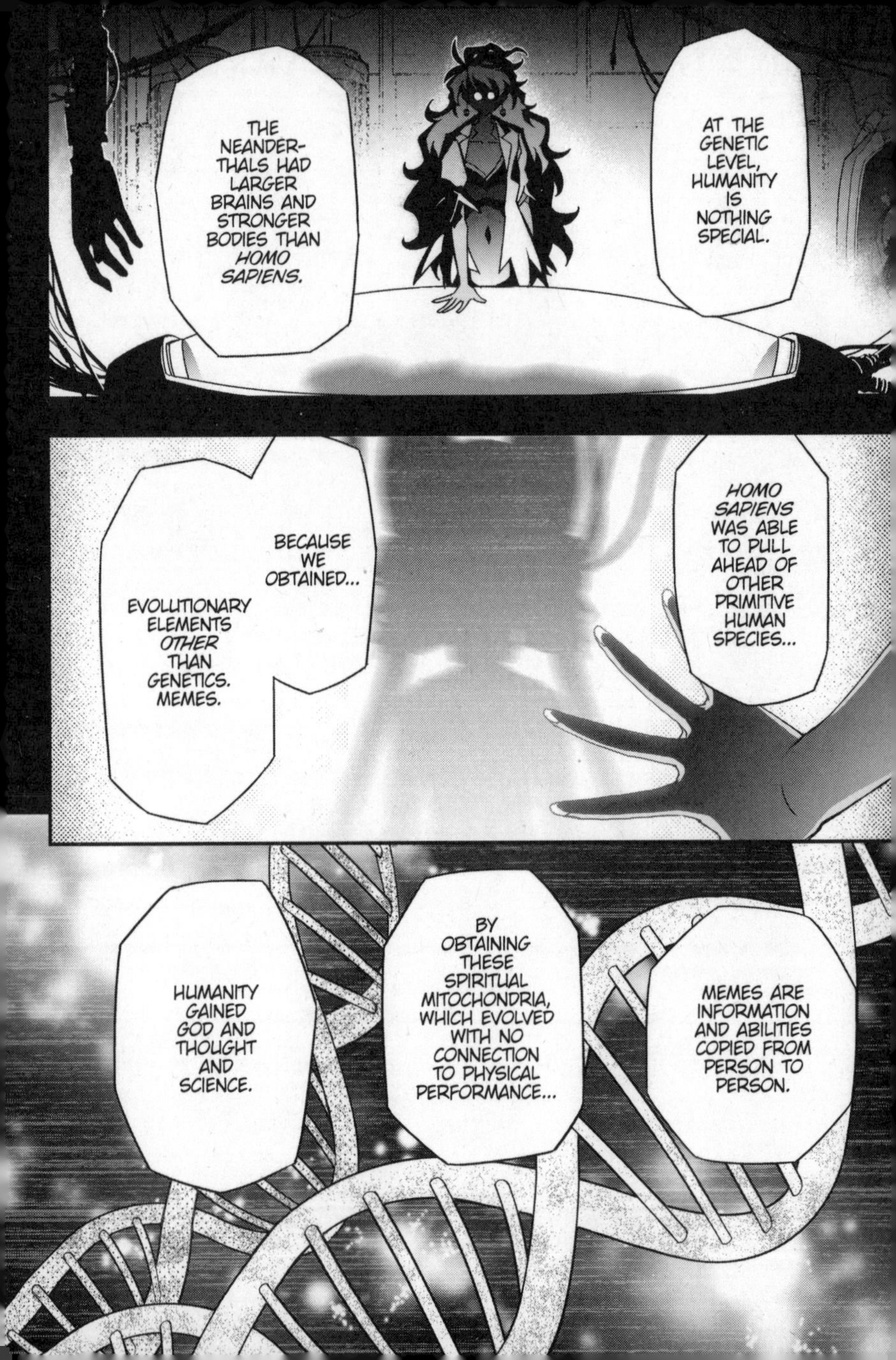
AT THE GENETIC LEVEL, HUMANITY IS NOTHING SPECIAL.
THE NEANDER-THALS HAD LARGER BRAINS AND STRONGER BODIES THAN *HOMO SAPIENS.*
HOMO SAPIENS WAS ABLE TO PULL AHEAD OF OTHER PRIMITIVE HUMAN SPECIES...
BECAUSE WE OBTAINED...
EVOLUTIONARY ELEMENTS *OTHER* THAN GENETICS. MEMES.
MEMES ARE INFORMATION AND ABILITIES COPIED FROM PERSON TO PERSON.
BY OBTAINING THESE SPIRITUAL MITOCHONDRIA, WHICH EVOLVED WITH NO CONNECTION TO PHYSICAL PERFORMANCE...
HUMANITY GAINED GOD AND THOUGHT AND SCIENCE.

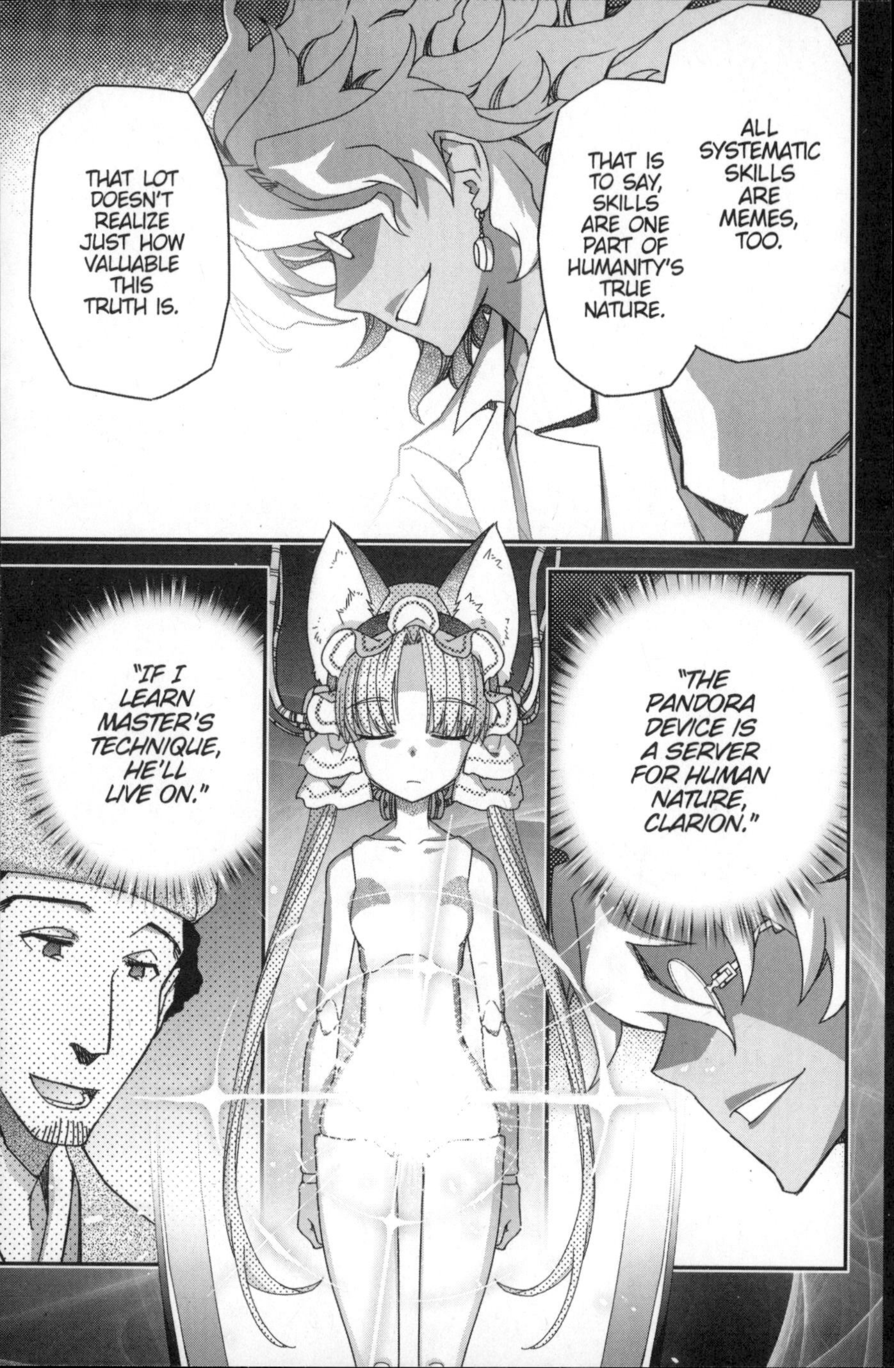
ALL SYSTEMATIC SKILLS ARE MEMES, TOO.
THAT IS TO SAY, SKILLS ARE ONE PART OF HUMANITY'S TRUE NATURE.
THAT LOT DOESN'T REALIZE JUST HOW VALUABLE THIS TRUTH IS.
"THE PANDORA DEVICE IS A SERVER FOR HUMAN NATURE, CLARION."
"IF I LEARN MASTER'S TECHNIQUE, HE'LL LIVE ON."

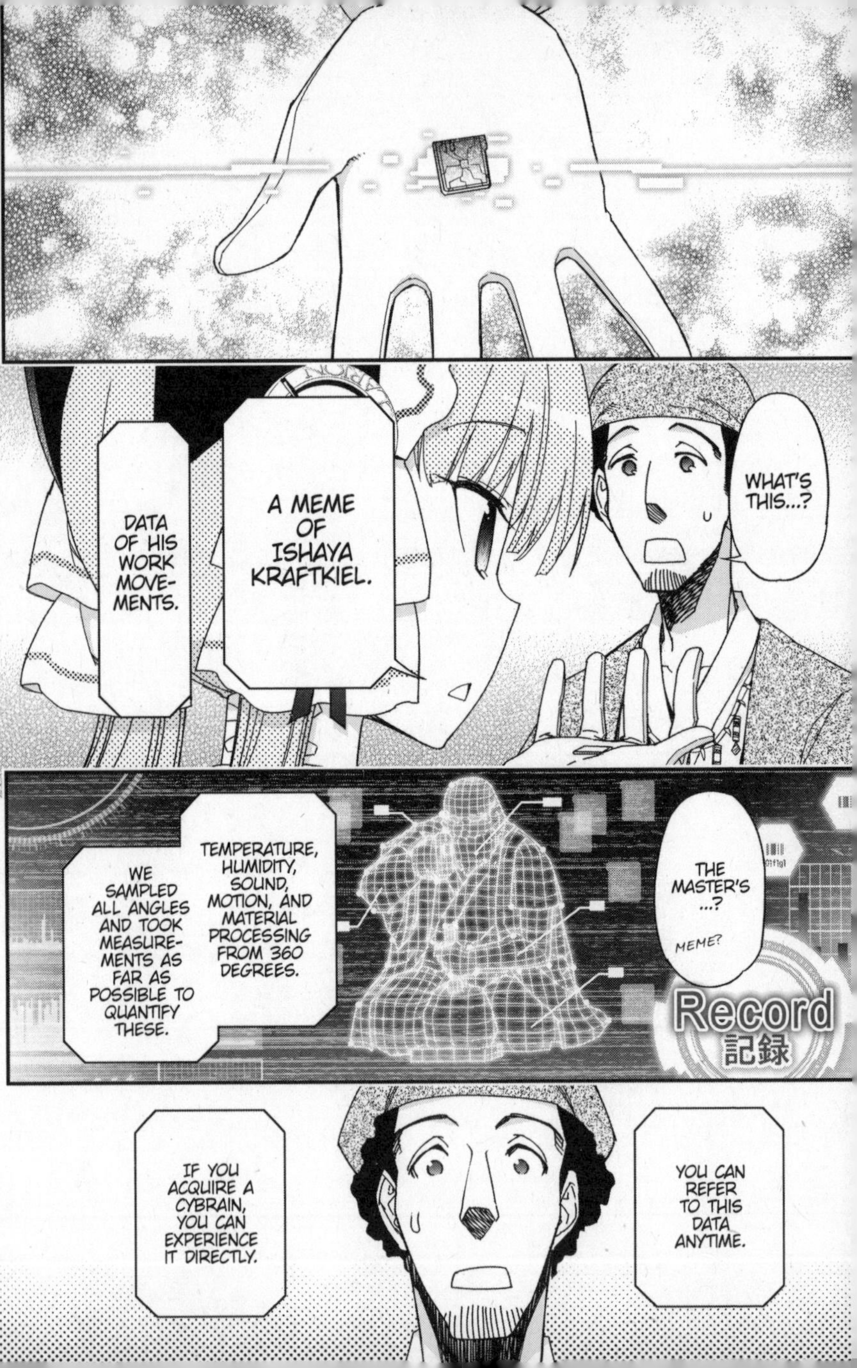
WHAT'S THIS...?
A MEME OF ISHAYA KRAFTKIEL.
DATA OF HIS WORK MOVEMENTS.
THE MASTER'S ...?
MEME?
Record
記録
TEMPERATURE, HUMIDITY, SOUND, MOTION, AND MATERIAL PROCESSING FROM 360 DEGREES.
WE SAMPLED ALL ANGLES AND TOOK MEASUREMENTS AS FAR AS POSSIBLE TO QUANTIFY THESE.
YOU CAN REFER TO THIS DATA ANYTIME.
IF YOU ACQUIRE A CYBRAIN, YOU CAN EXPERIENCE IT DIRECTLY.

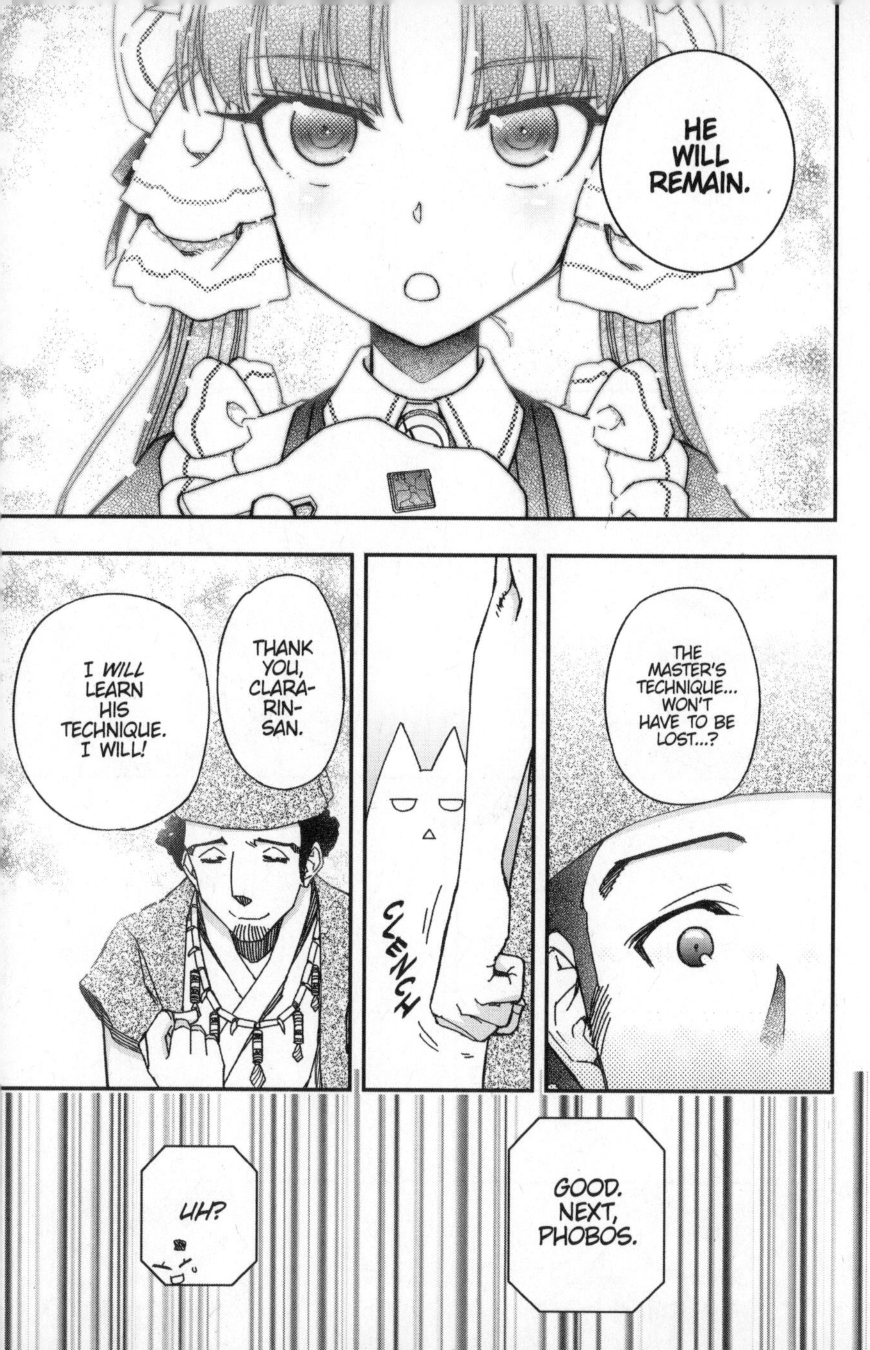
HE WILL REMAIN.
THE MASTER'S TECHNIQUE... WON'T HAVE TO BE LOST...?
CLENCH
THANK YOU, CLARA-RIN-SAN.
I WILL LEARN HIS TECHNIQUE. I WILL!
GOOD. NEXT, PHOBOS.
UH?

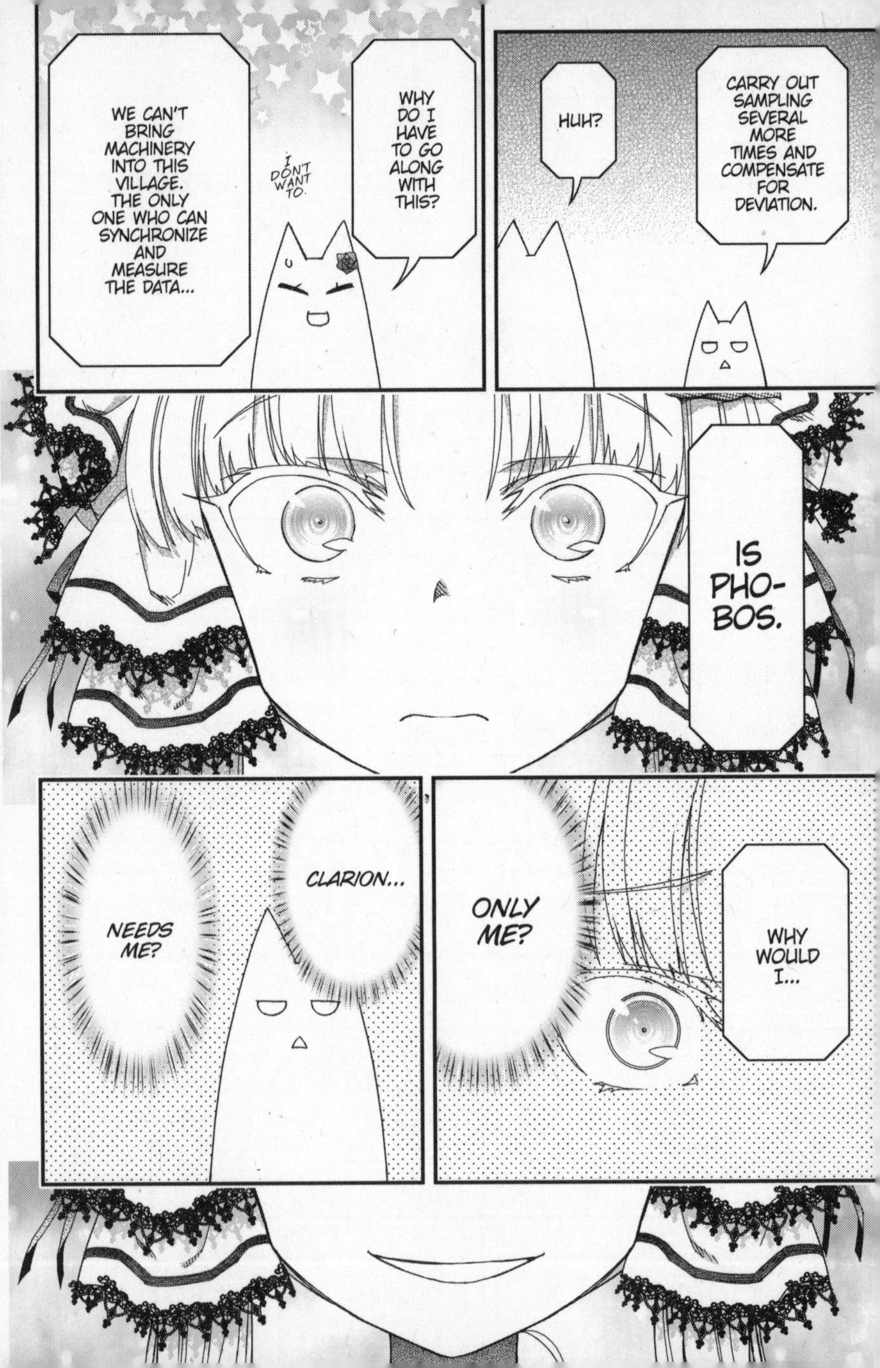
CARRY OUT SAMPLING SEVERAL MORE TIMES AND COMPENSATE FOR DEVIATION.
HUH?
WHY DO I HAVE TO GO ALONG WITH THIS?
I DON'T WANT TO.
WE CAN'T BRING MACHINERY INTO THIS VILLAGE. THE ONLY ONE WHO CAN SYNCHRONIZE AND MEASURE THE DATA...
IS PHO-BOS.
WHY WOULD I...
ONLY ME?
CLARION...
NEEDS ME?

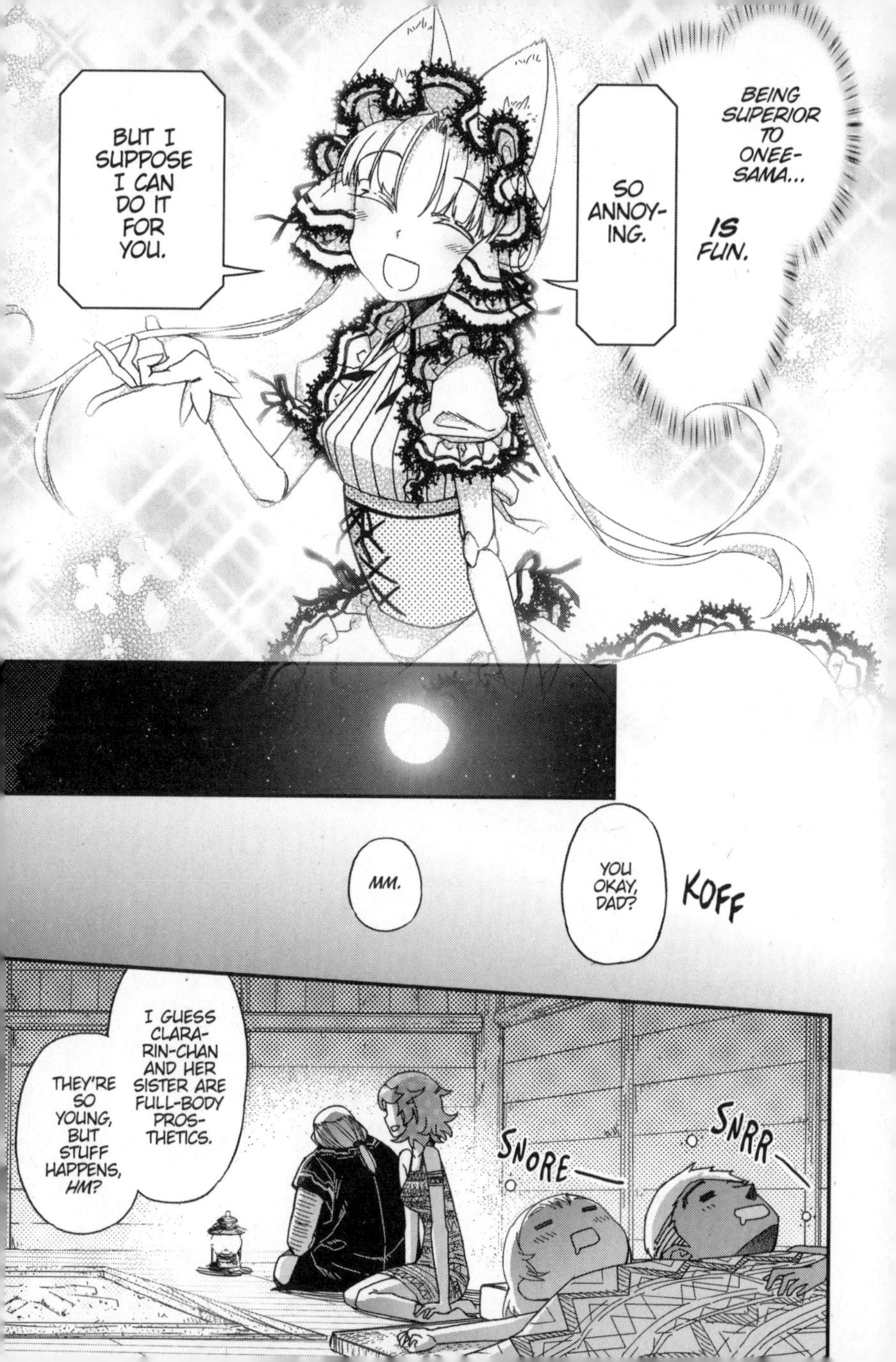
BEING SUPERIOR TO ONEE-SAMA... IS FUN.
SO ANNOY-ING.
BUT I SUPPOSE I CAN DO IT FOR YOU.
KOFF
YOU OKAY, DAD?
MM.
SNRR
SNORE
I GUESS CLARA-RIN-CHAN AND HER SISTER ARE FULL-BODY PROS-THETICS.
THEY'RE SO YOUNG, BUT STUFF HAPPENS, HM?

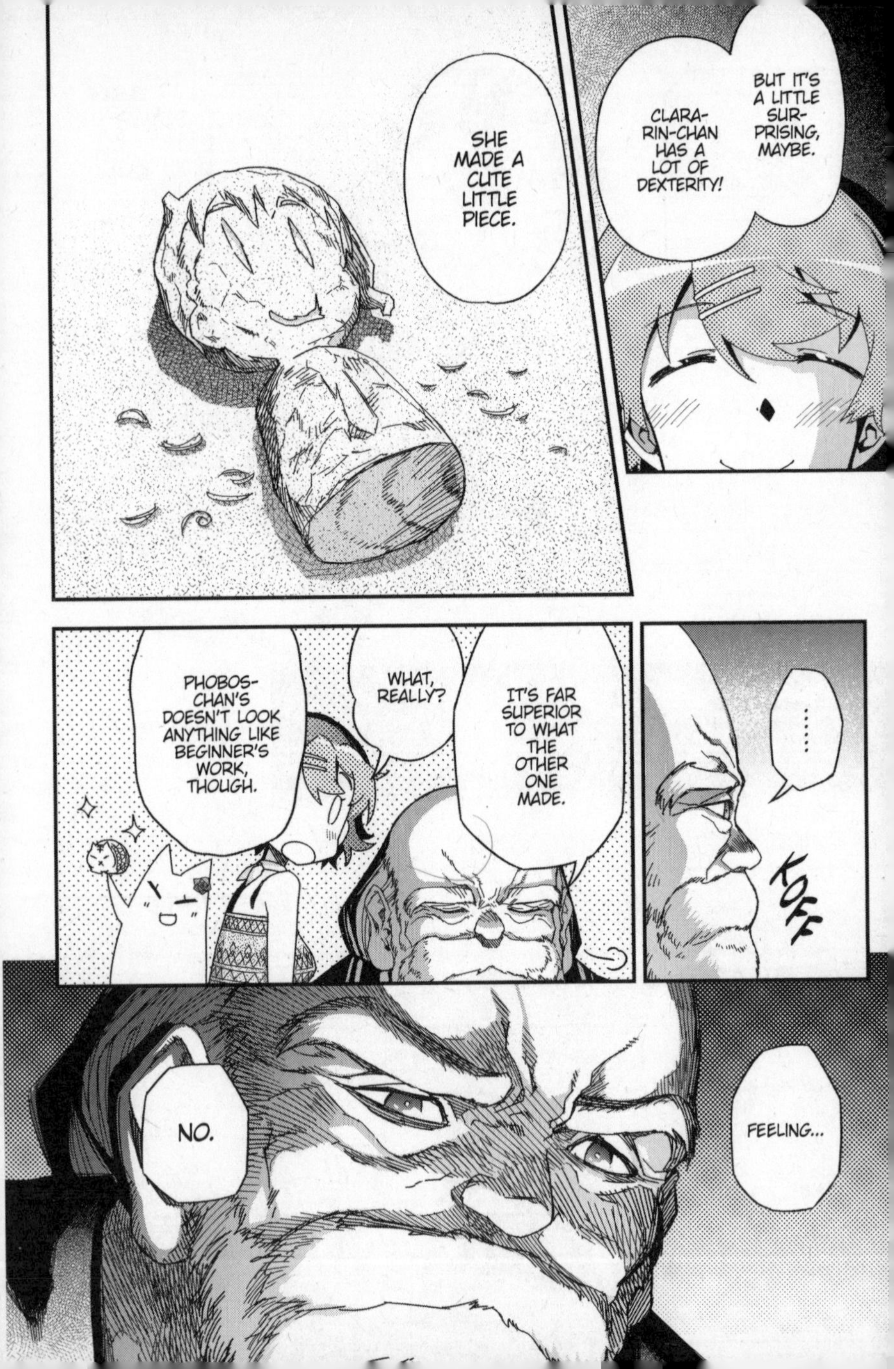
BUT IT'S A LITTLE SUR-PRISING, MAYBE.
CLARA-RIN-CHAN HAS A LOT OF DEXTERITY!
SHE MADE A CUTE LITTLE PIECE.
......
KOFF
IT'S FAR SUPERIOR TO WHAT THE OTHER ONE MADE.
WHAT, REALLY?
PHOBOS-CHAN'S DOESN'T LOOK ANYTHING LIKE BEGINNER'S WORK, THOUGH.
FEELING...
NO.

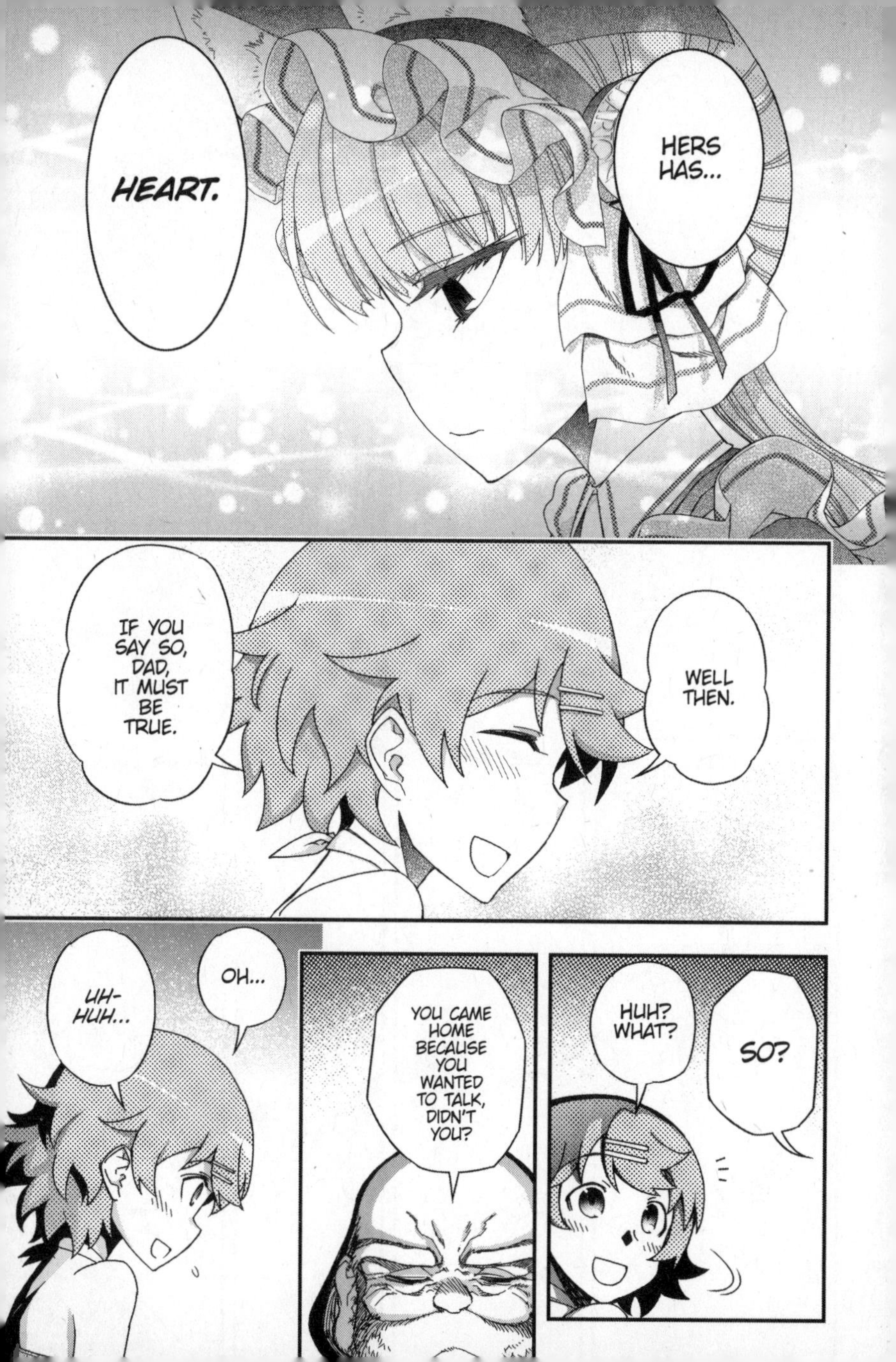
HERS HAS...
HEART.
WELL THEN.
IF YOU SAY SO, DAD, IT MUST BE TRUE.
SO?
HUH? WHAT?
YOU CAME HOME BECAUSE YOU WANTED TO TALK, DIDN'T YOU?
OH...
UH-HUH...

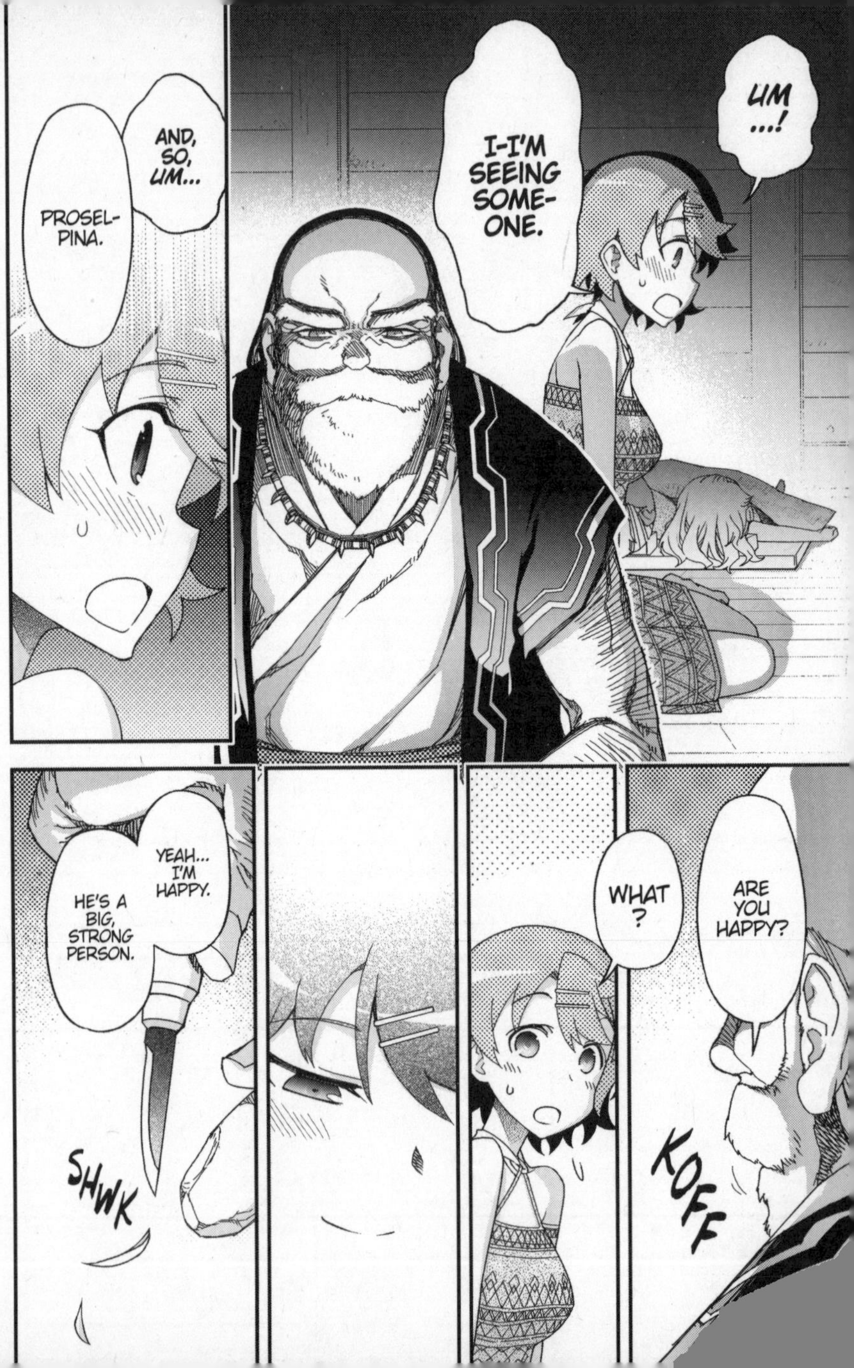
UM ...!
I-I'M SEEING SOME-ONE.
AND, SO, UM...
PROSEL-PINA.
ARE YOU HAPPY?
KOFF
WHAT?
YEAH... I'M HAPPY.
HE'S A BIG, STRONG PERSON.
SHWK

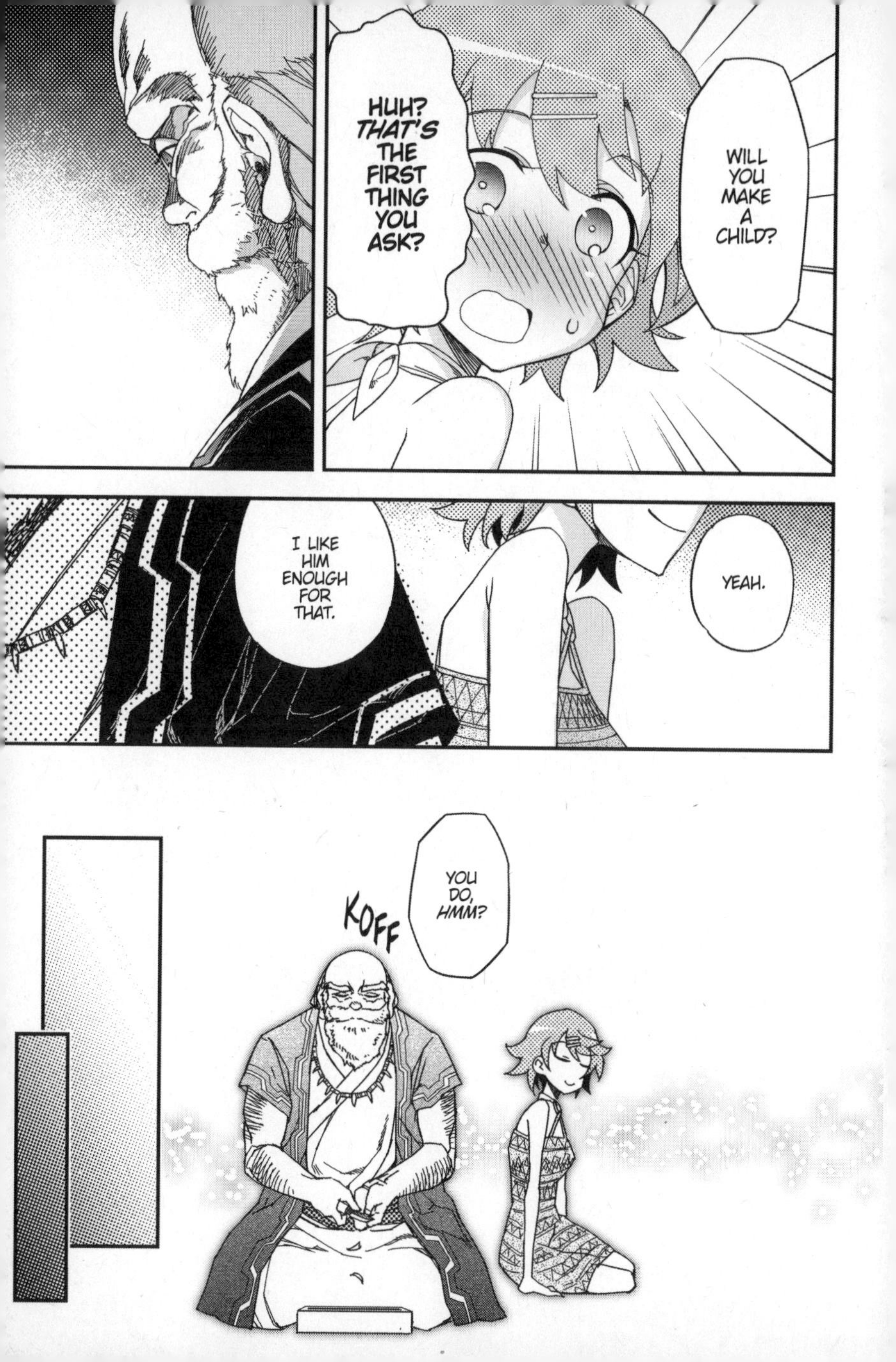
WILL YOU MAKE A CHILD?
HUH? *THAT'S* THE FIRST THING YOU ASK?
YEAH.
I LIKE HIM ENOUGH FOR THAT.
YOU DO, *HMM?*
KOFF

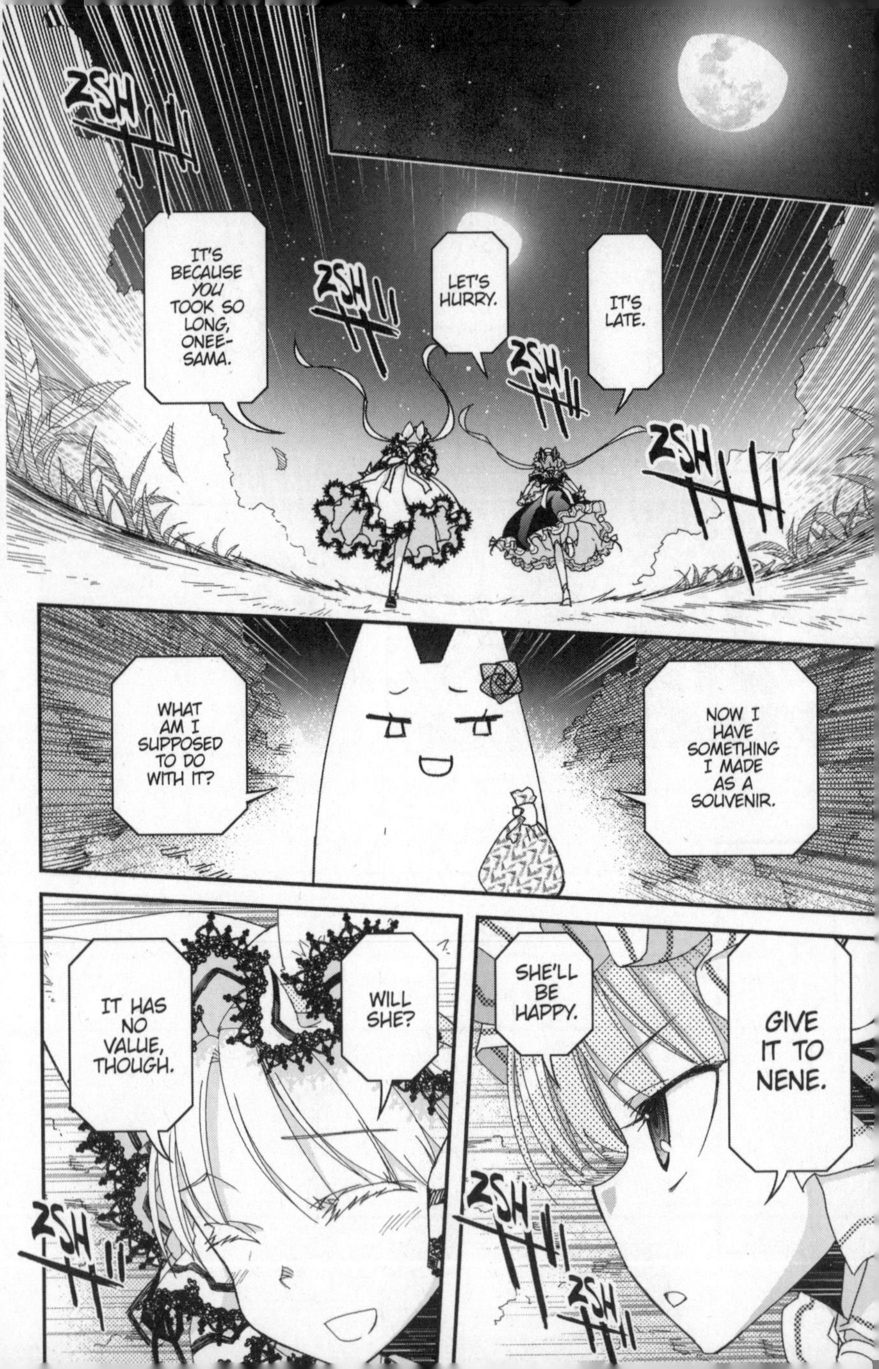
ZSH
IT'S LATE.
ZSH
LET'S HURRY.
ZSH
IT'S BECAUSE YOU TOOK SO LONG, ONEE-SAMA.
ZSH
NOW I HAVE SOMETHING I MADE AS A SOUVENIR.
WHAT AM I SUPPOSED TO DO WITH IT?
GIVE IT TO NENE.
SHE'LL BE HAPPY.
ZSH
ZSH
WILL SHE?
IT HAS NO VALUE, THOUGH.
ZSH

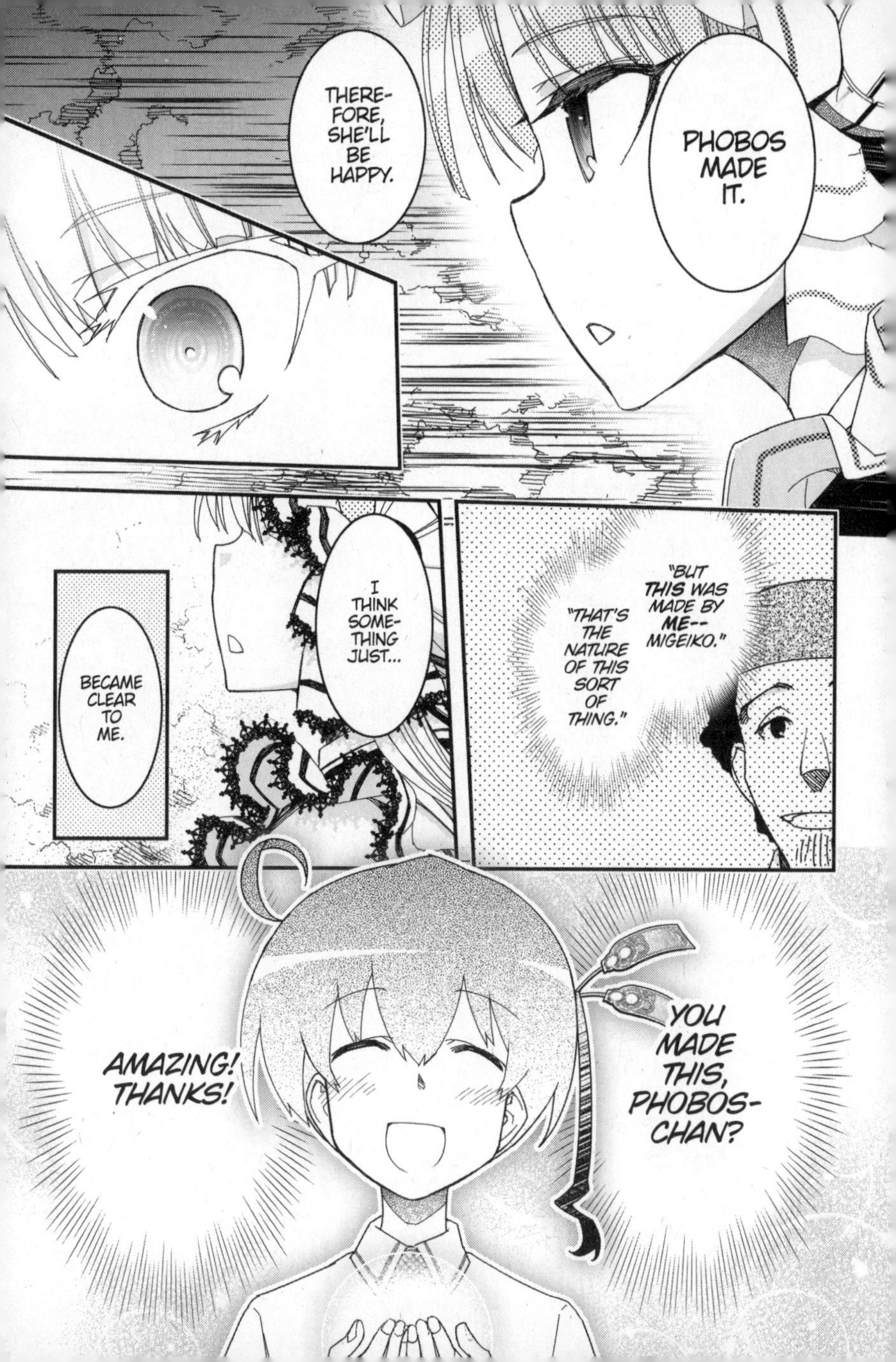
PHOBOS MADE IT.
THEREFORE, SHE'LL BE HAPPY.
"BUT THIS WAS MADE BY ME-- MIGEIKO."
"THAT'S THE NATURE OF THIS SORT OF THING."
I THINK SOMETHING JUST...
BECAME CLEAR TO ME.
YOU MADE THIS, PHOBOS-CHAN?
AMAZING! THANKS!

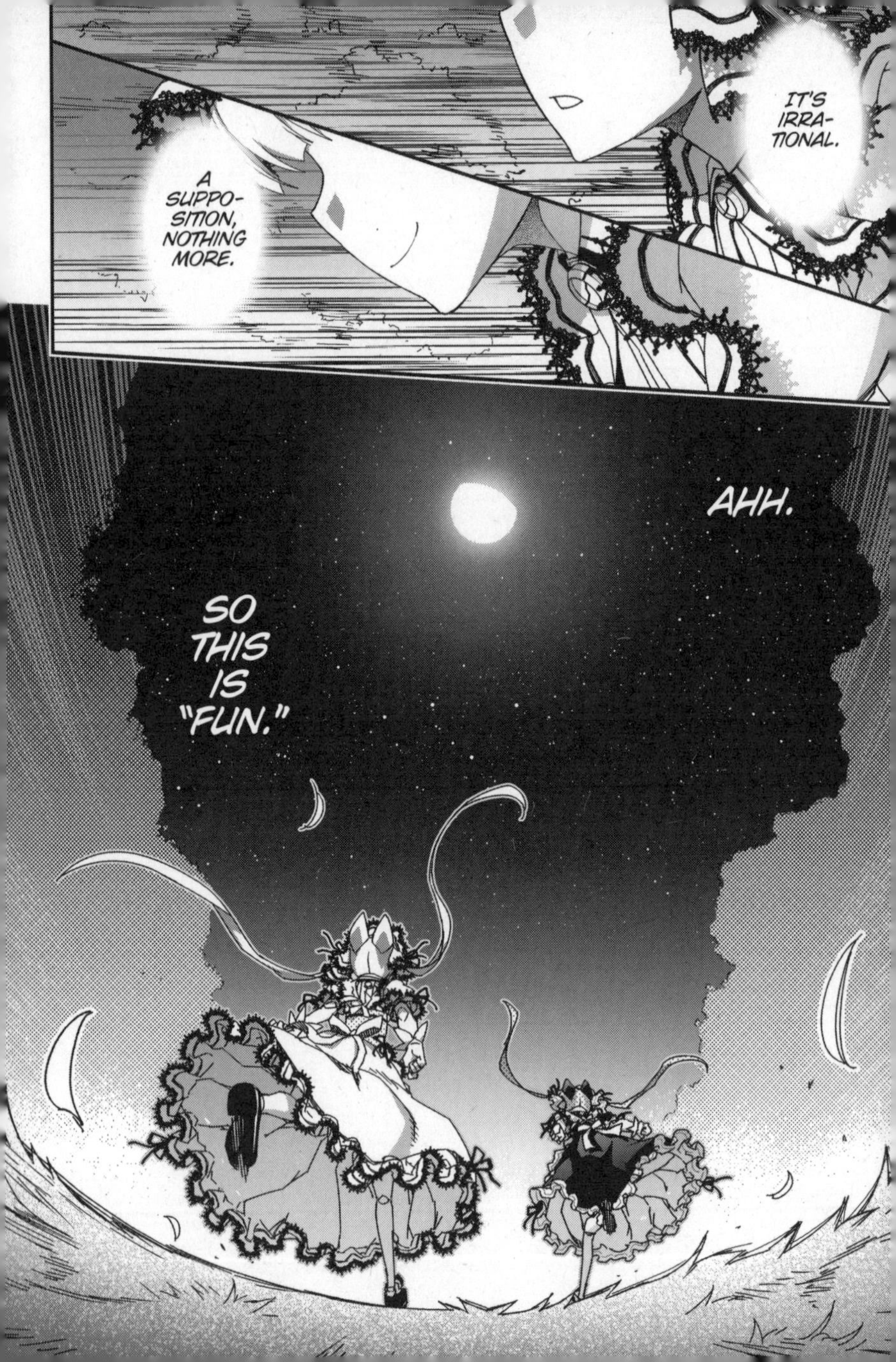
IT'S IRRA-TIONAL.
A SUPPO-SITION, NOTHING MORE.
AHH.
SO THIS IS "FUN."

...TO BE CONTINUED

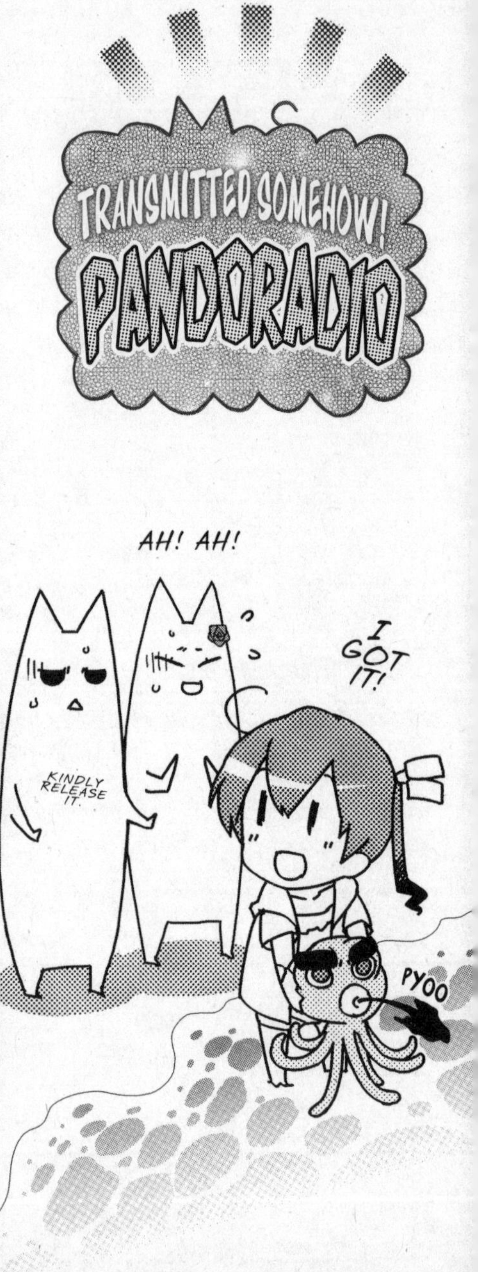
TRANSMITTED SOMEHOW!
PANDORADIO
AH! AH!
I GOT IT!
KINDLY RELEASE IT.
PYOO

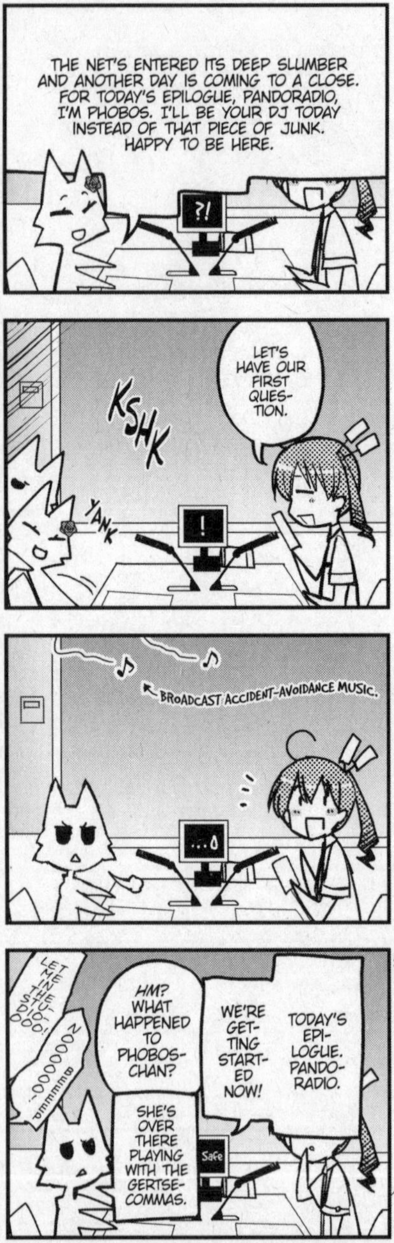
THE NET'S ENTERED ITS DEEP SLUMBER AND ANOTHER DAY IS COMING TO A CLOSE. FOR TODAY'S EPILOGUE, PANDORADIO, I'M PHOBOS. I'LL BE YOUR DJ TODAY INSTEAD OF THAT PIECE OF JUNK. HAPPY TO BE HERE.
?!
LET'S HAVE OUR FIRST QUESTION.
KSHK
YANK
!
BROADCAST ACCIDENT-AVOIDANCE MUSIC.
...
TODAY'S EPILOGUE. PANDORADIO.
WE'RE GETTING STARTED NOW!
HM? WHAT HAPPENED TO PHOBOS-CHAN?
LET ME IN THE STUDIOOO!
NOOOOOO-MMMMM
SHE'S OVER THERE PLAYING WITH THE GERTSECOMMAS.
Safe

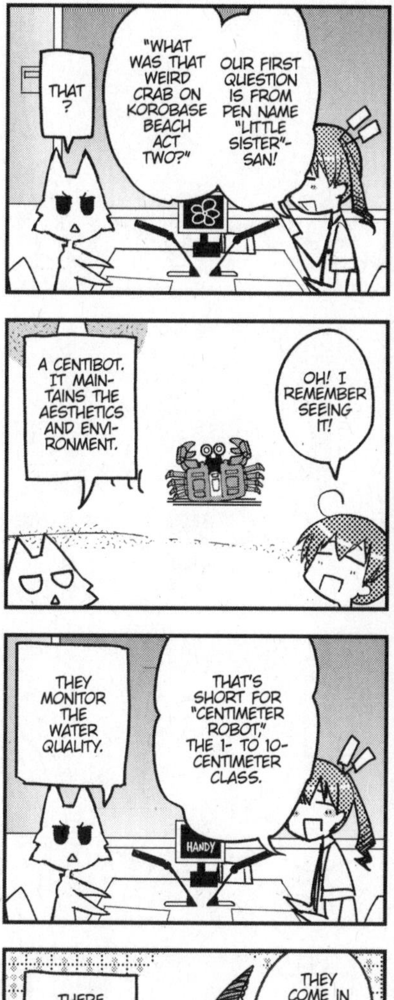
OUR FIRST QUESTION IS FROM PEN NAME "LITTLE SISTER"-SAN!
"WHAT WAS THAT WEIRD CRAB ON KOROBASE BEACH ACT TWO?"
THAT?
OH! I REMEMBER SEEING IT!
A CENTIBOT. IT MAINTAINS THE AESTHETICS AND ENVIRONMENT.
THAT'S SHORT FOR "CENTIMETER ROBOT," THE 1- TO 10-CENTIMETER CLASS.
THEY MONITOR THE WATER QUALITY.
HANDY
THEY COME IN ALL SHAPES--SHELL, HERMIT CRAB.
THERE ARE MANY INSECT TYPES NEAR THE BEACH.
YOU'RE DIFFERENT.
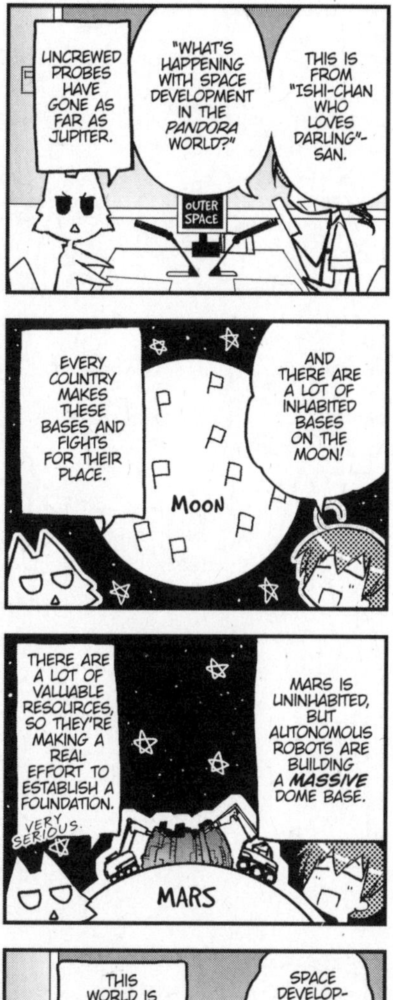
THIS IS FROM "ISHI-CHAN WHO LOVES DARLING"-SAN.
"WHAT'S HAPPENING WITH SPACE DEVELOPMENT IN THE *PANDORA* WORLD?"
UNCREWED PROBES HAVE GONE AS FAR AS JUPITER.
OUTER SPACE
AND THERE ARE A LOT OF INHABITED BASES ON THE MOON!
EVERY COUNTRY MAKES THESE BASES AND FIGHTS FOR THEIR PLACE.
MOON
MARS IS UNINHABITED, BUT AUTONOMOUS ROBOTS ARE BUILDING A ***MASSIVE*** DOME BASE.
THERE ARE A LOT OF VALUABLE RESOURCES, SO THEY'RE MAKING A REAL EFFORT TO ESTABLISH A FOUNDATION.
VERY SERIOUS.
MARS
SPACE DEVELOPMENT'S MAKING REAL PROGRESS, HUH?
THIS WORLD IS DANGEROUS, SO WE'RE EXPLORING ALL KINDS OF PATHS FOR HUMANITY'S FUTURE.
ROMAN-TIC

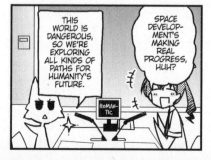

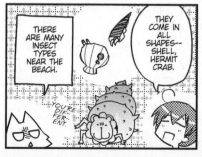

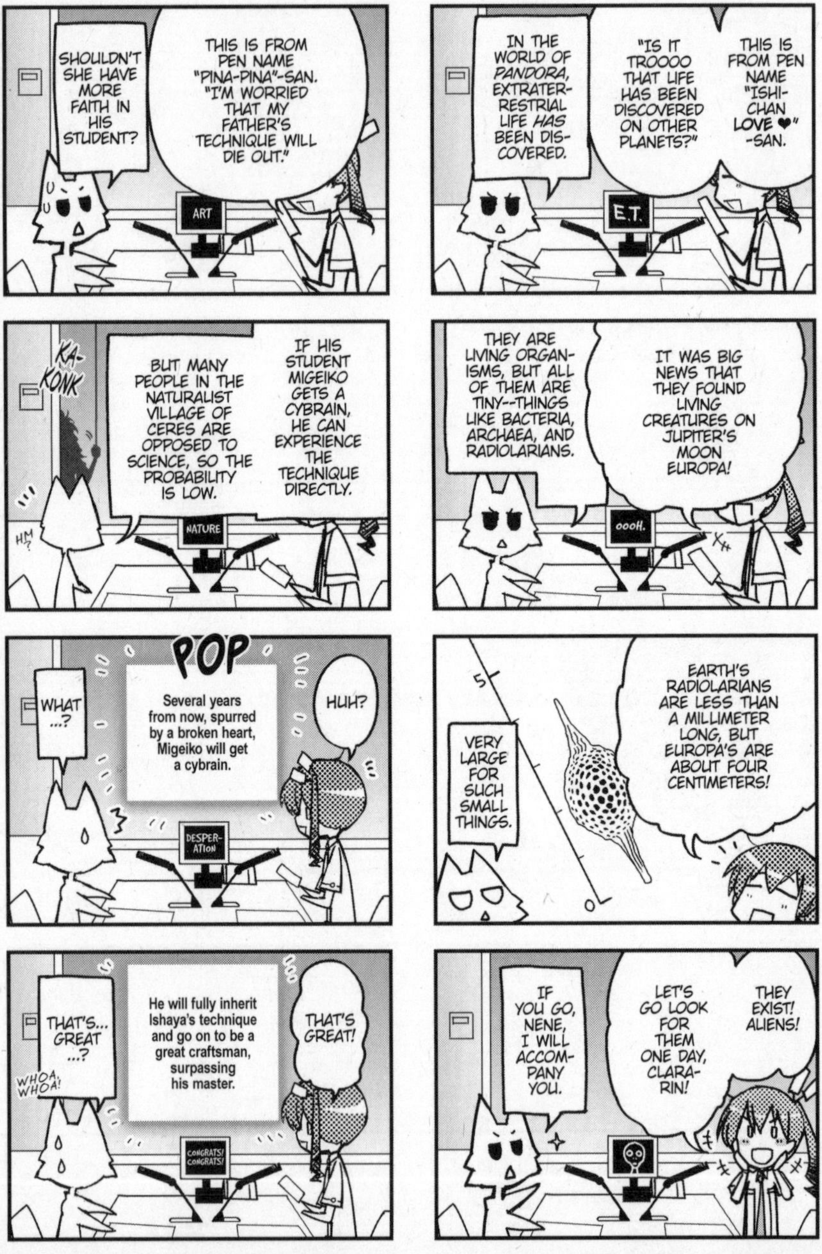
THIS IS FROM PEN NAME "ISHI-CHAN LOVE ❤" -SAN.
"IS IT TROOOO THAT LIFE HAS BEEN DISCOVERED ON OTHER PLANETS?"
IN THE WORLD OF *PANDORA*, EXTRATERRESTRIAL LIFE *HAS* BEEN DISCOVERED.
E.T.
IT WAS BIG NEWS THAT THEY FOUND LIVING CREATURES ON JUPITER'S MOON EUROPA!
THEY ARE LIVING ORGANISMS, BUT ALL OF THEM ARE TINY--THINGS LIKE BACTERIA, ARCHAEA, AND RADIOLARIANS.
OOOH.
EARTH'S RADIOLARIANS ARE LESS THAN A MILLIMETER LONG, BUT EUROPA'S ARE ABOUT FOUR CENTIMETERS!
VERY LARGE FOR SUCH SMALL THINGS.
5
0
THEY EXIST! ALIENS!
LET'S GO LOOK FOR THEM ONE DAY, CLARA-RIN!
IF YOU GO, NENE, I WILL ACCOMPANY YOU.
THIS IS FROM PEN NAME "PINA-PINA"-SAN. "I'M WORRIED THAT MY FATHER'S TECHNIQUE WILL DIE OUT."
SHOULDN'T SHE HAVE MORE FAITH IN HIS STUDENT?
ART
IF HIS STUDENT MIGEIKO GETS A CYBRAIN, HE CAN EXPERIENCE THE TECHNIQUE DIRECTLY.
BUT MANY PEOPLE IN THE NATURALIST VILLAGE OF CERES ARE OPPOSED TO SCIENCE, SO THE PROBABILITY IS LOW.
KA-KONK
HM?
NATURE
POP
HUH?
Several years from now, spurred by a broken heart, Migeiko will get a cybrain.
WHAT ...?
DESPERATION
THAT'S GREAT!
He will fully inherit Ishaya's technique and go on to be a great craftsman, surpassing his master.
THAT'S... GREAT ...?
WHOA, WHOA!
CONGRATS! CONGRATS!

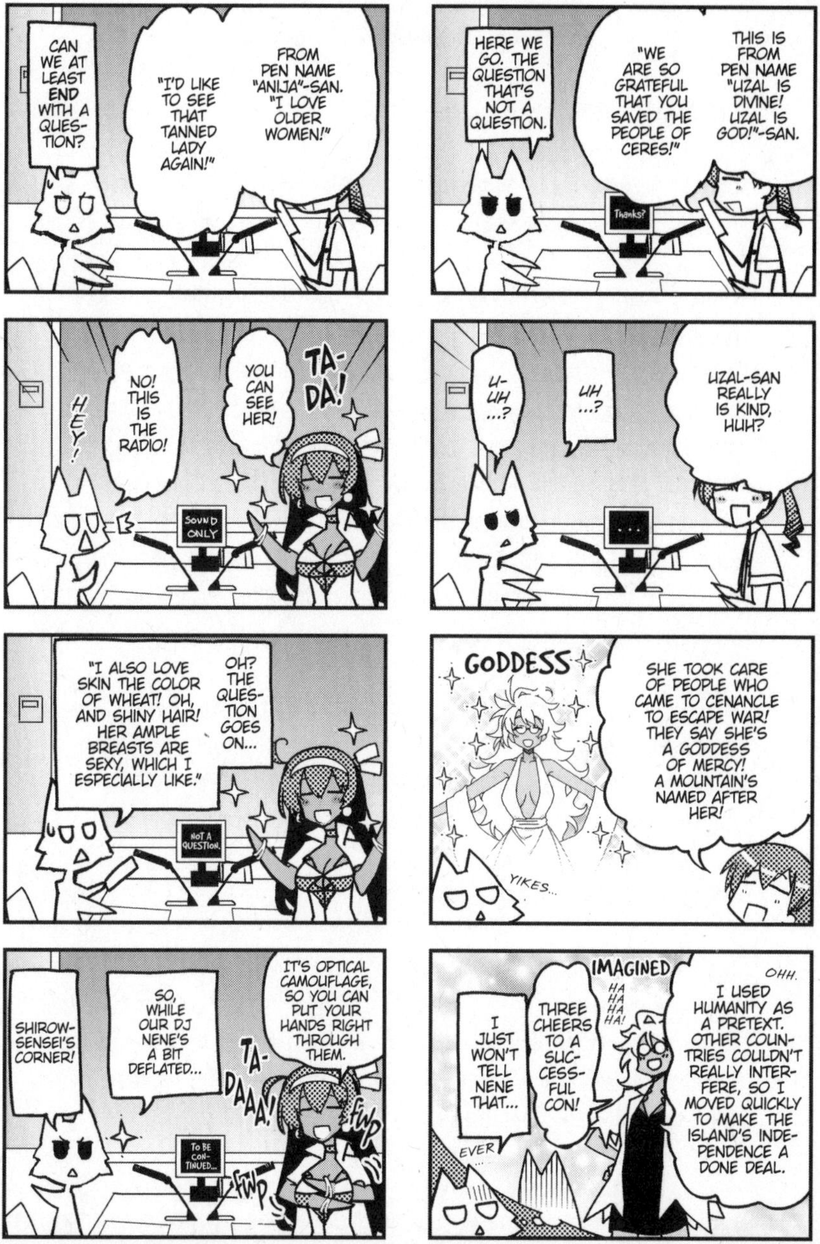
THIS IS FROM PEN NAME "UZAL IS DIVINE! UZAL IS GOD!"-SAN.
"WE ARE SO GRATEFUL THAT YOU SAVED THE PEOPLE OF CERES!"
HERE WE GO. THE QUESTION THAT'S NOT A QUESTION.
Thanks?
UZAL-SAN REALLY IS KIND, HUH?
UH ...?
U-UH ...?
...
SHE TOOK CARE OF PEOPLE WHO CAME TO CENANCLE TO ESCAPE WAR! THEY SAY SHE'S A GODDESS OF MERCY! A MOUNTAIN'S NAMED AFTER HER!
GODDESS
YIKES...
OHH.
I USED HUMANITY AS A PRETEXT. OTHER COUNTRIES COULDN'T REALLY INTERFERE, SO I MOVED QUICKLY TO MAKE THE ISLAND'S INDEPENDENCE A DONE DEAL.
HA HA HA HA!
IMAGINED
THREE CHEERS TO A SUCCESSFUL CON!
I JUST WON'T TELL NENE THAT...
EVER...
FROM PEN NAME "ANIJA"-SAN. "I LOVE OLDER WOMEN!"
"I'D LIKE TO SEE THAT TANNED LADY AGAIN!"
CAN WE AT LEAST END WITH A QUESTION?
TA-DA!
YOU CAN SEE HER!
NO! THIS IS THE RADIO!
HEY!
SOUND ONLY
OH? THE QUESTION GOES ON...
"I ALSO LOVE SKIN THE COLOR OF WHEAT! OH, AND SHINY HAIR! HER AMPLE BREASTS ARE SEXY, WHICH I ESPECIALLY LIKE."
NOT A QUESTION.
IT'S OPTICAL CAMOUFLAGE, SO YOU CAN PUT YOUR HANDS RIGHT THROUGH THEM.
TA-DAAA!
FWP
FWP
SO, WHILE OUR DJ NENE'S A BIT DEFLATED...
SHIROW-SENSEI'S CORNER!
To BE CONTINUED...

Greetings (for the thirteenth time)!

Dearest readers, thank you for coming back for Volume 13 of *Pandora in the Crimson Shell*.

Coming from me, since I simply wrote notes on a tentative plan and some rough ideas, perhaps this is a bit much, but I ask that you resign yourself to this once more. (Deep gratitude) Vlin-whatever-san has also been safely (?) put in place (expressive gratitude), and since this is originally Rikudou-shi's creative work—the script, the construction, the storyboards, the big plots, the small plots—when it comes to this greeting, I've been thinking it would be more authentic to leave this to him, instead of me. But inertia carries me onward. (LOL) That said, my repeated thanks to you readers and to everyone involved in the production has nothing to do with inertia. It's always the truth. A thousand thanks!

Now, as for *Pandora in the Crimson Shell* itself! With me and Rikudou-shi combined, with our powerful, poisonous darkness like a coating of white chocolate, *Pandora* finished its first half (the Kurtz arc), then went through a retrenchment arc. Adding in Hitotose-shi's sprinkles and frills, we passed through the "good magical girl"-type midgame, and now we're finally heading toward the endgame.

Every time I look back at any element, I am so grateful to Rikudou-shi and everyone involved in the production for polishing the "science fluff" (so-called, Rikudou-shi), rather than the gloomy cyber punch with no hope of salvation, into the girls' cyber story, so that you can laugh and have fun (with an extra-large helping of parody).

There is absolutely no malice behind these meandering, irritating messages that I write, for all that they seem to be trying to decrease your visual acuity, and I would never complain, either. This is simply how I am. I'd ask that you readers resign yourselves to it, given that you have encountered a strange bald man. (Deep gratitude)

It's not that there's no longer an option of adding to the good magical girl story (and no, this is not the final volume...there will be a little more), but since neither Rikudou-shi nor myself are of the mainstream shonen manga school of continuing the story for as long as possible...while it's popular in terms of structure, the idea is that *Pandora* should fulfill its role as a work of art progressing as it has been.

Still, Takumi-chan... Although there were cute pictures when she first appeared, she's now thoroughly a funny-faces character (LOL), but she still has the desire to dissect and investigate. Things just happened to not go in this direction, but if Nene hadn't met Uzal and Clara-rin, she might be having her brain dissected right about now... Scary. ((((٧ ° △ °)))))))

Shirow Masamune
May 28, 2018

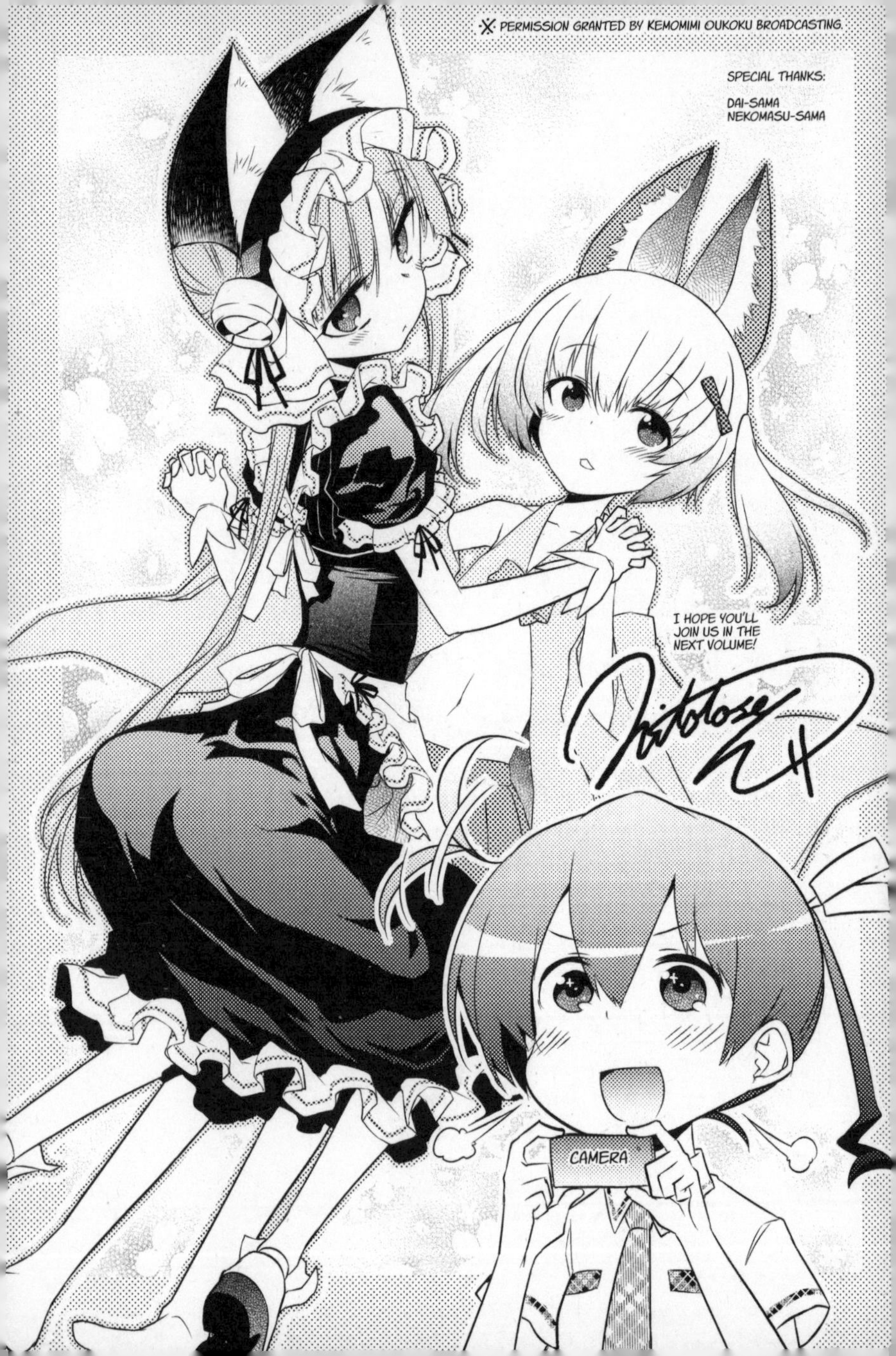
※ PERMISSION GRANTED BY KEMOMIMI OUKOKU BROADCASTING.
SPECIAL THANKS:
DAI-SAMA
NEKOMASU-SAMA
I HOPE YOU'LL JOIN US IN THE NEXT VOLUME!
CAMERA

13 STAFF

Original story	Shirow Masamune (in cooperation with Crossroad)
Production/Composition	Rikudou Koushi
Art	Hitotose Rin
Direction assistance	Takepon G
Assistant	Unamu Kibayashida Mekabu Chashibu
Editing	Koichiro Ochiai (Kadokawa) Kinoshita Kosuke (Kadokawa)
Design	Noriyuki Jinguji (Zin Studio)
SPECIAL THANKS	Seishinsha Co., Ltd.

GHOST URN

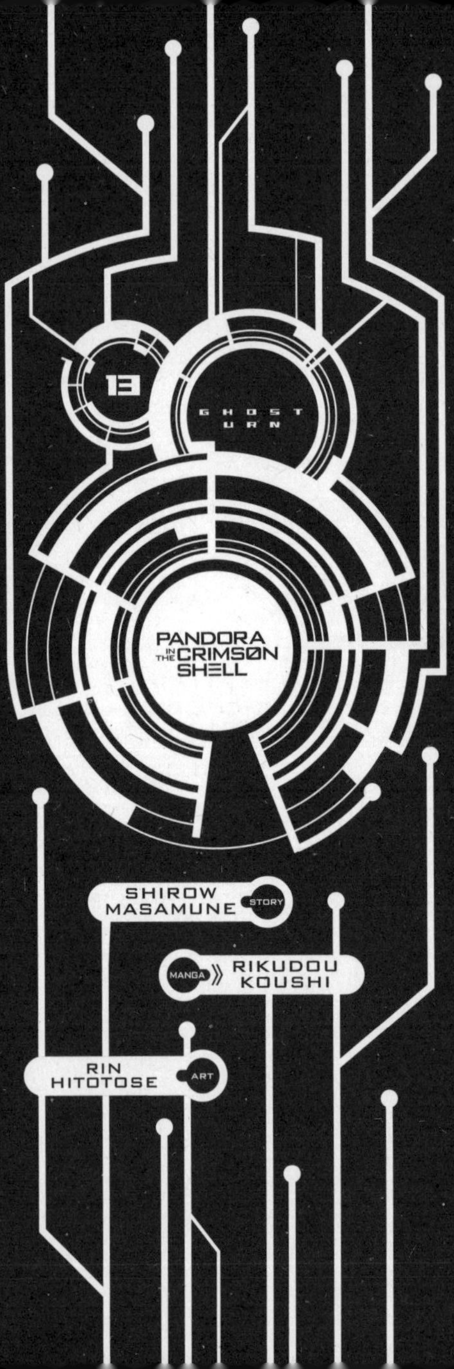
13
GHOST URN
PANDORA IN THE CRIMSON SHELL
SHIROW MASAMUNE
STORY
MANGA
RIKUDOU KOUSHI
RIN HITOTOSE
ART

GHOST URN

GHOST URN

SEVEN SEAS ENTERTAINM

PANDORA in the CRIMSØN SHELL

GHOST URN vol.13

story by **SHIROW MASAMUNE** / art by **RIKUDOU KOUSHI**

TRANSLATION
Jocelyne Allen

ADAPTATION
Ysabet Reinhardt MacFarlane

LETTERING AND RETOUCH
Roland Amago
Bambi Eloriaga-Amago

COVER DESIGN
Nicky Lim

PROOFREADER
Danielle King

ASSOCIATE PUBLISHER
Adam Arnold

PUBLISHER
Jason DeAngelis

KOUKAKU NO PANDORA Volume 13
© Koushi Rikudou 2018
© Shirow Masamune 2018
First published in Japan in 2018 by KADOKAWA CORPORATION, Tokyo.
English translation rights arranged with KADOKAWA CORPORATION, Tokyo.

Printed in Canada
First Printing: September 2020
10 9 8 7 6 5 4 3 2 1

FOLLOW US ONLINE: *www.sevenseasentertainment.com*

READING DIRECTIONS

This book reads from *right to left*, Japanese style.
If this is your first time reading manga, you start
reading from the top right panel on each page and
take it from there. If you get lost, just follow the
numbered diagram here. It may seem backwards at
first, but you'll get the hang of it! Have fun!!

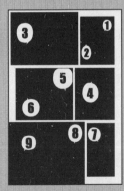